The Franklin Automobile Company

By Sinclair Powell

The History of An Innovative Firm, Its Founders, The Vehicles It Produced (1902-1934), and The People Who Built Them.

Published for The H.H. Franklin Club, Inc.

by Mark H Chaplin

Second Edition 2014

Second Edition

Copyright © 2014 Sinclair Powell   All rights reserved

Licensed to:
Mark Chaplin
The H.H. Franklin Club, Inc.
Cazenovia College
Cazenovia, NY 13035
www.franklincar.org

ISBN 978-0979584145

This book is affectionately dedicated to
the memory of the late
DAVID TEMPLAR DOMAN

Loyal friend, wise counselor, an engineer's engineer, whose work
with
The H.H. Franklin Club and the
Ford Motor Company
testified to his interest in both the history
and the future potential of the automobile.

Herbert H. Franklin

1866—1956

John Wilkinson

1868—1951

Table of Contents

PREFACE TO SECOND EDITION vii

ACKNOWLEDGEMENTS ix

TECHNICAL PIONEERING BY FRANKLIN xix

TIME LINE xxi

PROLOGUE xxxv

CHAPTER 1	Two Men and an Idea 1
CHAPTER 2	Entrepreneurship and Vision: The Birth of a New Organization (1901-1905) 43
CHAPTER 3	Technical Progress in a Growing Industry (1906-1910) 77
CHAPTER 4	A Maturing Company (1911-1918) 109
CHAPTER 5	The Postwar Era (1919-1924) 149
CHAPTER 6	The Tempo of the Twenties (1925-1929) 201
CHAPTER 7	The Years of Decline (1930-1933) 255
CHAPTER 8	The Demise of the Company (1934-1940) 311
CHAPTER 9	The People Who Built the Cars 345
CHAPTER 10	The Leaders of the Organization 397
CHAPTER 11	Inside the Company: Management, Marketing, and Engineering 429
CHAPTER 12	Summary 473

Notes 485

Research Sources 501

Bibliography 507

Index 513

About the Author 523

PREFACE TO SECOND EDITION

The First Edition of the book describing the history of the Franklin firm of Syracuse, New York, and the car it produced, entitled "The Franklin Automobile Company," was published in 1999. The book received generally splendid reviews and several major awards including the Cugnot Award from The Society of Automotive Historians in 2000, and The McKean Memorial Award from The Antique Automobile Club of America in the same year.

Published by the Society of Automotive Engineers' Press, the First Edition of the Franklin book went through several printings, with a total of 2,400 copies ultimately produced. All of the books printed have been sold, and copies can only be obtained on the used book market at often inflated prices.

Recognizing that many persons wish to obtain a copy of this book, The H.H. Franklin Club has decided to sponsor a second edition. The author has been developing this new work during the past several years. While retaining the full body of the First Edition, certain desirable additions are incorporated in this new edition. Additional information giving a timeline of the Franklin firm in the overall context of the American Automobile industry has been added. Certain newly discovered and quite pertinent images also have been placed in the new edition.

The author wishes to extend his sincere thanks to Mark Chaplin, who has spent a very extensive amount of time in preparing this second edition for publication. Thanks also are extended to Chuck Richardson and Brian McEntee for giving substantial assistance in revising the text and the pictures in this new edition.

Good Reading!

Sinclair Powell, Author
April 2014

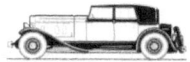

ACKNOWLEDGEMENTS

When I started the Franklin project in the summer of 1986, I greatly underestimated the scope of the work I was about to undertake. Completing this challenging activity was to consume nearly eleven years, with research and writing continuing into 1997. The reader may well be interested in hearing how this effort got under way; why a public affairs lawyer chose to devote a considerable segment of his life to the vast amount of research necessary to produce a book on the history of a motor car company which went out-of-business over sixty years ago.

The late David T. Doman was the catalyst largely responsible for my undertaking this long-term effort. Learning that I was considering early retirement from legal practice, and also recalling that I had been exposed to training in historical research prior to entering law school at Cornell, David urged me to consider examining in depth the history of the H.H. Franklin Manufacturing Company of Syracuse in order to determine if a professional-quality book on this pioneer automotive firm might be produced. David's background was responsible for his keen interest in seeing such an undertaking get under way. Member of a family which has contributed an extraordinary four generations of engineers to the American automobile industry, and whose father and grandfather played significant roles in the development of the Franklin car, he was keenly aware of the qualities which made this marque a standout in its day. David felt strongly that the time had come for a serious effort to be made to recognize the contribution of Franklin to the American automobile scene during the first third of the twentieth century. David's enthusiasm proved to be infectious, and I soon decided to move ahead with both the research effort and development of

THE FRANKLIN AUTOMOBILE COMPANY

the manuscript.

The genesis of the Franklin project having been described, it next is essential to express thanks to the large number of persons who contributed to my research and helped review my writing. Among these individuals two stand out. The late W. F. (Frank) Robinson, president of the Society of Automotive Historians in 1979 and 1980, learned of my project soon after its inception and quickly offered advice and assistance. During a visit to his home in Bellevue, Washington, he turned over to me his large collection of Franklin-related articles and pictures, covering the period from John Wilkinson's work with the New York Automobile Company in 1900-1901 to the demise of the Franklin firm in 1934. A second key person was Dr. Theodore (Ted) Wallin, holder of the Franklin Chair of Transportation Management in the Crouse School of Business at Syracuse University. Dr. Ted, on hearing of the study, promptly offered me the use of office facilities whenever I was in the Syracuse area (I soon was to discover the value of this offer during some fifty or so visits!) and contacted on my behalf a number of persons with Franklin-related information. Ted Wallin's invitations to attend the annual Salzberg Transportation Seminars at Syracuse University also were greatly appreciated, as was the award of the Franklin Medallion in 1993 in recognition of my research efforts.

Within Syracuse a number of important sources of information were quickly unearthed. Since the 1950s the staff of the Onondaga Historical Association, particularly Richard Wright, long-time former director, collected a large amount of Franklin-related material. During my years of research I often found occasion to examine these many items, which were of substantial value. While a number of staff members at the historical association's research center assisted me, Suzanne Etherington and Judy Haven were my principal contacts, and deserve my sincere thanks.

Walter Miller, Syracuse collector of vintage car literature, kindly allowed me to ransack his numerous files and use Franklin-related items

ACKNOWLEDGMENTS

found therein. The Automobile Club of Syracuse proved to be an unexpected (but very good!) source of information on early automotive activity in the area, and Betty Rothfuss of the club staff was most helpful in making records and pictures available for my use.

Libraries invariably are prime sources of information for the historian, and this was decidedly true in my Franklin-related research. Staff members of the Special Collections Division of Syracuse University's Bird Library, particularly Carolyn Davis and Amy Doherty, located and made available for my use important correspondence and records relating to H.H. Franklin's ties to the university and his service on the school's governing board. At Cornell's Olin Library, archivist (now retired) Kathleen Jacklin and her staff produced for my review numerous files of Cornell alumni who had participated in early automobile development at the H.H. Franklin Company and other firms. At the University of Michigan in Ann Arbor, assistant head, Engineering Transportation Library, Sharon Balius discovered various items involving the Franklin Company and competitor firms. The staff of the National Automobile History Collection (NAHC) at the Detroit Public Library has rendered vital assistance to some two generations of automotive historians, and proved to be equally helpful in my case. Ronald Grantz initially, and his successor Mark Patrick, assisted in finding numerous Franklin-related historical items among NAHC's vast inventory. At the University of Rochester (New York), manuscript librarian Karl Kabelac unearthed Franklin-related pictures and auto show records dating to the 1920s. Through the kind assistance of the late Professor Richard Scharchburg, Franklin items at the research library of GM Engineering and Management Institute (now Kettering University) in Flint, Michigan, were made available for my review. At the Philadelphia Free Library's automotive section, Louis Helverson made it possible for me to inspect a variety of items involving the Franklin automobile.

A number of museums across America were found to hold collections of Franklin-related items. At the Auburn-Cord-Duesenberg Museum in Auburn, Indiana, archivist Gregg Buttermore unearthed for my pe-

THE FRANKLIN AUTOMOBILE COMPANY

rusal a substantial number of items dealing with both the H.H. Franklin Company and several competitor firms. The recently-opened Franklin Foundation Museum in Tucson, Arizona (established through a generous bequest by the late Tom Hubbard, well-known collector of both Franklin cars and company historical items), contains holdings which include Franklin pictures plus correspondence of Herbert H. Franklin, and these were quickly made available to me through the courtesy of curator Bourke Runton, himself a highly-knowledgable Franklin historian (the museum's splendid collection of Franklin vehicles proved to be equally interesting). On the west coast the Los Angeles County Museum of Natural History held Franklin-related collections which later were transferred to the new Petersen Automotive Museum. Through the fine assistance of curator Leslie Mark Kendall of the Petersen Museum, I was able to examine documents relating to both the Franklin firm and its vigorous Southern California distributor-dealer, Ralph Hamlin. In the Hudson River community of Coxsackie, New York, where H.H. Franklin began his business career in 1886, town historian Raymond Beecher produced documents from the Vedder Library outlining the activities of Herbert Franklin, and also guided me to the building near the Coxsackie riverfront (still in splendid condition and fully occupied!) in which the future automobile magnate set type over 110 years ago. The transportation division of the National Museum of American History (Smithsonian), Washington, D.C., holds numerous Franklin items, and Roger White of this division kindly made them available for my use.

A number of Syracusans added a great deal to this book through their first-hand knowledge of the leaders of the Franklin firm. The late Anne Wilkinson Sherry, daughter of the designer of the Franklin car, John Wilkinson, granted me numerous interviews in her comfortable home, and produced a diverse collection of pictures and other memorabilia relating to her talented father. These documents plus the interviews made it possible for me to reconstruct her father's life from his days as an engineering student at Cornell to his long period of service as engineering leader of the Franklin firm. Hope Wilkinson Yeager, granddaughter of John Wilkinson, together with her mother,

ACKNOWLEDGMENTS

Mary Van Duyn Hill (daughter-in-law of John Wilkinson), also were helpful in recalling incidents in the life of the air-cooled vehicle expert, and provided numerous pictures. Helen Stringer, daughter of Edward Dann, a long-time member of the board of directors of the Franklin Manufacturing Company, was well-acquainted with Herbert H. Franklin, and through numerous interviews with her I was able to obtain a well-rounded picture of the automobile company chief executive. Helen, ever hospitable and helpful, also put me in touch with other Syracusans who were familiar with Herbert Franklin and the company he headed. Millie Franklin (Mrs. John) Moreland provided important pictures and records of H.H. Franklin and his company. Retired newspaper editor Barbara Rivette made available information on H.H. Franklin's early business career in Coxsackie, New York.

Various other persons from the Syracuse area gave key assistance in my research efforts, including several members of the bar. The late Caleb Candee Brown, Esq., associated for some years with the law firm which represented the Franklin company, made numerous suggestions on research sources. Lawrence Sovik, Esq., with his broad knowledge of bankruptcy matters, assisted me in securing from the Federal Archives the bankruptcy records of the H.H. Franklin Manufacturing Company, and answered a number of questions which I raised on technical aspects of insolvency proceedings. Lawrence, a member of the Syracuse University golf team during law school days in the 1920s, also recalled his experiences as a golfing partner of Herbert H. Franklin and John Wilkinson! Brothers and law partners David Fraser, Esq., and Henry Fraser, Esq., were able to unearth research leads, with David very kindly giving me free access to his personal library containing a number of books and documents dealing with the industrial history of Syracuse in the 1890s.

Luke and Joseph Ganley, sons of an early Franklin company mechanic and test driver, provided valuable assistance in my efforts to contact one-time employees of the Franklin firm. Luke set up a series of luncheon meetings at Weber's Restaurant on the old north side of Syracuse, to which he invited various persons who either formerly worked

THE FRANKLIN AUTOMOBILE COMPANY

for the air-cooled vehicle manufacturer or had parents or relatives once employed there. Joe Ganley, well-known columnist at the *Syracuse Newspapers*, aided greatly by mentioning my research work on a number of occasions in his articles, and urging persons with helpful information to get in touch with me (many responded). Joe's fellow-columnist, Richard Case, also assisted in publicizing my research efforts, with useful results. Frances Hares, well-known retired Syracuse architect, aided me in my efforts to learn more about Alexander T. Brown, Syracuse inventor-industrialist whose important role in the affairs of the H.H. Franklin Company from the 1890s-on deserves full recognition. Marion (Mrs. Donald) Napier discovered and made available important papers of her father, Edward Marks.

In other upstate New York communities several persons provided assistance in my research efforts. John B. Johnson, editor and publisher of the *Watertown Daily Times*, unearthed several items relating to the Franklin firm and the Babcock Body Company. Perry Hastings, of Pulaski, provided me with information on Franklin factory procedures, and made available a manuscript describing the involvement of his family with a series of Franklin cars. George Peter and Edward Kabelac, of Aurora, produced important material on the life of Captain Roswell Franklin, ancestor of Herbert Franklin and the initial settler in that community. The late J.D. Franklin of King Ferry, member of another branch of the Franklin family, located pictures of Herbert H. Franklin and provided me with detailed information on his ancestry. The late Robert ("Bob") Murphy, son of Ralph Murphy, onetime H.H. Franklin Company vice-president, recalled incidents of his father's life in the 1920s and 1930s. Village historians Betty Gurnett of Liverpool and Donald J. Stinson of Skaneateles helped unearth Franklin-related items.

Despite the many decades which have passed since new Franklin vehicles could be purchased at retail, three old-time dealers still were available for interviews. The late Justin Fleming of Jackson, Michigan, made perceptive comments to me about the key features of the air-cooled vehicle which appealed to customers. R.K. Lorenz of Lan-

ACKNOWLEDGMENTS

sing, Michigan, took time from his current duties as a Buick dealer in the mid-1980s, to relate how he left his parent's farm sixty-five years earlier to open a small Franklin agency in Michigan's capital city. Donald Douglas described how he dropped a career in another field to gamble on becoming a Franklin dealer in Fort Wayne, Indiana, during America's great depression of the 1930s.

Such a large number of members of The H.H. Franklin Car Club assisted me in various ways that only a sampling of those persons can be mentioned here. Joseph Aronson, of Highmount, New York, a dedicated student of Franklin history, located and sent me pictures, field service letters, and early issues of the *Franklin News*. Arnold Christiansen of West Ossipee, New Hampshire, made available a major collection of Franklin dealer records, which I found of substantial value in analyzing dealer business practices plus factory-dealer relationships. William Tuthill, of Binghamton, New York, located and turned over to me a book containing company sales messages sent to the dealer network in the very early 1920s. Mirhan Melkonian, also of Binghamton, assisted in tracking down pictures of Franklin vehicles plus related historical data. Roland Kemp of Andover, New York, provided help in several ways, locating pictures and other Franklin items. Gary Rink of Jordan, New York, aided by placing on bulletin boards at various antique car meets in upstate New York a poster describing my research and urging anyone with information on the Franklin company to contact me (a number did). Peter Kunan, owner of an early Franklin "cross-engine" vehicle, went beyond the normal call of duty at a national H.H. Franklin Club "Trek" in fulfilling my request for an evening drive so that the effectiveness of the vehicle's lights could be evaluated. In seeking to ignite an acetylene lamp prior to our commencing an initial run the gas vapor suddenly exploded, attracting a huge crowd and ending any immediate possibility of a driving test. Peter then took me out the following year without incident!. Betty Doman (sister of David) made available extensive records of her father, Carl Doman, which helped fill many gaps in my research. Henry (Hank) Manwell of Liverpool, New York, on several occasions brought to my attention key items relating to Franklin history. Rich-

THE FRANKLIN AUTOMOBILE COMPANY

ard McKnight, of Tully, New York, provided me with early Franklin company bulletins plus employee-related materials. Roy Canfield, of Washington, D.C., brought to my attention several U.S. patents involving features of early Franklin cars. Mario Cuniberti, of Columbus, Ohio, obtained for me a book describing tests of early Franklin engines conducted at Cornell University. Other club members who rendered assistance include Dr. George Boyer, James Crippen, Lloyd Davis, William Gewand, Frank Hantak, Fenton Meredith, Bobbie dine' Rodda, John Stein and Gary Vorel.

From the beginning I intended to devote a substantial portion of this book to the reminiscences of the people who built the Franklin car. Because of the advanced age of all surviving employees (nearly everyone was over eighty; a number were in their nineties; and one had passed the century mark), it was important that interviews be conducted as quickly as possible. The *Syracuse Newspapers* at the very beginning cooperated by publishing a story describing the research effort about to get under way, and urging all persons once employed by the air-cooled vehicle manufacturer to contact me. A number of people did so, and on subsequent visits to the Syracuse area I met with them and recorded their stories. Ultimately, the word spread and additional persons were unearthed, together with relatives of employees who also had interesting tales to tell of the activities of grandparent, parent, brother, sister, uncle or aunt at the Franklin firm. The very large number of people interviewed (well over one hundred) makes it impossible to personally acknowledge the contribution of each. The stories of a many such persons are recorded in the various chapters of the book; to the remainder I must express a collective "thank you" as a means of recognizing their fine help. This book could not have been developed in its present form without the outstanding support and cooperation of these individuals.

This book was produced in an old-fashioned manner; a handwritten original; an initial typed copy; and finally a computer version on disc. I wish to express my heartfelt thanks to Joan Doman, widow of David, for volunteering to decipher my written words and turn them into a

ACKNOWLEDGMENTS

typed version. Following corrections and changes Anaira Clavo then worked her magic on the computer, and produced the final manuscript (and over many months had to deal with amended versions ad infinitum!).

Several persons proved willing to review and edit my manuscript. Dr. Wallin stepped forth to go through the first four chapters, raising questions and making incisive comments about a number of items. Two MIT trained engineers of widely-separated years, Richard Haven of Fulton, New York, and Seth Gussow, of Ann Arbor, Michigan, between them carefully edited some eight chapters of the manuscript. Their work was of decided value. The key chapter covering interviews with the people who built the car was examined by Ann Heybey, of Ann Arbor and George Peckover, of Toronto, Canada. Both made important recommendation on wording, content and organization. All of the above persons deserve my warmest thanks.

Finally, my wife Suzanne contributed enormously to all aspects of this endeavor. From filling in frequently on the typewriter and computer and assisting in organizing notes and pictures to reviewing drafts of the manuscript for clarity and providing overall encouragement to my efforts, she played a pivotal role. Above all, she deserves a major award for enduring over a period of a decade and more the disorganization in a home which served as the base for a good-sized research study. My deepest thanks are extended to her.

These persons, together with countless others, are the background contributors to this manuscript, and I owe a major debt to all of them. Any factual errors or mistakes in judgement, however, are my sole responsibility and mine alone.

Sinclair Powell
December 20, 1997

THE FRANKLIN AUTOMOBILE COMPANY

TECHNICAL PIONEERING BY FRANKLIN

Franklin led the American automobile industry in many technical areas, achieving such "firsts" as the following:

First air-cooled, four-cylinder, valve-in-head engine (1902).

First in developing throttle control (1902).

First in utilizing float-feed carburetor (1902) (utilized in conjunction with throttle control).

First in developing air-cooled, six-cylinder engine (late 1905). Engine exhibited at 1906 New York auto show.

First in pioneering scientific light-weight combined with flexible construction. This incorporated such fundamentals as light unsprung weight, wood frame, tubular axles and full-elliptic springs (1902-1905).

First to employ transmission service brake (1906).

First to adopt automatic spark advance (1907).

First to develop concentric valves and auxiliary exhaust system.

First to use individual recirculating pressure feed oiling system in engine (1912).

First to use exhaust jacket for heating intake gasses (1913).

First to incorporate closed bodies in standard vehicles (1913).

First to utilize an electric carburetor primer to facilitate cold weather starting (1917).

First to introduce case-hardened crankshaft in regular production (1921).

First to employ narrow steel front body pillar construction (1925).

First to develop and place in production an air-cooled V-twelve engine (1932).

The author wishes to attribute much of the above material to the late Carl Doman's writing.

THE FRANKLIN AUTOMOBILE COMPANY

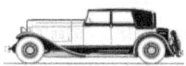

TIME LINE OF FRANKLIN'S PLACE IN THE HISTORY OF THE AMERICAN AUTOMOBILE,

1. April 6, 1865. The American Civil War ended, with the North victorious. The war helped create enormous economic development, as steel mills, manufacturing plants, cotton mills, railroad shops and other factories mushroomed across the land. Should this development continue, America in the decades ahead could well become a world leader in industrial technology, and particularly in transportation.

2. Sept. 1, 1866. Herbert H. Franklin was born on a farm located in the Caldwell Settlement, midway between the hamlets of Upper Lisle and Nanticoke, in western Broome County, New York State (Herbert was younger than three other future auto industry pioneers, William Durant, Henry Ford and Ransom E. Olds, who were born in 1861, 1863 and 1864 respectively). Herbert's father, Charles Risden Franklin, taught school as a young man, but some years prior to Herbert's birth turned to farming as an occupation. The father undoubtedly expected that Herbert, one of six children, would continue to work on the farm when he reached manhood.

3. February 11, 1868. John Wilkinson was born in Syracuse, New York. John's ancestry was an impressive one–his paternal grandfather, also named John, was a pioneer lawyer and businessman, who received credit for giving Syracuse its name. The grandfather also was active in the field of transportation–he took a leadership role in organizing railroad lines operating east and west of Syracuse. Young John's father, Forman Wilkinson, together with relatives, organized and managed an important bank in downtown Syracuse.

4.	1872. George Bailey Brayton, an American inventor, developed a two-cycle internal combustion engine powered by gasoline and later oil. This early engine, given the popular name "The Brayton Ready Motor," was used to power an occasional boat, streetcar and omnibus, with modest success. Prior to Brayton several other American inventors had developed early versions of internal combustion engines, with the pioneer being Samuel Morey, who produced such a power plant in the early 1820s.

5.	1877-1879. George B. Selden, a Rochester, New York, patent attorney, designed a road vehicle which was to be powered by a three-cylinder Brayton-type engine. Selden applied for a patent on this proposed vehicle (it was never actually built until many years later), but by filing a series of amendments to the patent application succeeded in delaying the granting of the patent until 1895. By this time an infant auto industry was emerging in America, and the Selden group sought to enforce royalty payments on each automobile manufactured.

6.	1885. John Wilkinson entered the Sibley School of Mechanical Engineering at Cornell University, where he would balance academic achievements with an outstanding record in intercollegiate sports. Interestingly, he was preceded at Cornell by another talented young person, Kate Gleason, of Rochester, New York, possibly the first woman in America to study engineering. Later Ms. Gleason would play an innovative role in the development and marketing of complex machine tools, a number of which were used in the fledgling automobile industry.

7.	1886. Herbert Franklin departed from his home near Lisle, New York, where he had worked (reluctantly!) on his father's farm and also spent a short time sanding wood bodies in a small sleigh shop. His new venture was in the upper Hudson River town of Coxsackie, New York, where he would become an apprentice (or "printer's devil") in the printing shop owned by a relative. Young Herbert swiftly mastered technical aspects of printing, and having also developed writing skills took over the editorship of the *Coxsackie News*, a

TIMELINE

small weekly newspaper.

8.   Late 1880s and early1890s. Several persons in Pennsylvania, Ohio, Indiana and Wisconsin experimented with road vehicles powered by internal combustion engines. These early machines actually ran short distances on local public streets, but were never developed to the point where they could be produced commercially.

9.   1892-1893. Two brothers, J. Frank and Charles Duryea, originally from southern Illinois, came to Springfield, Massachusetts, where they developed what is generally regarded as America's first fully successful automobile powered by an internal combustion gasoline engine. Their vehicle quickly began winning road races both at home and abroad, thus gaining valuable publicity for the brothers and their car. They were able to put these victories to practical use in manufacturing and selling a tiny number of motor cars in the mid-1890s, a first in America.

10.   1894-1899. In southern Indiana in 1894, Elwood Haynes developed a small motor vehicle powered by an internal combustion engine originally designed for use in a boat! Also in 1894, in New York City, Stephen Balzer produced a three-cylinder air-cooled radial engine which was used to power a tiny car. In Michigan, Charles Brady King of Detroit, a Cornell classmate of John Wilkinson, in March 1896, drove a four-cylinder "testing wagon" on the streets of his city. A few months later Henry Ford of Detroit guided his "quadricycle" around the downtown area of that city. In Lansing, the state capital of Michigan, Ransom E. Olds, after first experimenting with steam-powered vehicles, in the late summer of 1896 developed a gasoline motor car which ran on city streets and nearby country roads. Olds, obtaining financial support in Lansing and later Detroit, built and sold a tiny number of vehicles over the next several years. Following this accomplishment he constructed a factory on the east side of Detroit for building motor cars. In Cleveland a Scottish immigrant, Alexander Winton, built in 1896-97 two experimental gasoline cars, and in 1898-99 established a small factory for regular production of motor

THE FRANKLIN AUTOMOBILE COMPANY

cars. In 1899 production of the Winton possibly reached 100 cars. This may have marked the beginning of true manufacture of gasoline-powered vehicles in America.

11.   1897-1900. Another pair of brothers (twins!) located in Massachusetts, the Stanleys, in 1897-1898, developed a light-weight steam-powered road vehicle, which promised to sell in respectable numbers. However, the Stanley patents were soon sold to others, most notably the Locomobile Company, which ultimately built its steam car in very substantial volume in a Bridgeport, Connecticut factory (the Stanleys resumed steam car production by 1901-1902). The White Company, which built high-quality steam-powered cars in Cleveland, Ohio, was another successful producer of this type of vehicle. In the electric vehicle field the Columbia was manufactured in Hartford, Connecticut, although much of its production involved taxicabs. Other electric vehicles were built in several Eastern and Midwestern states. By 1899 electric and steam vehicle production far exceeded that of gasoline-powered motor cars.

12.   1898-1901. In Springfield, Massachusetts, a young technically-trained man, Harry Knox, developed an air-cooled gasoline powered motor car. Cooling of the engine was in part accomplished by insertion of hundreds of small pins in the walls of the cylinder, thus increasing the area exposed to the current of air. The "Waterless Knox" was placed on the market during the year 1900, and by 1901 it achieved an annual sales level of approximately 100 cars.

13.   1893-1901. Herbert Franklin, during his seven years of living in Coxsackie, achieved a moderate degree of success as editor of the *Coxsackie News*. He also dabbled in several other areas, including the sale of real estate and bicycles. However, by 1893, seeking further worlds to conquer, he began investigating economic opportunities in larger cities in New York state. Finally, meeting a young engineer who had developed a technique for casting small metal parts in volume (called die-casting) Franklin removed to Syracuse, where he opened a tiny factory to produce such cast parts. After many early

TIMELINE

ups-and-downs the new Franklin venture achieved success.

14.   1889-1901. Following graduation from Cornell John Wilkinson worked as a technician and engineer at several companies in Syracuse and elsewhere. Becoming identified with the Syracuse Bicycle Company as its chief engineer, John both designed and raced bicycles with considerable success. However, his primary interest turned to motor cars, and in his free time he designed several gasoline motors cooled by air. In 1899 John secured modest financial support from a group of Syracuse businessmen, and completed his first car featuring an air-cooled engine at the beginning of the year 1900. A second car followed, but interest on the part of the businessmen flagged, and John realized he must look elsewhere for financial backing.

15.   1901-1902. John Wilkinson met Herbert Franklin, demonstrated his air-cooled vehicle, and secured financial support from Franklin and a wealthy Syracuse inventor, Alexander T. Brown, who together formed a partnership for development of a more advanced motor car. The new car was highly successful in road tests, and following the merger of the Franklin-Brown partnership with the original Franklin die-casting firm, the road ahead was clear for the production of Franklin air-cooled motor vehicles. In June 1902 the first Franklin car was sold. An initial factory building was erected, and the small firm was ready to compete with other companies in the East and Midwest in an American motor car industry.

16.   1900-1905. While the Columbia electric car tended to fade from the picture after the year 1900, the Locomobile steam vehicle took first place in sales in 1901 and 1902, in the steadily-expanding American automobile industry. However, in the Midwest the gasoline-powered car moved to the forefront, and by 1903 the top three vehicles in sales, Oldsmobile, Ford and Cadillac, all were Detroit-based, with the Kenosha, Wisconsin, Rambler holding down the fourth spot. In 1904 and 1905 these cars again claimed the top four positions in sales, but in fifth place was a newcomer–the Syracuse-based air-cooled Franklin!

THE FRANKLIN AUTOMOBILE COMPANY

17.   1900+. The "Auto Show" was utilized early on by motor car companies to display their latest models. The first national-level show was held in November 1900, at Madison Square Garden in New York City, and became an annual event each year thereafter (many other cities soon held their own shows). At the initial New York City show a test track was installed, probably to demonstrate to the many skeptics that this new form of highway transportation was safe and reliable!

18.   1897-1906. During the early days of the American automobile the typical motor car manufacturer sought to demonstrate the durability of its product by engaging in long-distance runs and related endurance contests. In the late 1890s Alexander Winton twice drove the experimental vehicles he built from Cleveland to New York City, an impressive achievement in that era (Winton also made every effort at race tracks to show that his company's cars were capable of astonishing feats of speed). A trip across America was certain to generate wide publicity for any brand of automobile successfully achieving such a feat, and here Winton again led the way when a New England physician piloted this make from the West to the East coast. Shortly after the doctor left San Francisco on his trip two other makes of cars, a Packard and an Oldsmobile, joined in the cross-America competition. Few roads of any type existed in the western part of the nation in this era, thus all three vehicles took from sixty to seventy-five days to make the trip. The Winton was the first to arrive, although the Packard had the shortest elapsed time. In 1904, however, the Franklin firm decided to try its hand at such an undertaking with one of its light but strongly-built four-cylinder cars, and shattered the previous record by cutting the time required for the cross-country run to thirty-two and a fraction days. Two years later, not content with its previous achievement, the Syracuse-based company utilized its powerful new six-cylinder model for another across-America trip. The earlier record was easily eclipsed, with the time required for the run reduced to a mere fifteen days!

19.   1901-1908 As the American automobile industry constantly expanded, the more successful firms undertook major building pro-

grams. In Lansing, Michigan, the Oldsmobile firm constructed a good-sized factory, while in another Michigan city, Flint, the now-well-known entrepreneur, "Billy" Durant, began the development of a substantial plant for the manufacture of the increasingly successful Buick car. In Detroit the Ford Motor Company, after beginning manufacture of its vehicles in a rented frame building, erected a good-sized brick factory to meet heavy consumer demand. Also in Detroit, the Packard Motor Car Company utilized the services of talented architect Albert Kahn to develop a series of buildings for the efficient production of its high-quality automobiles. In Syracuse, the Franklin firm continued its steady expansion of factory and office facilities. In mid-1907 Franklin employed over 1600 people, among the highest in the American auto industry.

20.   1904-1909 Technical advances were swiftly occurring in the automobile industry, as engineers constantly sought to design more reliable cars. In Detroit, Henry Leland, now head of the Cadillac Motor Car Company, enforced strict standards of precision in the manufacture of parts for his company's vehicles. In Indianapolis, Indiana, Howard Marmon utilized his technical background to design advanced motor cars. At the Franklin plant in Syracuse John Wilkinson organized an engineering research staff which was considered tops in the auto industry. In New York City, in 1905, the Society of Automotive Engineers was established, with Henry Ford and John Wilkinson named vice-presidents.

21.   1908. While many auto manufacturers in the early era of motor car development tended to build large and increasingly expensive vehicles, one auto builder, Henry Ford of Detroit, constantly thought of producing an "universal car," simply constructed and low-priced. Ford achieved this goal in 1908 when the Ford Motor Company unveiled its "Model T." Priced at a low $850 it swiftly took top rank in sales among American auto firms, and would hold that position for many years.

THE FRANKLIN AUTOMOBILE COMPANY

22. 1902-1910 The commercial truck made its appearance on the automotive scene very shortly after the introduction of pleasure cars. At first a passenger car chassis often was used, with a light panel body–or even a box–attached at the rear of the frame in which to pack items for quick delivery. Soon, however, purpose-built trucks of a heavier-duty type were constructed, with substantial carrying capacity available in the rear area behind the driver. Steam-powered trucks were used in the very early days, but they proved to be ungainly, and gradually disappeared from the scene. Electric-powered units lasted much longer, particularly for use in cities. Packard and other manufacturers in the Midwest produced powerful gasoline trucks, as did the Mack firm in eastern Pennsylvania. In Syracuse, Franklin was building trucks by 1906, many of them featuring the driver-over-engine configuration. The air-cooled automobile firm also built taxicabs for use in New York City and a few other major municipalities.

23. 1902-1911. The majority of American automobile firms (including Franklin) chose to recognize as valid the 1895 Selden patent covering gasoline-powered motor cars, and established in 1903 an organization–the Association of Licensed Automobile Manufacturers (ALAM)–to enforce the patent (and payment of royalties) against all other auto builders. A few "outsiders," led by the Ford Motor Company of Detroit, refused to acknowledge the validity of the patent, and fought the issue in Federal Courts. After losing in the Federal District Court in 1909, the Ford firm appealed the decision, and in 1911 won a resounding victory in the Federal Circuit Court of Appeals. Out of this decision of "no infringement" came an agreement by American auto manufacturers to allow substantial interchange of innovations, with a more formal cross-licensing program arriving a few years later.

24. 1911. While efforts to develop an effective self starter for gasoline-powered automobiles dated back to the 1890s (Wilkinson's air starter being one such device), no really satisfactory unit was developed until some years later. Then, in 1910-1911, the talented Charles F. Kettering perfected a practical electric starter which was used on the 1912 model Cadillac automobile, and soon thereafter adopted by

substantially all motor car firms. This development insured the triumph of automobiles powered by internal combustion engines over the steam or electric-powered vehicle, whose production faded into insignificance.

25.   1910-1915. As Americans became better and better acquainted with the merits of the motor car, the annual increases in production of these vehicles were little short of astounding. The year 1910 saw just under 190,000 cars and trucks pour off the assembly lines of the various manufacturers, a huge jump from a few years earlier. However, this was only the beginning. By 1913 the annual total of some 485,000 vehicles were built, with this figure almost doubling to approximately 970,000 two years later. In both cities and rural areas ever greater numbers of persons were finding that ownership of a motor vehicle was indispensable for personal and business use. Farm families particularly were relieved from isolation by this new means of transportation.

26.   1913. As the vast increase in production of motor cars was taking place, it became apparent to executives at America's leading motor vehicle manufacturer, the Ford Motor Company, that new methods of building such vehicles needed to be developed. The answer was the assembly line, which featured cars moving steadily along a chain-driven line as workers attached parts to the vehicles. Such a technical innovation resulted in vastly increased production at reduced cost. Ultimately, this approach was adopted by all the major companies in the automobile industry, and even by the minor firms.

27.   1908-1915. The Franklin car–light-weight, precision-engineered and carefully-built–clearly was capable of being a leader among American-built automobiles in economy of operation. This leadership was demonstrated as early as 1908, when in a monitored contest a Franklin stock vehicle outdistanced all other American cars in fuel economy. Then, in mid-1913, a four-cylinder Franklin driven by S.G Averell, the first purchaser of a Franklin back in 1902, achieved an astonishing 83.5 miles per gallon in a test run on Long Island (ad-

THE FRANKLIN AUTOMOBILE COMPANY

mittedly, this vehicle was equipped with special gears and carburetor).

28.   1910-1915. During the period from 1910 to mid-1913 the H.H. Franklin firm offered several series of motor cars for sale, ranging from a relatively small four-cylinder vehicle to a large, luxurious six-cylinder machine. Since the company also offered commercial units to buyers during this time, it became clear that the Franklin factory was being highly-stressed to manufacture this broad variety of vehicles. The company therefore took decisive action to deal with the situation. The commercial vehicles were eliminated, and the several lines of pleasure cars were consolidated into a single series, a moderate-sized six-cylinder unit. Efficiency in the Franklin factory was upgraded by installation of the Taylor System in Franklin management. These new approaches, assisted by the pioneering in the area of closed body styles, put the company back on track in terms of profitable operation.

29.   1914-1917. The period from 1914-1916 saw several of the American auto companies which produced upper-middle and high-priced vehicles introduce larger and more powerful motor cars. Leading the way was the Cadillac firm, which late in 1914 unveiled a powerful vee-type eight-cylinder automobile. Not to be outdone, the Packard Motor Car Company in 1915 placed on the market a twelve-cylinder machine of imposing size. Led by its engineering head, John Wilkinson, the Franklin Company, in developing an advanced vehicle, moved in a totally different direction from the above firms. In mid-1916 it introduced its new Series 9 motor car, a light, flexible vehicle which would combine smooth operation with excellent fuel economy. This new offering sold in substantial numbers, moving the Franklin firm toward the forefront of what might be called the "small" producers of cars in America.

30.   1917-1918. After maintaining neutrality for over two-and-one-half years, America entered the First World War in the early spring of 1917. The Federal government quickly enlisted the automobile industry in its effort to equip the armed forces of America and its allies

TIMELINE

with modern weapons of war. In addition to a large output of trucks, the industry produced guns and gun parts, ammunition, tanks, Liberty aircraft engines, small ships and numerous minor items. Franklin participated by producing aircraft engine parts, a tank transmission and a trench lighting system. Auto production virtually came to a halt by mid-1918.

31.   1919-1923. With the end of World War I occurring in November 1918, the American auto industry swiftly resumed building pleasure cars. Throughout 1919 and the first half of 1920, the demand for new automobiles by the public was substantial, and auto companies went all-out to produce vehicles. By mid-1920, however, car prices had soared to very high levels, and there was a sharp fall-off in sales. The Ford Motor Company, quickly followed by the Franklin firm, reduced prices, and sales gradually returned to normal levels. In 1920-1923 the Franklin firm was challenged by other producers of vehicles utilizing air-cooled motors. The Holmes and Fox firms, plus the Chevrolet division of General Motors, all sought to invade the air-cooled field. They were not successful, however, and Franklin emerged as the nation's sole builder of air-cooled vehicles.

32.   1921-1925. As the decade of the 1920s unfolded, the American automobile industry assumed giant proportions. Huge factories were built, employing many thousands of workmen, as companies sought to meet consumer demand. Literally, every American family appeared to want a car! The development of the closed car (here Franklin was one of the leaders) increased the popularity of the motor vehicle. At the same time new highways were being built across the nation, making long-distance travel by autos steadily more popular.

33.   1924-1925. With automobiles becoming ever more reliable mechanically, the American public by the mid-1920s had become more and more conscious of the "looks" of the motor cars they purchased. Franklin became sharply aware of this fact in 1924, when its 10-C model, a well-engineered vehicle, failed to sell in satisfactory numbers due to its somewhat obsolete appearance. Herbert Frank-

THE FRANKLIN AUTOMOBILE COMPANY

lin, following pressure by one or more of its dealers, retained a well-known automotive stylist to design a more attractive, up-to-date car. The result was the Series 11, with a handsome appearance featuring an upright radiator shell. However, Franklin's colleague, the brilliant engineer John Wilkinson, upset by the new design, left the company.

34.   1928-1929. The American auto industry prospered greatly during the closing years of the decade of the 1920s. Peak auto production was reached during the first nine months of 1929, with nearly all companies setting records. However, in October of that year came the great stock market crash, which resulted in a swift drying-up of demand for new cars. A substantial number of firms, including Franklin, found themselves with large stocks of unsold cars on hand at the end of 1929, which did not portend well for the future.

35.   1930-1932. As the depression of the 1930s took hold in America, the auto industry found itself swiftly and sharply affected. Sales of pleasure cars dropped substantially in 1930, fell off even more in 1931, and literally collapsed in 1932. The "big three", General Motors, Ford and Chrysler, having low-priced vehicles to sell, managed to weather the storm in respectable fashion (although with heavy lay-offs of workers in their plants). The same could not be said of the small "independent" auto companies, which one-by-one found themselves with their backs to the wall. Only a few of the minor firms had the financial reserves needed to design and manufacture cars and sell them in sufficient numbers to ensure a profit.

36.   1930-1932. The H.H. Franklin firm was typical of the small auto producers facing difficult times in the early 1930s. Having taken out large bank loans in 1929 to greatly expand production of vehicles during that year, the company in 1930 and 1931 found itself having to dispose of its unsold earlier cars at fire sale prices. Thus, despite having placed on the market an attractive and more powerful new model car in 1930, the firm began incurring substantial losses. The red ink continued throughout 1931, with the company now unable to repay the bank debt. The creditor banks reacted by installing at the end of

1931 a manager who to a major degree ran the Franklin firm.

37.   1932. Amazingly, despite the abysmal economic conditions in America in 1932, a number of auto firms introduced huge–and expensive–twelve-cylinder models at the beginning of that year (a year or two earlier Cadillac introduced a "Sixteen" and a "Twelve," and Marmon a "Sixteen"). Packard, Pierce-Arrow, Auburn and Lincoln were among the luxury car builders offering these vehicles, with Franklin joining the group in the spring of the year. Franklin sold few "twelves," which further impaired its already weak financial condition. The Syracuse firm fared much better with its new Olympic model, a medium-priced vehicle which combined a REO chassis and a Hayes body with a Franklin engine. Sales of this car, on each of which the Franklin firm made a small profit, may well have saved it from immediate bankruptcy.

38.   1933-1934. The American automobile industry struggled to regain momentum in 1933, but found the going difficult. The carnage during the depression years among the small independent auto firms had been appalling, with such old-line companies as Marmon, Stutz, Peerless, Elcar, Kissel and Moon closing their doors. The "big three" auto firms, having the funds needed to modernize their plants and produce new, low-cost models, took an ever-larger share of auto sales. The surviving small production companies such as Franklin struggled to continue operating, hampered by huge layoffs of key personnel and run-down factories.

39.   1934. In early 1934 it was clear that the end was approaching for the old-line Franklin firm. Sales of the company's face-lifted 1934 models were tiny; the firm could not meet the bills of its suppliers; and ultimately it could not even pay its workers. The creditor banks continued to press hard for payment of their outstanding loans. Abandoning hope for survival, the company filed a voluntary petition in bankruptcy in Federal court in early April of 1934. The petition was swiftly approved, and the bankruptcy process got under way.

THE FRANKLIN AUTOMOBILE COMPANY

40.   1934-1935. As the trustees in bankruptcy wound up the affairs of the Franklin firm, it was hoped that some group might purchase the assets of the failed company and produce a new, moderately-priced car under the Franklin name. For a time this appeared to be a possibility, but unlike the Studebaker and Willys bankruptcies of the same period which resulted in these firms resuming operations, all efforts to rescue the Syracuse firm failed. The company's old factory was used for some years for other purposes (building air conditioners!) by another firm, but in the 1970s it was demolished. The era of Franklin was over–it became one of the two thousand or more American automobile firms which did not survive in the marketplace.

41.   1936-1939. Two senior engineers from the Franklin firm, Carl Doman and Edward Marks, had earlier organized a small company which was retained in 1936-1937 to design and build a small, three-wheeled vehicle powered by an air-cooled motor. The small car was never placed in production, but its motor was adapted for use in a light delivery truck built by the White Motor Company of Cleveland, Ohio. The same motor, with largely aluminum components, also was utilized in light aircraft. A final effort to employ air-cooling in an automotive engine prior to World War II was undertaken by the Crosley Company of Cincinnati, Ohio. This firm built a tiny motor car utilizing a two-cylinder engine originally designed to power a garden tractor! The midget vehicle attracted a great deal of attention, but sold poorly.

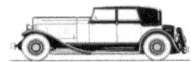

PROLOGUE

The reader, on examining this book initially, might well ask certain pointed questions. Why should several hundred pages of print be devoted to a history of the H.H. Franklin Company, the people involved in it, and the car produced? What possibly could justify a detailed examination of a firm which built a dimly-remembered automobile in an upstate New York community far distant from the center of the motor car industry? What did the company—or the car—stand for to merit such serious attention?

These are reasonable inquiries, which deserve adequate responses. It should be noted initially that since the late 1890s as many as three thousand firms across America have sought to manufacture automobiles. Most were both inconspicuous and short-lived, and out of that vast multitude only three indigenous ones remain today. One of those which ultimately was compelled to close its doors, but only after producing some 150,000 motor vehicles of splendid quality over a period of nearly a third of a century, was Franklin. From 1902 to 1934 this company could claim the distinction of building America's only truly successful gasoline-powered motor car incorporating an air-cooled engine, a feature which a number of competing auto manufacturers, large and small, sought to emulate but were unable to accomplish.

The Franklin firm began manufacturing automobiles as the result of a unique partnership of two men possessing different talents, who together forged a significant enterprise. Each was a product of post-Civil War upstate New York , and each was individualistic to the point

THE FRANKLIN AUTOMOBILE COMPANY

of stubborness, but here the similarity ended. Herbert H. Franklin, for whom the car was named, was a self-made man thoroughly attuned to the business world and its ways. Without exposure to higher education, and compelled to work under the handicap of a physical defect which restricted his ability to express himself orally, he nonetheless guided a diminutive company through struggling infancy into long years of vigorous maturity. A man gifted with impressive talents in the areas of advertising and public relations, Franklin could claim only limited acquaintance with the world of science and technology, but this was of little consequence. The other member of the partnership, John Wilkinson, met this need in superb fashion. With formal engineering training at a premier university, plus earlier experience in the design of another innovative form of transportation, the bicycle, this able and imaginative young engineer developed an automobile which in terms of both reliability and performance was a pacesetter in its day.

Fortunately, there was a receptive market awaiting the debut of this new vehicle at the dawn of the twentieth century. The American public, conditioned by development of the steam-powered train and the electric trolley, wanted a machine which could equal these modes of transportation in swiftness of movement. Through exposure to millions of bicycles in the 1890s, Americans had tasted the pleasures of independent personal mobility, and thus also sought a vehicle which would be responsive to the bidding of its owner. The Wilkinson-designed car, light, easily-managed and speedy, satisfied these twin demands in full measure. In endurance runs which spanned the breadth of the continent the machine also demonstrated that its driver need not fear that bugaboo of the typical pioneer motorist, a vehicle which due to mechanical shortcomings would break down on even a modest journey.

Conditioned by writers and others who sought to forecast the future, the public in those early days of the motor car was certain that in addition to meeting the need of personal convenience this new form of transportation would produce a host of other benefits. One of the most

PROLOGUE

important of these was to be the clean and sanitary city. No longer would communities have to put up with the unsightliness, the odor and the health hazard caused by the deposit of vast quantities of horse-produced wastes in local streets. It was fortunate, perhaps, that few had the foresight to realize that in abandoning the four-legged beast for the pleasures and obvious advantages of the speedy, self-propelled road vehicle, a new cluster of problems would ultimately arise. Urban decay, suburban sprawl, traffic congestion, a grim annual death toll from accidents and the pollution of the atmosphere by motor car exhaust, all were blissfully hidden from the view of the early enthusiast. Adoption of the automobile was to generate vast changes in American society, both for better and for worse.

The Franklin Company throughout its life was noted for more than the production of a top-quality air-cooled vehicle. As a pioneer in engineering research, it was one of a limited number of auto manufacturers where in the early years of the twentieth century the testing laboratory replaced cut-and-try methods of motor car design and manufacture. The firm also blazed new trails in the introduction of modern methods of production planning and control, adopting the principles of America's renowned efficiency engineer, Frederick W. Taylor, in its operations well before the First World War. Equally important, this was not a factory run on the lines of the massive, impersonal Midwestern motor-car plants, where total emphasis on high volume production required that the employee be viewed as little more than an automaton wearing a badge. Instead, at Franklin the typical worker to a surprising degree retained his individuality, and was expected to demonstrate both a dedication to craftsmanship and a willingness to contribute ideas for improvements in auto manufacturing methods. The iron discipline which characterized the typical good-sized American factory of that era was alleviated at the Franklin plant by band concerts, athletic contests, and other enjoyable recreational activities featured during the lunch break and after working hours. In short, the Franklin operation to a surprising degree sought to humanize the demands of tedious twentieth-century manufacturing employment.

Both the company and its product thus 'marched to the beat of a different drummer', and were unique in their time. The history of the Franklin firm, its founders, the vehicles it produced and the people who built them, is a fascinating one and deserves to be recorded. This book seeks to set forth that story.

– One –

Two Men and an Idea

It was late fall of the year 1899. In a modest suite of rooms on the top floor of a small factory in Syracuse, New York, a young engineer and his mechanic helper had been working for several months to complete construction of a gasoline-powered motor vehicle. All across America in this period men endowed with mechanical talents were attempting to produce successful road machines, some powered by gasoline, others by steam or electricity. However, this youthful Syracusan, John Wilkinson, was determined to perfect in his vehicle certain unique features, particularly an unconventional solution to the problem of cooling an internal combustion engine.

Until recently John had been employed by a local bicycle company as its chief (and only!) engineer. His imagination, however, was attracted to another type of moving vehicle, a gas-powered "horseless carriage." An independent thinker, he sought to design for this machine a power plant combining simplicity with efficiency. In order to dissipate the blistering heat produced by explosions of the gasoline-air mixture in each cylinder, John chose not to follow the lead of many American gas-engine experimenters, who incorporated in their plans elaborate systems of pumps, pipes and storage tanks to circulate quantities of water for cooling purposes. Instead, he decided to use a flow of air to directly cool the superheated cylinder walls. The engine was to be a multi-cylindered one, since he reasoned that such a unit, with overlapping power impulses, would be far smoother in operation than the typical "one-lunger" utilized in most other vehicles of the day. Less is known about his plans for the chassis of the new machine, but its design clearly stressed simplicity of construction along with light weight.

However, despite these progressive concepts, John Wilkinson was to experience many frustrating months before he could unveil his innovative automobile to the American public. First, he had to find an individual who could contribute qualities that complemented his own engineering gifts. He met such a person in Herbert H. Franklin, a man with limited mechanical know-how, but endowed with sound business judgment and well-honed entrepreneurial skills. Franklin was the catalyst who made possible the successful production and marketing of the new machine. The two men formed a partnership which endured for many years, and produced a significant impact on the American automobile industry.

John Wilkinson and Herbert H. Franklin first worked in other fields before entering automobile manufacturing. Thus it is essential that the backgrounds of the pair be described at some length in this chapter, so that the reader may fully comprehend those personal qualities and early experiences which helped insure their later achievements.

The city of Syracuse in the 1890s provided a uniquely hospitable environment for the efforts of John and Herbert. While never more than a medium-sized community in terms of population, the municipality nonetheless achieved considerable technological prominence in late nineteenth-century America. It was no typical upstate New York knitting mill town, as was its eastern neighbor, Utica. Instead, it became a vital center of invention and diversified industry, even playing a substantial role in the establishment of one of the nation's great technical societies. We now will examine this interesting community and its history.

TWO MEN AND AN IDEA

If a stratospheric airplane had been available in the pioneer era, its pilot would have observed two natural transportation routes in upstate New York, intersecting at or near the point where the city of Syracuse ultimately would be located. One route crosses the state from east to west beginning in the Albany-Troy area, follows the Mohawk Valley to Utica, and sweeps westward just north of the Finger Lakes to the Niagara River and Lake Erie. The other begins in the north near the point where Lake Ontario pours its waters into the St. Lawrence River, follows south along the east shore of this lake, and then continues parallel to the Tioughnioga River down to the northern boundary of Pennsylvania. Geographical factors, therefore, undoubtedly have favored the establishment of a transportation-oriented community at this key crossroads.

Human efforts soon supplemented the natural advantages of the area as a transportation center. Construction in the early 1800s of the Mohawk and Hudson Turnpike running from Albany westward through the Mohawk Valley, and the great Genesee Road extending from the Utica area west through Onondaga to the towns of Geneva and Canandaigua, made it possible for the area to enjoy primitive stagecoach service. Various wagon roads of lesser importance–some decently-constructed and maintained toll-routes, others little more than dirt trails–were gradually developed, further linking the area with nearby districts. One of America's earliest "plank" roads, constructed of rough-hewn pieces of timber with a flat side turned upward to provide a smooth surface, was built to connect Syracuse with several small communities lying to the north.

About the time Syracuse came into existence as a tiny, unincorporated community, water became a major transportation medium. The Erie Canal, New York Governor DeWitt Clinton's "Big Ditch," reached the village in 1820, triggering a wild celebration by the citizens and immediately providing a cheap, although slow, means of moving goods and people. Construction of this key east-west transportation link helped assure the permanence of the small community and advance its economic growth. The town became a stop-over site for persons making long journeys by stage or canal barge, a transfer point for shipment of freight, and a trading center for the surrounding countryside.

In about 1830, a very few years after construction of the canal, the steam railway began revolutionizing land transportation in America, and soon became immensely important to the young town of Syracuse. Because of the limited ability of the steam locomotive to climb steep grades, the route to be followed by railroads across upstate New York had to largely parallel the rights-of-way of the stagecoach roads and the Erie Canal. Initial development of the railroad from the upper Hudson River to the west began in 1831, when tracks were laid to establish a sixteen-mile link between Albany and Schenectady. This short section soon was extended westward along the Mohawk River Valley through construction of the Utica and Schenectady Railroad by 1836. Then, also in 1836, a number of business and professional men in Syracuse took the first step toward linking their community by rail to the outside world. The group's leader was John Wilkinson, a local lawyer and grandfather of the automotive inventor introduced earlier.

Largely due to the elder Wilkinson's energy and determination, surveys for a railway stretching east from Syracuse to Utica were undertaken and construction of the 53 mile line completed in July 1839. Syracuse now enjoyed a rail connection to cities further east, and passengers flocked aboard the tiny cars to take advantage of the speedy new service. Wilkinson assumed the presidency of the Syracuse and Utica Railway Company, and in an astute and vigorous manner met the challenges which confronted a pioneer rail transportation firm. The new line had to contend with flocks of cattle wandering on the tracks and causing accidents, with requests for free tickets from both rich and poor, and with the demand by New York State that the railroad compensate its competitor, the Erie Canal, for freight carried during the water shipping season (the state, which operated the Canal, did not wish to see its revenues shrink).

As rail linkages to the East were being developed, efforts also got under way to lay tracks lines westward toward Buffalo and Lake Erie.

TWO MEN AND AN IDEA

Work on a line from Syracuse to Auburn was completed as early as 1838, although for the first year the cars were laboriously drawn by horses. In 1839, a steam locomotive was finally secured to pull the trains at a much greater speed. A short time later the railroad was extended on to Rochester, and finally in the early 1840s completed all the way to Buffalo. At last the rail passenger could travel, with numerous transfers, across upper New York State to the Great Lakes at a speed many times that of stagecoach or canal boat. When, in 1853, the various local rail segments became part of the massive New York Central System, with its linkages to major Eastern Seaboard cities and ultimately to Michigan, Ohio, and other fast-developing states in the West, the future of Syracuse as a community located on a high-speed national transportation network was assured.[1-1]

The initial basis for the industrial economy of Syracuse can be expressed in one word–salt. Production of this vital substance, first by Indians and later by white settlers, got under way in the late 1700s and intensified in subsequent years. The salt was recovered from brine (pumped out of deep wells) by alternate processes, usually through the heating of kettles filled with the fluid over a wood or coal fire, but in some instances by solar evaporation. The primitive transportation network was then called on to carry the finished product–salt in bulk–from the tiny community to faraway customers in other states and even in Canada.

Introduction of rail facilities, and later the coming of the Civil War, helped Syracuse evolve from a small town into a community where industry quickly gained a solid foothold. Throughout the 1860s numerous firms sprang up in the city to meet America's increasing demand for manufactured products. Well before 1870 two good-sized steel companies had been established, both featuring advanced production methods. One, the Sweet's Manufacturing Company, pioneered in the use of gas furnaces for heating and even melting steel. These firms, together with an iron works in nearby Geddes, successfully competed with the great iron and steel mills of Pittsburgh, serving a market area extending from New England to Chicago. Syracuse-based manufacturers of plows, mowers and reapers participated in the young nation's expanding agricultural economy. Hunters throughout America and around the world found Syracuse-made rifle telescopes to be of exceptionally high quality.[1-2]

By the 1880s and early 1890s the city was fast becoming a regional-level center of technologically-based industry. From forge and foundry, mill and machine shop, poured a wide range of fabricated articles, including hand tools, locks, typewriters, lanterns, pumps, coffins, fare-boxes for street cars and springs for vehicles. It was in this era that transportation-related products began to occupy a definite niche in the Syracuse economy. The Moyer Wagon Works moved to the city from a small nearby town in the very early 1880s, and swiftly achieved importance. Producing horse-drawn vehicles of high quality, the firm also pioneered in utilizing modern industrial techniques in its factory. Moyer was among the first companies to divide its manufacturing and assembly operations into specific segments, with each employee assigned responsibility for one task. The concern also sought to mechanize its manufacturing processes, underwriting the development of a unique hub-boring machine, which was used under patent by numerous other wagon and carriage firms throughout the country. Several additional vehicle companies were organized in the city about the same time. The Whitney Wagon Works, Thomas D. Lines, J. S. Leggett, and O. H. Short all produced carriages, wagons and "buckboards," while the Central City Wheel Works and the Syracuse Dash Works manufactured wagon parts.

Syracuse, with a population approaching 100,000 in the mid-1890s, now was recognized as a business hub of considerable importance, not only in upstate New York but generally throughout eastern America. While not achieving the size of such cities as Buffalo, Cleveland or Detroit, Syracuse nonetheless had become relatively cosmopolitan in nature. Electric lights and telephones could be found in numerous homes and business places, motorized streetcars clanged along many thoroughfares, several theaters and opera houses had opened their doors in the downtown area, and the city had become the site of a flourishing university. With the dawn of the twentieth century fast approaching, the community clearly was ready to play a role in the development and manufacture of any new products which might be sought by the American public.

A community does not develop technologically-related industry by happenstance. Such an achievement requires major contributions by people, particularly individuals endowed with inventive and organizational talents of a very high order. Three men of exceptional abilities contributed significantly to Syracuse industrial growth during the decades of the 1880s and 1890s. The trio were John Edson Sweet, Charles Ehle Lipe, and Alexander Timothy Brown.

By far the oldest of the three, John Edson Sweet was born in the village of Pompey, located near Syracuse, in 1832. Receiving only a common school education, he was apprenticed to a local carpenter at the age of 17. Subsequently he worked as a draftsman and builder in an architect's office in Syracuse during the decade prior to the Civil War. After going abroad in 1862, Sweet patented a nail-making device in England, and a few years later produced an early type-setting machine which was displayed at the Paris Exposition of 1867. On returning to America he became designer and manager of a manufacturing company in Syracuse, and subsequently supervised the construction of bridges throughout central New York State. It was while engaged in bridge-building activity in the early 1870s that he met Ezra Cornell, who a few years earlier had founded the university bearing his name. Cornell, also a self-made man who felt that practical instruction should be an important part of an engineering education, engaged Sweet to teach mechanic arts and direct the machine shops at the new university. From 1873 to 1879, Sweet taught in the fast-developing engineering program at Cornell. While there, he helped build the nation's first dynamo, and won the loyalty of a substantial group of students. However, his lack of traditional academic credentials, plus his emphasis on the shop approach to engineering education, proved upsetting to certain other members of the faculty. He therefore left the university late in 1879, and returned to Syracuse. For decades thereafter, Sweet's onetime pupils gathered at an annual dinner in New York City to pay tribute to their beloved teacher.

While still at Cornell, Sweet had been asked to develop a list of prominent mechanical engineers who might be interested in the establishment of a national organization to represent their area of technology. With assistance from several other knowledgeable persons Sweet completed the list, and a letter was sent from Syracuse in January 1880, inviting a number of persons to a meeting in New York City to undertake the formation of a mechanical engineering society. A short time earlier Sweet had pioneered in organizing a local mechanical association in Syracuse, where university-trained technicians and skilled shop workers met on common ground. The organization established as a result of the New York meeting was the American Society of Mechanical Engineers (ASME), which effectively brought together persons with both theoretical and practical knowledge of this branch of engineering. The new society quickly gained national stature, and Sweet's reputation was such that he was elected its third president, serving in 1883-84. Meanwhile, in Syracuse he had established the Straight-Line Engine Company, which manufactured a high-speed, reciprocating steam engine designed by Sweet while at Cornell and particularly well-adapted for use in generating electricity and powering the special machinery needed by America's swiftly expanding factories.

Charles Ehle Lipe also was a product of upstate New York, having been born in 1852 in the Mohawk Valley town of Fort Plain, some distance east of Syracuse. He was an early engineering graduate of Cornell, coming to Syracuse in 1874. Lipe's career was largely spent in research and experimentation, and prior to his untimely death in the mid-1890s he made major contributions to the technology of the period through a series of key inventions. Perhaps his greatest achievement, however, was the creation of what might be termed an "industrial incubator," a facility where a number of talented people, working both independently and jointly, developed machines or products which ultimately could be manufactured by new or existing companies. This unique facility was located in the machine shop Lipe opened on South Geddes Street in Syracuse in the early 1880s.

Lipe and his fellow experimenters achieved such inventions as an universal milling machine (important in the field of gear cutting), a time clock (used extensively by the large new factories which were springing up across an increasingly industrialized nation), a hulling machine (which would quickly strip the shells from coffee beans), a marine engine, the hub-boring machine utilized by the Moyer Wagon Company, and even such utilitarian products as machines to roll cigars and sew brooms. These inventions and others equally notable formed the basis for establishment of a host of major and minor business enterprises in Syracuse, thus giving the city an economic boost of considerable significance.[1-4]

Alexander Timothy Brown was born on a farm in Cortland County, south of Syracuse, in 1854. During over fifty years of adulthood he was to play a vital role as an inventor and manufacturer in the life of his adopted city. At the age of 22 he first came to Syracuse to work at $2.50 per day for a firearms manufacturer. This firm subsequently became the L.C. Smith Gun Company, and while employed as its designer Brown developed a series of improvements in firearms, including a breech-loading shotgun and a safety catch for gun locks. Brown then designed for the Smith firm a double-keyboard typewriter which proved to be immensely popular, enabling the company to become one of the leading American builders of these essential office machines. Shifting his remarkable inventive talents next to the field of transportation, Brown produced a pneumatic bicycle tire mounted on a "clincher" rim which he sold to the Dunlop Brothers of Great Britain for a small fortune. By this time Brown had joined Charles Lipe

THE FRANKLIN AUTOMOBILE COMPANY

*Alexander T. Brown was an inventor and partner of H.H. Franklin.
(Courtesy of Frances E Hares)*

at the "incubator" on South Geddes Street, and the two men jointly developed a dual-speed device for bicycles called the Hy-lo Bi-gear. Despite its value to bike-riders in easing the strain of hill-climbing, it was not immediately accepted by cycle manufacturers because of its cost. However, it formed the basis of a new firm which went on to develop gears and clutches for what ultimately was to become a vastly more important market. The new "horseless carriages," which were being constructed in small but steadily increasing numbers around the turn of the century, were in serious need of such devices to transmit power from engine to wheels. The Brown-Lipe Company found it advantageous to reserve space at early national auto shows to display its products, and the firm's reputation grew to the point that auto pioneers from other parts of America reportedly came to Syracuse to obtain its assistance in solving power transmission problems.[1-5]

TWO MEN AND AN IDEA

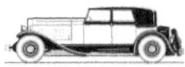

In this bustling city of the 1890s, with its rapidly expanding industrial base plus its cadre of talented engineers and inventors, arrived a young businessman who also claimed roots in upstate New York. He did not come to Syracuse directly from his fifty-mile-distant farm home, however, but first spent a number of years of early adulthood gaining valuable experience as an entrepreneur in a small Hudson River community.

Herbert H. Franklin was born slightly more than a year after the end of the Civil War, September 1, 1866, on a farm near the village of Lisle, New York. He thus was a few years younger than fellow auto pioneers Henry Ford and Ransom Olds, who were born in the Midwest in 1863 and 1864 respectively. Franklin's ancestors could be counted among the earliest settlers in the Finger Lakes Region of New York State. A great-great grandfather, Captain Roswell Franklin, after barely escaping death in an Indian massacre in Northeastern Pennsylvania, moved to the shores of Lake Cayuga in the late 1780s, where he constructed the first log cabin in what is now the village of Aurora.[a]

Descendants of Roswell sought their livelihoods in nearby communities, usually by tilling the soil, with the branch of the family which produced Herbert moving to the Lisle area about 1835. Herbert's father, Charles Risden Franklin, spent a short period in his late teens as a teacher in the nearby town of Cortland, but had turned to farming long before Herbert's birth. His mother, born Hannah Bliss, was a product of another small Finger Lakes community. Together with the two brothers and three sisters who reached maturity, young Herbert assisted his father in farm work during the crop-growing months of the year and attended school during the winter. While his childhood was relatively uneventful, one thing became certain at an early age–Herbert

---

a   Bad luck continued to haunt Roswell Franklin. Following a treaty between New York State and the Indian tribes, he was thrown off his land and, in despair, took his own life. The fascinating history of Roswell Franklin can be found in *Collections of the Cayuga County Historical Society*, No. 7, Auburn, NY, 1889, pp. 132-152.

had no desire to succeed his father in operating the family farm!^b In later years he recalled vividly his dislike of farm chores, particularly milking cows ("My father said the cows gave short measure when I milked," he related). An entry in his personal diary dated February 7, 1883, when he was sixteen, makes his views abundantly clear:

> Doesn't feel he can stand to work on the farm another season, but has to so supposes he must.

The young man's diary for the year 1883 includes notes on activities which did hold his interest. On March 31 he records the building of a work bench with two drawers, and on June 28 mentions visiting the wagon factory at Lisle. On August 18 an excursion trip north to Syracuse is briefly described, with his father paying one dollar for the train ticket and advancing Herbert twenty-five cents for spending money plus a five-dollar-bill for use in emergencies. He returned without having had to touch the latter.[1-6]

Farm chores were largely distasteful to Herbert, but book learning was not. The young man, after completing the common school grades locally, attended the Lisle Academy.^c He usually made the daily five-mile trip to and from the academy either on foot or riding a horse, but in the depths of the harsh upstate New York winter roomed in Lisle during the week, bringing food supplies from the farm to use in preparing meals. Contemporaries stated that Herbert was a bright youngster, quick to learn. During much of the period when he attended the academy it was headed by a capable young graduate of Amherst College, Giles Stilwell. The acquaintanceship which Franklin made with his principal would have important consequences for his future career.[1-7]

---

b Around the same time in southeastern Michigan, young Henry Ford also was making it clear to his father that work as a mechanic in the nearby city of Detroit was of greater interest than farm life.

c Lisle, situated 18 miles north of Binghamton and boasting of a population of several hundred inhabitants during Franklin's youth, functioned as a service and trading center for the surrounding agricultural area. In addition to the academy, Lisle could claim a half-dozen stores, two physicians, and a handful of small industries. The Franklin farm was located on a country road west of the village, in an area of low hills.

Having successfully completed the course of study at the academy, it was essential that the nineteen-year-old Franklin find employment. He first obtained a job with a small manufacturer of sleighs in a neighboring town, and quickly demonstrated considerable shrewdness in dealing with people. Put to work sanding the sleigh bodies, he observed that the shop employees, paid a fixed sum daily, tended to dawdle at their tasks. Franklin convinced the proprietor to base his compensation on the number of sleighs sandpapered, which resulted in more money for Herbert and more production (and profit) for the concern. The other employees soon followed suit, and the entire shop began operating on a piecework basis. The owner, impressed with the result, wanted Franklin to remain as his assistant, but the young man decided that his talents lay in areas other than sleigh-building.

At about this time Herbert met an older cousin, William Franklin, who published a weekly newspaper and operated a job printing shop in the small Hudson River town of Coxsackie. The cousin suggested that the ambitious youngster join him there. Herbert, sensing an opportunity to gain valuable experience at a place some distance from home, immediately accepted the offer, moving to Coxsackie on July 22, 1886, shortly before his twentieth birthday. Since as a teen-ager he had printed a tiny newspaper in his local neighborhood around Lisle, the work would not be totally foreign to him. Coxsackie, with a population at the time of some 1800, contained a number of churches, a shipbuilding yard in the lower part of town along the river, and one or two other minor industries. It was obvious from the start that "Cousin Will" (as Herbert called him) would display no partiality toward his young relative–he considered him simply low-cost help. Herbert's initial responsibility would be to aid his cousin in setting type–i.e., he would begin as a "printer's devil" or "apprentice to the trade." However, once he could perform basic printing tasks, his cousin held out the promise that he also might assist in some of the business aspects of the operation. The young man kept busy (occasionally toiling all night) in the print shop during his early months on the job, setting type and turning out items such as auction bills, envelopes, letterheads and tickets. By May of 1887 his duties also included helping make up the

THE FRANKLIN AUTOMOBILE COMPANY

Office of The Coxsackie News *in the Hudson River town of Coxsackie, New York, circa the late 1800's when H.H. Franklin worked there. (Courtesy of Barbara S. Rivette)*

The building that formerly housed The Coxsackie News, *as it appeared in 1997. (Sinclair Powell Collection)*

paper and billing customers.

Having skillfully mastered the printing shop procedures, Herbert quickly became a valued employee. At the end of the first year of his apprenticeship, in July 1887, he thus felt justified in requesting a salary for the duties he was performing, in addition to the room, board and clothes for which he had initially agreed to work. Personal feelings between the cousins tended to be cool (on weekends while off the job they seldom spoke to each other), and Will resisted for a time before finally agreeing to a payment of $150 per year (at the same time requiring Herbert thereafter to purchase his own clothes).

After some additional months had passed, however, it became apparent that a totally new relationship would have to be worked out if Herbert was to stay. The young apprentice, therefore, leased the newspaper operation, becoming associate editor and business manager, while Cousin Will, although retaining the title of "proprietor" of the paper, concentrated on the printing function. Herbert found the new position a demanding one, and took his responsibilities seriously. His diary for 1889 shows that he spent day-after-day at his desk, preparing copy, writing articles, getting the paper printed on an old-fashioned, flat-bed press, and sending out and collecting bills. The paper's mailing deadline each week was Friday morning, and he breathed a vast sigh of relief when all copies had been delivered to the local post office! Herbert authored stories about local activities in Coxsackie, covering such functions as the volunteer firemen's fair, and attended services at the various community churches, obviously to report Sunday sermons and related activities. For news from the outlying villages in the county he sought to secure locally-based correspondents, and did so in such a thorough manner that areawide coverage became outstanding.

The youthful editor clearly was proud of his new status as an emerging community leader in Coxsackie. Despite suffering all his life from a hare-lip and cleft palate, twin congenital defects which in that era could not readily be repaired surgically and limited his ability to speak to groups of any size, Herbert was succeeding in an expanded range of activities. In the 1889 diary he relates in some detail his successful efforts to organize a local board of trade, and expresses obvious pleasure at being elected secretary and a member of the executive committee of the new body. Clearly, for a young man of 23 he was moving steadily forward. He helped cement sound relations with local farmers by participating in the formation of a cooperative creamery, and together with other board of trade members promoted a waterworks for the municipality.

His newfound prominence was not appreciated by everyone—the editors of rival newspapers in the area, perhaps upset by Herbert's aggressiveness and his success in expanding the circulation of his publication, occasionally went after him with sharp language. On July 29, 1889, he wryly records in his diary being called a "pin-feather rooster" in the columns of the nearby *Hudson Register*! Such petty criticism only strengthened the energetic young entrepreneur's resolve to succeed, however. Herbert's social life began to blossom during this period also. The diary describes his taking-in a "leg show" (musical revue) in nearby Albany early in October 1889, and later in the same month going on a "double date" with a friend and two young women in a twin-seated wagon ("very pleasant time," he relates). He found time to be fitted with a badly-needed pair of glasses, and to order a quite expensive suit of clothes, with a "Prince Albert" coat.

Herbert Franklin now had reached his adult stature, standing just over five feet eight inches in height, and of slender build. Other distinguishing aspects of his appearance were his ever-present round-lensed spectacles, an impeccable wardrobe, and a moustache he grew in an effort to conceal his disfiguring harelip. Herbert undoubtedly enjoyed being able to fulfill family obligations by finding a place for his younger brother, Fred, in the newspaper's printing shop. The young editor at all times was a cool-headed, profit-conscious business manager. On numerous occasions he made it clear to persons sponsoring events in the village that publicity in the newspaper would depend on the placing of advertisements in its pages.

TWO MEN AND AN IDEA

During the next several years Franklin successfully expanded his printing and publishing activities to include an interesting new magazine for teachers, entitled *The Common School*. In 1891, together with a friend, Frank Bedell, he established a real estate and insurance business, and also sold bicycles and operated a ticket reservation service. The youthful editor raised "weather flags" on a pole in front of the newspaper office, thus giving local citizens warning of approaching storms. Franklin now had begun to spend a considerable amount of time on trips to various cities in the state–his diary records several journeys to Syracuse within a relatively short period of time, as well as visits to New York City. Much of this travel was recreational, but a part involved the seeking of new industries for the quiet river com-

The real estate office of Franklin & Bedell in 1891, in Coxsackie, New York. H.H. Franklin is the man on the left, wearing light trousers. His sister Mary is holding the bicycle. (Courtesy of Barbara S. Rivette)

munity in which he lived. He clearly displayed a genuine interest in the welfare of Coxsackie and its inhabitants.

On New Year's Day of 1893 Franklin, as was his habit, lists in his diary the positions he holds and evaluates the progress he has made during the previous twelve month period (by now he had become editor and publisher of the paper). He sums up the year 1892 as having been "fairly successful." However, a careful reading of his diary makes it clear that the ambitious businessman, no longer quite so young and inexperienced, had grown a bit dissatisfied with life in Coxsackie. Such a feeling is understandable–the often tedious day-to-day routine of newspaper work, coupled with the limited range of social activities available in a very small community, at the end of six years must have made his life seem a bit dull. Early in May 1893, he records a desire to leave Coxsackie. This somewhat tentative decision is reinforced a week or two later when a love-affair with a young woman ended in disaster. He literally cries out in his diary, "Fool that I am...parted with Clara for good...but there is one consolation...she will forget... young love will die." By late June he had completed arrangements with Cousin Will to take the newspaper off his hands, and began to bid farewell to friends.

It seems probable that Franklin initially hoped to seek expanded opportunities through a continuation of his newspaper career in a larger community, such as Syracuse or Buffalo. In a visit to Buffalo about this time he took his bicycle along in the baggage car of the train, so that on arrival he might have a ready means of touring the city and judging its future prospects. However, a few days before leaving Coxsackie he met an employee of the local valve works, H.G. Underwood, who had developed a new industrial process called "hydrostatic molding." Franklin now was sufficiently knowledgeable of business matters to recognize the commercial potential of this invention, which involved the insertion under pressure of molten metal into a form or die, with the metal assuming the desired shape as it cooled. He renamed the process "die-casting," and reached an informal understanding with Underwood to purchase the invention.

Departing from Coxsackie for good early in July 1893, Franklin went to Syracuse to attempt to interest such established companies as L.C. Smith Typewriter in using parts produced by the die-casting system. No immediate orders were forthcoming, but throwing caution aside, at the beginning of August he entered into a written agreement with Underwood to develop and utilize the new process. The contract called for all rights of the invention (including patents) to be assigned to Franklin, in exchange for which he was to provide capital for product development and manufacture and guarantee Underwood ten percent of the net profits plus employment for a stated period. With the agreement in place Franklin late in the summer of 1893 opened a small manufacturing shop at 241 West Onondaga Street in Syracuse. The rent for the new quarters was modest ($15 per month), as were the surroundings. Franklin's next-door neighbor was a tailor, while across the street a planing mill produced boards and shingles and a short distance to the west a Chinese laundry gave off clouds of steam. By late August Franklin and Underwood had installed a casting machine

The first Franklin "factory" located on West Onondaga Street in Syracuse. (Courtesy of Joseph Aronson)

and commenced operations in the tiny factory.[1-8] The young entrepreneur had taken his first step toward a future as an important American industrialist.

The months which followed saw many ups-and-downs in the life of the new venture. There were occasional successes in molding small products such as a match strike and a window sash, but these were offset by a substantial number of failures. The die-casting process was still in the experimental stage, and unremitting effort was necessary to produce satisfactory items. Franklin clearly was fighting a grim race against time–he had to manufacture soundly-crafted articles and market them successfully before his very limited capital ran out. The expense of the entire operation was his responsibility alone, as Underwood now was on his payroll. Both men performed such menial tasks as stoking the coal-burning furnaces and sweeping the shop floor in order to conserve funds. The two usually arrived shortly after six o'clock each morning to get daily activities under way. Pick-up of raw materials and delivery of finished products locally often were done by Herbert on his bicycle, since the small concern could not possibly have afforded the luxury of its own horse-drawn delivery wagon.

As the year 1893 drew to a close Franklin's financial situation had become critical. Orders were trickling in very slowly, and bills for machinery and supplies kept piling up. In late October Herbert commenced borrowing money from a young woman with whom he had become acquainted socially, and also from a male friend, Henry Chadwick. Established members of the Syracuse business community occasionally stopped by to examine the die-casting process, but clearly were reluctant to invest in such a small, unproved enterprise. In mid-November Franklin records in his diary that an effort to melt scrap brass in a new furnace was a failure, and that the bottom had been burned out of the shop's iron pot. By early December 1893, despite receiving a small order from nearby Rochester, Herbert had run out of funds–he unhappily notes in his diary on the 9th of that month that he is "blue busted" and "entirely broke," and that efforts to raise money by borrowing on his insurance policy and even by selling his fine watch had been unsuccessful. The nadir of the tiny enterprise had clearly been reached, and it was touch-and-go as to whether it possibly could survive.

At that critical point help came from a new source in the form of an advance of funds and some very useful advice. Giles Stilwell, Franklin's old academy principal in Lisle and now a well-established Syracuse lawyer, loaned Herbert several hundred dollars with the promise of more later, and counseled the aspiring businessman on organizing his small firm in a sound manner. With this assistance the corner had been turned, and disaster averted. Orders began coming in with increasing frequency, and the complex die casting process was gradually perfected. By July 1894, Franklin was able to buy out the minority interest in the firm held by Underwood, and a month later, obviously acting on Stilwell's advice, he formed a co-partnership. Members of the new organization, named the H.H. Franklin Manufacturing Company, were Franklin, Stilwell, Chadwick, James Pass and A.P. Seymour (Pass and Seymour were local manufacturers who had invested funds in the firm). Herbert received a more-than-one-third interest in the partnership and, of equal importance, was to be paid a salary of $100 per month as general manager of the enterprise, which would help restore his badly depleted personal finances.

By the beginning of 1895 conditions at the small company had vastly improved. Two men and two women now were employed in the shop, and various types of metal castings were being produced and shipped on a regular basis. In a diary entry for February 15, 1895, Franklin records the packing of a Chicago order, on which the firm would make a profit of $350. Additional items had been developed for the market–a cyclometer for use on bicycles, plus specialized parts for the various new high-technology firms springing up across America. With its innovative manufacturing processes now working well the company, while still of limited size, had entered the ranks of successful Syracuse industries. Somewhat larger quarters were obtained on North Franklin Street in the fall of 1895 to enable the firm to operate more efficiently. In December of that year the concern was incorporated under the same name as the former co-partnership, with James Pass as President, Giles Stilwell Vice President, H.K. Chadwick Secretary, and Herbert H. Franklin Treasurer and General Manager. At this time Franklin's business associates began addressing him as "H.H.," a nickname which clung to him for the remainder of his life.

During 1896 orders for die-castings reached a temporary plateau, a condition which caused the aggressive H.H. Franklin some concern. The maturing industrial executive, realizing that the firm needed to publicize itself and its products, occasionally prepared descriptive articles and advertisements for insertion in newspapers and trade journals. He also began scheduling extensive business trips to call on potential customers, with his diary for June 8, 1896 recording a meeting with Thomas Edison at the Orange, New Jersey, laboratory of the famous inventor. Franklin showed Edison samples of his die-cast products, and Edison, expressing pleasure at their quality, said that H.H. could expect to hear from him. There is no record as to whether any business relationship ever developed with the Edison interests, but at this point it was not of great importance. The value of the die-casting firm and its patented processes steadily increased (occasional "buy-out" offers were received), as did the volume of its production. Shipping records of the company for 1897-99 show that customers now included such nationally-important industrial firms as the General Electric Company of Lynn, Massachusetts, and the Western Electric Company of New York City and Chicago, as well as numerous small concerns located in states as far distant as Minnesota and Texas.[1-9] Arrangements were made with the renowned Lipe machine shop on South Geddes to produce dies and molds for the expanding H.H. Franklin Company, and early in 1899 the entire operation was moved to that location. Later that year the firm decided to exhibit samples of its products at the forthcoming Paris, France, Exposition, where it ultimately shared in the award of a silver medal. The company in subsequent years was credited by many authorities with originating the commercial die-casting process.

As a rising company manager Herbert Franklin now found time to participate in the social life of his adopted city. He remained a bachelor, securing room and board at the home of a married sister, Caroline Moser. The nearby lakes, with their dance pavilions and picnic areas, offered inviting opportunities for recreation, while parties at private homes plus occasional music recitals and plays gave a still youthful man additional means for enjoying himself. H.H. joined the Citizens Club of Syracuse in the late 1890s, and occasionally traveled to the Thousand Islands, long a favorite summer vacation spot for well-to-do Syracusans. However, evenings frequently found him foregoing social events to work at his desk in the factory, and on occasion he would don coveralls to assist shop employees in getting out a rush order. H.H. was able to offer employment in his firm to an older brother, Howard, who had gone west in the late 1870s to seek his fortune in the California gold mines.

From time-to-time the H.H. Franklin Manufacturing Company under Herbert's leadership sought to broaden its scope through the development of new products. An advertisement was inserted by the firm in the Scientific American magazine in the late 1890s, offering to purchase ideas or processes.[d] By the year 1900 the now-prosperous company was paying regular dividends to its small group of stockholders, and in addition depositing substantial surplus funds in a local bank. What the future might bring to the firm in terms of even greater business success was not entirely clear, but Herbert Franklin, with his hard-earned experience, was ready to guide it toward any promising new opportunity. H.H. also sought to explore profitably his keen interest in such areas as advertising and public relations. He regularly exchanged letters with leaders in these fields, at times offering his services on a consulting basis. The man had become a vigorous turn-of-the-century entrepreneur!

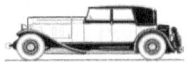

---

[d] The advertisement carried the attention-getting headline, "$5,000. We offer cash for ideas." *Scientific American*, April 24, 1897, p. 271.

THE FRANKLIN AUTOMOBILE COMPANY

John Wilkinson was born into a socially prominent and wealthy Syracuse family on February 11, 1868. His ancestors had been among the early settlers in the area, with his great-grandfather, a veteran of the American Revolutionary War, hewing a farm out of the forested wilderness near Skaneatales in 1798. This pioneer, an early John Wilkinson, shortly thereafter was killed in a barn-building accident, and one of his sons, also named John, gained an education by walking long miles through uninhabited territory to the nearest school. The son subsequently received legal training in the office of a local judge, and as a young lawyer was credited with giving Syracuse its name. This able attorney and businessman was the John Wilkinson who, as noted earlier, played a major role in railroad development in the Syracuse region. He also was an important civic leader, planning and laying-out the new community, serving as the town's first postmaster and representing the area in the state legislature. His son, J. Forman Wilkinson, also was active in railroad construction as a young man, but following service in the Civil War entered the banking field, in which for many years he prospered greatly. J. Forman was the father of the auto designer, the third John Wilkinson, whose career we will want to examine now.[1-10]

The future automobilist, after graduating from Syracuse High School at the age of seventeen, entered the Sibley School of Mechanical Engineering at Cornell University in September 1885. Young John had come to Cornell for instruction in his chosen field at a particularly fortunate time. A pioneer technical educator, Robert Thurston, who served as the first president of the American Society of Mechanical Engineers, also had just arrived at the university, and as director of the school was in the process of revolutionizing the engineering curriculum. Since Thurston was a renowned specialist in the technology of moving vehicles from one point to another by the application of power (he had analyzed and tested a gas engine as early as the mid-1870s), John could expect to receive unusually broad training in this subject. While steam was the key method of providing the force necessary for such vehicular movement in the mid-1880s, developments in the field of electricity also were occurring rapidly, and during his

TWO MEN AND AN IDEA

years at Cornell young Wilkinson and his classmates would have the extraordinary opportunity to work with both Brayton and Otto oil and gas-powered engines which had been installed in the university's testing laboratories.[e]

It became clear shortly after John's arrival, however, that the engineering school would have to relinquish him frequently to out-of-class activities that called for physical skills as well as mental ones. A splendid athlete, the young student was soon participating in a

Cornell University's first football team, fall 1887. John Wilkinson is in the middle row on the right. (Courtesy of Hope Wilkinson Yeager)

---

e   The Brayton motor, a primitive two-cycle unit utilizing first gas and later oil as a fuel, was developed in New England in the early 1870s and used to propel (at pitifully slow speeds) an occasional boat, streetcar, and omnibus. It also was used at Cornell in 1875 to power initially the dynamo which John Edson Sweet helped build. The Brayton motor was so weak that Sweet finally substituted his straight-line steam engine to drive the dynamo more effectively. Although it remained on the market for several years, the Brayton unit had fallen into disuse by the 1890s. The Otto engine, a four-cycle type, was adapted by the German motor car pioneers Gottlieb Daimler and Karl Benz for use in self-propelled road machines. In updated form the Otto engine powers the gasoline automobiles of today.

half-dozen sports, and excelling at most of them. Shortly after his arrival on campus he joined the "polo" team, which played a game now-long-forgotten, stick hockey on roller skates. The Cornell "polo" team faced off against Hobart College in its maiden game in the fall of 1885, with John Wilkinson, as "first rusher," scoring all the goals in a 3-0 shutout. John then went on to play third base on the varsity baseball team, competed for top honors in tennis, and was a member of Cornell's first intercollegiate track squad. Score cards recording his successful baseball and tennis contests still survive today.

In 1887 John and his fellow-students learned with joy that an earlier prohibition on university participation in another recreational activity, football, had been lifted. Cornell's aristocratic first president, Andrew Dickson White, was vehemently opposed to intercollegiate competition in this sport, which he regarded as crude and ungentlemanly. When Cornell students received a challenge from their counterparts at the University of Michigan in the 1870s to meet for a football game in Cleveland, Ohio, White had curtly rejected the request for faculty approval, issuing the celebrated statement: "Never will I permit thirty young men to travel four hundred miles to agitate a bag of wind!" White's successor as president, Charles K. Adams, took a more tolerant view of the students' interest in vigorous athletic contests, and John competed in the fall of 1887 for a position on Cornell's first football team. As a strong, aggressive 170-pound end he played a rugged game on the gridiron both offensively and defensively. The coaching given the neophyte eleven was unique, with a graduate student who had enjoyed some exposure to football while enrolled earlier at Yale assigned to instruct the squad as best he could in the fundamentals of the sport. Since his experience was so limited he usually was compelled to await the receipt of a weekly package of written instructions mailed by his former coach at Yale before running the team through its practices. With such an elementary level of coaching it hardly could be expected that the inexperienced squad would triumph against more seasoned opponents, and this proved to be the case. The young team put forth a valiant effort in its initial game against Union College, but an early lead was lost when several members of the untutored Cornell aggregation, as Wilkinson many years later recalled, made the mistake of questioning a referee's decision without taking the essential step of calling for a time out. Their more savvy opponents seized the opportunity to march down the field for a quick score, and taking advantage of one or two similar blunders soon put the game beyond reach. A second contest then was scheduled with Lehigh University, to be played on a neutral field in nearby Elmira, New York. Spectators' hats and canes flew in the air when the Cornell squad put over an early touchdown, but ultimately the heavier and more experienced Lehigh eleven carried the day. Any hard feelings between the opposing teams in those early days of intercollegiate athletics swiftly vanished after the end of each game, however. The erstwhile opponents usually sat down to a hearty dinner at a common table, with sufficient liquid refreshments served to enable the participants to quickly forget the black eyes and aching heads suffered in an era when no self-respecting player would go into a game wearing a helmet!

In addition to participation in sports, it also is obvious from early records that the young man led an active social life on campus. He was a member of Psi Upsilon fraternity, and participated in sufficient dances, "smokers," and boat rides on nearby Lake Cayuga to relieve any tedium caused by class and laboratory responsibilities. His out-of-classroom activities were so extensive that his daughter, Anne Sherry, remarked a century later: "Heavens, when did Dad ever find time to attend to his engineering studies?"

Obviously John did devote sufficient effort to school matters to enable him to successfully complete Cornell's demanding mechanical engineering course, since he was awarded his ME Degree in 1889. As the young man prepared to move from college into the world of work, his financial circumstances would be vastly different than during the period of his boyhood. The private Wilkinson Bank, owned and managed by his father and an uncle and long an anchor of the Syracuse financial community, had closed its doors about the time John began his engineering studies in the mid-1880s. With this collapse of the family fortunes coupled with the death of his father a few years thereafter, John would be compelled to make his way in the world largely through his own efforts.

The young Cornell graduate chose to return to his home community to begin his career. This was an era when the college-trained mechanical engineer was a new phenomenon, still struggling for recognition by American industry. Many firms, doubtful of the value of theoretical instruction, preferred to utilize persons with a shop background to fill engineering and design positions, and thus John found that despite his excellent education he would have to start at the bottom. He initially secured a position with the Sweet steel manufacturing firm, but soon moved on to the E.C. Stearns Co., where he worked for a period in the machine shop. Seeking experience further afield he spent some months with the Henry Worthington Pump Company in Brooklyn, but by 1891 had come back to Syracuse as a draftsman and machine designer at that large industrial concern, the Solvay Process Company. John spent some four years with this firm, during which time he was able to develop broad skills in the area of engineering design.

The drafting board alone, however, scarcely offered enough of a challenge to claim the undivided loyalty of this energetic and talented young man. Not unnaturally for an action-oriented individual, his attention had begun to turn to the field of moving vehicles. In the early 1890s a new form of personal transportation, the bicycle, burst upon the American scene and threatened to sweep everything before it. For decades a variety of technically-minded pioneers in France and England as well as America had experimented with such a vehicle, which gave a mounted rider, using his own legs for propulsion, a considerable degree of mobility. Many combinations were tried, but finally one was settled on–the so-called "safety" bicycle, incorporating equal-sized wheels front and rear plus a chain and sprocket drive which through the use of foot pedals enabled the rider to keep the vehicle in motion. About the same time the pneumatic tire came into use, providing an air-cushioned ride which appealed greatly to the new cycling enthusiasts.

The bicycle literally revolutionized individual transportation during most of the 1890s. The new vehicle sold by the hundreds of thousands annually, and bicycle exhibitions held at major halls and arenas were given immense publicity, often drawing as many spectators as would auto shows a generation later. Dealers sprang up by the dozens in towns of any size, and repair shops were available everywhere to keep each rider's cycle in top operating condition. The social effects of the bicycle were widespread. Cycling clubs were organized in communities large and small across the nation, and Sunday tours out into the countryside achieved vast popularity. Numerous clergymen, perhaps chagrined by the absence of young men and women at church services on the Sabbath, issued scathing denunciations of this "immoral pastime." The female sex in particular openly welcomed the two-wheeled machine. The huge skirts worn by women in that era soon began to give way to more utilitarian clothing necessary for comfortable bicycle riding. The "bloomer," while shocking the conservative, quickly became a recognized form of dress for female cyclists. A new sense of freedom was enjoyed by women, who for the first time had an easily-manageable personal vehicle available for use.

Other aspects of American urban life also were impacted by this popular new form of transportation. Police bicycle patrols were introduced to control speed on city streets. Persons who exceeded the legal speed limit, usually a sedate eight miles per hour, were prosecuted for "scorching," but city ordinances typically covered other misdeeds as well. One of the individuals affected was H.H. Franklin, shortly after his arrival in Syracuse in 1893. The youthful businessman ran afoul of the law when he illegally operated his cycle on the sidewalk, but successfully defended himself against the charge by proving that the street had been obstructed. Franklin, perhaps still a newsman at heart, in the mid-1890s took time from his manufacturing activities to contribute numerous anonymous items to the Syracuse papers, with several of these championing the rights of bicyclists.[1-11] Bicycle owners soon felt the need to organize to protect themselves against unfair treatment, with the League of American Wheelmen effectively representing cyclists on a national scale. The League plus local bicycle clubs also sought to have the rough, poorly-maintained streets in cities across America upgraded to a satisfactory level. Progress was slow, but it was at least a modest beginning of the "good roads" movement which would snowball two or three decades later during the automobile era.

The advent of the bicycle helped bring into being the modern American transportation industry. It was essential that the new two-wheeled vehicle be produced in vast numbers at a low per-unit cost if it was to successfully meet the demands of a mass market. This meant that broad-scale mechanization of the production operation would be required, with rows of special-purpose machines installed in cycle factories to turn out identical parts in large quantities. Advanced standards of mechanical precision were called for, since gears, shafts and hubs on a bicycle had to be fitted to very close tolerances. With tough new steels needed to stand up under the stresses imposed by use of the cycle (bicycle parts had to be both light and strong) the science of metallurgy also developed rapidly. The sheer size achieved by many of the new cycle factories stunned observers of the industrial scene. A company in Indianapolis hired its first employee in 1891; by 1897 during peak periods some 1,500 persons were producing two to three hundred bicycles daily in its vast plant. With these large operations came innovative methods of management control. The president of a New England bicycle concern employing 1,000 hands installed in his office a cluster of electrical devices which enabled him to monitor all factory departments effectively, and even check the temperature of the ovens used to bake paint on the cycle frames.[1-12] The forms of industrial organization and the operating methods developed for bicycle production were to be of immense value when the nation later turned to large-scale manufacture of other types of personal transportation.

Having a strong technological base to draw on, the City of Syracuse became one of the major centers of American bicycle production. In 1869 the Syracuse-based Sweet steel firm briefly produced a predecessor vehicle, the velocipede, a heavy contrivance with pedals directly connected to the front wheel. Later, in the early 1890s, the E.

C. Stearns Company developed a modern, light-weight cycle which achieved immediate popularity with male and female riders alike. Naming its product the "Yellow Fellow" ("catchy" advertising was pioneered by the cycle companies), the Stearns organization expanded to the point where its big bicycle factory, operating night and day, employed as many as 1,200 persons during rush periods and achieved an annual production of over 25,000 units in 1896. The Syracuse Cycle Company in the same year occupied another of the large factories in the community, with some 800 hands engaged in bicycle production and an additional 250 salesmen working on the road. This company turned out the "Crimson Rim" machine. Other local firms, including the Barnes, Empire, Olive, Dodge, Tourist and Frontenac Companies, also were important competitors. Syracuse bicycles soon were being shipped to nearly every part of the civilized world, and local cycle enterprises played a major role in the economic life of the city.

The year 1897 saw the peak of the cycle era locally. An enormous bike show was featured at the Alhambra Hall, with page after page in the Syracuse newspapers devoted to a description of the highlights of this premier event. Bicycle paths surfaced with cinders had been established through much of the city and out into the surrounding countryside, with cycle owners required to purchase license tags as a prerequisite to their use. Six men riding a bicycle along the New York Central railroad track just outside the city had been able to outpace a crack steam train over a short distance. It was estimated that in this period more than one out of eight Syracuse workers was employed by the bicycle industry or a related supplier firm.

The many companies which produced the new two-wheeled vehicles engaged in fiercely competitive merchandising practices. One of the most common of these was the sponsorship of bicycle racing, and in the early 1890s this activity inevitably drew the interest of John Wilkinson. The muscular young man began spending nearly all his free time training for cycle races, and quickly entered competition as a member of the Syracuse Amateur Athletic Association's racing team. Winning one contest after another, he acquired the title "curly-headed crimson king" of Syracuse bicycle racing (the color, of course, was that of the bicycle he favored). After vanquishing the local opposition he even competed occasionally in races against nationally-ranked cyclists, and reportedly did well in several such events.

The desire to become totally identified with this exciting two-wheeled vehicle finally became irresistible to John Wilkinson. The young engineer resigned his position at the Solvay firm late in 1895, soon thereafter transferring his allegiance to the Syracuse Bicycle Company. An initial assignment by his new employer was the design of a

At the peak of his bicycle racing career in the 1890's, John Wilkinson competed as a member of the Syracuse Amateur Athletic Union, as indicated by the "S" on his shirt. (Courtesty of the late Anne Wilkinson Sherry and John Sherry)

tandem (two-person) bicycle, which he promptly accomplished. The new machine was put to practical use when Wilkinson married Edith Belden in April 1896. The bride found herself being taken on a "bicycling honeymoon" through the several New England states (history does not record whether the petite young lady fully appreciated the cycling aspect of her wedding trip). At about this time John also developed a "quadruplet" on which he and three sinewy co-riders, whizzing around the Syracuse Velodrome, established a national speed record for such a type of cycle.

Having changed from the somewhat prosaic task of designing chemical processing machinery to more stimulating work in the bicycle field, it was hardly surprising that John Wilkinson soon expanded his

John Wilkinson (second from left) developed this "quadruplet" bicycle that set a national speed record. (Courtesy of the late Anne Wilkinson Sherry and John Sherry)

range of interests to include other methods of road transportation. As the decade of the 1890s swept along it had become apparent that the American public was ready to embrace further progress in development of the moving vehicle. The bicycle had demonstrated to the people of the nation the joys of independent personal mobility, and this feature appealed to all. At the same time the steam train and the electric street car displayed the advantages of power applied to a transportation medium utilizing steel rails, with the result being high speeds and the ability to cover long distances.

Clearly, the best of two worlds might be achieved by use of a motor of modest size to propel an individually-operated road vehicle. For a long period of years experimenters had groped with this idea, crudely at first but later in a more sophisticated manner. The first candidate for propulsion was steam, and since the 1700s numerous vehicles utilizing this power source had been tested on the roads of France, England, America and other nations. While some success was achieved, most of the early steam vehicles proved to be too heavy, dirty and dangerous to be tolerated by the regulatory authorities, and too complex to be operated by anyone other than a highly-skilled driver. A typical steam-powered unit, the massive Dudgeon wagon, was run for some months on the streets of New York City as early as 1857, but ultimately withdrawn from service. In the 1890s, though, thanks to advances in technology, lightweight steam runabouts were being designed for general use on public highways. The electric-powered vehicle, another favorite in this decade, enjoyed the advantages of complete cleanliness and relative ease of operation over limited distances. However, a third option, the internal-combustion engine, using an explosion of fuel within an enclosed cylinder to generate power, had been developed by various pioneers in Europe and America over a number of decades. It now offered a fairly reliable source of power, and thus was exciting the interest of a number of pioneer automobilists across America as a means of propulsion for road machines. It was this type of motor which John Wilkinson sought to utilize in a vehicle.[1-13]

It is impossible to pinpoint an exact date when Wilkinson began seriously attacking the problem of designing a gas-powered road machine. Clearly by the early summer of 1898, while still employed at the Syracuse Bicycle Company, he had begun such work. Since he was kept busy during daytime hours with his duties at the cycle concern, design activity for the most part took place in the evening, at a drafting table in his own home. The motor itself received John's initial attention, and from the beginning his internal combustion engine designs incorporated the principle of air cooling. He first developed a single-cylinder air-cooled engine, which was built but never utilized in a vehicle. Some machining and assembling of parts for the engine was done, perhaps a bit surreptitiously, at his employer's factory during the noon hour. It was about this time that John Burns, a fifteen-year-old Syracuse youngster employed as a shop helper at the cycle company, began to assist Wilkinson by handing him the tools he needed for his work. Wilkinson was able to test his early engine in the well-equipped mechanical laboratory at Cornell University, some sixty miles distant.

By the spring of 1899 Wilkinson had developed at least general plans and possibly some detailed designs for a four-cylinder gasoline power plant, also air-cooled. This motor in addition incorporated an auxiliary two-cylinder mechanism, a combined air-compressor and engine, which would work in conjunction with the gasoline unit. This ingenious device, acting first as a compressor while the car was driven, built up a charge of air in a storage tank. When released this charge would permit the device, now working as an air engine, to generate sufficient power to get the vehicle under way, with the gasoline motor taking over the operating task once a modest speed had been reached. The car thus did not require a clutch to control its forward movement, nor would it need to be started by hand-cranking (there was no transmission). All-in-all it was a complex design, but one which might appeal to a public concerned about the danger of attempting to get a gas motor operating initially by use of a crank.

THE FRANKLIN AUTOMOBILE COMPANY

By this time John Wilkinson was not the only person in Syracuse seeking to advance the cause of a self-propelled road vehicle. Practically all the local bicycle companies, now confronted with a saturated market for their two-wheeled product, were experimenting with some type of "horseless carriage." At least one firm was considering steam for motive power, and a second electricity, while others had turned toward the gasoline engine. In visits to these concerns John observed at one plant a partially constructed, air-cooled gas engine. In addition to such experimental efforts, several Syracuse citizens had purchased motor vehicles built outside the city, and occasionally operated them on local streets. While records are far from complete, the initial gasoline-powered car to appear in the city apparently was a single-cylinder Haynes-Apperson, which was delivered new to local businessman

The first gasoline-powered car in Syracuse, New York, April 1899, The Haynes-Apperson car was owned by Syracuse businessman Ted Wilkin. (Courtesy of the Automobile Club of Syracuse)

TWO MEN AND AN IDEA

Ted Wilkin in 1899, and quickly displayed to the public. However, this vehicle may have been preceded by one or more electric or steam-powered machines, and perhaps even by a pioneer gas-driven unit.[1-14] In the spring of 1899 a highly-successful bicycle company sales manager, C. Arthur Benjamin (an early competitor of John Wilkinson on the bike racing circuit), opened the first auto salesroom and service facility in the city, featuring the Locomobile steam car. In the field of commercial vehicles, by late 1899 an electric delivery van had been placed in service by a local A & P grocery store.

The automobile thus was very much "in the air" in Syracuse as the nineteenth century neared its end. Elsewhere in the nation, following development of various experimental gasoline, steam and electric vehicles throughout the decade of the 1890s, one manufacturer, Duryea, had offered a few gasoline-powered cars for sale as early as 1896, and several others were advertising similar products on a regular basis by the year 1898. Electric and steam powered cars were being built in New England in respectable numbers for sale to the public during this period, and two Midwestern companies, Haynes-Apperson and Olds, in 1898-99 erected the nation's first automobile manufacturing plants.

Aware of the swift progress being made elsewhere, John Wilkinson, armed with the plans for his unique gas-air engine, in the late spring of 1899 sought to convince a group of Syracuse business and professional men to sponsor development of an automobile. The group, which included Ernest White, a lawyer, Frederick White, a local capitalist, and Arthur Peck, general manager of the Barnes Bicycle Co., displayed keen interest in the Wilkinson concept. In a series of meetings held through the summer of 1899 the group discussed a possible partnership with Wilkinson for construction of a vehicle incorporating the gas-air engine. Before a partnership was established there appeared to have been an informal agreement reached by the parties to proceed with building an automobile, with Wilkinson to contribute his time and the others funds to pay for labor and material. Consequently, some work on parts for the engine was begun immediately at several local factories, with John Wilkinson coordinating the activity. At the end of the summer of 1899 the Syracuse Bicycle Company closed its doors, leaving Wilkinson without permanent employment and able to devote full time to motor vehicle development.[1-15]

A formal partnership agreement was entered into by Wilkinson with Ernest and Frederick White and Arthur Peck on September 19, 1899. The work on development and construction of an automobile then intensified, with John Wilkinson now assisted by Edward Moore, a former bicycle company machinist who was employed by the partnership. Two rooms were rented in the so-called Industrial Building on East Water Street (nicknamed the "Beehive" because of the many diverse activities taking place there) as a location for machining and fitting parts for the car. John and his assistant worked steadily through the remainder of the year, and on the first day of January 1900, unveiled an initial motor vehicle. This automobile featured the Wilkinson gas-air engine mounted amidships in the vehicle, under the seat. A rather crude "surface carburetor" was used to mix gasoline and air for combustion in the cylinders. Contemporary pictures indicate that the two-seat body may have been adapted from another motor car, possibly the Locomobile runabout. With the machine ready to run it was brought to the large top floor of the building owned by the Leggett Carriage Company on State Street, where it could be demonstrated indoors to interested persons.

During January and early February of 1900, the new vehicle, in addition to being operated on a "track" during indoor demonstrations, was taken on outdoor trips through downtown Syracuse. An initial drive was cut short when failure of a connecting rod bearing caused the engine to stick as the car was crossing the New York Central Railway tracks. The auto had to be pushed back to Leggett's by Wilkinson and Moore. A second journey was made without incident, and following a third trip the car was placed in storage, first at the Benjamin automobile garage and later at the Lipe machine shop on South Geddes.

It seems obvious that everyone regarded the first vehicle as simply a model to show what could be done. Consequently, design work on a second car, incorporating a larger motor and other changes, was commenced late in February of 1900. Wilkinson and Edward Moore undertook this work jointly, with the drawings and plans being prepared in various temporary quarters. The second car was constructed in the Lipe machine shop principally by Moore, with assistance from Lipe personnel. On its completion about the beginning of June 1900, it proved to be far superior to the first model in operating capabilities. The new vehicle was soon being used successfully in daily demonstrations, and as many as 100 persons rode in it on short trips around Central Syracuse during the summer months. Wilkinson undertook a longer out-of-town journey, to South Bay on Oneida Lake, in the early fall of 1900 as part of an automobile club run. About a dozen other machines participated in the tour, indicating that use of motor vehicles was now sharply increasing in Syracuse. On this trip the car's otherwise smooth performance was marred by a brief period of overheating, requiring John Wilkinson to splash water on the cylinders to aid in the cooling process.

Shortly after design work began on the second vehicle the members of the White-Peck-Wilkinson partnership together with several additional investors took steps to incorporate the New York Automobile Company. Those involved in the original partnership turned over to the new company all partnership property, receiving stock in exchange. Following completion of incorporation on March 1, 1900, the company entered into a formal employment contract with John Wilkinson. Under its terms John would be paid a salary of $100 per month as superintendent-engineer and assigned a considerable amount of stock, in exchange for which he was to convey to the New York Automobile Company all patent rights related to discoveries and inventions he might make while in its employ. Despite the large authorized capitalization of the new company, $350,000, only a total of six to seven thousand dollars actually was paid into the treasury of the firm to meet expenses.

Some limited efforts were made by key investors in the New York Automobile Company to move toward actual production of the second

THE FRANKLIN AUTOMOBILE COMPANY

Wilkinson automobile. After receiving a relatively optimistic report from John in September 1900, about the potential marketability of the vehicle, committees were appointed by the board of directors of the firm to report on the cost of machinery necessary to manufacture the car and on the availability of factory sites. No follow-up action was taken by the company toward purchasing such machinery or securing a facility for manufacturing, however. In the meantime John Wilkinson continued testing and seeking to improve the second model car. The air starter was removed in order to lighten and simplify the vehicle, the position of the engine was changed from horizontal to vertical, and the valve arrangement was modified. John conferred from time-to-time with the technically-knowledgeable Alexander T. Brown, who had invested money in the New York Automobile Company, on solutions to other problems which existed in this second vehicle. The company at one point decided that another motor, designed by Brown, would be built for experimental purposes, but because of limited funds this was not done.

By the spring of 1901 it was apparent that conditions at the New York Automobile Company were far from auspicious. The company had failed to take any further steps whatever toward organizing itself as a manufacturing concern. It not only lacked a factory, but apart from an informal arrangement at the Lipe machine shop for storage of the two Wilkinson-designed cars, did not even have a place of business. Its key directors appeared to be focusing their efforts primarily on attempting to raise capital from outside sources, and displayed little interest in making additional investments themselves. John Wilkinson's suggestion that development of a marketable air-cooled car by the firm would require construction of yet a third model was not acted on (the second car still lacked a transmission, and thus could be operated only on a single forward speed, with no reverse gear whatsoever). The company treasury now was empty, and the firm had ceased to pay John a salary. Clearly, at this point the New York Automobile Company was drifting aimlessly with no apparent goal or purpose.

What was wrong appeared all too clear. The struggling firm did not contain an individual who could balance John Wilkinson's inventive genius with the practical business qualities and personal dedication needed to insure success for the enterprise in the marketplace. Without such a person the group lacked focus and direction, and the innovative research and experimentation which had been undertaken to develop a sound air-cooled vehicle was in grave danger of becoming meaningless. It was obvious by this time that the automotive effort was little more than a sideline with many of the shareholders of the firm, mostly prominent Syracuse business leaders whose futures were not dependent on the success or failure of a tiny, undercapitalized enterprise. Such decidedly was not the case with John Wilkinson. All of his time plus his limited resources had been thrown unstintingly into the effort to develop a successful car. As months continued to go by without a salary being paid he appeared to have his back against the wall financially, encountering problems in meeting bills. Finally, at the end of June 1901, John resigned his position with the New York Automobile Co. The future thus looked bleak indeed for the talented inventor and his pace-setting automobile. Other Syracuse firms, particularly the Stearns Company with its electric car, had been moving forward with the development of marketable vehicles, and soon might be expected to leave the Wilkinson-designed product in the dust.

At this critical juncture one of the shareholders in the New York Automobile Company, the able inventor-manufacturer Alexander T. Brown, determined that a radical change in the existing course of events was necessary if the Wilkinson air-cooled automobile ever was to be produced successfully. Brown therefore decided to enlist the services of a businessman in whose abilities he had confidence. The great partnership was about to be born!

THE FRANKLIN AUTOMOBILE COMPANY

– *Two* –

Entrepreneurship and Vision: The Birth of a New Organization (1901-1905)

During the winter of 1900-1901 the directors of the New York Automobile Company had occasionally discussed the need for a general manager of the operation, to serve on either a full or part-time basis. A bicycle manufacturing executive first was approached, but proved to be uninterested in changing employment. Some time later Alexander T. Brown suggested that Herbert Franklin be considered for such a position. At that point the two were well acquainted, as Brown had invested a substantial sum in the H.H. Franklin Manufacturing Company in the late 1890s, becoming president of the firm at the same time. Finding the New York Automobile people somewhat receptive to utilizing Franklin's services, Brown took steps to bring the two parties together.

At an initial meeting with an officer of the New York Automobile Company, Alexander Brown introduced H.H. Franklin as a person he felt was well-qualified for the position of operating head of the organization. Franklin was informed by the Automobile Company officer, however, that a manager was sought who could put fresh money into the enterprise, perhaps as much as $10,000. The ever-cautious H.H.

asked for time to consider this. A few days later he informed New York Automobile representatives that he had little interest in managing their company on these terms, and if he invested in the automotive business at all it probably would be on his own account.[2-1]

As these discussions proceeded, certain very important related developments were taking place. Immediately after resigning from the New York Automobile Company John Wilkinson discussed his future and that of the air-cooled car with H.H. Franklin in a momentous meeting at the Lipe Machine Shop. Legend also has it that about this time Franklin was given a ride in the Wilkinson-designed automobile, and found himself favorably impressed with both the vehicle and its builder. In any event, a few days later John entered the employ of H.H. Franklin and Alexander Brown, who had formed a partnership for the purpose of manufacturing automobiles. Franklin and Brown felt strongly that development of a sound air-cooled car without further delay was essential, and determined to jointly underwrite the cost of such work by John Wilkinson. The goal would be the swift creation of an automobile of marketable quality, and to achieve this John, following initial consultations with Brown and one or two other persons, quickly began the preparation of new plans and drawings. The four-cylinder air-cooled engine concept was to be retained, but otherwise the car would represent a generally fresh approach.

As Wilkinson's work got under way, H.H. Franklin continued intermittent discussions and negotiations with officers of the New York Automobile Company. Despite additional urging Franklin stood firm in his determination not to become manager of the automobile firm. Possibly H.H. felt he would be spread too thin in attempting to oversee the work of both his own die-casting operation and a separate motor car company; or perhaps he simply questioned the wisdom of attempting to rescue the obviously shaky automotive concern. The suggestion also was made that Franklin buy out New York Automobile, but H.H.'s modest offer was spurned as inadequate, and finally withdrawn. The key people in the automobile concern then advanced the idea of a consolidation of their firm with Franklin's, but H.H., backed by Brown (by now totally in his corner), would have none of this. When New York Automobile's officers expressed unhappiness at John Wilkinson working for Franklin and Brown, H.H. stated that this step had been taken to conserve time, and informally indicated that if no agreement of any nature was reached, the results of Wilkinson's new work might be turned back to the Automobile Company on repayment of Brown and Franklin's out-of-pocket costs.

Negotiations between the parties finally collapsed in September 1901. At that time a representative of the New York Automobile Company requested that H.H. Franklin render a statement of expenses incurred in the new development work being undertaken by John Wilkinson, and turn the end product back to them. This H.H. refused to do, indicating that in addition to John's work ideas of others now had been incorporated in the new model being developed. The New York Automobile people were acutely unhappy with the outcome, implying that Wilkinson and his concepts had been unfairly appropriated and that Franklin had got "something for nothing." As a result a sharp schism developed, with New York Automobile officers at a later date filing a lawsuit against Franklin, Brown, Wilkinson and the H.H. Franklin Manufacturing Company, in which they sought substantial damages.

While the businessmen negotiated and bickered, John Wilkinson lost no time in moving ahead with his work. The infusion of cash from Brown and Franklin had made it possible for the enthusiastic young engineer to proceed immediately with the design and development of a prototype production vehicle. Seated at a drafting board in space rented by the die-casting firm on the second floor of a wooden structure known as the Lipe Building annex, Wilkinson laid out plans for an air-cooled car of advanced design. His blueprints were quickly shaped into metal in the Lipe shop by a small team of machinists and mechanics, and in an incredibly brief time the vehicle was assembled and ready. On October 1, 1901, while H.H. Franklin was at lunch, Wilkinson, without any preliminary testing, ran the machine out into the street and off to the open country. Later in the day H.H. joined his designer in trying out the car, and any resentment which he might

THE FRANKLIN AUTOMOBILE COMPANY

have felt at not having been included on the initial run soon vanished as he observed the mechanical excellence of the new vehicle. Over twenty miles were covered on that historic first day, with the small automobile demonstrating the ability both to whiz along the straightaways and readily climb the steep hills in which the Syracuse area abounds. The other partner, Alexander Brown, was given a ride two days later, and endorsed Franklin's comment that the new car was a great success. The total direct cost of producing the new vehicle was the minute sum of $1,100.

With the mechanical soundness of the vehicle fully demonstrated Franklin, always the practical businessman, turned his attention to the need to restructure the die-casting firm to encompass the new operation. A proposal to expand the scope of the H.H. Franklin Company to include automobile manufacturing was submitted to the board of directors, and unanimous approval received. The problem of funding was dealt with initially through a decision to increase substantially the authorized capital of the company. These changes were reflected in revised articles of incorporation adopted by the concern and submitted to the State of New York in mid-November of 1901.[2-2] At the same time the Company bought out the Brown-Franklin partnership (which included rights to the newly-designed vehicle) for $50,000, payable in stock. Alexander Brown continued as president of the reorganized corporation, with Franklin serving as its treasurer and general manager, W.C. Lipe as vice-president, and, H.K. Chadwick as secretary. The new automobile would bear the name of the company which was to produce it—Franklin. John Wilkinson, perhaps somewhat surprisingly, made no objection to this decision. Ultimately Wilkinson, in recognition of his work in designing the new car, was given a portion of the company stock received by Brown and Franklin.

These necessary organizational changes having been made, the H.H. Franklin Company now could move ahead with plans to manufacture its new automobile. There can be little doubt that for a number of reasons the timing of this step was propitious. While by 1901 Americans in most sections of the country found public transportation to be generally satisfactory, with fast trains meeting the traveler's long-distance needs and electrified streetcars plus the new interurban trolleys readily available for shorter trips, the same was not true of the personal vehicle. As had been the case for centuries, the horse-drawn wagon or buggy continued to furnish for most persons the basic means of private travel. The bicycle, which had sold in such huge numbers throughout much of the decade of the 1890s and seemed for a time to offer a new and exciting means of free-ranging individual transportation, now was fast fading in popularity. The public clearly had become sharply aware of the limitations of this two-wheeled vehicle, propelled at modest speeds through vigorous muscular effort on the part of its rider. The cycle more and more was perceived as a practical means of transportation primarily for short distances in pleasant weather, and even then suitable for use only by a single individual who was not burdened with large packages or extensive luggage. As the populace recognized these shortcomings annual production and sale of bicycles dropped precipitously, from nearly a million and a quarter in 1899 to less than one-fourth of that amount a few years into the new century.[2-3]

At the same time the vast publicity being given the new "horseless carriage" was making Americans also aware that a greatly improved means of personal transportation now was at hand—one which could offer speeds nearly competitive with those of the streetcar or train, coupled with an ability to convey the vehicle's driver and passengers directly from one point to another at a time of their own choosing.

Certain factors did exist which in the pioneer days of the automobile tended to limit its use. One was capital cost–the typical self-propelled vehicle still involved a far larger initial investment than did the horse and wagon or the bicycle. However, by the turn of the century America's economic prosperity had generated a large and constantly-growing body of professional and business persons who had the fiscal ability to invest in promising new means of personal transportation. Two other important limitations were abominable roads in rural areas (many city streets were little better), sharply restricting long-distance auto travel, and the lack of mechanical reliability of all-too-many of the early vehicles. Transforming muddy, rutted country lanes into decent, hard-surfaced highways would require the long-term attention of the great mass of citizens and their governments; the problem of reliability of the new machines on the other hand could be dealt with directly by each individual motor car company. Fortunately, in the case of the Franklin automobile those who built it were from the very beginning determined to produce a simple, sound and reliable car, which could be fully depended on by its purchasers to perform well under even the most adverse conditions.

There would be ample competition facing the H.H. Franklin Company in late 1901 and early 1902 as it prepared to bring its new product to market. The 1900 U.S. Census of Manufactures noted that fifty-seven establishments were producing automobiles at that time but this may well have been a less-than-complete count.[2-4] Throughout the nation, from major metropolis to tiny village, during this period could be found numerous concerns which had developed self-propelled vehicles and were offering them for sale to a generally receptive public. The great majority of these were underfinanced, poorly managed operations, which typically might produce a few units and then close their doors forever. A number of leaders in the industry already were emerging, however. In Michigan, despite having been crippled for a time by a fire which destroyed its factory, the Olds Motor Company in 1902 was achieving an annual production volume of gasoline-powered vehicles measured in the thousands, with the firm even utilizing a primitive assembly line. The small "curved dash" Olds was seen briefly in Syracuse in October 1901, when youthful Roy Chapin, a rising star with this Detroit and Lansing-based auto maker, drove through the city en route to New York (because of the pitiful condition of public roads he often utilized towpaths found along the banks of the Erie Canal as his route). This trip was intended to demonstrate to the public the capabilities of the light, simply-constructed $650 runabout which

ENTREPRENEURSHIP AND VISION

Olds now was manufacturing following disastrous earlier experiments with larger, more complex models. Various other concerns also had reached considerable size, among them the Bridgeport, Connecticut, based Locomobile Company, which for several years had produced in substantial numbers a very successful steam-driven vehicle under patents purchased from the Stanley brothers and was preparing to offer a gasoline car for sale in the near future. The air-cooled vehicle field already had been entered by the Knox Automobile Company, a Massachusetts firm now selling a small, gasoline-powered, three-wheel runabout whose "one-lunger" engine featured vast numbers of steel pins screwed into the cylinder to assist in dissipating heat (it was appropriately nicknamed "Old Porcupine"). Annual Knox production by the year 1901 had passed the 100 mark, and soon would go much higher.[a] The electric-powered vehicle, despite being handicapped by heavy batteries and limited cruising range, found numerous buyers, particularly for urban use. In New York City electric taxicabs had furnished service since 1897, and substantial numbers of women now were driven to shops and social events in this metropolis by chauffeurs in broughams propelled by this type of motor. Future industry leaders such as Packard and Pierce-Arrow had begun the manufacture of gasoline-engine machines, with the first National Automobile Show held at Madison Square Garden in New York City early in November 1900 (electric and gas motor cars had been displayed earlier at a bicycle exhibition held in New York in February 1899, attracting thousands of curious onlookers). In the Syracuse area efforts were being made to market such cars as the Stearns, which by 1901 had produced small numbers of both electric and steam vehicles, and the Century.[2-5]

Before placing an automobile on the market for sale H.H. Franklin and his associates prudently decided to develop still another experimental vehicle. This car was ready by early 1902, and on March 3 of that year was given its first out-door run. Modernized through

---

a   Harry Knox, of Springfield, Massachusetts, organizer of the automobile company bearing his name, and Steven Balzer, of New York City, may have been the first Americans to develop motor cars powered by air-cooled gasoline engines. Knox claimed to have driven his vehicle on local roads in 1897. Balzer, whose tiny quadricycle utilized a three-cylinder radial motor spinning around a stationary crankshaft, alledgedly tested his machine on city streets a year or two earlier.

placement of the engine in front and installation of wheel steering it proved to be a splendid machine, particularly adept at hill-climbing. By early summer the second car was being used for out-of-town trips of some distance, with Brown and Franklin driving to H.H.'s home town, Lisle, and back without experiencing problems of any nature. Wilkinson and his handful of assistants clearly had performed their development task in a first-rate manner.

The long period of experimentation and testing having been completed, the young company now was ready to introduce the initial Franklin automobile to a hopefully receptive public. A "Type A" light roadster, with two individual bucket seats, was put on display for the first time on June 19, 1902, at Leggett's Carriage Shop in downtown Syracuse. Local citizens did not demonstrate any great readiness to purchase the vehicle, however, and on June 23 it was sold to S.G. (Sylvester Gilbert) Averell of New York City, a Cornell classmate of John Wilkinson. The new owner left immediately with his vehicle for a return trip to New York, but encountering roads in the Albany area which were literally impassable due to rain he placed the car on a Hudson River steamboat for the balance of the journey. Averell's payment of $1,200 for the roadster was unquestionably welcomed by the fledgling auto firm–after briefly considering framing the check the practical H.H. Franklin instead had it photographed, and then quickly deposited it in the concern's bank account ("We needed the money," he was frank to state later). A second vehicle was sold not long afterward to Herman Casler, the inventor, and a third to a Mr. E.F. Shepard. Yet another was delivered in mid-September to J.A. Seitz, a Syracuse photographic supply store owner. Seitz would give his car hard business use during the ensuing winter, often running the heavily-loaded machine through snow drifts so deep that the local trolley cars were unable to function.[2-6] Correspondence of H.H. Franklin indicates that a purchaser late in the year was the sportsman-industrialist Max Fleischmann, then mayor of Cincinnati. Some thirteen vehicles had been disposed of by the Franklin firm when the initial model year came to an end. The company now could consider itself successfully launched in the automobile business.

ENTREPRENEURSHIP AND VISION

This photo, taken in 1994, shows the initial production Franklin car of June 1902, as it exists today. The car was acquired by the Smithsonian Institution in 1937.

For the technically-minded a brief description of the initial production vehicle is desirable. The new car weighed a bit over 900 pounds, some twenty-five percent lighter than the first product of the Ford Motor Company, which, powered by a two-cylinder water-cooled engine would be displayed in Detroit a few months afterward. The wheelbase of the Franklin was 71 and a fraction inches,[2-7] with transmission and differential brakes utilized to stop the vehicle. The frame was constructed of angle iron, and the tiny body made entirely of wood. Four full-elliptic (over and under) carriage-type springs were used to suspend frame and body on the axles of the vehicle, which were of tubular construction in order to minimize unsprung weight. The "bicycle-style" tires were three-inches in width, and were mounted on 28-inch diameter wire-spoke wheels. The car was controlled by means of a steering-wheel located on the right side, with the throttle and ignition advance levers positioned on the steering post just beneath the wheel. The four cylinder, overhead valve, air-cooled engine of equal bore and stroke (3¼ x 3¼ inches), developing some seven horsepower, was placed transversely in the front of the chassis, and thus received the name "cross-engine." In order to insure adequate cooling from the

THE FRANKLIN AUTOMOBILE COMPANY

The initial production Franklin shown in its early days. (Courtesy of Elizabeth A. Doman)

natural flow of air (no fan whatever was used!) each cylinder was cast individually, and was encircled with fins about 1/16 of an inch thick to help dissipate the heat. A planetary transmission located at the left side of the engine provided two forward speeds and reverse, and was connected to the differential in the rear by means of a long chain. The gear ratios were twelve-to-one for low and four-to-one for high, with the gear shift lever mounted at the right side of the vehicle and the reverse pedal placed on the floor. A speed of fully thirty miles-per-hour could be attained on high gear. The car utilized jump-spark ignition and a float-feed carburetor, with the engine splash-lubricated. The air-starter used on the vehicles Wilkinson built for the New York Automobile Co. was not incorporated in this car, thus hand-cranking was necessary.[2-8]

The new vehicle's conception was unusually advanced for its day, and reflected fully the innovative thinking of John Wilkinson. This early master of automotive design recognized that a four-cylinder engine would be far superior to a "one lunger" in flexibility and smoothness, and would produce maximum power at a relatively modest speed (the contemporary Packard car utilized a single-cylinder engine, and while well-constructed lacked both the Franklin's freedom from vibration and its ability to achieve cruising speed quickly). The slowly-rotating Franklin engine also would reduce the number of explosions taking place within each cylinder in a given time period, and thus permit air-cooling to do an effective job. The light weight of the auto, coupled with the use of full-elliptic springs, gave the vehicle exceptional stability on rough roads and saved the passengers from the harsh ride typical of most cars of this era. Above all the vehicle was constructed in a simple, uncluttered fashion, free from excess bulk and economical to operate. The feature of air-cooling meant that it could be driven during the icy temperatures of an American winter, without the ever-present danger of "freeze-up" found in water-cooled cars.

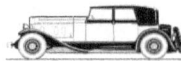

During this early period the H.H. Franklin Company's experimental and production activities were conducted in a series of rented buildings located in the southwest section of Syracuse, none of which was found to be particularly satisfactory for automotive-related purposes. A substantial amount of money was spent initially in rehabilitating two floors of an old four-story factory located at the corner of West Fayette and South Geddes Streets for vehicle manufacture. Unfortunately, a very few days after operations got under way in this structure it was totally gutted by fire, resulting in a loss of much newly-acquired equipment and severely delaying company progress. Another leased unit on South Geddes then was used to assemble the first production car, while the die-casting functions plus machining of auto parts continued in the Lipe building.

Obviously, use of such scattered, largely makeshift facilities must have galled the disciplined business mind of H.H. Franklin. It is not

THE FRANKLIN AUTOMOBILE COMPANY

The original Franklin factory, erected in late 1902, measured only 50 by 110 feet. The structure was located at the corner of Marcelus and South Geddes streets and later became part of the General Office Building of the firm. (Courtesy of the late David T. Doman)

surprising, therefore, that as the company began to meet with increasing success in the manufacture and sale of cars in 1902 (the die-casting operation also was thriving), attention was given by Franklin to the need for permanent quarters. A tract of vacant land located on South Geddes Street a block below the Lipe shop was acquired, and plans for an attractive new brick structure were promptly prepared. Following a formal ground-breaking ceremony in mid-September 1902, ("A great many people got full on the cider," H.H. Franklin reported), construction progressed swiftly, and in January 1903, H.H. could triumphantly report that the firm had initiated activities in its new multi-story factory, "with power on and the wheels turning." The die-casting operation followed auto manufacturing in the move to the new plant.[2-9]

Once fully under way the company continued its physical growth with unabated momentum. The nineteen hundred and three model year (to November 1) saw 181 vehicles built and sold–an increase in excess of one thousand per cent over 1902.[b] Further plant expansion thus be-

---

[b] Year-to-year production and sales figures for the Franklin automobile during this period are far from easy to ascertain, largely because "model year" and "calendar year" usually differed. The firm often began manufacture of a model year vehicle during the fall of the previous calendar year, with a number of retail sales possibly occurring during this period also. It is not clear how such sales were reported.

came necessary immediately, and late in June 1903, ground was broken for a major addition to the initial building. Its completion a few months later gave the automotive concern a tall, impressive red brick structure stretching well over two hundred feet along South Geddes Street in which to house its offices and factory operations. However, even this splendid facility soon proved to be of insufficient size to enable the lusty young auto firm to meet the burgeoning demand for its product. Sales of the Franklin car again were to increase several fold to a total of just over 700 in the 1904 model year, and manufacturing space once more would be at a premium. By July of that year the crash of a steam-powered piledriver could be heard sinking the underpinnings for a new wing, which would be joined to the rear of the main Geddes Street unit at approximately a ninety-degree angle and extend some 160 feet to the west. Completion of this five-story structure, together with a number of auxiliary buildings including a powerhouse, a test facility, and a repair shop, made it possible for the firm at least for the present to carry on its ever-expanding level of activity efficiently.

Young industrial organizations do not develop at the tempo achieved by the H.H. Franklin Manufacturing Company without access to two key items–money and personnel. Unfortunately, fiscal records covering the early days of the company presently are unavailable, and its financial history must be reconstructed from a number of ancillary sources. The Franklin firm, as it began to build automobiles, could of course utilize any fiscal surplus built up during the die-casting period. However, start-up expenses undoubtedly were heavy in the new area of activity (particularly for such items as buildings and machinery), and until a number of cars were sold and the profits generated thereby could be realized, additional cash funds would be needed. This meant that the heads of the organization, as was true of practically all early auto entrepreneurs, had to address almost immediately the problem of finding additional sources of capital. In this effort, however, the company's key executive, H.H. Franklin, could draw on his background of fund-raising experience in the early days of the die-casting operation in Syracuse.

THE FRANKLIN AUTOMOBILE COMPANY

The two major investors in the concern as it began to design and manufacture automobiles were Alexander Brown and H.H. Franklin himself. Each soon contributed new funds to help meet additional company expenses; Brown about $20,000; H.H. some $10,000. Brown easily was able to produce such a sum from his own ample resources, but H.H. may have been compelled to borrow his share through a personal note to a bank. The Lipe family plus their associate, H.W. Chapin, also invested in the company, and Giles Stilwell and other shareholders in the original die-casting concern increased their holdings in the new combined operation. A sprinkling of other local people also purchased stock, including A.J. DeMott, E.H. Dann, W.H. Warner, F.E. Cable and Dr. D.H. White. In the early months of auto manufacture H.H. Franklin occasionally would offer a car for sale at a reduced price contingent on the prospective purchaser becoming a stockholder (there were few takers). He also sought to enlist new investors by offering several such persons a bonus half-share of stock from his own holdings for each new full share purchased. Companies which supplied Franklin with parts and raw materials occasionally agreed to take stock in the firm in lieu of cash payments. Well-to-do Syracusans generally, however, did not rush to back the new venture with their assets.[2-10] This in part may have been the result of ill-feeling engendered by the New York Automobile Co. dispute, but it also appears that due to the rapid pace of industrial development attractive opportunities for placement of venture capital existed elsewhere in Syracuse at that time (the city enjoyed excellent diversification of industry, and was fast becoming a leader throughout the world in the manufacture of typewriters). Major investment banking firms in New York City and other Eastern financial centers showed little interest in risking money anywhere in the young and struggling automotive industry during this period–they followed the conservative practice of making their funds available primarily to businesses with proven earnings records, such as steel and railroads. Officials of many such banks for some years viewed motor car companies as little more than out-and-out speculations.

H.H. Franklin clearly left no stone unturned in his efforts to obtain additional capital for his expanding firm from potential outside investors. A number of surviving letters written by him to friends in Coxsackie and to business acquaintances in other cities demonstrate the vigor of his fund-raising efforts. These early letters also testify to something else–the confidence of the man in both his company and the future of the automobile, and his ability to project these beliefs through the written word. Whatever difficulty Franklin may have had in expressing his thoughts orally, the following excerpts from one of these letters demonstrate his facility in written expression:

Frank F. Bedell
Coxsackie, N. Y.

August 8, 1901

My Dear Frank:

    Before long I expect to be doing things in the automobile business. It is the coming business. Did you know that?
    The business isn't coming in a night like the foolish mushroom. It is coming fast though, and a lot of folks are going to wonder why they didn't see it coming. About that time it will be too late to get on the "ground floor"...
    Getting in right is what is going to count...
    I have been watching developments since '93. I have watched with eyes open. I am convinced that as a business proposition now is the time. It is neither too late nor too early. It is "it."
    ...Maybe you think automobiling is only a fad. But don't. As a factor in industrial and financial operations it has come as a permanent fixture. Its development and progress is as certain as the sun...
    ...Whatever may be the improvements in other things the power vehicle can't be let go of.... People will walk. But they will also ride. A self-propelling conveyance is the limit–not the horse, no rails, no trolley pole.
    What's this to you? Just this: the H.H. F. Mfg. Co. is going into the automobile business. The company is already a solid institution. It has brains (emphasis on the brains) and capital. It has made its way by purely business methods. Stock schemes, manipulations and rake-offs have never been its stock-in-trade...
    Our folks are going into the business on business principles.
    We are going in to win.
    Our machine is right. It embodies what others have learned as well as what fresh brains have conceived. If you or your friends are looking for an investment that promises good, look us up...
    We think the situation with us is extremely favorable. Experiments have been done. Future expenditure will be for assets and products only...
    The stock will be sold at par. Shares $100 each.
    Anyway isn't it time you made me a visit?

                      Yours truly,
                      (signed) H.H. Franklin

THE FRANKLIN AUTOMOBILE COMPANY

Despite this and other similarly eloquent letters there is no indication that any important investment ever was made in the firm by an out-of-town person. Consequently, Franklin and his Syracuse colleagues had to proceed largely on their own in funding the spectacular growth of their promising new venture. This undoubtedly took both skill and careful management, but H.H. and his aides proved fully equal to the task. The fact that automobile manufacturers in this era could obtain payment for the cars they produced from a dealer or other purchaser quickly (a "sight draft," calling for payment on delivery, accompanied each vehicle shipped), while settling accounts with parts suppliers in a somewhat leisurely fashion, helped Franklin and other pioneer motor vehicle companies remain solvent.

The swift success met by the H.H. Franklin Company in manufacturing and selling vehicles triggered a parallel need for rapid expansion of the firm's work force. In finding qualified personnel the company unquestionably was aided greatly by the precipitous decline in demand for bicycles and the consequent vast cut-backs in employment made by the once-thriving cycle companies. Nearly all the numerous good-sized bicycle manufacturers which earlier operated factories at peak capacity in Syracuse now had closed their doors, and the plants either lay idle or had been converted to some other use (Franklin ultimately was to utilize one for body manufacturing). Thus from the ranks of displaced bicycle plant employees the Franklin organization obtained many of the typical skilled and semi-skilled workers needed in an early auto factory–tool makers, machine operators, fitters and assemblers. Surprisingly, the manufacturers of horse-drawn vehicles did not suffer from the same abrupt drop in production in the first few years of the new century, and thus this industry contributed relatively few persons to the motor car firm's work force. Employment at the Franklin Company, which utilized only thirteen employees to initiate auto manufacturing (some thirty-five others worked in the die-casting division in 1901-02), grew steadily through 1903 and even more rapidly in 1904, reaching the level of 570 toward the end of the latter year. The firm thus had swiftly attained an important position in the ranks of Syracuse industrial concerns. The original die-casting operation now

ENTREPRENEURSHIP AND VISION

Frank Barton served in administrative capacities for the Franklin organization for more than 30 years. (Franklin Automobile Company dealer's brochure)

found itself completely overshadowed by motor-vehicle building.

Several persons who were to play significant roles in the affairs of the Franklin Company joined the organization in these very early years. Frank Barton resigned his position with a small industrial concern in a nearby town to enter the company's employ as assistant manager and purchasing agent on February 1, 1902. Barton, the brother-in-law of H.H. Franklin, would serve for over thirty years in important administrative capacities with the firm. At the beginning of 1904 a young but experienced manufacturing executive, Frederick Haynes, joined the organization as assistant engineer. After receiving training in engineering at Cornell in the 1890s, Haynes entered the bicycle field, working briefly with John Wilkinson at the Syracuse Cycle Company and ultimately becoming superintendent of the Toronto, Canada, plant of the E.C. Stearns Company. When this unit was bought out by the bicycle "trust" at the turn of the century, the young man served under rough-and-tumble John Dodge of Detroit in one of the Canadian factories of the consolidated organization. A year or two later, when Haynes had moved on to head a machine-building concern in Marquette, Michigan, Dodge, recalling the demonstrated capabilities of the young engineer, urged him to take the position of superintendent of a recently organized Detroit auto manufacturer in which Dodge had become an investor, the Ford Motor Company. However, after inspecting the tiny Ford factory Haynes declined the opportunity, feeling that the Detroit concern simply looked too down-at-the-heels to be able to pay him the substantial salary offered. With know-how in the areas of both engineering and manufacturing Haynes would play an important role in the Franklin Company during its formative years, and later rise to top positions elsewhere in the auto industry.[2-11]

The rapidly-expanding Franklin firm attracted additional talented individuals in both office and shop. Giles Stilwell, H.H. Franklin's attorney, remained in the company's employ on a part-time basis (he continued independent law practice, also), later becoming a vice-president. Stella Tague, after a short period of training in a local business school, joined the company during its die-casting era as secretary to H.H. Franklin. Despite her youth (she wore her red hair in braids), Miss Tague quickly made herself indispensable both to Franklin personally and to the organization as it moved ahead in the complex business of auto-building. John Burns, who had continued for a time in the bicycle field after John Wilkinson left it and subsequently worked for a rubber products manufacturer, rejoined his old chief at the Franklin Company in September 1904. Burns, an extraordinarily versatile man endowed with both great technical ingenuity and immense physical energy, was to perform notable services in many capacities for the firm over the next three decades. Still others would join the young organization. C. Arthur Benjamin, the "boy wonder" bicycle and auto salesman of Syracuse, came on board as Franklin's first general sales manager on October 1, 1902, and swiftly initiated a campaign to develop a nation-wide organization to market the company's product. Dealers were quickly secured in such cities as Chicago, Boston, New York, Pittsburgh, Indianapolis and Denver, with arrangements made to exhibit the Franklin car at the New York Auto Show to be held in January 1903. At this time, H.H. Franklin also sought to interest an English businessman, Oliver Wethered, in producing and selling the Franklin car in Great Britain, on a royalty basis. Despite numerous highly persuasive letters from H.H., Wethered ultimately rejected the offer, thus depriving the new Syracuse auto manufacturer of the op-

ENTREPRENEURSHIP AND VISION

Herbert H. Franklin (right) greets John Burns (left), almost a half-century after Burns joined the H.H. Franklin Manufacturing Company in 1904. The photo was taken around 1954. (Courtesy of Automotive Hall of Fame)

portunity to pioneer in building and selling an American car abroad.

Practically all automobiles in this pioneer period to a greater or lesser degree were "assembled" vehicles–that is, outside suppliers were relied on by motor car companies to provide a variety of essential parts. In its very early years Franklin followed this approach, and looked to local and out-of-town manufacturers for a number of items needed to complete construction of its vehicles. Thus the John Leggett Carriage Company of Syracuse initially produced the small but beautifully-crafted wooden bodies used on Franklin runabouts; as the volume of its production shot upward Franklin also purchased this key component from the Hill Body Company of Buffalo.[c] Ultimately the firm began constructing its own bodies, largely of aluminum. The adjacent Brown-Lipe Company furnished steering gears, differential units and transmission parts for the vehicle, all of very high quality, with the Penn Spring Company in nearby Baldwinsville providing the spring leaves necessary to cushion the vehicle's ride. The tiny kerosene lanterns which provided limited illumination for those drivers brave enough to venture forth at night were principally obtained from such well-known lamp manufacturers as R.A. Dietz of Syracuse and C.M. Hall of Detroit. The oiler used on the car to provide lubrication, and the dynamo utilized to generate electric current, were furnished by manufacturers from other cities, while engine bearings were produced in the Franklin die casting shop.

Together with other early leaders in the automobile industry, the top executives of the H.H. Franklin Company were quick to recognize the immense amount of free publicity which might be obtained by entering their product in racing and endurance events. During this pioneer period newspapers and popular magazines devoted almost unlimited space (and headlines) to describing the competitive achievements of various automobiles and their drivers, and many an unknown make of vehicle became a household word literally overnight following a contest in which it had emerged victorious.

---

c   The Hill firm also produced bodies for a competitor air-cooled car, the Cameron, as well as for the Thomas Motor Company of Buffalo.

ENTREPRENEURSHIP AND VISION

*Taken circa 1903, this photo shows the early "cross-engine" Franklin vehicle.
The identity of driver is unknown.
(Courtesy of American Automobile Manufacturers Association)*

In this era the heads of many of the pioneer auto companies themselves were quick to doff their business suits and don the goggles and dustproof coats which constituted the racing uniform of the day. The fiery Alexander Winton of Cleveland was ready at a moment's notice to pilot the cars produced by his company in a variety of contests across America, and even the more cool and calculating Henry Ford of Detroit risked his life to set a world's speed record on the frozen surface of Lake St. Clair.[2-12] The Franklin Company fortunately had a member of its own organization who in speed and endurance contests could compete with the best. John Wilkinson, with his impressive background in bicycle racing and other competitive sports, quickly rose to the challenge and proved that he was no deskbound engineer by participating in a number of exciting events. Driving a ten-horsepower Franklin runabout in several races at Yonkers, New York, on

THE FRANKLIN AUTOMOBILE COMPANY

July 25, 1903, John handily defeated a number of competitors who piloted various makes of domestic and imported light cars. This contest demonstrated decisively to the numerous (and often highly vocal) critics of the air-cooled car that the company's product could display a somewhat surprising turn of speed.

Later in the same year Wilkinson was to prove that the vehicle which he had designed was tough and durable, as well as swift. As one of a team of six drivers who piloted three Franklin cars, he competed in a brutal 800 mile endurance contest from New York City to Pittsburgh, via Buffalo and Cleveland. The conditions encountered throughout much of the race were well-nigh unbelievable–pelting rains turned the primitive roads into quagmires, and at one point collapse of an unrepaired bridge resulted in a Franklin car sliding into a deep stream. The drivers as well as the vehicles were subjected to harsh stresses and strains–when the mud-spattered John Wilkinson entered his hotel in Buffalo he had not taken his clothes off for fifty hours. Two of the rugged little Franklin cars nonetheless were able to complete the entire trip with high scores. These triumphs were particularly pleasing to the company sales manager, "Art" Benjamin, who shrewdly utilized the resulting favorable publicity to excellent advantage.

Then, in the summer of 1904, Franklin Company officials made the decision to subject their small four-cylinder car to the most challenging of all possible tests, a transcontinental run. Two experienced drivers, L.L. Whitman, who held the cross-country record for water-cooled cars (achieved in an Olds vehicle), and C.S. Carris set out on August 1, 1904, from San Francisco for the east coast in a stock Type A Franklin. In addition to a generous supply of spare parts and a good-sized kit of tools, the two men also carried a pair of items which were to prove indispensable on the trip–an axe and a shovel. The following excerpt is taken directly from L.L. Whitman's description of the run in the Franklin Company pamphlet: "From Coast to Coast in a Motor Car:"

Leaving Sacramento after lunch...we headed for the mountain pass... as we neared that point, the road gradually grew worse. Large boulders had rolled into the road.... At Colfax we stopped for the night. When we left early in the morning the summit was over fifty miles away...we climbed on the low speed gear for hours...at 5 PM the last grade was mounted and the Franklin stood 7,256 feet above sea level.... We looked over our brakes...and then started downhill over ledges and rockstrewn trail.... Next forenoon we ran down to Reno.... We reached Clark, a desert station...a little after dark.... Seventy-five miles away was the town of Lovelock, and no sign of life in-between except the railroad.... On this desolate waste...not a blade of green grass, not a tree, not a drop of water are to be found.... Many times a day we had to use axe and shovel as the machine would flounder in a hole or catch on a stump or high ridge in the road...at times we were obliged to get the car up on the railroad track

This small four-cylinder Franklin car set a record in the 1904 transcontinental run, cutting the former record almost in half. The two drivers were L.L. Whitman and C.S. Carris. C. Arthur "Art" Benjamin is probably the man on the left. (Courtesy of American Automobile Manufacturers Association)

and bump over the sleepers...the washes, ruts, stones and sand were a test for any automobile...between Rock Springs and Rollins (Wyoming) our rear axle caught on a telegraph pole that had been cut off a foot above the ground. We brought up good and solid and both of us flew out over the front of the car in regular circus fashion!... we looked over the machine and discovered only a bent truss rod... at noon on the sixteenth day we entered Denver. On we sped, and at noon on the fourth day from Denver we rolled into Omaha...our next point was Chicago...Toledo...Cleveland...Buffalo...then Rochester. Early next morning we were off again, being due in Syracuse in the afternoon. The reception and the banquet we were given at Syracuse were in reality for the little car that stood outside. The next morning dawned clear and fine for the run to Albany and the Hudson River...the day following we arrived at the New York Automobile Club's building at 1:20 PM...thirty-two days, twenty three hours and twenty minutes had passed since leaving San Francisco.

As the previous time for crossing the continent in a water-cooled car had been 61 days, the two drivers in their Franklin came very near to cutting the former record in half! This highly successful run generated substantial publicity in numerous metropolitan newspapers, undoubtedly of priceless value to the company in marketing its vehicles.

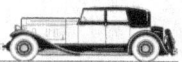

While the Franklin car was demonstrating its worth on the nation's primitive roads, the leaders of the firm which produced it sought to deal effectively with the numerous business problems which confronted a company active in a newly-established industry. One of the more important early decisions reached by the board of directors was to join the ranks of the Association of Licensed Automobile Manufacturers (ALAM), which the H.H. Franklin Manufacturing Company accomplished by signing Articles of Agreement on March 5, 1903 (such other well-known pioneer motor car firms as Olds, Pierce, Packard, Locomobile, Peerless and Winton became members of ALAM at the same time). The ALAM organization was far more than a mere autobuilders' national trade association. ALAM members acknowledged the validity of Rochester, New York, attorney George Selden's controversial claim, through an 1895 patent, of having invented in 1877 the gasoline-powered vehicle in America, and agreed to take legal action against those manufacturers, including Henry Ford, who refused to pay royalties to the assignees of the patent. Many will find it surprising that a company with a highly-independent person, H.H. Franklin, at its helm, would join an organization which throughout its existence was tagged with the label "monopoly." This action in part may be ascribed to the fact that while H.H. had a mind of his own, he also was essentially conservative in dealing with business matters. The threat of lawsuits by the assignees of the Selden patent rights may well have concerned the leader of a company which only recently had achieved success in its operations. Whatever the reason, the Franklin Company not only joined the organization, thereby making itself responsible for payment of a small licensing fee on each car produced, but its executives actively participated in ALAM affairs. H.H. Franklin became treasurer of the association, serving in this capacity until his resignation of the post in 1908, and on at least one occasion appeared to advocate sharply limiting new entries in the automotive field.[2-13] Giles Stilwell was named a member of the trades committee and vice-president of ALAM's important patents subsidiary, while John Wilkinson served on the organization's technical standards committee with such other renowned pioneer automotive engineers as A. L. Riker of Locomobile, Russell Huff of Packard, Hiram Maxim of The Electric Vehicle Company, and Charles Brady King of The Northern Auto Company.

The broad-scale acceptance by the public during this period of the Franklin product could be attributed largely to two factors; manufacture of a well-engineered and carefully-constructed motor car and the development of an astute publicity campaign to bring to the attention of potential buyers the merits of the vehicle offered for sale. Several attractive brochures intended for broad public distribution were developed by H.H. Franklin and his aides, extolling (often in a witty fash-

THE FRANKLIN AUTOMOBILE COMPANY

ion) the virtues of the Syracuse air-cooled product. Officials of the company also made effective use of advertisements in both technical journals and magazines of general circulation during the early years of the firm's existence, with $25,000 appropriated in December 1903, to carry on a broad advertising campaign. Numerous well-written ads were developed to provide maximum appeal to individuals with some prior knowledge of the automobile, as well as to relatively uninformed persons contemplating their first purchase. These ads pointed out in persuasive language the advantages of the Franklin car's light weight, simplicity of design, economy, and air cooling. An advertisement in the *Scientific American* for January 28, 1905, tells the reader:

> The car you want is not the car with the most horse-power, or with this frill or that, but the car that does the most at the least expense... The car you don't want is the complicated, heavy car that wears out tires fast, uses gasoline extravagantly, costs a lot for repairs, and is clumsy besides.

Then, in conclusion the ad relates:

> "The Franklin gets its power by masterly engineering and its light four cylinder air-cooled motor!"[2-14]

With an ability to put across such telling points it is not surprising that Franklin sales registered another excellent gain in 1905, rising to just under eleven hundred. At this time the company had achieved a level in national sales which placed it among the top four or five members of ALAM.[2-15] (Olds, Cadillac and Winton were its key competitors.) Obviously, Franklin was marketing its product exceptionally well by any standard, with 92 dealers across America now handling the Franklin car.

Sales success helped produce early financial prosperity for the concern. Capital stock issued and paid for jumped from $138,500 on December 31, 1903 to $260,500 a year later. The first dividend was declared in 1903, in the amount of $8,900, followed by distribution of the more healthy sum of $26,050 in 1904. These were highly satisfactory returns on investment for a relatively new automobile manufacturer. No dividend would be paid in 1905, due to a decision by management to reinvest earnings in continued expansion of the company's facilities. Such a farsighted policy, however, would benefit holders of stock many times over in future years as the company grew and prospered.

Renewing the earlier dispute, a lawsuit was brought by officers of the now almost defunct New York Automobile Company against H.H. Franklin, John Wilkinson, Alexander T. Brown and the Franklin Manufacturing Company in December 1904. The case was tried in special term of the New York Supreme Court in July 1905, before the experienced Judge W.S. Andrews. As plaintiffs, New York Automobile Company officials charged that the Franklin interests took Wilkinson from them, used certain unique ideas which he had developed while in Automobile Company employ, and converted to its (Franklin's) use plans which the Automobile Company had paid John to carry out. The defendants denied all this, with Wilkinson noting frankly that he never had claimed to be the first person to have developed an air-cooled gasoline engine. Theodore Hancock, former New York State Attorney General and now co-counsel for the defendants, introduced a degree of levity into the proceedings by moving to have the suit thrown out of court on the ground that the plaintiffs could claim no property right in the air or atmosphere! After spending several months evaluating the testimony, in December 1905, Judge Andrews found totally in the defendants' favor and dismissed the matter. The judicial decision pointed out that no patents had been granted Wilkinson for work done on a four-cylinder air-cooled motor while in the employ of New York Automobile, thus a charge of infringement could not be sustained. It went on to state that the Automobile Company did not appear able to demonstrate loss of any other right, since it obviously could not claim a property right in the skill and experience which Wilkinson had gained while in its employ. Any informal promise made by H.H. Franklin during the course of negotiations to turn back to New York Automobile the results of John Wilkinson's work done for H.H. and

THE FRANKLIN AUTOMOBILE COMPANY

Alexander T. Brown lacked consideration and thus was without validity, the court determined. The judge also sharply rapped the knuckles of New York Automobile for its delay in bringing the suit, implying that it may well have done so only after the Franklin Company had achieved success in automobile manufacturing.[2-16] The opinion clearly took a progressive view toward the interchange of ideas in the early automotive industry, and numerous companies in addition to Franklin may well have been the beneficiaries. The decision was appealed by New York Automobile to higher state courts, but was upheld in all aspects.

With its continuing concern for high quality, the Franklin Company in 1905 took steps to organize a formal research and testing program (an informal one had existed from the beginning of the auto manufacturing period). A mechanical laboratory was established in September of that year, enabling the company to experiment with new devices and conduct extensive tests to insure reliability and long life for each individual component of its product. Early the following year the laboratory was expanded to include physical and chemical units, giving the company what undoubtedly was one of the best engineering research facilities in the young automobile industry.[2-17]

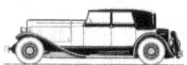

The H.H. Franklin Company followed a conservative policy in the models it offered the public during its initial years of automobile manufacturing. The two-passenger runabout introduced in 1902 was continued largely unchanged as the company's only series through 1903, although late in that year buyers were given the option of ordering a removable aluminum tonneau (rear seating compartment), which would increase carrying capacity to four persons. For 1904 the company broadened its offerings. The small runabout, the Model A, had its wheelbase extended to seventy-eight inches and featured artillery-style wooden wheels. The body now was aluminum throughout, with the car weight totaling 1,100 pounds and the price nudged upward to $1,400. The Model B would be similar in size, but with the addition of a tonneau sold for $1,650. These vehicles continued to use the small four-cylinder "cross engine," now rated at ten brake horsepower. The two basic models, however, would be supplemented by a larger and far more expensive Model C. This new version was capable of transporting five passengers, incorporated a ninety-six inch wheelbase, and weigh a full 2,200 pounds. It would feature a twenty-four horsepower engine (still four-cylinder) placed lengthwise rather than transversely, with the "natural" air cooling supplemented by use of a fan.[2-18] The base price would be a resounding three thousand dollars, with a collapsible top costing an additional $250.

This modest expansion of the Franklin product line was followed by a proliferation of models in 1905. No less than four variations of the small cross-engined vehicle were offered, two essentially of the roadster style (one of these did have a detachable tonneau), and two others with permanently-attached rear compartments. There also were two top-of-the line touring models, designated the D (one-hundred-inch wheelbase; twenty horsepower, forty miles per hour top speed) and the C (one-hundred-ten-inch wheelbase; thirty horsepower; 2,400 pounds in weight; capable of fifty miles per hour). The new 1905 cars, while continuing to utilize four-cylinder engines exclusively, would feature important technical advances. Additional use would be made of aluminum in both engine and body construction; this would keep car weight at a modest level (well below that of water-cooled competitors) despite increases in size. Laminated wood frames were now utilized in the two larger models. The overhead engine valves would be supplemented by an auxiliary exhaust port located near the bottom of each of the four cylinders; such an innovation would help the engine rid itself of burned gases and thus reduce any tendency to overheat. The two larger cars, both with longitudinal engines, also would feature three-speed sliding gear transmissions, an important step toward modernization of the vehicles. The company now was manufacturing automobiles in two distinct price classes; the small cross-engine units would sell in the $1,400-$1,700 range, while the pair of senior vehicles carried price tags of $2,500 and $3,500.

THE FRANKLIN AUTOMOBILE COMPANY

In addition to repositioning its automobile product line to enable it to compete in the semi-luxury price range, the Franklin Company by late 1904 had begun to explore the possibility of developing commercial vehicles. Initial efforts appeared to be somewhat limited in scope, and probably consisted of little more than placing a small pick-up or panel delivery body on a passenger car chassis. However, statements by former employees plus company records indicate that by the beginning of 1905 experimentation on vehicles specifically designed for hauling commercial loads was under way, with Aurin Chase, a young engineer, spearheading the work.[2-19] The company thus could anticipate being able to compete in a new field of activity in the near future.

By 1905 auto manufacturing had gained a modest but steadily expanding foothold in the ranks of American industry. The Census of Manufactures published that year–actually covering 1904 operations–listed 178 establishments producing motor vehicles (this total included body and parts manufacturers as well as actual motorcar builders). These motor vehicle concerns employed 12,049 hourly wage earners and 1,181 salaried employees, indicating clearly that the typical auto or auto-related factory was a small one. The overall volume of motor vehicles built during 1904 was 22,800, with some eighty-five per cent of those powered by gasoline engines. Total value of product was $30,033,000, with two cities, Detroit and Cleveland, together accounting for over 36 percent of this amount. The auto industry, however, was broadly-decentralized–while in terms of volume Detroit now had become the nation's leading automotive manufacturing center, such cities as Cleveland, Indianapolis and Buffalo offered important competition, and many small and medium-sized communities in such states as Indiana, Connecticut, Massachusetts and New York contained companies which produced substantial numbers of vehicles. It should be noted, however, that the 1905 census report showed very clearly that the auto industry still was insignificant in relation to carriage and wagon manufacturing. The total output of vehicles by carriage factories was given as 937,000, with the wagon builders producing an additional 644,000 units.[2-20]

ENTREPRENEURSHIP AND VISION

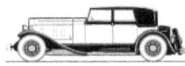

As the year 1905 neared an end H.H. Franklin and his colleagues undoubtedly viewed with satisfaction the impressive progress their organization had made in the highly-competitive motor car field in a brief period of time. Building a vehicle which emphasized technical innovation and sound quality of workmanship, the firm had swiftly carved out for itself a significant position in the ranks of American automobile manufacturers. Although beginning auto production later than another upstate New York builder of high-caliber cars, Buffalo-based Pierce-Arrow, the level of Franklin sales quickly surpassed that of Pierce despite the strong reputation for reliability the Buffalo firm had achieved in the initial Glidden Tour. Total American auto industry production reported for 1905 rose slightly from the year before to just over 24,000 units; thus Franklin now was building nearly five percent of all American automobiles.[2-21] Local competition for the firm largely had disappeared, since the Syracuse-based Stearns and Century automobiles both had faltered before entering volume production, and output of the Iroquois motor car (built at various times in Syracuse and nearby Seneca Falls) was insignificant. A local Syracuse engine builder, the Brennan Manufacturing Company, also produced a few vehicles, some in kit form for "do it yourself" auto assemblers.

Internally the Franklin Company saw a specific division of responsibilities taking place between H.H. Franklin and John Wilkinson. In the realm of overall business management, including finance and marketing, H.H. would be in complete control, assisted by such key lieutenants as Frank Barton, Giles Stilwell and C. Arthur Benjamin. Barton supervised all details of office operations, while Benjamin continued to contribute his vast enthusiasm and energy to the company sales effort. Stilwell, a mature and skillful attorney, was of great assistance as an advisor to the firm not only on legal matters but in the important area of industry relations as well (governmental relations were of minor importance in this era; the auto industry was subject to little public regulation). In the fields of engineering and plant operations John Wilkinson now was in overall charge, although his title would be only that of engineer for several more years. Wilkinson's principal deputy in the area of manufacturing was the hard-working, serious Fred Haynes. A man of both ability and integrity, Haynes supported without reservation the dedication of his chief to production of a high-quality automobile. It should be noted that in developing this major division of responsibility within the organization the Franklin policy strikingly paralleled that of the young Ford Motor Company of Detroit, where Henry Ford headed engineering and manufacturing functions and James Couzens directed all business affairs.[2-22]

The steady expansion of Franklin Company operations made it necessary to increase the work force continually, and by mid-1905 employment had reached the 1,270 range.[2-23] To a considerable degree this swift rise appears to have been due to a decision by management to make more and more parts in the company's own shops, a policy which Franklin would follow to unusual lengths throughout its corporate history. The H.H. Franklin Manufacturing Company thus had speedily become one of the major employers in the City of Syracuse, and one of the top half-dozen in the entire auto industry. By comparison, total employment at the Ford Motor Co. of Detroit was only 300 at this time, due to the Ford being largely an "assembled" car. Of equal importance, it should be observed that the Franklin firm had served its community well in taking up much of the slack in local employment caused by the abrupt closing of all the bicycle plants in Syracuse. As noted earlier, this discontinuation of bicycle production threw hundreds of blue-collar employees out on the street. By supplying many of these persons with jobs, the company kept a large number of individuals in the community who otherwise might have been forced to relocate.

In evaluating its potential future position in the industry, the H.H. Franklin Company now could expect to encounter increasing competition from other firms. The company had achieved a significant early advantage by producing a smoothly performing four-cylinder vehicle at a time when practically all its competitors offered less satisfactory one or two-cylinder autos. This was changing rapidly, as additional manufacturers had begun to develop and produce similar multiple-cylinder machines. As yet the price of the typical four-cylinder vehicle remained high; however, this would soon change as manufacturers steadily reduced costs of production. In addition, the market for the small two-passenger runabout, which during the first three years of production (1902-1904) had been the basic Franklin model, appeared to be gradually diminishing. The public now increasingly began to demand vehicles of the so-called touring car variety, with a permanent second seat in the rear and some type of collapsible top for protection against the elements (the "closed" car–one with a fixed top and solid windows–was still some years in the future). In effect the automobile was beginning to be considered a means for transporting an entire family, not simply a male adult.

To meet these potential new challenges Franklin began planning for introduction in the 1906 model year of an automobile which would incorporate an engine larger than the four-cylinder unit used so successfully by the company in its initial several years of motor car manufacture. Such a vehicle could be expected to position the company in the forefront of advanced technical design. It also was hoped that the new offering would keep the company's name before the public, and thus help generate an even more satisfactory sales performance than in the past. We will want to look closely at this new car in the next phase of company history.

THE FRANKLIN AUTOMOBILE COMPANY

– *Three* –

Technical Progress in a Growing Industry (1906-1910)

The American public by the end of 1905 no longer dismissed the automobile as an extravagant curiosity, of interest only to a few sportsmen. Over the previous eight years some 77,000 individuals across the nation, mostly from the ranks of the well-to-do, had purchased this appealing new convenience. The motor car was perceived by more and more people to be of substantial value in carrying on a variety of day-to-day activities. Professional and business men had discovered they could use the four-wheeled machines for speedy trips to-and-from their offices, while on weekends such vehicles also might serve as a handy means of transporting entire families on enjoyable jaunts into the countryside. A variety of progressive-minded department stores and specialty shops, seeking to provide in-town customers with prompt service, now utilized light trucks (often propelled by electric motors) for delivery and related purposes. Physicians in particular were becoming keenly aware of the superiority of the motor car over the unwieldy horse-drawn buggy. When summoned in the middle-of-the-night to deal with an emergency the doctor could get under way in his gas-powered machine with the spin of a crank, rather than have to undertake the laborious and time consuming task of "hitching up" (the

THE FRANKLIN AUTOMOBILE COMPANY

An early advertisement for a closed Franklin car. The American public no longer dismissed the automobile as an extravagance. (Courtesy of American Automobile Manufacturers Association)

H.H. Franklin Company was quick to proclaim the value of its product to the medical profession–as early as February, 1903, it published a letter from a New York City physician describing the Franklin car as a little gem). Together with its advantages as a personal conveyance, the automobile in this early period also demonstrated a striking ability to provide badly-needed assistance during a major calamity. Hundreds of motor vehicles were commandeered by desperate army personnel for service in the aftermath of the great San Francisco earthquake and fire of 1906, with observers testifying to the spectacular role played by the new machines in performing a multitude of emergency tasks in that stricken city.

Despite its ever-increasing usefulness for business and pleasure, however, this new mode of personal transportation at times displayed enough faults to cause skeptics to shake their heads about the automobile's future. Motor cars had not as yet fully emerged from the experimental stage; thus owners all-too-frequently experienced annoying mechanical failures on the road. The operator of an ailing vehicle might be required at any time to demonstrate competence as a mechanic, or suffer the humiliation of seeing the stalled machine towed home by its slow-moving but dependable rival, the horse. The "Get Out and Get Under" melody of the period was a trifle too near the truth to be entirely amusing. Tires were a particular curse of the early automobilist, with even brief runs frequently interrupted by a vexing "flat," necessitating on-the-spot repair. Practically all female owners of motor cars, and even many men, found it desirable to employ a chauffeur both to drive and to deal with the ever-present possibility of vehicle breakdown. The lack of a reliable, low-cost self-starter for gas-powered cars also caused more cautious individuals to abstain from a purchase. Winter weather tended to sharply restrict motor car use, with numerous owners placing their vehicles in storage during the cold season after first taking the precaution of draining radiators and engine blocks to protect against "freeze-up" (here Franklin and the handful of other makes featuring air-cooled power plants enjoyed a significant advantage–they quite truthfully could advertise their products as "year-around" vehicles). The kerosene lanterns used on the

THE FRANKLIN AUTOMOBILE COMPANY

typical vehicle produced so little illumination that driving after dark tended to be a somewhat risky affair (acetylene lamps gave more light but could be hazardous if mishandled). With open cars used almost exclusively, most motorists found it advisable throughout much of the year to shelter themselves from the elements. Fur coats, hats with ear muffs and heavy lap robes were indispensable adjuncts on winter runs, while the clouds of dust raised by motor cars on unpaved country roads throughout the summer made it necessary during that season for both sexes to wear ankle-length protective coats, accompanied by wide-brimmed caps, goggles and, in the case of women, veils.

The industry which produced these self-propelled vehicles now receiving widened acceptance across America was becoming organized in an increasingly sophisticated manner. The plants of such leading auto manufacturers as Franklin, Olds, Cadillac, Locomobile, Ford and Rambler were divided into a number of good-sized departments—machine shops, body-building and paint rooms, final assembly areas and testing bays. Each such division was given a specific group of re-

The June 1910 issue of "The Franklin News" *showed as its headline photo this group of young female employees of the Franklin office on an annual trip. Sixteen touring cars transported the picnickers to Rexford Falls.*
(Courtesy of Joseph Aronson)

sponsibilities, with operations becoming more and more mechanized. An article describing the Franklin factory of the period noted that no less than two hundred machine tools were in use in the big Syracuse-based plant, with a number of these labeled "automatics"–machines which could produce identical parts in volume, with little attention needed from an operator other than feeding-in the raw stock and removing finished items (major advances in the American machine tool industry significantly aided automobile development during this era). The article also observed that a level of precision had been attained in the Franklin machine shops which made it possible to interchange one finished part with another.[3-1] This was a significant step forward in technology, as a few years earlier no American auto manufacturer could have made such a claim. A key result was that assembly of motor vehicles was becoming simplified. The "fitter" of an earlier period, who often was required to perform finishing touches on numerous parts to enable them to be used in a vehicle, now was being replaced by the "assembler," whose sole function was to put various components together swiftly to create the final product. The availability of precision-finished, interchangeable parts not only was resulting in better automobiles, but soon might be expected to lead to development of revolutionary new factory procedures in the assembly of motor cars.

An increasing number of employees in the larger motor vehicle plants were becoming specialists–that is, they worked exclusively on a single operation. The day when a general-purpose machinist might be called on to perform a wide variety of tasks in an auto factory was gradually vanishing. A major advantage of this new approach was the potential for expanded production. The specialist employee, particularly when utilizing a machine designed for one operation only, could be expected to develop far greater speed in accomplishing his single assigned duty than one who undertook a broad range of functions. Since the typical auto plant sought to achieve a greater output each year to meet rising consumer demand, this stepped-up productivity was of decided value. The small-scale auto builders, of course, did not follow this pattern to the same extent, since they could not afford the specialized machine tools so heavily utilized by the larger manufacturers.

THE FRANKLIN AUTOMOBILE COMPANY

Although changing in nature due to increased size and more advanced production techniques, many automobile factories in these initial years still operated on a somewhat personalized basis. Foremen typically had risen from the ranks of lower-level employees, thus their relationships with the workers under them often tended to be informal. Even plant superintendents and chief engineers frequently might be found on the shop floor discussing with skilled hands such as tool and die makers solutions to the vast number of problems which arose in the design and manufacture of early motorcars. This manager-worker cooperation undoubtedly was essential if the typical automobile company of the period was to upgrade its product regularly and remain competitive in the marketplace. It also should be noted that while specialization now had increased sharply, a considerable number of workers could still be considered skilled or semi-skilled. Many a task at machine or bench required a period of training before full proficiency was attained, thus numerous employees enjoyed a status above that of an unskilled hand. In January, 1909, the H.H. Franklin Manufacturing Company reported that thirty-three different trades were represented among its workforce.[3-2] Pay in the auto plants was modest–during this era the typical person in the Franklin factory received some 22 to 25 cents per hour. The work week was a lengthy one, lasting 59 hours (six full days) for practically all shop personnel (during summer months the Syracuse-based company closed on Saturday afternoons, but expected no drop-off in weekly production!).

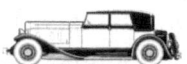

As the year 1906 opened the H.H. Franklin Manufacturing Company could consider itself one of the strongest and most prosperous firms in the fledgling American automobile industry. The young organization was carrying on its manufacturing, engineering and business operations in a cluster of thoroughly modern buildings, thus keeping abreast of such competitors as the Detroit-based Packard Motor Car Company, which also had invested in handsome new production facilities. Franklin company personnel in substantially all areas, technical and

John Wilkinson directed engineering at the Franklin firm from 1901 to the mid-1920's. With an analytical mind and impressive problem solving skills, he was an important influence on both the H.H. Franklin Manufacturing Company and the U.S. automobile industry.
(Courtesy of Hope Wilkinson Yeager)

administrative, were regarded throughout the industry as an outstanding group of individuals. John Wilkinson had few peers in the automotive field as an engineering leader, with his ability and personality serving as a magnet to attract young men of promise from engineering colleges of leading universities to the Franklin organization. Remaining active on the technical standards committee of the Association of Licensed Automobile Manufacturers, John, in conjunction with several other top-flight motor car engineers, initiated an important effort to obtain standardization of basic parts for the new industry.

THE FRANKLIN AUTOMOBILE COMPANY

This 1906 Franklin limousine was one of the few enclosed models offered during this period. (Source Franklin Marketing Materials)

Wilkinson also was a key participant in the formation (in January, 1905, in New York City) of the motor car industry's first professional organization, the American Society of Automobile Engineers (SAE), of which he was named second vice-president. Recognition for his innovative work at Franklin came from various knowledgeable groups. John was awarded the Certificate of Merit at the St. Louis Exposition for designing the Franklin car, and during 1907 Franklin's technical research was considered to be tops in the industry.

TECHNICAL PROGRESS

The automobiles placed on the market by Franklin in 1906 bore eloquent testimony to the capabilities of the company's engineering and design staff. A new six-cylinder model became the firm's pacesetter, probably the earliest motor vehicle containing this number of cylinders to be placed in volume production by any American automobile manufacturer. Designated the Model H, this advanced car featured a fan-cooled engine rated at thirty horse power, and incorporated a 114-inch wheelbase. The powerful motor was mounted under a lengthy, barrel-shaped hood, and the equally long, low-slung touring body comfortably seated as many as seven passengers. The vehicle weighed some 2,400 pounds, and could attain a speed of fifty miles per hour. The advertised cost was $4,000, thus placing the company's new entry in the high-priced range of American automobiles. In its other models the firm continued to offer, in two sizes, the tried-and-true four-cylinder engine with which it began initially. The larger four was the Model D, carried over from 1905, with a 100-inch wheelbase and a 20-horsepower motor. It was priced at $2,800, positioning it cost-wise in the upper-middle sector of the automobile market. The smaller twelve-horsepower, four-cylinder vehicles included the Model G runabout and light touring cars, with the engine placed "in line" in the chassis, plus the holdover, cross-engined Model E "Gentleman's Roadster." The prices of the smaller fours ran from $1,400 to $1,800.

At this point the Franklin cars all utilized a laminated wood frame, unique in the industry and superbly designed to cushion both vehicle and passengers from the shocks produced by America's rough, largely unpaved roads.

This proliferation of new models, encompassing a wide range of sizes and prices, in part may have been the Franklin Company's answer to the threat of competition from other makers of air-cooled vehicles. The pioneer air-cooled auto manufacturer, the Massachusetts-based Knox firm, no longer was as important a competitor, since following the resignation of its founder, Harry Knox, it now was encountering a variety of problems, administrative and financial. However, a company from the same state, the Waltham-Orient, was offering a

*Franklin introduced a light-duty truck in 1906.
(Courtesy of Cycle and Automobile Trade Journal)*

simple one-cylinder car plus a more sophisticated four-cylinder vehicle, both with direct air-cooling. Yet another New England product, the Cameron, gave prospective purchasers the opportunity to enjoy the advantages of direct cooling by the atmosphere. Several midwestern concerns also had brought forth technically advanced air-cooled cars, which if effectively marketed might well challenge Franklin's supremacy. The Frayer-Miller, manufactured by the Oscar Lear Automobile Company of Columbus and Springfield, Ohio, was a splendid machine (initially offered in a four-cylinder model; later a six, also), incorporating a highly-effective forced-air-cooling system. This pace-setting car quickly gained broad recognition through outstanding performances in races and endurance runs. The Marmon Company of Indianapolis, a long-established manufacturer of mill machinery, built a V-type air-cooled four-cylinder unit which appeared to have substantial sales potential. Another Indianapolis-based concern, the Premier, also offered an air-cooled vehicle of good quality.[3-4]

In addition to these challenges, the Franklin Company had to keep a careful eye fixed on its water-cooled competitors, a number of which were now offering improved multi-cylinder models to the car-buying public. Even the steam automobile, while far less of a threat than it had been several years earlier, still could not be completely ignored. The White Company of Cleveland had developed a high-quality vehicle with an efficient "flash" boiler, which competed effectively with Franklin and other gasoline-powered cars (through 1906, White's annual output of steam-driven machines fully equaled Franklin production). Electric-powered vehicles now were falling behind in customer acceptance, other than as in-town delivery trucks, since they could not match the performance capabilities of the gasoline vehicle. They continued to be a favorite with numerous members of the female sex, however, due to their easy handling characteristics. This period was one in which new automobile manufacturing companies were being established across America at the rate of several each month, all eager to take advantage of what appeared to be virtually unlimited public demand for the four-wheeled motor car.

By early 1906 Franklin also had developed and placed on the market a light-duty truck capable of carrying a load of 2,000 pounds at a speed of up to twenty miles per hour. This new vehicle was expected to appeal to merchants and other business concerns in need of such a unit for local delivery work. It utilized the small, four-cylinder air-cooled motor car engine mounted longitudinally in a stiffened frame. This pioneer Franklin commercial vehicle also featured a sliding-gear transmission, and incorporated heavy-duty springs, axles and wheels. The driver was perched on an elevated seat high above the engine, thus saving space for payload, and the vehicle rode very firmly indeed on solid rubber tires. Within a few months the United States War Department ordered one of the new light trucks for use by the Quartermaster Corps at an army depot in Pennsylvania. This purchase, one of the earliest made by the army of a commercial-type unit, forecast extensive use of such vehicles by the armed services in America[3-5].

To ensure that the capabilities of its new and powerful six-cylinder model were brought fully to the attention of the public, the company in mid-1906 again retained L.L. Whitman to lead a team of drivers in a assault on the cross-country record, already in Franklin's possession by virtue of the earlier 1904 run. In this attempt to lower the previous mark the new "six" was to be kept in motion continuously, day and night, from San Francisco to New York by the three-member driving team of Whitman, C.S. Carris and C.B. Harris, with two other men, M.S. Bates and James Daley, serving as guides. The group, working in relays (two handled the car while the others boarded trains operating on parallel routes to rest and eat), left San Francisco, which was almost destroyed by the catastrophic earthquake of that year, on August 2, 1906. The rugged vehicle which the men piloted overcame obstacle after obstacle in crossing vast expanses of arid desert plus range after range of steep mountains. The drivers were compelled to ford numerous streams, fight their way through untold miles of deep mud, and bump over broad areas of wasteland containing few if any roads worthy of the name. An irritating delay was experienced in Iowa, where after passing a farm wagon being jerked in one direction after another by a skittish horse the Franklin driving team was abruptly halted in a town a few miles down the road by constables armed with guns. The group was required to return to the scene of the "crime" and charged with having damaged the farm wagon by frightening the horse! Arguments were of no avail, and the drivers were compelled by a local judge to "pay up" before they were allowed to continue their run.

Just outside Conneaut, Ohio, a much more serious incident occurred, which nearly ended the trip. In attempting to round a curve at high speed one of the drivers skidded into an embankment, resulting in minor injuries to the crew and damaging the vehicle to the extent that 36 hours was required for repairs. Undaunted, members of the driving team sped on, reaching New York City in a blaze of glory. They had cut the former record in half, requiring only fifteen days and two hours to cross the country. The publicity received by the Franklin Company for accomplishing this feat was overwhelming, with newspapers, magazines and scientific journals all acclaiming the pace-setting run. The same car then was brought back to the Midwest and immediately

TECHNICAL PROGRESS

used to establish a new time record for the trip from Chicago to New York City–just under fifty-seven hours.[3-6]

If achieving new cross-country and Chicago-New York records did not convince potential motor car purchasers of the merits of the Franklin vehicle, the results of an economy test run conducted during the same year in New Haven, Connecticut, by the Automobile Club of America should have done so. A Franklin cross-engine runabout, driven by Arthur Holmes, a young Wilkinson engineering aide, totally outclassed a broad field of competitors in efficient use of fuel. While the Franklin victory was based on a pound-mile formula, the vehicle actually covered a total of 87 road miles on two carefully measured gallons of gasoline (to prove that this was no fluke, the same car achieved a

In the first decade of the twentieth century, endurance runs were often used to prove the durability and speed of automobiles. This Franklin vehicle was used in a run from New York to Boston. The identity of the driver and passenger are unknown. (Courtesy of American Automobile Manufacturers Association)

THE FRANKLIN AUTOMOBILE COMPANY

95-mile distance on an identical two-gallons a few days later). This economy record was so impressive that H.H. Franklin felt it necessary to reassure the public that the carburetor used on the test car's engine was a normal stock unit, not a special one.[3-7]

Following this string of victories the Franklin Company late in 1906 introduced its 1907 models. The principal change was the abandonment of the small, simply-constructed four-cylinder cross-engine Model E, which was now replaced by a somewhat larger runabout with a longitudinally-placed motor and a three-speed sliding-gear transmission. The new model thus received the configuration which automobiles more and more were beginning to assume, with an extended hood up front plus increased wheelbase and overall length. However, the price of the car also was increased nearly thirty percent, to a full $1,800. This meant that Franklin no longer expected to compete in what might be termed the "basic transportation market," but instead decided to restrict its offerings to the middle-price range and above. Clearly this denoted a major change in company policy, which might well have important consequences in the volume of cars produced during the years to come (while Franklin was repositioning its offerings upward, Henry Ford in Detroit was laying plans to build a low-cost four-cylinder vehicle which he felt would appeal to a broad range of automobile purchasers). The other three models offered by the Syracuse firm were similar to those of the preceding year, with all four series incorporating a variety of technical improvements. The company sought to use light-alloy steels whenever possible for moving parts, thus insuring great strength together with minimum weight. Aluminum was even more extensively utilized than earlier in both chassis and body, further lightening the vehicle. The six-cylinder model featured a seven-main bearing engine, resulting in extreme smoothness of operation, and had its wheelbase extended to 120 inches, thus placing it among the industry's largest cars.

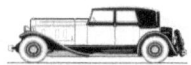

With sales throughout 1906 continuing at a high level, and employment at its plant growing by leaps and bounds, the Franklin Manufacturing Company once again faced the need to expand its physical facilities. Work on building "M" began on July 16, 1906, and was completed several months later. This five-story unit, an extension of the east-west-oriented building located behind the original Geddes Street structure, provided the firm with over 15,000 square feet of additional floor space for manufacturing and various related activities. Other buildings completed during late 1906 and early 1907 included a wooden structure to be used for shipping purposes, plus a saw mill and millwright shop. By this time spur lines from the Delaware, Lackawanna and Western Railway had been brought into the plant site, making it possible to load or unload bulky items quickly. The railroad also began furnishing "auto cars"–rail cars with special doors which permitted swift loading of the high motor vehicles of the period. These additions to the plant, together with departmental and staff reorganizations carried out at the same time to better utilize space and improve operating efficiency, resolved the overcrowding problem for at least the near future. While expanding physical facilities the company also did not neglect the appearance of its buildings and grounds. Trees and shrubs were placed in the lawn abutting South Geddes Street, and ivy was planted along the walls of the office structure. Clearly, through such efforts at beautification the firm sought to demonstrate to Syracuse its intention to be a good corporate citizen.[3-8]

Late in 1906 a vitally important reorganization occurred at the top level of the Franklin Company. The key management group at the firm, H.H. Franklin, Giles Stilwell, John Wilkinson and Frank Barton, purchased most of the stock holdings of A.T. Brown, W.C. Lipe, and H.W. Chapin. Franklin, who acquired the largest block of stock changing hands (borrowing heavily to do so), henceforth was to hold a controlling interest in the company. Brown continued as nominal head of the organization for a brief additional period, but at the annual meeting of the firm held on January 23, 1907, H.H. took command. From that time on he served as president and general manager of the concern, with Giles Stilwell named vice-president, Frank Barton secretary, and H.B. Webb treasurer. The directors of the organization included Franklin, Stilwell, Barton, and Wilkinson, together with Brown, Lipe, and E.H. Dann (Dann headed a local firm which for years had supplied the Franklin die-casting division with specialty metals). Wilkinson and Stilwell joined H.H. Franklin as members of the company's executive committee.[3-9]

There was no indication that this major shift in control was anything other than an amicable one. Alexander Brown, Willard Lipe and H. Winfield Chapin were operating gear companies of a highly-profitable nature, which supplied key parts to a number of automobile manufacturers across the country. Undoubtedly these men–particularly Brown, who also headed several other Syracuse manufacturing concerns–felt it desirable to devote the bulk of their time to the demands of their own firms, thus reducing direct participation in Franklin. However, the change meant that Herbert Franklin, just over forty years of age, for the first time was fully in charge of the manufacturing company carrying his name. The man who, bearing the handicap of a mild speech impediment, abandoned the family farm as an inexperienced youth some twenty years earlier to seek his fortune in the outside world had assumed the position of chief executive of a company of decided importance on the national automotive scene. H.H. thus joined the ranks of a group of relatively young men, often from modest backgrounds, who had risen to the top of the small but fast-growing American automobile industry. The influence of the new company president radiated far beyond the local Syracuse business community. H.H.'s views on a number of subjects relating to the auto industry–overall market conditions, cost of manufacturing, benefits of light weight vehicles–were sought by editors of publications reaching a nation-wide audience.

Together with this change in top leadership came other innovations affecting the firm. To strengthen the sales effort the Franklin Automobile Company was established; this new subsidiary henceforth was to serve as the marketing arm of the manufacturing concern. The first annual company sales conference was held in Syracuse in August of 1906. The event, which lasted three full weeks, undoubtedly constituted an effort both to build up the company's network of dealers and improve relationships between the home office and the field. The company now was shipping cars to far distant points, with sales recorded in Canada, Mexico, and Puerto Rico. The first Franklin reached the Pacific Coast province of British Columbia, Canada, in 1906, and in the same year an aide to the governor of Puerto Rico expressed great satisfaction about the hill-climbing abilities of his Franklin when driving over the irregular terrain of that island. Early in 1907 a traffic department was established by Franklin management; this unit sought to deal with the twin problems of securing prompt delivery of materials needed by the company in the manufacturing process and efficient shipment of completed motor vehicles.[3-10]

During the 1906-07 period certain significant personnel changes and additions took place in the Franklin firm. The ebullient Arthur Benjamin, seeking new worlds to conquer, departed for Buffalo and the Babcock Electric Carriage Company. He was succeeded as sales manager by the equally vigorous Fred R. Bump, a young Cornell graduate. To further strengthen the marketing of its product the company appointed an advertising manager, J.E. Walker. In the factory Frederick Haynes was named general manufacturing superintendent, with George DeAlbert Babcock, a recent graduate of Purdue University, chosen as his assistant. Babcock was an example of the Franklin Company's extraordinary ability even at this early date to attract to its staff persons of competence from a variety of fields. Intellectually inclined, the young executive previously had served as an instructor in mechanical and industrial engineering at Syracuse University, and earlier had conducted independent research at Purdue in the field of electrophysics. With an inquiring and innovative mind, Babcock was to play a vital role in company affairs during the next decade. The very heavy burden resting on the shoulders of John Wilkinson in the broad area of technical development was eased somewhat when Arthur Holmes, a youthful graduate of the University of Michigan, began assuming increasing responsibility in the fields of experimental engineering and testing.

THE FRANKLIN AUTOMOBILE COMPANY

Various other items of note relating to the forward-looking and successful firm should be commented on briefly. The company's interest in obtaining adequately-trained shop personnel was emphasized when it made a handsome contribution toward the establishment of the Sweet Artisan School, founded by the earlier-mentioned John E. Sweet, still active on the Syracuse industrial scene at age 75. The primary function of the new school was the instruction of young men in the mechanical arts.[3-11] A department heads' society of the H.H. Franklin Manufacturing Company was formed in the spring of 1906, with the obvious goal of strengthening relationships among key personnel in a fast-growing organization. An electrical laboratory was established late in 1906, thus rounding out the excellent research facilities sponsored by the company. In the same year Marcus Lothrop joined the company as its first metallurgist, and immediately began research directed toward finding additional light, tough steels for use in gears and other vital car parts (Lothrop decades later became president of the Timken Roller Bearing Co.). The Franklin firm shortly thereafter became a member of the American Society for Testing Materials, thereby underscoring its commitment to maintenance of high quality in its products.[3-12] The vast increase in the size of the company labor force, and the prevalence of industrial accidents in a period when safety was not too fully emphasized, led to the opening of a first-aid room in the plant in March, 1907. The new facility was heavily used, with a company report of the era noting that over 1,800 accidents occurred annually in the factory, or an average of more than one per employee. The report concluded with the statement that fortunately none of these numerous mishaps to date had involved anything more serious than a loss of fingers![3-13]

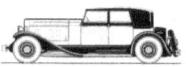

Continued expansion of auto production was experienced by the Franklin Company throughout 1906. The total number of cars shipped during that year was nearly 1,300, an increase of eighteen per cent over calendar year 1905. Company advertisements claimed that during the first half of 1906 Franklin sales were second in number and third in value among all makes of motor cars in America. A fair proportion of the vehicles manufactured in 1906–approximately ten-to-fifteen per cent–were said to be of the six-cylinder model. It was clear, however, that the four-cylinder units, which competed in a more moderate price range, still constituted the bread-and-butter models of the firm. With this very satisfactory level of operations having been attained, the company resumed dividend payments. The sum of $13,025, exactly five per cent of paid-in capitalization, was distributed to shareholders in 1906. While not a large return on investment (profits still were being utilized heavily to fund plant expansion), those who held stock in the company also could note with satisfaction that each share now represented ownership in a firm whose underlying value was increasing swiftly from day-to-day.

The entire American auto industry looked forward to a highly successful 1907. The nation had been experiencing an unprecedented degree of economic prosperity during the early years of the twentieth century, with the overall standard of living rising and more and more families enjoying substantial incomes. An ever-larger number of such well-to-do people continued to shift from horse-and-buggy to the new form of motorized transportation. This also was the period when public demand for large and expensive automobiles reached a peak. The Franklin line of vehicles, priced from the middle to the upper ranges, appeared to be well-positioned to take advantage of this trend. Late in 1906 H.H. Franklin made optimistic comments about the overall state of the economy and the condition of the auto industry. In an article in *Motor Age* (November 29, 1906), H.H. was quoted as saying with respect to the motor car, "the puzzling question that today confronts manufacturers is not the selling, but how to manufacture in quantities and in time to meet the season's demand." In line with this statement a spokesman for the company observed that a production level approaching 2,000 vehicles might realistically be anticipated by Franklin for the coming year.

As 1907 unfolded, the motor car picture did indeed appear to be a bright one. A record number of vehicles was shipped by the Franklin Company in January, and at the end of that month seven hundred unfilled orders were on the books. By spring some 42 cars per week were being manufactured, and total company employment had reached nearly 1,650 (a new high), making the H.H. Franklin Manufacturing Company one of the two largest employers in the entire Syracuse area. Further plant expansion was authorized, with an addition to Building B begun in the summer. When completed this would give the company a multi-story structure on Geddes Street nearly 350 feet in length. Numerous parcels of property adjacent to the factory were being purchased in contemplation of additional expansion, and the firm leased the former Syracuse Bicycle Company plant in West Fayette Street for use as a paint shop and storage area. At the second annual sales conference held early in August, 1907, it was announced that the firm planned to employ seven field sales representatives together with two traveling mechanics to assist dealers with marketing and service problems.[3-14] On September 1 a New York City sales branch was opened, at the corner of Broadway and 73rd Street. This mushrooming economic prosperity was reflected in a generous dividend policy on the part of the company. Quarterly dividends now were to be paid, with the total distribution for 1907 reaching $87,500, or a resounding 33 1/3 per cent return on capital invested.

Franklin's success was matched by other leading manufacturers elsewhere in the auto industry. The Cadillac Motor Car Company in Detroit announced an employment level in its plants of 2,000 and a production rate in peak periods of 50 cars per day; while in Buffalo, Pierce Arrow noted that its office and manufacturing facilities were being consolidated entirely within the imposing new factory which it had recently constructed. Also in Detroit, the young Ford Motor Company had gained useful publicity by entering its large six-cylinder car in a variety of races, but now was concentrating production efforts on a basic four-cylinder vehicle which would sell at the incredibly low price of $600.

Suddenly, as the year 1907 neared its close, disaster struck. The finan-

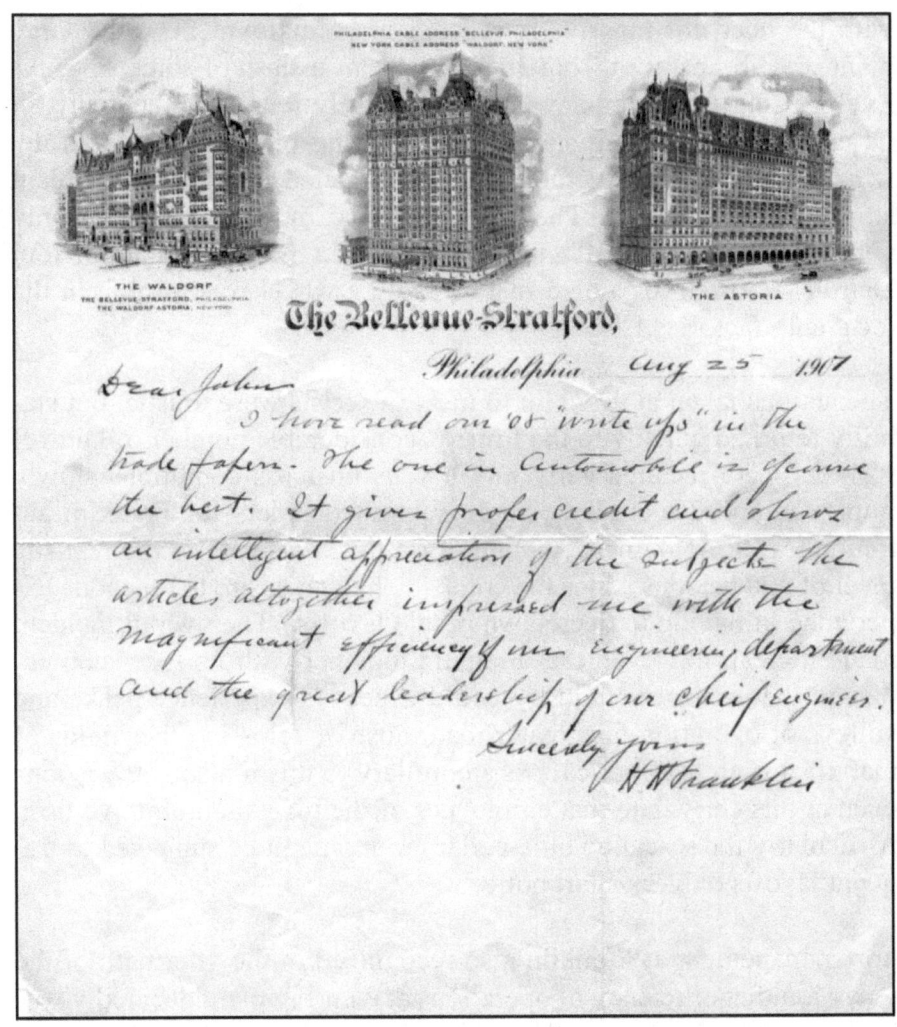

A letter to John Wilkinson from H.H. Franklin in August 1907. Franklin obviously was pleased with his chief engineer in this time of prosperity.

cial panic of November 1, 1907, hit the nation and many segments of industry swiftly and with hurricane force. Franklin was typical of the motor car companies quickly and harshly impacted. Orders for cars vanished overnight and the firm, whose problems heretofore had involved the expanding of facilities and workforce to meet a constantly increasing demand for its vehicles, instead found itself forced to deal with the need for massive retrenchment. Employment at the large plant was abruptly cut from 1650 to 418, or a slash of some seventy-five per cent (the company, however, wisely retained practically all its talented engineering staff). The building program was held up, with construction of several partially-completed additions to the plant stopped for the present. The H.H. Franklin firm was far from the only vehicle manufacturer affected by the panic. Business reports from Detroit late in 1907 noted that scarcely a wheel was turning in the local auto factories.[3-15]

The actions taken at Franklin to meet the crisis were drastic, but stability returned quickly to the firm. A considerable number of laid-off workers were recalled early in 1908, as business conditions slowly improved and dealers once again submitted orders for Franklin automobiles. Employment, though, for a time was kept to the realistic level of 900 persons, since the company had no desire to repeat its experience of having to decree wholesale layoffs. The overall incident made it clear, however, that Franklin together with its sister companies in the motor car industry could expect to experience peaks and valleys of operation far greater than those of firms in other fields of manufacturing in America. As a corollary to this it also was obvious even at this early date that employees of the typical automotive firm, particularly the so-called blue-collar group, might be subjected to frequent layoffs on very short notice.

Top management at Franklin also recognized in the aftermath of the recession that efficiency of operations at their big plant decidedly was in need of improvement. The ratio of workers to cars produced had been substantially higher than that of most competitor motor car manufacturers (other than those few companies building a tiny number of high-priced cars to order). If company profitability was to be maintained in a market where substantial fluctuation in sales levels might often occur, an approach which involved more thorough planning of the production process plus improvement of operating methods in the factory was required. Other automobile manufacturers reached similar conclusions. Such major motor car producers as Buick, Ford and

Cadillac were taking steps to upgrade efficiency in every step of vehicle production through such measures as rearrangement of machinery and simplification of employee tasks.

The Franklin Company, led by its alert new assistant manufacturing superintendent, George Babcock, looked carefully into various means of improving output and controlling costs. To its credit, however, the company did this in a rational manner, recognizing that fairness demanded that the interests of its shop workers be given adequate consideration in any move to strengthen overall operating efficiency. After examining various approaches to improvement of productivity, Babcock and other executives of the firm opted to follow the so-called Taylor plan. Developed by Frederick Winslow Taylor, the acknowledged dean of American efficiency engineers, this approach involved central planning and control of production together with careful analysis of each segment of machining and manufacturing operations to identify techniques which might be used to upgrade employee output and reduce costs. Such a plan could be expected to take a number of years to implement fully, but would provide the company with a method of management control of the production process particularly well-suited for a moderate-sized firm.[3-16]

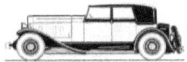

As the recovery of automobile sales got under way following the 1907 panic, the Franklin organization for the first time decided to feature a major display of its products in a local show. Taking over the large Alhambra Hall in downtown Syracuse, the company in late January, 1908, unveiled for public viewing a variety of models of the Franklin car, including a taxicab. At the same time the executives planning the show sought to give the citizens of the community a convincing demonstration of the value of a vehicle which emphasized light weight and sound engineering. Two tiny model automobiles were positioned at the bottom of a steep incline; one a replica of a light-weight Franklin, the other a miniature of the typical heavy American motor car currently in use. When an equivalent amount of force was applied through strings connected to each, the Franklin replica quickly shot up the slope, leaving the heavyweight "competitor" far behind. While perhaps a bit simplistic, the test did help fix in the minds of the public one major advantage of a vehicle whose weight had been carefully pared down–given equal power it would travel further and faster than a more bulky product. An additional exhibit was utilized to show the nicely-balanced design of the Franklin car–when each of the four wheels was placed on a scale, the recorded weights matched to within a very few pounds. Still another feature of the show was a "non-stop" car–a vehicle whose engine was started at the beginning of the show and never shut off until the end. Those attending the show thus were assured that the Franklin air-cooling system could perform effectively over long periods of time. The local event was rounded out by a dis-

John Burns driving the Governor of New York State, Charles Evans Hughes, in a 1908 Model D.

TECHNICAL PROGRESS

play of the manufacturing processes utilized at the Franklin plant, including methods used to insure quality of product.

The 1908 Franklin models incorporated a number of technical improvements in their motors, designed both to increase power and permit more effective cooling. From early days the Franklin car had featured spherical combustion chambers in its cylinder head, thus helping insure smoothness of engine operation. Now, in order to improve power output this feature was to be supplemented with a highly-unusual concentric-valve arrangement. This meant that the overhead intake and exhaust valves occupied the same space, with one positioned inside the other. The auxiliary exhaust port at the bottom of each cylinder was retained to aid in the quick elimination of the hot burned gas. To further speed heat elimination new phosphor-bronze cooling

Demonstrating the Franklin One Man Top.

fins were shrunk on each cylinder, with the number of flanges varying according to the distance of a cylinder from the front-mounted cooling fan. Carburetion and ignition systems on the new models also were upgraded, as was motor lubrication. To facilitate ease of control a selective-type gear shift now was used on certain of the larger models. As a result of these changes, coupled with a modest increase in the sizes of the various series of engines, the small four-cylinder unit now was rated at eighteen horse-power; the larger four at twenty-eight; and the six at forty-two. Since company engineers through careful design and choice of materials had been able to keep overall car weights at the same levels as 1907, the performance of the new vehicles was exceptionally brisk.

Models introduced in the following year, 1909, were in most respects similar to the 1908 series. The six-cylinder and the larger four again featured selective-type transmissions, permitting gear changes to be made by the driver swiftly and positively. Ease of operation was even further improved by an arrangement of gears and operating levers which made it possible to shift from one gear to another without disengaging the clutch. By 1909 the company included an occasional closed car model among its offerings, although the price of such a vehicle was so greatly in excess of that of an open roadster or touring car that relatively few were sold.

The 1910 models, the last to be constructed with the so-called round or barrel-type hood, incorporated an improved cooling system developed by the ever-forward-looking Franklin engineering department. The new approach featured vertical steel flanges cast into each cylinder to aid in heat dissipation. The gear-driven front-mounted fan used previously to furnish a vigorous blast of air for the purpose of cooling the engine now was eliminated. To replace it, a suction fan incorporated in the flywheel at the rear of the engine drew a strong current of air downward through sheet metal sleeves surrounding each individual cylinder. This approach increased the amount of air flowing over the cylinders with less expenditure of power, thus improving both cooling and engine efficiency. The 1910 purchaser could choose

TECHNICAL PROGRESS

A 1910 Franklin Taxi.
(Courtesy of American Automobile Manufacturers Association)

from among three series: A small four-cylinder Model G, mounted on a 91½-inch wheel base; a large four-cylinder model D, with the wheel base increased to 106 inches; and the company's pacesetter, the six-cylinder model H, featuring a luxurious 127 inches wheelbase. Prices ranged from $1,850-up for the new models.

Together with its pleasure cars the company expanded its manufacturing and sales activity to include commercial and special purpose vehicles. By early 1908 a short-wheelbase taxicab utilizing the small four-cylinder motor and chassis had been placed on the market. The passengers enjoyed the comfort of a fully-enclosed rear section; the cab driver sat in front completely exposed to the elements. This vehicle, designed for quick maneuverability on crowded city streets (it could soon be seen in considerable numbers on the avenues of New York City), was light in weight and economical in operation. Franklin also developed police patrol wagons for several cities, with a small, solid-tired unit delivered to the Syracuse police department in the summer of 1908, and a somewhat larger, 3000-pound model shipped to the Washington, D.C., law enforcement agency a year later. The Washington vehicle was equipped with medicine chest and stretcher, thus permitting it to be quickly convertible for use as an ambulance.[3-17] During 1908 the company pioneered a plan by which mechanics were sent out from the factory to inspect vehicles recently purchased by customers and make any necessary adjustments and repairs.[3-18] In this period the Franklin firm developed a typewriter for possible sale, but never put it on the market.

As the first decade of the twentieth century drew to a close the American automobile industry was enjoying spectacular expansion of sales of its product. Despite the sharp national recession experienced toward the end of 1907, during that year a total of 43,000 motor cars plus a thousand trucks had been placed in the hands of waiting customers. The following year, 1908, saw a further increase of close to fifty per cent in motor vehicle sales, with nearly 65,000 units produced by the automobile factories. Another major jump was registered in 1909, when some 127,200 cars and trucks were shipped, while in 1910 the total reached 187,000. The wholesale value of all cars and trucks sold by the factories in 1910 attained the impressive figure of $225,000,000. In an era when the gross domestic product was only a tiny fraction of what it is today, sales of this magnitude meant that the automobile was successfully competing for a steadily increasing share of the disposable income of the consumer. The U. S. Census of Manufactures showed that in 1909 employment in automotive firms actually exceeded that of wagon and carriage builders .[3-20]

Within the motor vehicle industry itself important trends could be de-

TECHNICAL PROGRESS

Building Franklin cars, circa 1908-1910. In 1909 sales of Frankllin vehicles reached the 2,000 mark.

The Franklin Factory, circa 1905.

tected. Perhaps the most noteworthy was the increase late in the decade in purchaser acceptance of the moderately-priced motor car. In 1907 the average wholesale price of each automobile sold in America was $2,125; this represented a peak not again equaled until the inflationary era which followed World War II. A large drop in average per-car price to approximately $1,600 was recorded in 1908, with a further decline to $1,300 experienced in 1909. The trend continued in 1910, when the average wholesale price shrank to $1,200. These drops clearly reflected major production and sales increases by several Midwest-based builders of lower-priced cars–particularly the Ford Motor Company, which by mid-1908 had placed on the market its revolutionary "Model T" automobile, and almost immediately found itself unable to keep up with the avalanche of orders. Another trend of lesser note was the sharp reduction in imports of foreign vehicles. While a considerable number of Americans purchased European-built machines in the very early years of the twentieth century, this tendency had diminished sharply by 1910. The typical domestic vehicle now was seen as better adapted than most foreign autos to withstand the primitive road conditions found in many parts of America, with the result that use of foreign machines was largely confined to a few major cities. America was in the process of becoming an exporter rather than an importer of the motor vehicle.

The Franklin Company continued to be an important competitor in the American automobile industry in the period from 1907 through 1910, although no longer occupying the commanding position it held a few years earlier. Production of automobiles by the company in 1907 reached well over 1,500 (with sales income nearing $4,000,000), but in 1908, for the first time in its history, the organization experienced a modest decline in output to some 1,000-1,100 vehicles. This would be reversed in 1909, when production jumped to the 2,000 range, but fell again in 1910 to under 1,200 (during June and July of that year not a single vehicle was assembled in the Franklin shops). This meant that the firm's share of American motor vehicle production had dropped well below one per cent, a far cry from the nearly five per cent achieved in 1905. Obviously, the company's decision to concentrate its offerings in the middle and higher-priced ranges at a time when, as noted, the average price paid for an automobile was trending sharply downward, seriously affected its competitive position. It also should be observed that other prestigious automobile companies were competing aggressively in the price ranges occupied by the various Franklin models. Packard by 1909 was offering an attractively-styled four-cylinder vehicle for $3,200, or just slightly in excess of the cost of the Franklin Series D, while Cadillac, now enjoying an international reputation for mechanical excellence, in the same year had placed its own four-cylinder Model 30 on the market for approximately $1,500, well below the price tag of any Franklin.

In 1910, however, the Franklin firm experienced one significant advantage–it now without question was the leading American company offering a good-quality air-cooled vehicle to prospective purchasers. Of its earlier air-cooled competitors, Frayer-Miller had gone out of the pleasure car business, while Marmon, Knox and Premier had decided to shift almost completely to engines which would utilize water as a cooling medium. Thus, so long as its talented engineering department continued to improve the process of direct air-cooling to meet the demands of the ever-more-powerful motors being developed, Franklin would enjoy a unique position among American automobile manufacturers.

To strengthen its appeal to potential customers, the Franklin company decided in 1910 that a major change in styling of the vehicle it produced was necessary. The "barrel" front now looked somewhat outdated, particularly when measured against several other medium and high-priced American cars which featured massive radiator shells and long, imposing, square-shaped hoods. The firm, therefore, sought to modernize the appearance of its new offerings for the 1911 model year, and at the same time incorporate a design which would identify the car more distinctly as an air-cooled vehicle. This was no minor decision, since the degree of acceptance of new styling by the public might well be an important factor in determining the level of sales for some years to come. We will evaluate the success of this effort shortly.

― *Four* ―

A Maturing Company
(1911-1918)

1911 could well be considered a watershed year for the youthful American automobile industry. Throughout the previous decade motor vehicle builders had been engaged in an aggressive effort to establish themselves as a force to be reckoned with on the nation's business scene. Beginning with the output of a few thousand "horseless carriages" during the opening year of the twentieth century, motor car manufacturers had confounded the skeptics by producing an increasing number of units in each succeeding twelve-month period. Now, with 1911 production anticipated to reach 200,000 or more vehicles, it was apparent to every observer that the industry had cast off its garments of infancy and was entering a period of vigorous adolescence. Total automobile registrations in all states passed the 500,000 level early in 1911, demonstrating clearly that ownership of the motor car no longer was confined to a privileged few, but now encompassed an ever-broadening segment of society. This trend toward widened ownership, while particularly strong in cities, also was extending increasingly to small communities and even farming areas. It should be noted, however, that despite an impressive automobile registration figure the estimated number of horse-drawn vehicles in use throughout the nation was no less than 7,000,000! In addition, the U.S. Census of Manufactures showed that as late as the year 1909 the number of carriages and wagons produced exceeded the output of motor cars by a ratio of over eight to one. The public, then, still tended to rely on the four-legged beast to meet a large proportion of its individual transportation needs, particularly in rural areas.[4-1]

The degree to which the motor car was coming into much more general use was attested to by the rapid development of associations of auto owners in numerous cities throughout America. The Syracuse Automobile Club was everywhere viewed as one of the most enterprising and active of such bodies. This vigorous organization, founded by a sprinkling of motor car enthusiasts at the turn of the century, had achieved the imposing total of 600-plus members by 1911 (its executive secretary was quiet, diplomatic Forman Wilkinson, younger brother of John). While it could boast of a large number of top-level local citizens on its rolls, including H.H. Franklin, and sponsored a profusion of road rallies and tours through the countryside for its members' enjoyment, the group was far more than a mere social body. As its primary function the Syracuse club carried on a wide-ranging and aggressive program to make possible the safe and effective use of motor vehicles throughout the city and the surrounding region. For decades a number of privately-owned roads in the area had imposed tolls on users, and the auto club through lawsuits and vigorous lobbying of elected officials sought to end this archaic and annoying practice. The year 1911 saw such efforts crowned with success by elimination of the last toll highway in metropolitan Syracuse. Since little had been done as yet by local or state governments to place signs along country roads or even city streets giving directions or warning of hazards, the club took independent action to remedy this deficiency, hiring a man to cover the area in a small cart and post signboards wherever needed. At the top of the dangerous Camillus Hill west of Syracuse one of the first illuminated (the source of light was a kerosene lantern furnished by a local farmer) caution signs to be found along any highway was installed. The Syracuse Club on one occasion even undertook the extraordinary step of repairing at its own expense, after unsuccessful appeals to public agencies, a particularly poor stretch of dirt road in which many autos had become mired, and in another instance paid for completion of work on a rural bridge when the state and county governments could not reach agreement on a formula for sharing the cost.[4-2] The condition of roads throughout America now was receiving steadily increased attention, with auto clubs at both the national and local levels joining other concerned groups in seeking to address this problem.

Beginning in 1901 the various American states one-by-one had enacted legislation requiring motor vehicles to be registered by their owners, with some type of identification plate displayed on the car (in many states the owner initially had to provide this item himself!). Most jurisdictions contented themselves with assessing only a nominal fee for such registrations, but a few went far beyond this. New York State, alert to the possibility of the self-propelled vehicle serving as a source of revenue, imposed ownership fees which were directly scaled to the horsepower, and thus presumably the value, of each car. The Empire State also broke new ground in a related area, requiring that the thousands of chauffeurs who were employed to operate automobiles in New York City and other parts of the state submit to a test of their driving abilities (owner-operators as yet did not have to demonstrate their competence, making it legal in some instances for 13- and 14-year-olds to pilot their own motor cars). Since horse-drawn vehicles and their drivers for years had escaped most forms of public regulation and taxation (an occasional municipality did require registration of carriages), many automobile enthusiasts tended to look askance at being singled out for such special attention. State legislatures, of course, may well have viewed the carriage and wagon users as constituting a much larger and more influential segment of voters at that time than the new motor car groups, and thus acted accordingly. However, with automobile owners becoming increasingly vociferous in their demands for upgrading of roads, state governments undoubtedly felt that the cost of such work should be placed on the shoulders of this noisy—and presumably well-heeled—group through new forms of taxation. Concerned about the steadily increasing number of accidents involving the motor car (such occurrences rated flamboyant headlines in the press), the various governmental units also kept themselves busy enacting endless numbers of laws regulating in almost minute detail the speed at which a motor vehicle could be driven. Such speed limits often were set at absurd levels–in one instance the driver of an automobile was overtaken by a police officer riding a bicycle and charged with exceeding the eight-mile-per-hour maximum set by local ordinance. A demand for additional legislation in New York State brought a quick rejoinder from the head of the H.H. Franklin Manufacturing Company. In an article in *The Horseless Age*, H.H. demonstrated that he could still wield the sharp pen of a former newspaper editor. Noting that New York State and most of its cities had already enacted an almost mind-boggling variety of laws controlling speed and providing heavy penalties for any violation thereof, Franklin tartly suggested that law officers and judges concentrate their efforts on more effective enforcement of existing regulations before seeking to burden the public with yet another cluster of restrictive acts.[4-3]

While auto ownership was becoming widespread across America, the centers of motor vehicle manufacture increasingly tended to be restricted to a few geographic areas. By the beginning of the second decade of the twentieth century it was clear that the Midwest was to be the unchallenged leader of automobile production. The New England states, which in the very early days led the way in building "horseless carriages," now had dropped behind. The electric and steam machines in which Connecticut and Massachusetts-based companies specialized had fallen by the wayside as the gas-powered vehicle surged ahead to become an overwhelming favorite of the car-buying public. Among the Midwestern states Michigan was swiftly outdistancing all competitors. The first eight months of 1910 alone saw the amazing total of 92 new motor car and parts manufacturing companies organized in the Wolverine State, with nearly three-quarters of these located in Detroit. Nearby Ohio and Indiana furnished the principal challenge to Michigan for leadership in motor car production. During this period, however, New York was able to maintain its position as headquarters for a number of motor car concerns, ranking fourth in number of motor vehicles produced in 1914, behind Michigan, Ohio, and Indiana.[4-4] Franklin continued to be the only manufacturer of consequence building pleasure cars in Syracuse, although the Moyer Wagon Company had developed and was producing in small numbers a very-high-quality automobile. In the commercial vehicle field Franklin was compelled to meet a more serious local challenge. The three-cylinder, air-cooled Chase motor truck at this time had achieved a considerable degree of popularity on a national basis, with its year-to-year production showing steady increases. This vehicle, designed by former Franklin engineer Aurin Chase, featured a wood frame and sold at prices well below those charged by Franklin for its commercial units. Still another local firm, the Sanford-Herbert Company, built the Sanbert truck on a limited scale. The City of Syracuse had now become a motor car parts manufacturing center of considerable importance, with transmissions, clutches, rear axles and steering gears all produced in substantial volume and marketed throughout the nation.

The H.H. Franklin Company joined other members of the Association of Licensed Automobile Manufacturers in displaying its newly-styled 1911 models at New York's Madison Square Garden Automobile Show (the non-members of A.L.A.M. sponsored a separate show at the Grand Central Palace in the same city). The new Franklin offerings featured an almost revolutionary change in appearance, with the former barrel hood replaced by a sloping, coffin-shaped front section obviously pirated from the French Renault automobile. Mechanically only one modification of any importance could be noted–the integral intake and exhaust valve introduced in 1908 had now been replaced by separate single-purpose valves mounted side-by-side in the cylinder head. Franklin purchasers could chose from no less than four distinct series of cars, two four-cylinder models and two sixes, with prices ranging from just under $2,000 for the small four up to $4,500 for the 48 horsepower senior six-cylinder touring car mounted on a lengthy 133-inch wheelbase. A sleek "torpedo" body could be obtained by those buyers who sought the equivalent of modern-day sports-car styl-

THE FRANKLIN AUTOMOBILE COMPANY

The 38 HP 1911 Franklin Torpedo, as illustrated in the Company's 1911 Sales Brochure.

The Franklin Torpedo of 1910. A 75-mph model of this car was built for H.H. Franklin's personal use. (Courtesy of Elizabeth A. Doman)

ing. This attractive body style had been pioneered by the company in a few custom units during the previous year, including a seventy-five mile-per-hour model for H.H. Franklin's personal use.

Stiff sales competition would be offered Franklin in this period by a wide range of other makes of motor vehicles. In the upper price echelon could be found such competitors as the prestigious Pierce-Arrow and Peerless automobiles; the former offering a massive 66-horsepower touring car featuring a 140-inch wheel base and selling for $6,000, and the latter seeking to attract well-to-do customers with a luxury-class six-cylinder limousine carrying a price of $7,000. The Premier car also ranked as an elite vehicle, with its stately limousine available to a prospective purchaser at $5,000; while immediately below this level a Locomobile touring car might be had at $4,800 and a Lozier or a Simplex for a few hundred dollars less. It should be remembered that these whopping price tags existed in an era when highly-skilled machinists in industry were fortunate to earn as much as eight or nine hundred dollars a year, and experienced public school teachers usually toiled for an even smaller amount.

While these high-quality vehicles would compete with Franklin's luxury six-cylinder model, it was not from this price range that the most serious challenge came. A new cluster of automobiles, all well-designed units selling at highly competitive prices, had been offered to the motor car buyer in the past year or two. Among the better known of these were two vehicles built in Detroit, both developed by the able automotive engineer Howard Coffin. The Chalmers car sold at a price a notch below that of the smallest Franklin, but offered equally-fine performance plus sound quality of construction (although in ride and road-handling Franklin could boast of clear superiority). The Hudson automobile, also a good-quality car, was priced at a level even below that of the Chalmers. In addition to these two products a number of other makes, including Buick, Oakland and Maxwell, enjoyed broad market appeal and excellent name recognition by the public. Yet another gifted automotive engineer, John Wilkinson's Cornell classmate, Charles Brady King (who in 1896 had operated the first motor car

THE FRANKLIN AUTOMOBILE COMPANY

seen on the streets of Detroit), introduced a moderately-priced vehicle bearing his name which featured the innovative combination of left-hand steering and center control. Franklin clearly would have to merchandise its newly-restyled product line vigorously if it was to maintain sales share in the crowded medium and high priced fields. In the lower-priced sector the Ford Model T by this time was totally outdistancing all competition, and undoubtedly taking sales away from companies offering more costly lines.

The pleasure automobiles produced by the Franklin company were supplemented by a varied line of business-oriented vehicles. At the national commercial car show which opened in Chicago on February 6, 1911, the Syracuse firm displayed new flat-bed delivery trucks with both open and enclosed cabs for the driver, plus a van with a closed panel body and also a small ambulance. Other commercial body styles had been developed for specialized purposes–two light 12-passenger buses were delivered to an amusement park in Paterson, New Jersey, and a ten-passenger omnibus was placed in service by one of the largest hotels in Winnipeg, Canada. A Franklin was chosen specifically by the management of this hotel because its air-cooled motor made it possible for the vehicle to be used throughout the bitter-cold Western Canadian winter. A New England company found an innovative means of making a single Franklin delivery truck with a quickly demountable body do the work of two. As the vehicle and its crew delivered packages to customers, a second body was simultaneously loaded at the warehouse, ready to be swiftly substituted for the first when the truck returned from its route. A particularly unique use was found for a Franklin runabout in Brownsville, Texas. When a flood made it impossible to bring conventional railroad rolling stock into this town, the Franklin was fitted with flanged wheels and pressed into service to pull along the rail tracks two small flat cars loaded with passengers and baggage. This impromptu "locomotive" usually made better time than the heavy steam trains which normally serviced the route. An important use for motor vehicles was demonstrated during the Christmas season of 1911 in Syracuse, when an automobile replaced several horse-drawn wagons in collecting mail from postal

A MATURING COMPANY

substations for delivery to the central post office. The motorized fire truck was fast taking the place of earlier horse-drawn units, with several big aerial rigs purchased by New York City during this period (the H.H. Franklin Company did not seek to compete in this specialized field).

Events of major importance were occurring in the auto industry at this time. The 1911 New York auto shows had barely opened when on January 9th of that year a decision of the United States Second Circuit Court of Appeals struck with the effect of a bolt of lightning. The court, speaking through Circuit Judge Walter Noyes, found that the Selden automobile patent was valid only for the obsolete Brayton motor, and had no applicability whatever to the modern four-cycle internal combustion engine being utilized generally by American motor vehicle manufacturers.[4-5] The decision rejecting any claim of infringement represented a stunning victory for leading Selden patent opponent Henry Ford of Detroit, who became a hero overnight among the American public. The court's finding not only ended any prospect of a monopoly being exercised by the holders of the Selden patent interests, but opened up an era in which interchangeability of ideas would be a key feature of the motor car industry. The now-influential Society of Automobile Engineers a year or two earlier had replaced the old mechanical branch of the Association of Licensed Automobile Manufacturers in providing technical leadership for motor car builders, and under the guidance of such outstanding men as Henry Souther, Howard Coffin and John Wilkinson was pressing hard for standardization of a large number of parts used in motor vehicle manufacturing. The various companies also began moving swiftly at this time toward a flexible policy on industry-wide sharing of patents. Most automobile firms quickly endorsed this new approach (with a formal agreement on cross-licensing entered into a few years later), although the H.H. Franklin Company, apparently concerned about retaining control of certain of its key patents covering unique air-cooling processes not in use elsewhere in the industry, was somewhat reluctant to do so.[4-6]

In mid-1911 the Franklin firm announced with some fanfare that it no longer would offer to the car-buyer annual new models. However, in November of that year what in effect constituted a new group of Franklin cars for 1912 was introduced to the public. Designated the "New Series" (consecutive numbers henceforth would be used to identify Franklin models–thus the New Series became Series 1 at the next model change, introducing the Series 2 cars) these vehicles were available in no less than five types, with varying combinations of engine and chassis sizes. Two large six-cylinder vehicles were offered, each with a thirty-eight horse-power motor (the huge "48" had been dropped), plus a newly-developed smaller six (Model M) of thirty horse-power. Two four-cylinder machines also were listed, one a twenty-five horse-power touring car and the other a small runabout with an eighteen horse-power engine. The key mechanical change in the vehicles was the elimination of the auxiliary exhaust valve located at the bottom of each cylinder, which for several years had been a much-talked-about feature of the Franklin engine. The company's explanation for this modification was that exhaust manifold design was rendered unduly complex by the special valve, and that owners now could safely rely on an improved suction cooling system to dissipate the heat in a fully effective manner without use of the auxiliary device. The range of prices for the 1912 Franklin cars was extraordinarily broad. The two-passenger runabout could be bought for a modest $1,650, while a limousine in the larger six-cylinder series sold for a resounding $5,000!

In terms of business success the period from mid-1910 through 1912 was far from an outstanding one for the Franklin company. Clearly the firm during these years was encountering vexing problems in establishing a satisfactory identity with the swiftly expanding American car-buying public. While the early Franklin automobiles had appealed to purchasers as well-built, reliable, no-nonsense vehicles, concentrated largely in a single price-range, the models now being offered encompassed a wide variety of engine and chassis sizes and sold in a broad price spectrum. The firm appeared to be having difficulty deciding which model it wished to emphasize, with the result that buyer demand for the car declined alarmingly. Introduction of the new "Renault-nose" model had not helped appreciably. In 1911 the total number of pleasure vehicles manufactured was only a trifle over 1,000, little more than one-half the 1909 figure, with output not substantially better in 1912 (industry-wide sales during the same period were soaring to unprecedented heights). This slump meant that production of the firm's more expensive cars, such as the large six-cylinder models, must have been so limited as to have made them uneconomical to build.

These sales problems were soon reflected in company earnings and dividends. The handsome return on investment enjoyed by Franklin stockholders a short time earlier–as recently as the spring of 1910 the firm had paid dividends of 33⅓% in cash and 12% in stock–now literally had vanished. Only a modest 12 percent cash dividend was declared in 1911, with no payment whatever made to shareholders the following year.[4-7] The company was tardy in paying many of its suppliers' bills during 1912, clearly seeking to conserve its fiscal resources.[4-8] As a closely-held corporation Franklin did not publicly announce its earnings during this period, but the company's net profit must have been modest in 1911 and probably close to non-existent in 1912. By comparison, Detroit's Packard Motor Car Company, despite trailing Franklin by several years in developing a six-cylinder engine and pricing its various models at higher levels than the Syracuse-based firm, continued to exploit its image as builder of a "prestige" automobile with amazing success. This company produced 3,617 cars in its fiscal year 1912, and reported net earnings of $1,832,000 after payment of preferred dividends, thus achieving a profit of over $500 per vehicle sold. Packard's balance sheet did show three million dollars in outstanding debenture notes (issued largely to provide additional working capital), while Franklin was free of any similar indebtedness, but with its strong earning power the Detroit luxury car builder was experiencing no problem in accumulating reserves adequate to meet all debt payments as they came due.[4-9]

THE FRANKLIN AUTOMOBILE COMPANY

This reduced ability of the H.H. Franklin Company to market its product was reflected in other aspects of its business operations. The number of persons employed by the firm during most of the 1911-1912 period did not exceed 1,100, and at times dropped below that figure. Franklin thus was falling far behind competing Midwestern motor vehicle builders in size of workforce as well as in output of vehicles. In mid-1911 such major Detroit-based auto manufacturers as Studebaker and Packard could claim employment levels of over 6,400 persons in their factories, while the Cadillac Motor Car Co. trailed only slightly with 5,400. Other big employers in this booming Midwestern city were the Ford Motor Co. with 3,600 hands (many Ford parts continued to be built by outside suppliers such as Dodge Brothers; thus the firm's employment as yet did not fully reflect its huge output of vehicles) and Chalmers with 2,400. Smaller Detroit auto builders included Regal with 400 employees and Herreshoff with a modest 45.[4-10] The importance of the Packard plant in the city which was becoming the world's motor car capital may be judged by the fact that the Detroit Public Library established a branch reading room at the factory. Franklin, after completing its major building program in the period 1902-1909, also was proceeding much more slowly with further physical expansion. By 1910 the company had acquired numerous parcels of property in the large block bounded by Geddes, Marcellus, Magnolia and Gifford Streets (the major exception was the Kallfelz Bakery building), but only a structure containing a test shop and mechanical laboratory plus a saw-toothed building intended to house a sundry machine shop and case hardening operation were completed in the next few years.

As 1912 neared an end Franklin management had been compelled to review its motor car manufacturing program carefully and begin outlining plans for the development of a more desirable product line. One important decision was already behind it–the firm had dropped the manufacture of all commercial units, and thus would concentrate its future efforts entirely in the area of pleasure cars. The trucks, busses and related business vehicles built by Franklin had been more costly than similar commercial units manufactured by competing firms, and thus while undoubtedly of high quality failed to sell in any substantial volume. Due to the fact that many of these units were built to special order, they also tended to impede the normal production process in the factory. With respect to its four-cylinder pleasure cars, the firm also had to recognize that Franklin offerings were far higher-priced than similar vehicles being built by most other manufacturers. By late 1912 a four-cylinder automobile of only medium size costing nearly $2,000 clearly was not competitive with products of other reputable companies selling for hundreds of dollars less. Likewise, the large six-cylinder Franklin machines, perhaps lacking the prestige of Packard and Pierce Arrow, continued to find only limited numbers of purchasers. The small six which had been introduced in 1912 now appeared to be the vehicle holding the greatest promise for the future, particularly if its cost could be kept at a moderate level.

At the beginning of 1913 Franklin introduced an initial group of vehicles, designated the Series 2, which in most respects were little different from the 1912 Series 1 cars. Some months later in the same year the company brought out its Series 3 cars, which apart from some de-emphasis of the four-cylinder offerings continued the traditional model line. The principal change in the 1913 units was the adoption of electric starting and lighting on the six-cylinder models (the electric self-starter had been pioneered by Cadillac a year earlier, and vastly increased the gas-powered automobile's appeal to the general public). The new Franklin electrical system featured an unique combined starter-generator, which gave the car no-stall characteristics–so long as the ignition switch remained on, a stopped engine re-started automatically. Obviously, these two series of vehicles represented a holding action by the Syracuse firm, pending development of a car with stronger public appeal.

Then, in the fall of 1913 the Franklin company broke with recent tradition and consolidated its product line. Its Series 4 cars for 1914 were based on a single engine and chassis, an updated version of the small six-cylinder Model M first introduced in 1912. The large six plus the four-cylinder were no longer offered to the car-buying public. The new car, named the Six-Thirty, featured a number of technical changes and improvements in engine, drive line and chassis. From the standpoint of the customer, however, one modification was all-important. The steering wheel was moved to the left side of the vehicle, with the gear shift and hand brake levers placed in the middle of the front compartment, giving so-called center-control. The new series, while continuing to feature the basic roadster and touring car models, also incorporated four smartly-styled closed bodies, including a coupe, sedan, limousine and berline. All bodies regardless of size, however, were interchangeable on the one chassis. Both the limousine and berline models were intended to be chauffeur-driven, with the operator of the vehicle seated in the open in the limousine and in a closed separate front compartment in the berline. The sedan, a body style which Franklin together with Hudson largely pioneered in production motor cars, was intended to be an owner-driven model. Certain of the new offerings, most notably the touring car, were built with lower bodies and more pleasing lines than earlier Franklins.

With this attractive new car the Franklin firm now had a modernized single product line on which it could concentrate its sales and manufacturing efforts. The vehicle, mounted on a 120-inch wheelbase, fully incorporated the features of flexibility and light weight for which Franklin had become famous, with the basic touring model tipping the scale at a modest 2,700 pounds. Prices were established at $2,300 for the two open body styles, the roadster and touring car, moving upward to the $2,950-$3,400 range for the various closed models. The company clearly had determined that its future lay with a medium-sized vehicle which sold in the upper-middle price range, but offered an effective challenge to competitors with its air-cooled engine, top-quality workmanship, ease of handling, and overall durability.

The H.H. Franklin Company, whose products in earlier years had outdistanced all other gas-powered vehicles, small and large, in fuel economy, decided to demonstrate in mid-1913 that it could still claim such leadership. A 1911-model four-cylinder Franklin, owned by S.G. Averell–who, it will be remembered, was the purchaser of the company's first production car back in 1902–was fitted for an economy trial with a light-weight, streamlined body plus special rear axle gears and a modified carburetor. A single gallon of gasoline was poured into the dashboard fuel tank and the vehicle sent on its way over a route on Long Island. The test car covered an amazing 83.5 miles before it stalled for lack of fuel! The record established was an extraordinary one, and since the trial was conducted under the auspices of the Automobile Club of America, there could be no question of its validity. While the vehicle used bore little resemblance to a stock model, obviously having been specially equipped for the test run, the record achieved nonetheless demonstrated the inherent economy of operation of the Franklin product.

In order to drive home to the public the fact that Franklin's new Six-Thirty model also would have a limited thirst for fuel, the company next scheduled an economy test throughout all its American sales outlets. On the morning of May 1, 1914, each Franklin dealer across the nation, using a stock model automobile, was to disconnect the normal fuel line from gas tank to carburetor, attach a one-gallon can, and under the supervision of impartial observers determine how many miles could be covered by the vehicle. With driving conditions varying greatly on that day from one sector of the country to another, the mileage actually achieved by the different cars on the single gallon of gas ranged from over fifty-one in Milwaukee, Wisconsin (in fine, fair weather) to only seventeen in Georgetown, Texas (heavy rain). An average of 32.8 miles per gallon was attained by the ninety-four cars tested, which was exceptional for a vehicle of Franklin's size. Since the car, with its flexible springs and light weight, seldom wore out a set of tires, the company could without undue exaggeration assure those persons who paid an upper-middle-range price for the new Franklin product that much of their initial investment would be recovered over the life of the vehicle in low cost of operation!

With the economy of the new model adequately proven, the company next turned to the important area of durability. Again using its retail sales outlets as guinea-pigs, the Franklin firm scheduled a nationwide test of the ability of its air-cooled engine to function under extraordinary stress. On September 24, 1914, each dealer operated a Franklin Six-Thirty model for 100 miles entirely in low gear, with the hood closed, no oil added, and the motor kept running continuously. One hundred sixteen vehicles were driven in this manner, with only a handful actually failing to finish. Each car was accompanied by an observer, often a newspaper man, and the routes chosen were far from easy, frequently including runs up good-sized mountains. The company felt that the success of its cars in this test did more than merely demonstrate the efficiency of air-cooling–it also showed that under the hood throbbed a tough, durable engine, able to stand up to any demand made on it. In the same period the Worcester Polytechnic Institute, after conducting carefully-monitored tests in its engineering laboratory, certified that 84.4 per cent of the power generated by the Franklin motor was delivered to the rear wheels. Losses due to friction, slippage and other causes were kept to a minimum due to precise engineering design of the vehicle.

While top-level company executives in Syracuse kept busy devising these varied tests to prove the Franklin car's worth, two of the dealers in the field decided to demonstrate Franklin prowess in a more vigorous fashion. Ralph Hamlin, the shrewd, aggressive Franklin distributor in the Los Angeles area, like John Wilkinson had won his spurs in bicycle racing contests before the turn of the century. Still a fiery competitor years later, Hamlin since 1908 had piloted a Franklin in the annual 500-mile Los Angeles to Phoenix across-the-desert-race, and on his fifth attempt, in October 1912, took first place in this grueling contest. His victory, in the Franklin 6-cylinder model D, was particularly impressive when it is noted that he outperformed several well-known professional racing drivers who were behind the wheels of such big, prestigious vehicles as Simplex and Mercedes. Hamlin then turned to mountain climbing, and in the fall of 1913 piloted a Franklin to the highest altitude yet attained by a motor car in California–10,600 feet, very near to the top of the Sierra Nevada range. A year and a half later the Franklin dealer in Walla Walla, Washington, was able to devise a torture test for one of his showroom models that few sellers of competing makes would have attempted to emulate.

PRACTICAL AMERICA—
AND THE FRANKLIN CAR

AMERICANS are at heart a practical people. There is something in them that responds to Thrift; something that makes them ashamed of extravagance and waste.

They may get off the track occasionally, but they always come back to the main road of efficiency and common sense.

$300,000,000 Wasted in Gasoline and Tires Every Year

The average American is busy. Outside his business he lets others do his thinking. He thinks with his crowd.

He did this on motor cars. He bought dead weight and rigidity, ponderous machinery and big wheel base.

He lugged around radiators and plumbing, a water-cooling system of 177 parts.

He *paid the price* in upkeep and depreciation, tire destruction, gasoline waste

It cost him about $600,000,- 000 a year and did not give him the comfort of the flexible, easy riding Franklin, with its *world's record of economy in cost of operation.*

There is no middle ground in this Thrift question.

A car has it—or it has not.

Like easy riding comfort—if Thrift is there it proves itself.

Take the tire question, for instance.

If the owner of a *heavy machine* uses his car as freely as the Franklin owner uses his scientific-light-weight car, in three years he will buy *four sets of tires* to the Franklin's two—and the tires alone will cost him nearly *three times* what they cost the Franklin owner.

There never was a more complete demonstration of a *principle* than the way every *thrift* record in the fine-car class has been established by the *Franklin Car*.

Efficiency Standards Established for Motor Cars

Gasoline! Franklin National Economy Test, May 1, 1914— 94 Franklin Cars in all parts of the country averaged 32.8 miles to the gallon of gasoline.

And again, May 1, 1915— 137 Franklin Cars averaged 32.1 miles to the gallon.

And again, in the Yale University Fuel Economy Test, when Professor Lockwood and Arthur B. Browne, M. E., established the fact that the Franklin Car uses less gasoline per mile than any other car with six or more cylinders.

Oil! In the New York to Chicago Oil Test the Franklin Car ran 1,046 miles on one gallon of oil.

Power! Efficiency Test by the Worcester Polytechnic Institute demonstrated that the Franklin delivers 84.4 per cent of its engine power at the rear wheels.

Tires! The five-year National Tire Average of Franklin owners is 10,203 miles.

Investment Value! If you can find a used Franklin for sale, you will pay *twenty per cent more for it* than for any other fine car in proportion to its first cost and the use it has had.

American Motor Cars Carry More People than the Railroads

The more this country gets down to stern *realities* the bigger place there is for the Franklin Car.

There is nothing new in the Thrift of the Franklin—only more people are recognizing it.

The Franklin owner has nothing to change, nothing to explain or excuse.

He is using his car more instead of less, because it is primarily a car of *utility*, owned and operated on a *Thrift basis*.

It must be gratifying to him that he saw these things *before* the call to National Thrift.

Touring Car	2280 lbs.	$1950.00
Runabout	2160 lbs.	1900.00
4-pass. Roadster	2280 lbs.	1950.00
Cabriolet	2485 lbs.	2750.00
Sedan	2610 lbs.	2850.00
Brougham	2575 lbs.	2800.00
Town Car	2610 lbs.	3100.00
Limousine	2620 lbs.	3100.00

All Prices F. O. B. Syracuse

FRANKLIN AUTOMOBILE COMPANY
SYRACUSE, N. Y., U. S. A.

This advertisement emphasizes the practical reasons to purchase a Franklin car.
(Courtesy of National Geographic Magazine*)*

THE FRANKLIN AUTOMOBILE COMPANY

Removing second and third-speeds and then sealing the transmission to insure complete honesty, he successfully drove the Franklin 880 miles in low gear from Walla Walla to San Francisco, California, without once turning off the engine. The trip, over some of the most rugged terrain to be found anywhere in the nation, involved 83 hours and 40 minutes of trouble-free non-stop operation.

These splendid achievements on racing circuit and primitive rural road, coupled with able merchandising of the new single-chassis Franklin automobile, produced a major turn-about in company fortunes. Sales volume, which had been a modest 1,300 in 1913, moved

Throughout the early 1900s, highly publicized test runs were commonly used to prove the durability and economical operation of a vehicle. This Franklin vehicle participated in a fuel economy test run in 1919. The driver is Horace Turner; the other two gentlemen are unidentified. (Courtesy of Bill Simpson)

A MATURING COMPANY

up impressively to 2,500 the following year when the full effect of the popular Six-Thirty model was felt. A company document issued early in 1915 provides an interesting breakdown on 1914-year sales. The leader among Franklin dealers was the dynamic Ralph Hamlin of Los Angeles, who disposed of 129 cars, followed by distributors in San Francisco, Chicago and Boston, who delivered 122, 118 and 106 vehicles respectively. Many dealers operated on a very small scale, a substantial number selling only two-to-five Franklin cars annually and numerous others merely one apiece. The strong sales recovery continued in 1915, when the company was able to market a record 3,300-plus units. It is interesting to note that by this time the Franklin's dealer network included representatives in far-distant Johannesburg, South Africa, as well as in Mexico City and various Canadian communities.

The Franklin factory organization moved aggressively forward to keep pace with the increase in sales. A major change in production management took place in June 1912, when Frederick Haynes resigned as manufacturing manager to take charge of the big Dodge Brothers' plant in Detroit. The Dodge firm undoubtedly sought to utilize Haynes' broad talents in the development of its proposed new car, which would be introduced with considerable fanfare to the public in 1914, and prove to be an instant success. Haynes ultimately was to head the Dodge Company, first as president in the early 1920s, and later in that decade as chairman of the board. His successor as Franklin manufacturing chief was cool, precise (but very likeable) George D. Babcock. On assuming his new position Babcock immediately sought to move ahead swiftly with installation of the Taylor plan of production control and work simplification throughout the factory. Vital to such an approach was the development of a more systematic manufacturing process, whereby employees performing assembly duties had necessary parts continuously supplied to their work stations. This made it possible to build Franklin cars both more efficiently and in steadily-increasing numbers each year. Within the relatively low-output Franklin factory final assembly had not yet been mechanized; cars were pushed from one work station to another as the building of each vehicle progressed. It would be some years in the future before a conveyor-type moving assembly line similar to that utilized by the Ford Motor Company was installed. Early in 1915 the company also reinstituted its building program, constructing during that year major factory additions encompassing tens of thousands of square feet of new floor area, at a cost of over half-a-million dollars.

In the engineering sector other personnel changes took place. Early in the decade John Wilkinson received the title of vice-president and general manager of engineering and manufacturing; he was succeeded as chief engineer by Arthur Holmes. The design and production of automobiles in the Franklin organization thus continued to be separated from management, finance and sales. The company also organized its own technical training program following the closing of the Sweet Institute. The new Franklin school gave selected young men four years of indoctrination in factory methods, with each youth rotated through the various manufacturing departments of the company. This broad exposure to shop work was supplemented by academic instruction in mathematics, drafting and design, thus producing a well-trained automotive technician. The firm clearly felt this program to be of value in helping guarantee it a steady flow of skilled personnel, indispensable to the manufacture of an increasingly complex product.

Under the leadership of Wilkinson and his key aides the company engineering staff continued its vigorous campaign to simplify in every way possible construction of the Franklin automobile. Through a concentration of effort on the Six-Thirty chassis, numerous refinements were made in succeeding series which significantly scaled down the weight of the vehicle without in any way impairing its utility. When the Series 6 was unveiled late in 1914, it featured a Dyneto 12-volt starter-generator which weighed a full forty pounds less than a similar unit used on the previous model (the Dyneto device produced an electrical charge when the car traveled at twelve or more miles per hour; below that speed it functioned as a starting motor). This series also incorporated spiral bevel gears in the rear axle, thus helping achieve another feature constantly sought by Franklin engineers, that of silent

A MATURING COMPANY

The printing shop of the H.H. Franklin Manufacturing Company around 1915, established to support the expanding automobile firm. (Courtesy of Harley Willis)

operation. The Series 8, announced in mid-1915, showed continued attention being given to the development of an ever-more-trim vehicle. The company's engineering team had analyzed the car part-by-part to determine where bulk could be reduced without sacrificing durability, and the resulting weight decrease in several areas was striking. Fenders made of aluminum rather than steel pared off a total of 38 pounds, and similar substitution of the lighter metal in the dash and running-board assemblies eliminated another 30. This weight saving, of course, was part of a carefully thought-out plan to make the Franklin ever-more-economical to operate. In addition to featuring low gas consumption and tire wear the lightweight car also was more quickly responsive to a touch of the accelerator when its driver sought

THE FRANKLIN AUTOMOBILE COMPANY

Students of the H.H. Franklin Technical School enjoy an annual outing to a local lake in June 1913. (Courtesy of the late David T. Doman)

increased speed.

The engineering and manufacturing efficiencies achieved by the Franklin organization were promptly reflected in reduced prices for the consumer. The Series 6 open cars sold for $150 less than previous models, and the Series 8 price tags were trimmed by another $200, bringing the touring car cost down to $1,950. This effort to build a lighter, lower-cost car was in direct contrast to the approach taken by two of Franklin's long-time, Detroit-based competitors, who now chose to move in a totally different direction. The Cadillac Motor Company, which in its pioneer days had specialized in relatively small vehicles, introduced a powerful V-type eight-cylinder car late in 1914, and Packard followed suit some months later with an imposing V-12. Both of these vehicles sold in substantial numbers, but they clearly appealed to a clientele quite different from the typical Franklin purchaser. The superbly-designed Marmon Model 34 had been developed along lines similar to the Franklin, featuring extensive use of aluminum to reduce weight and thus provide a smooth ride plus ease of handling and brisk acceleration, but with its long wheelbase plus a price tag in the $2,900-and-up range it was very much a luxury vehicle. The Peerless V-8, introduced toward the end of 1915 at a price substantially below that of the company's massive earlier models, may well have been an important Franklin competitor, as undoubtedly were two attractive, moderately-priced six-cylinder vehicles, the high-performance Hudson car featuring the industry's first fully-counterbalanced crankshaft, and the crisply-styled, Cleveland-based Chandler automobile.

This was an era in which several gifted engineers had successfully developed technically-advanced vehicles for the motor car industry. Jesse Vincent of Packard, D. McCall White of Cadillac, Howard Coffin of Hudson, and Howard Marmon of the company bearing his name, all demonstrated impressive leadership skills in automotive design. How would the equally talented engineering leader of the H.H. Franklin Company, John Wilkinson, respond to these trailblazing performances by his peers? The answer was not long in coming.

In mid-1916 the Franklin engineering staff outdid all its previous efforts by introducing an automobile in which scientific light weight plus flexibility of operation were incorporated to an extraordinary degree. The new Series 9, while retaining all the features for which the marque previously had been renowned, weighed some 400 pounds less than the predecessor Series 8. Tipping the scale (in the touring car version) at only 2,280 pounds, the new model was claimed by the company to be fully the equal–or even the superior–of earlier Franklins in all respects, despite nearly every individual part having been reduced in weight and the car slightly diminished in size.

John Wilkinson and his assistants had achieved another triumph, developing a vehicle which through careful choice of materials (particularly the lavish use of aluminum) and elimination of each surplus ounce of metal was the lightest motor car of its class in the world. Since both front and rear axles had been substantially lightened, far less unsprung weight now had to be dealt with. The end result, despite a wheelbase

THE FRANKLIN AUTOMOBILE COMPANY

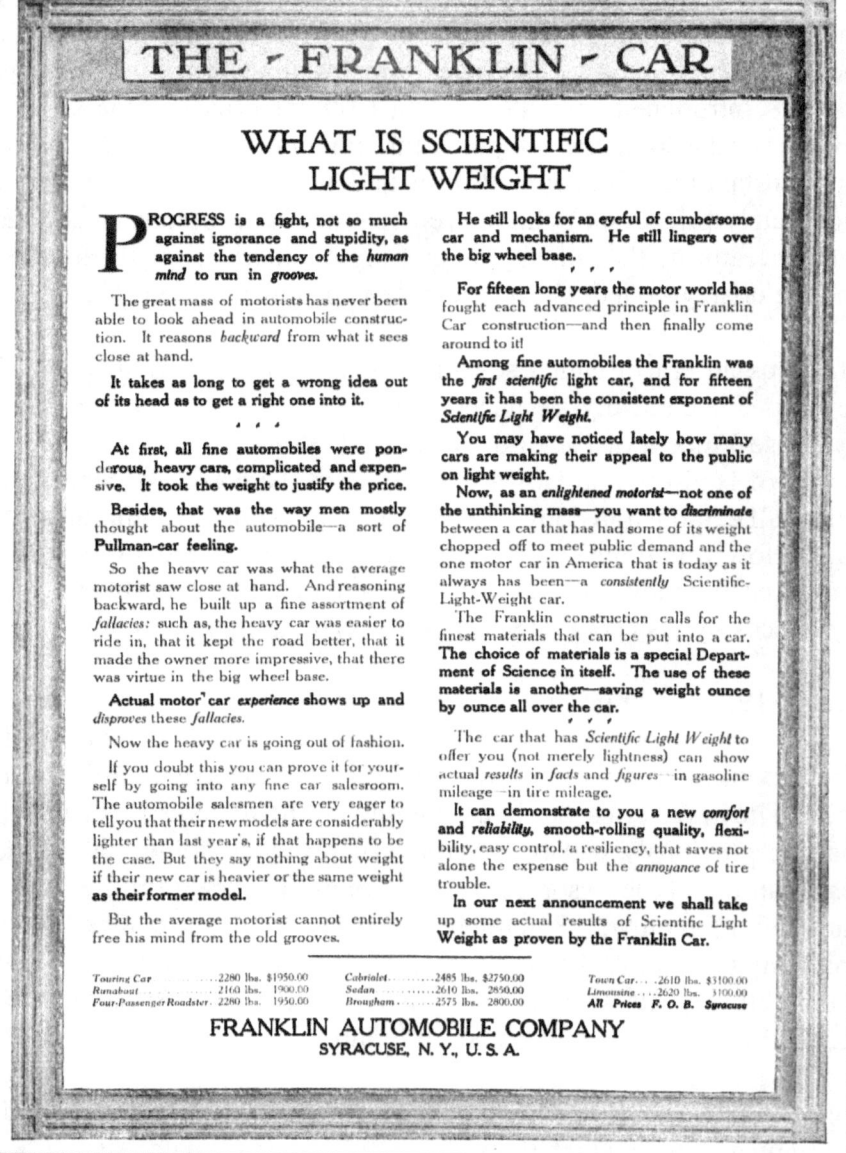

This advertisement for the Franklin car (circa 1917) emphasized "scientific light weight" as a major advantage of Franklin cars. This characteristic was important for most Franklin cars throughout the years. (Courtesy of National Geographic Magazine*)*

shortened to only 115 inches, was a very high standard of riding comfort and ease of control. The engine had been reduced in size at a time when nearly all American auto companies were featuring ever-larger power plants, the rationale being that less horsepower was required to propel this moderate-sized, light-weight car. Economy of operation also was emphasized in the new Franklin product, with owners having to make far fewer stops for now-more-costly gasoline and oil. Styling in the new model had been modernized, with square corners rounded and body lines smoothed out. To increase marketability prices were slashed even further, with the touring car and the four-passenger roadster carrying factory tags of $1,850, while the sedan now could be had for $2,750. In summary, the Franklin firm continued to pioneer in offering prospective purchasers a relatively small, agile car of high quality, not the bulky, ponderous type of vehicle championed by most of its competitors. The company had chosen to go very much its own way in automotive design, rather than seek to emulate the great majority of motor car builders.

During the early summer of 1916 the Franklin factory encountered a number of problems in manufacturing the first run of Series 9 cars, causing delays in shipments to dealers. Once these initial teething troubles had been mastered, however, the company moved at top speed to meet the explosive consumer demand for its vehicles. Improved business conditions, as well as the innovative new model, helped spur Franklin sales to extraordinary heights. As 1916 reached a close and the year 1917 began, a war-inflated economy had taken full hold in America. While the nation had not yet become a formal participant in the great military struggle raging in Europe, the effects of the First World War now had spread throughout the country. The receipt by America of huge orders for munitions, motor trucks, raw materials and foodstuffs from the Allied Powers, particularly Great Britain and France, had ignited a veritable explosion of business activity and produced widespread prosperity across the land, with the auto industry a major beneficiary. Demand for motor vehicles achieved record highs, with an increasing number of purchasers ordering cars with substantial price tags.

THE FRANKLIN AUTOMOBILE COMPANY

This 1917 advertisement for the Franklin car appeals to both luxury and practical car buyers. (Courtesy of National Geographic Magazine)

A MATURING COMPANY

By late January 1917, the Franklin Company was building an unprecedented thirty vehicles per day, nearly double the level of a year earlier. In mid-March the company announced that its factory output for the month would approach one thousand vehicles (a few years earlier this number had constituted nearly the total annual volume), and that floor space used for productive purposes had been increased by 150 per cent during the preceding twelve months. Late in May a further announcement was made that factory employment totaled 2,742, with an additional 340 persons engaged in office duties. The weekly payroll of the firm now averaged $73,000, or $23.70 per employee, while the value of new cars shipped each month was approximately two million dollars. The nation's extraordinary prosperity thus was being participated in fully by the Syracuse auto maker. In the early fall manufacture of vehicles at the South Geddes Street plant set another record, frequently exceeding fifty per day. Total Franklin production ultimately was to reach nine thousand vehicles in 1917, much more than double the 1916 figure of 3,800. The company therefore appeared to be taking giant strides toward once again becoming an important part of the nation's motor car industry.

This major turnabout in Franklin Company fortunes during the five-year period 1913-1917 produced important financial benefits for stockholders in the firm. At the beginning of 1913 authorized capital was increased to $900,000 in common and $600,000 in preferred stock, with holders of company common shares receiving a 200 percent stock dividend. As the year progressed a steady flow of earnings made it possible for the firm to resume cash dividends, with a four-and-one-half percent payout made on shares of common stock. In 1914, with increased company prosperity generating net earnings of three-quarters of a million dollars, the common dividend was raised to eighteen percent in cash. The year 1915 saw net income soar to the unprecedented level of $1,073,000, making possible a cash dividend on common shares of $396,000, or a stunning 44 percent! With the board of directors late in 1915 authorizing another increase (to $2,000,000) in the total amount of common stock, the company on January 1, 1916, announced a 100 percent stock dividend on the com-

THE FRANKLIN AUTOMOBILE COMPANY

This advertisement was intended to reach the wealthy luxury car buyer who would be willing and able to pay the large price tags for Franklin luxury cars. (Courtesy of National Geographic Magazine*)*

A MATURING COMPANY

mon, followed by a modest six percent cash payout. At this point the Franklin firm clearly chose to use most of its large annual net income for physical expansion; a similar policy was followed in the peak sales year of 1917 when only a limited four per cent cash payment was made on common shares. It should be noted that as early as 1913 the company for the first time sold a small amount ($126,000) of preferred stock. This issue was redeemed in mid-1915, and at the beginning of 1917 some $540,000 of new preferred was marketed, undoubtedly to help fund the continuing capital expansion program.

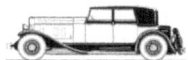

Skyrocketing production and use of motor cars during the period from 1912 to 1916 demonstrated emphatically that a spectacular new industry had shouldered its way onto the American business scene. While the building of 356,000 motor cars in the year 1912 broke all previous records, this number was minute when compared to the astonishing total of 1,526,000 units turned out in 1916. Never in the history of the nation had a manufacturing sector grown so swiftly in such a brief period of time. The adolescent motor vehicle industry of a few years earlier now had become a healthy young adult–and one displaying very large muscles indeed.

Registrations of all motor vehicles (cars and trucks) across America at the end of 1916 reached the imposing figure of 3,513,000. Of equal importance, however, was the extraordinarily broad distribution throughout the land of car and truck ownership. The nation's agricultural areas, which in an earlier period could claim only a modest number of motor vehicles, now were among the leaders in incidence of automotive registrations. Such largely rural Midwestern states as Iowa, Nebraska, South Dakota and Kansas recorded astonishing increases in automobile sales from year-to-year, and could claim more vehicles in relation to population than heavily industrialized New York, Massachusetts, New Jersey and Pennsylvania. The motor vehicle in one form or another, car or truck, obviously was well on its way to cap-

THE FRANKLIN AUTOMOBILE COMPANY

turing the hearts of Americans everywhere. The automobile industry also was kept busy furnishing large number of motor vehicles to other nations throughout the world. Over eighty thousand cars and trucks were exported in 1916, while Americans purchased only a handful of foreign-made units.

Unquestionably the one motor car most responsible for nationwide expansion of automobile ownership, particularly in small towns and rural areas, was the Ford Model T. Constructed in a simple but sturdy manner, cheap to acquire and operate, it was the car of choice of a huge number of persons throughout the nation. By the year 1916 the Ford firm was totally in a class by itself in terms of motor vehicle output, producing not far from fifty percent of all automobiles sold in America. However, during this period a number of other motor car builders also were playing important roles in the overall industry. These included such good-sized companies as Willys-Overland, Buick, Dodge, Maxwell, Studebaker and Chevrolet, each of which turned out from 60,000 to 140,000 cars per year. Not as large as these leaders but nonetheless well-known to the auto-buying public were concerns such as Oakland, Reo, Hudson, Cadillac, Chandler and Paige, all manufacturing from 12,000 to 35,000 vehicles annually. Innumerable smaller firms brought up the rear, building from a few hundred to 10,000 automobiles each twelve months. The H.H. Franklin Company could be found at the top of the small firm group.

The Ford Motor Company's leadership in developing the conveyor-type assembly line plus its broad-scale utilization of specialized machine tools enabled it to produce vast quantities of vehicles at a minimum cost per-unit, obviously a major factor in its ability to achieve top ranking in annual output and sales. Despite Ford's corner on a large portion of the automotive market, however, there clearly was a place in the industry during this era for the company of modest size. The automobiles built by Ford, as noted previously, were low-priced and durable, but they had limited appeal for a large number of Americans from the middle and upper economic classes, who often preferred a higher-grade, more individualized product. The non-Ford sector of the market thus was broadly open to numerous other motor car manufacturing firms and, during the 1916-17 period, accessible to this group on a relatively equal basis. Such important companies as Willys-Overland, Buick and others of similar stature took the lion's share of the non-Ford market, producing vehicles in sufficiently large volume to realize handsome annual profits and justify the construction of large factories. The lesser auto builders, while not operating on the level of the above-mentioned concerns, were often effective competitors. Some degree of consolidation of the industry into fewer companies had now begun, but the small motor car firm, if it was well-managed and offered a nicely-designed product with solid consumer appeal, could continue to thrive in the automotive marketplace. At this point in the history of the auto industry no harsh penalty was exacted for being a minor producer. It should also be noted that during this period no conglomerate existed which sought to blanket every sector of the market with a group of vehicles ranging from low-priced to costly. An organization such as General Motors in 1916 consisted of a somewhat loosely-knit aggregation of semi-independent motor car manufacturers, with limited top-level coordination of marketing plans and little interchange of engineering or manufacturing know-how among the various divisions.

By the 1916-17 period electric and steam-driven vehicles played an insignificant role in the automotive industry. Earlier mechanical shortcomings of the gas-powered car had largely been overcome, and it now could be relied on to transport driver and passengers to a destination swiftly and with little fear of breakdown. The development of an easy-to-operate self-starter, mentioned previously, removed the final obstacle to the dominance of the internal combustion engine. Such firms as Detroit Electric and Stanley continued to produce electric and steam-powered units, but a mere handful of buyers showed any interest in their offerings.

During this era Franklin was known across the nation as the only successful example of an air-cooled, gasoline-powered vehicle. It had outlasted all other makes using direct air-cooling, including the much publicized "cyclecars" of the 1913-1915 era. These undersized vehicles, mostly utilizing tiny, air-cooled, motorcycle-type engines and accommodating only two persons, enjoyed a brief period of popularity in this country. Once their limitations became known, however, they largely dropped out-of-sight in the United States, although continuing to be popular in Great Britain. Americans at this relatively early date made it clear that they wanted motor cars of adequate size and power.

The vast expansion of the automobile industry helped reinvigorate several medium-sized cities in the Midwest among them Toledo, Akron and Indianapolis. However, one community above all others in America's heartland reaped the full benefit of the motor vehicle boom. Detroit, which as recently as 1890 was a pleasant but somewhat slow-moving municipality of less importance than such competitor Great Lakes cities as Buffalo and Cleveland, now had mushroomed into an industrial colossus. Automobile and parts manufacturing plants thrust their way into one neighborhood after another of this swiftly expanding city, whose level terrain made large-scale industrial development particularly feasible. Foundries spewed out dense clouds of smoke as they sought to meet the almost insatiable demand for engine blocks and other large castings, while innumerable machine shops emitted a steady hum, day and night, in producing the torrent of parts needed to supply the fast-paced assembly lines. Engineers and entrepreneurs met in downtown hotels to plan the development and exploitation of new motor car technologies, while tough shop superintendents saw to it that vehicles were turned out efficiently and in ever-increasing volume by gangs of production-line workers. "High, wide and handsome" was the term which best described the atmosphere of the "motor city," where fortunes were made (and occasionally lost) literally overnight.

In upstate New York the city of Syracuse also was a beneficiary of the nation's new-found love for the motor vehicle, but to a decidedly lesser degree than Detroit. The Franklin firm, after its heady era of expansion during the early days of the twentieth century, subsequently experienced some years of steady but relatively moderate growth, and this was true of Syracuse generally. The big Detroit auto plants, with their emphasis on mass-production, welcomed huge numbers of unskilled workers from out-of-town, many of whom were recent immigrants struggling to learn a new language and adapt to a different culture. The Franklin firm, together with other Syracuse industries, tended to recruit the majority of new employees from the city itself, or from nearby towns and farming areas. This meant that population expansion of the city and surrounding area failed to match the explosive growth experienced by Detroit and other southeast Michigan industrial centers. It also meant that Syracuse was less subject to the severe social and urban development problems which all too often accompany unchecked community expansion.

The pay scale for Franklin factory employees had progressed steadily upward from the modest levels of the 1907-08 period, and by 1916 averaged a trifle over forty cents per hour. This, of course, was a far cry from the five dollars per day (for an eight-hour work shift) paid by the Detroit-based Ford Motor Company to a significant proportion of its employees. Working conditions at the Franklin plant tended to be generally satisfactory, particularly by the standards of the day. The Taylor system of work simplification and central planning now had been adopted throughout the South Geddes Street factory. George D. Babcock, however, was a consistently fair manufacturing manager, and while numerous jobs, particularly those on machines, were analyzed carefully in order to eliminate unnecessary motion and improve output, production standards were established at reasonable levels. This enabled Franklin employees to earn decent incomes without being forced to work at top speed throughout their shifts. Franklin's small personnel unit occasionally gave advice to employees about effectively managing their incomes ("stay away from bars" appeared to be a frequent suggestion), but did not carry on the intrusive investigations into family life allegedly undertaken by the sociological department of the Ford Motor Company in Detroit during this era. Turnover of personnel in the Franklin plant was moderate, reflecting the decent treatment of workers.

THE FRANKLIN AUTOMOBILE COMPANY

A much-discussed feature of the Taylor system in the Franklin factory was the establishment of production "control boards" in the central manufacturing office. These boards, which filled a good-sized room, were equipped with movable disks, making it possible first to plan and subsequently to track the progression of batches of parts through the plant. With such technological aids, plus an effective time-and-motion study office, the H.H. Franklin Company clearly had become a leader in progressive plant management during this period.

Somewhat surprisingly, neither H.H. Franklin nor any other top executive of the Syracuse auto firm played a significant role in the effort by members of the motor car industry, together with leaders of other vitally interested groups such as the American Automobile Association, to seek the development of a system of roads which would meet the needs of the army of new owners of automobiles. The abominable streets and highways found across the nation in the early years of the century desperately required upgrading if the true potential of the automobile was to be realized, and from 1912-on several heads of motor car companies banded together to help initiate this effort. Leadership came largely from the Midwest, however, with Henry Joy of the Packard Motor Car Company, Roy Chapin of the Hudson firm and Carl G. Fisher of Prest-O-Lite all playing prominent roles.

Initially the automobile industry group concentrated much of its efforts on obtaining construction of a major cross-country facility, called the Lincoln Highway, as a means of aiding the long-distance motorist. However, a far broader approach was adopted ultimately by all good roads advocates, and the modern era of highway development began with enactment of the Federal Aid Road Act in 1916. This act, while not establishing a specific national highway system, did provide an appropriation of $75,000,000 to assist states in the construction of so-called post roads over the ensuing five year period. It also required that each state, if it wished to share in the benefits of the act, establish a highway department which would directly supervise construction of all roads funded by the new legislation. The nation thus was poised to move forward in future years with large-scale highway development.

A MATURING COMPANY

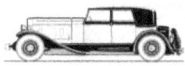

While Franklin during 1917 was smashing all past production records, and the auto industry generally was enjoying a period of extraordinary prosperity, events of earth-shaking importance were occurring at the national and international levels. After an extended effort to maintain the status of a non-belligerent, the United States in April 1917, entered World War I on the side of the Allies. Since it was obvious from the experience of Great Britain, France and Germany that this was a war requiring broad-scale mobilization of the nation's economy, American automobile manufacturers might expect to be affected in several ways. With the motor car industry incorporating major engineering know-how plus impressive productive capacity, it undoubtedly could anticipate being called on to help design and build a good-sized portion of the technical products needed to wage the first heavily mechanized war. Conversely, as its most important peacetime product, the pleasure car, was only indirectly useful to the war effort, the industry might expect to see the vast flow of raw materials required to support its factories gradually diverted to activities more closely keyed to national survival.

The H.H. Franklin Manufacturing Company plus many of its key personnel soon were tapped to assist the nation in the massive effort to produce the tools of war. Not long after America's entry into the World War the company was presented with a major challenge in the designing and building of a transmission for one of the new monsters of ground warfare, a tank. When another concern failed completely in its efforts to produce this vital part, the Franklin firm was asked to step-in, and given a three-week deadline to complete the task. Through a superb effort on the part of company engineers and production specialists the transmission was designed and a prototype unit built, with delivery made to Bridgeport, Connecticut, well within the allotted time!

As America's role in the war expanded the firm received other key as-

*Henry P Shaw was one of many Franklin employees who served in World War I.
(*The Franklin News, *May 1, 1919)*

signments. A small portable lighting plant, useful in providing illumination in the front-line trenches and in other locations where electricity was not readily available, was produced by the Franklin company in substantial volume. Contracts to build major engine components for Wright-Martin and Rolls-Royce aircraft were awarded to the Syracuse firm in the summer of 1918, and in short order over a million dollars worth of new, special-purpose machinery was installed in the South Geddes Street factory to permit this task to be effectively performed. The die-casting division also played an important role in the war effort, producing vast numbers of small parts for such diverse weapons as depth bombs and gun sights. The Franklin plant was compelled to recruit hundreds of new employees to help it meet those heavy production demands.

While the H.H. Franklin Company participated heavily in the production of war-related items, a key member of the firm, John Wilkinson, was called on to provide a different but vital type of assistance. A major effort had been made throughout 1917 and early 1918 by several top engineers in the American automobile industry to design a powerful engine suitable for use in aircraft. The end result was the development of a massive, twelve-cylinder motor, named the Liberty, which was rushed into manufacture by several automotive companies. Once mounted in airplanes and tested in flight, however, early models of the new power plant received a barrage of criticism, particularly on the basis of reliability. When even General John Pershing, commander of the American Forces in Europe, joined the circle of critics, the Army office in charge of airplane production realized that it must take immediate steps to deal with the complaints. A special Aircraft Board Committee consisting of prominent engineers was promptly appointed to conduct investigative tests and evaluate the soundness of the big engine. John Wilkinson was named a member of the Committee; he was joined by Henry M. Crane, another well-known automotive engineer (Crane-Simplex), and D. McCall White (Cadillac). These three engineering experts together with representatives of the air forces of several of America's allies quickly scheduled a series of tests to identify problem areas in the Liberty motor and recommend corrective measures. Testing was carried on throughout the spring and early summer of 1918, and reports submitted to top army personnel. Undoubtedly this investigative work was of substantial value in eliminating reliability problems in Liberty motors, and ultimately enabling the engine to play a significant role in the American war effort.[4-11]

Throughout the 1917-1918 period the transition of the American automobile industry from production of passenger cars to war work was a gradual one. While there were threats of shortages of coal in 1917, the industry came through the year relatively unaffected by the war. Even in the opening months of 1918 such manufacturing giants as the Ford

THE FRANKLIN AUTOMOBILE COMPANY

Motor Co. still were turning out large volumes of pleasure cars. By March of that year, though, due in part to reduced availability of raw materials and supplies, a series of sharp cut-backs began, and these deepened in succeeding months. The Franklin firm for the most part followed the overall industry trend. As 1918 began it was manufacturing nearly 300 cars each week, its highest level ever, and while this pace was not long maintained it continued building pleasure vehicles in considerable volume into the early summer of 1918. The pressures of the new aircraft engine contracts, plus the demands of the Federal War Industries Board that auto companies concentrate their efforts on products vital to national defense, were felt by the end of the summer, however. On September 10 the company indicated that its plant now was practically one hundred per cent on war work, and that its inten-

This photograph, taken at an early H.H. Franklin Club Trek, shows the old Franklin factory (no longer extant) in the background. In front are three Franklin cars (1911 Model G, 1918 Series 9, and another 1918 Series 9) owned by club members. (Photo by Bill Stevens, courtesy of the late David T. doman)

tion was not to produce any more Franklin automobiles until the war ended. By early October this decision had been fully implemented, and car production had ceased.

Suddenly, the great conflict was ended by the Armistice of November 11, 1918. A blizzard of telegrams quickly emerged from federal government offices directing the nation's manufacturing firms to terminate war production as swiftly as possible. No concern was shown for the obvious disruption this would cause in the operations of thousands of industrial plants, or in the lives of the vast number of employees who had been taken on to staff the war-related projects. The motor car companies soon were given a relatively free hand to reconvert to civilian production as quickly as they chose to do so. The Franklin factory was able to produce a token number of automobiles–four in all–the week following the Armistice, and during the month of December the total output climbed to 311.

Vast changes would confront Franklin and the numerous other motor car manufacturing concerns in the postwar era. Many firms had expanded their physical facilities enormously to meet the demands of war, and could expect to be faced with the necessity of utilizing this increased productive capacity effectively in a time of peace. Sources of raw materials and parts had been severely disrupted during the period of hostilities, and needed to be reestablished. The handling of a labor force which had become accustomed to a relatively high income during the 1917-1918 years might well present problems. Finally, questions related to market demand–the types of vehicles which would be sought by prospective purchasers in the months and years to come, and the prices they might be willing to pay–would have to be dealt with. Consequently, the next few years would be a period which would challenge the best efforts of Franklin and other firms in the now large and highly-competitive automotive field.

THE FRANKLIN AUTOMOBILE COMPANY

– *Five* –

The Postwwar Era
(1919-1924)

The year 1919 began on a note of hope and optimism in all regions of America. While the World War had disrupted the lives of millions of people across the nation, particularly those who served in the armed forces, the vast conflict also generated expanded opportunities and opened new horizons for many others. Workers' pay had shot upward throughout the war period, and although the cost of living also skyrocketed, on balance most persons in industry enjoyed a net gain (the picture was very different for those on relatively fixed incomes, such as teachers and civil servants). In rural districts an almost extraordinary prosperity reigned, with the combination of a huge wartime demand for agricultural products plus high price levels for foodstuffs resulting in enormous increases in the purchasing power of the typical farm owner.

In the postwar years the status of women would never again be the same, as the great armed struggle had swept away all vestiges of the Victorian Era. During 1917 and 1918 members of the female sex convincingly demonstrated an ability to work side-by-side with men in many areas of activity which previously had been forbidden them. Women operated fast-revolving machines on factory floors, assembled motors and other complex mechanisms, and in Detroit even drove electric-powered taxis throughout the war period. With this upgraded niche in society, it could be anticipated that a number of women soon would purchase their own motor vehicles, and that many more would strongly influence the type of automobile acquired by their spouses. Motor car manufacturers thus might find that features which appealed to women, such as ease of handling and auto bodies which gave year-round protection from the elements, could be very much in demand in postwar times.

With a vast amount of purchasing power available throughout a now-more-wealthy nation, and large numbers of persons anxious to obtain consumer-related products which often had been unavailable or in limited supply during wartime, America clearly appeared poised to advance into a splendid new economic era. And if an exciting period of business expansion and material prosperity was to highlight the nation's future, it also was apparent that the automobile industry would lead the way. The progress made during the previous few years by this vigorous newcomer to the country's industrial scene could only be labeled as astonishing. From having been a "plaything of the rich" a scant decade or so earlier, the motor vehicle more and more was considered a necessity by millions of Americans. Automobile ownership had become commonplace among business and professional-class persons throughout the country, and while the typical blue-collar worker or office clerk had yet to become a motor car buyer, it was not difficult to foresee this occurring in the years ahead. During 1917, the last year of full auto production prior to war-generated cutbacks, the wholesale value of vehicles produced had reached the astonishing level of one billion fifty-nine million dollars. The auto industry in that year gave employment to 280,000 persons, with motor vehicle manufacturing taking place in some thirty-two states. As this lusty giant achieved massive size its once-important competitor, the horse-drawn vehicle business, had dwindled into relative insignificance. Carriage and wagon factories were fast closing their doors across the nation as few persons bothered to replace worn-out buggies with new ones. The Studebaker Company, a renowned builder of high-quality wagons and carriages since the 1850s, soon was to terminate such production to concentrate totally on motor vehicles. The carriage houses found in many rear yards in urban areas more and more were being converted by their owners to garages for the storage of newly-purchased automobiles. Widespread use of motor vehicles for pleasure purposes, however, was only part of the total picture. The development of the motor truck, found indispensable by the armed services during the Great War, also had proceeded rapidly, and in most cities this vehicle, while slow and ponderous (many trucks still utilized solid tires!), was fast crowding out the horse-drawn delivery van. The bicycle had been totally left behind in the rush toward speedy personal transportation, although its gas-powered counterpart, the motorcycle, now enjoyed considerable popularity among young, active males.

During the early months of 1919 the pent-up demand for automobiles at all price levels appeared to be unlimited, with the available supply minute. Total production of passenger cars in 1918 had been approximately 926,000, little more than half the number built during the previous year. On December 31, 1918, nearly two months after the end of the war, manufacturers nationwide had only 15,500 finished motor cars available for shipment, less than a three-day output during a normal period. Hundreds of thousands of prospective automobile purchasers thus found it necessary to place their names on dealer back-order lists, and resign themselves to an extended period of waiting for delivery of that much-desired new touring car, runabout or sedan.

With such a bright future in sight, each car company quickly sought to increase assembly of automobiles to meet the clamor for its scarce product. By the end of January 1919, a leading luxury motor vehicle manufacturer, Cadillac, reached a production level of fifty-five cars per day. Such an output, however, was exceptional. Cleveland-based Winton, another producer of top-quality cars, was assembling and shipping only five vehicles daily, while Packard, a firm deeply involved for many months in war work and now encountering major reconversion problems, had not yet built a single postwar pleasure car (it was turning out many trucks, however). Apart from the time-consuming task of reestablishing factory assembly lines, various

THE FRANKLIN AUTOMOBILE COMPANY

other problems kept auto companies from quickly achieving satisfactory levels of production during the early months of the peacetime period. One of the most important of these was the severe wartime disruption of normal sources of parts and raw materials, which continued to adversely affect automobile manufacturers through the first half of 1919. Many motor car builders were frequently compelled to establish special departments in their plants to fabricate, often at high cost, items unobtainable in the marketplace but desperately needed to produce completed vehicles for shipment.

A second major difficulty facing many firms involved the recruiting and holding of a quality labor force. When war-related activities abruptly ceased in many factories, company labor policies often tended to be somewhat short-sighted, with numerous employees dropped without thought of future staffing needs. Workers with marketable skills who were laid-off even temporarily usually sought continuing paychecks elsewhere, and thus often were not available once an auto firm was ready to swing into volume production. In addition, in a number of cities the almost unprecedented expansion of motor vehicle and parts factories compelled car manufacturers to recruit huge numbers of new employees from distant areas. A vast torrent of people now were deserting the small towns and farms of the Midwest and South to seek their fortunes in the new centers of auto production.

Unfortunately, housing for this veritable army of transplanted workers frequently was totally unavailable in the industrial "boom towns." Newly-arrived factory hands often had to spend weeks or months in overcrowded rooming houses, while their families remained stranded back home. The story of workers employed on different shifts utilizing a single bed in successive eight-hour periods actually seems to have a degree of truth to it! In Flint, Michigan, which had mushroomed from a sleepy county seat town of 13,000 people to a bustling auto manufacturing center of nearly 100,000 in two short decades, incoming workers often were compelled to inhabit tents and tar-paper shacks along the banks of a local river. Ultimately, of course, more permanent living facilities had to be provided if the huge employee turnover rate—over 100 per cent each year in some motor car factories—was to be reduced and some degree of work force stability maintained. Due to the desperate situation in Flint the city's largest employer, the General Motors Corporation, felt compelled to construct a thousand houses for its burgeoning work force. In Akron, Ohio, the local chamber of commerce spearheaded a campaign to raise several million dollars to produce housing for the vast group of newcomers who poured into that city to help produce the huge quantities of tires absorbed annually by motor car companies.

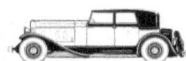

The H.H. Franklin Manufacturing Company was among the many motorcar builders seeking to return quickly to full-time building of automobiles in the early months of 1919. The limited output of vehicles achieved during November and December 1918, enabled the firm to announce that a total of some 6,700 cars had been built during this final war year. Production in January 1919, exceeded that of the previous month by only a narrow margin, and not until mid-February did the plant reach a level of 25 vehicles per day. The company projected a series of further production increases throughout the year, with the goal of building at least 10,000 automobiles in 1919. As wartime restrictions on use of materials were lifted, and credit terms on car sales eased by the Federal Reserve Bank Board, it was anticipated generally by leaders of the auto industry that manufacture of motor vehicles would attain normal levels by July of 1919.

Management of the good-sized Franklin factory had undergone a major change during the World War. Production chief George D. Babcock, now well-known throughout American industry for his advocacy of modern management techniques, obtained a leave of absence from the company in mid-1917 to accept a commission in the Ordnance Department of the Army. After service in France as a lieutenant-colonel, Babcock on his return to America resigned from Franklin, soon thereafter assuming an executive position with a large Midwestern tractor manufacturer. Named as new production head was William Dunk, an English immigrant who following active duty in the Spanish-American War during 1898-1899, entered the Franklin company as a machinist and rose steadily through the ranks. "Bill" Dunk, a vigorous, shirt-sleeved-type of administrator who was not above donning boxing gloves in order to engage in some vigorous sparring with factory hands at company picnics, quickly took steps during the reconversion period to further improve the overall production process. As machinery installed during the War to produce aircraft parts was either removed or adapted for motor vehicle production, the Syracuse motor car builder initiated the so-called progressive group plan of manufacturing at its plant, a system commonplace among the large-volume automobile companies but relatively new to Franklin. Under this approach machining and other work necessary to produce a part would take place sequentially on a number of special-purpose machines clustered together in a single area of the factory (previously a part to be manufactured might travel in and out of such totally disparate units as lathe, milling machine and grinding departments for a variety of operations, obviously an unwieldy and time-consuming process). Not long afterward the "control boards," the group of specially-designed panels which as noted earlier made it possible to monitor the flow of parts on their journey through the manufacturing process, were brought out of wartime storage and reinstalled in the production office.

The vehicle produced by the Franklin factory in the immediate postwar period continued to be the Series 9, first introduced in mid-1916. This lightweight but sturdy car had been modified somewhat during the 1917-1918 period, when the aluminum fenders–found to be all-too-subject to dings and dents in the rigors of everyday use–were replaced by more durable ones built of steel, and an electric carburetor primer (first in the industry) was adopted to facilitate cold-weather starting. The body subsequently was lowered an inch or two to give the vehicle a somewhat less top-heavy appearance. The trim, well-engineered Franklin product demonstrated a continued ability to render economical service to its owners when it swept the Los Angeles-Yosemite Economy Run held in the early summer of 1919. The Series 9 delivered an amazing 28.8 miles per gallon over a 375-mile distance, defeating not only several heavyweight vehicles (including Marmon and Peerless) in its price class, but also proving to be less thirsty of gasoline than even light four-cylinder cars in the low cost category! While the Franklin car produced thus was little-changed in size and economy of operation at the beginning of the postwar era, the same could not be said of its price. With the cost of materials skyrocketing during the wartime period, the base price tag of a Franklin touring car had shot up from the 1916-17 level of $1,850 to $2,450 late in 1918, and $2,650 in June 1919 (Pierce-Arrow raised its prices a stunning $800 per vehicle a short time afterward). Inflationary pressures continued to rage in the summer months of 1919, resulting in a further cost escalation for the touring model to $2,750 less than two months later.

Despite these hefty jumps in price, demand for the car on the part of an automobile-starved public increased steadily during all of 1919. On June 11 of that year S.E. Ackerman, sales manager, reported 3,100 unfilled orders for new Franklins entered on the books of the company. Vigorous efforts to increase production continued, but throughout this first postwar year shortages of parts and materials still plagued the firm, holding down output. During the early summer of 1919 company purchasing agents literally scoured the country seeking items essential for production of Franklin vehicles, with only a fair degree of success. The factory ultimately was compelled to establish a new department for the manufacture of gas tanks and mudguards, so that lack of these items would not delay output of vehicles. By July 1 a daily production rate of 35 cars was finally achieved, substantially below the 40-to-50 per day goal set early in the year.

Cut-backs in personnel made by the company in November and December 1918, following termination of war contracts, now were sharply reversed. Former employees returning from service in the Armed Forces were re-hired quickly, as were many new hands. On June 1, 1919, it was announced that Franklin employment totaled 3,805 persons, the highest number ever, and was being expanded even further.

THE FRANKLIN AUTOMOBILE COMPANY

Some 230 of these employees staffed a night shift (something new to Franklin in peacetime), making it possible to keep the machine shop and several other production departments operating continuously. By August 4 the weekly payroll of the company had reached the record level of $112,000. Because of the relative stability of the upstate New York labor market Franklin continued to fill most new openings with persons who came from either the city of Syracuse or within a forty-or-so-mile radius of the plant. At this time a company survey revealed that some two-thirds of all employees lived no more than a mile from the factory (however, this figure undoubtedly included a substantial number of people who lodged in rooming or boarding houses in the vicinity of the plant during the week, but journeyed to their more distant permanent homes on weekends). The Franklin firm was completely spared the labor unrest which erupted in the spring of 1919 in such major motor car manufacturing centers as Toledo, where employees of Willys-Overland, angered by company reluctance to continue benefits granted during the war period, engaged in a strike marked by substantial violence. A survey conducted in Michigan at this time disclosed that common labor in automobile plants generally was being paid 50 to 60 cents per hour, with skilled workmen receiving 65 cents up to $1.25. The typical skilled employee brought home a paycheck of from $35 to $50 per week, a substantial income for a factory hand of that period. A six-day work week was still standard in most auto factories, although employers were beginning to modify this so that their workers could enjoy a free Saturday afternoon.

Rapid expansion of Franklin production and the substantial increase in the number of employees resulted in heavy demands on the company's physical plant. The Franklin firm had found it difficult to undertake large-scale building activities during the wartime months, due to shortages of materials and of skilled construction workers. However, recognizing that development of major new facilities to house its manufacturing program would be required in the postwar period, the firm purchased nearly all the remaining independently-owned property located within the large block bounded by Geddes, Marcellus, Magnolia and Gifford Streets. Included in this acquisition program

THE POSTWAR ERA

was the well-known Kallfelz Bakery, which for years had supplied Franklin employees with a variety of delicacies. (At one time an aerial conveyor, stretching from a top floor of the plant to the bakery, was put in operation by enterprising Franklin workers, thus insuring a continuing supply of rolls, cakes and cookies "fresh from the oven.")

During the war years and the period immediately following the company met its needs for additional manufacturing and storage space by leasing all or major parts of five unused factory and warehouse buildings located in or near downtown Syracuse. Two of these structures were adapted for use as body plants during 1919, with sedans produced in a multi-story building on Richmond Avenue, and runabout and touring units built on the top floor of a warehouse on South Clinton Street. These operations were made necessary by Franklin's inability to obtain an adequate volume of auto bodies from its normal outside suppliers, including the Walker-Wells Body Co. of Amesbury, Mass., the Rubay Co. of Cleveland, the American Body Co. of Buf-

This aerial photograph of the expanded Franklin plant was taken in September 1923 and published in The Franklin News *on February 1, 1924. The massive brick chimney in the center was 250 feet high.*

falo and several other firms. However, manufacture of such items in these aged facilities scattered about the city undoubtedly added to production costs, and may well have impeded overall output of finished vehicles. Early in the summer of 1919, therefore, design work was begun on a seven-story manufacturing building, to be located at the corner of Marcellus and Magnolia Streets. This structure, with dimensions of 120 by 240 feet at ground level, was to be constructed of reinforced concrete, with large windows incorporated to provide adequate daylight for the employees working within. A contrast for erection of the new building was awarded at the end of July, with completion of the $400,000 facility scheduled for late in the year. Work on the foundation for this big unit had barely commenced when the company announced plans for erection of a new power plant of substantial size, incorporating a massive brick chimney which would tower over all other such structures in the Syracuse area. This new facility would supply much of the electrical power and all of the heat needed by the fast-growing company. No less than 1,225 piles had to be driven into the soft soil to support both the building and the heavy boilers and turbo-generators to be installed therein, while some nine railcar-loads of bricks were required for construction of the huge chimney!

In undertaking this substantial plant expansion program during 1919, to be followed by construction of a series of additional large buildings in 1920, Franklin management made certain basic decisions which would have important consequences in the years ahead. Factory development was to take place totally within the relatively small central city site owned by the company, hemmed in by an important public street on the east, a residential area on the south, other factories to the north, and a steep hill (on which was located a state mental institution) to the west. Faced with such tight space restrictions the Syracuse firm was compelled to expand by going up-in-the-air with multi-story buildings. However, by this time designers of large manufacturing facilities for the automobile industry favored the single-story, saw-toothed-roof factory, built with few internal support posts and columns and thus highly adaptable to the continuous assembly lines now being installed by more and more companies. Franklin's new structure thus faced the danger of being quickly rendered obsolete by rapidly-advancing production technology. In addition, the overall 1919-1920 Franklin building program was a large one, with total factory floor area to be increased by well over twice the pre-1919 level. The company planned this expansion with the goal of achieving a production volume of 18,000 or more automobiles annually, far in excess of previous annual sales. If this number of vehicles could not be marketed the firm would be burdened with a capital investment in substantial unused plant capacity, not a desirable situation.

During the years 1919 and 1920 the Syracuse firm was only one of many on the American automotive scene to engage in major plant expansion. Triggered by boundless optimism in Detroit and other auto centers practically all automotive firms, anticipating a huge growth in the market for motor vehicles during the immediate years ahead, moved swiftly to build and equip a vast number of new factories. The Ford Motor Company took the leadership role as it began development of the great River Rouge plant in Dearborn, Michigan, but others quickly fell in line. William Durant, again at the helm of the large and far-flung General Motors Corporation, initiated major expansion programs in Flint and Lansing, Michigan, for GM's Chevrolet, Buick and Oldsmobile divisions, and also constructed a new plant for the Corporation's Detroit-based Cadillac unit. The well-established Hudson Motor Co. of Detroit laid out a new factory for manufacture of its low-priced companion car, the Essex, while concerns such as Nash in Milwaukee, Marmon in Indianapolis, and Chandler in Cleveland all enlarged their plants. Several manufacturers now were planning either new or expanded branch facilities in Canada to serve the growing automotive market north of the border, and nearly all American auto firms of any consequence exported vehicles to various nations in Europe and elsewhere. During the month of June 1919, the Franklin firm announced the shipment of cars to Yokohama, Japan, Capetown, South Africa, and Christiana, Norway, while in July vehicles went out to such distant points as Montevideo, Uruguay and Copenhagen, Denmark. A total of over eighty Franklins were delivered to foreign purchasers in the entire year 1919, a solid achievement for a small

THE FRANKLIN AUTOMOBILE COMPANY

auto company.

The year 1919 brought the H.H. Franklin Company its first serious competition in nearly a decade from another manufacturer of air-cooled vehicles. Arthur Holmes, earlier chief engineer of the H.H. Franklin Manufacturing Company and vice-president of its marketing subsidiary, the Franklin Automobile Company, resigned in 1916, and soon after organized the Holmes Motor Car Company in Canton, Ohio. Working with capital provided by a number of well-to-do Canton business leaders, Holmes during 1917 began development of a vehicle undoubtedly intended to outshine the Franklin product. When introduced to the market in 1918 the Holmes car featured a soundly-designed engine with pressure air-cooling, a chassis somewhat larger and heavier than that utilized by Franklin, and body lines which best could be described as ungainly and awkward. In short, it was a technically-advanced car with totally unexciting styling, a dubious combination in an era when buyers were tending to demand attractive appearance as well as sound craftsmanship in the vehicles they were considering for purchase. This new Canton-based air-cooled offering also sold at a price a good deal higher than that charged for the Franklin product. Only a scattering of vehicles had been built by the Holmes concern during the wartime period, but in 1919 this firm sought to increase production, undoubtedly with the goal of supplying cars to some of the persons now becoming discouraged with the long wait for a post-war air-cooled Franklin.

In the overall field of pleasure automobiles the Franklin Company encountered a broad range of competition during 1919 and 1920. Ford, continuing to build exclusively its basic, low-cost Model T, now had achieved an enormous level of production in its far-flung group of plants, and was easily the sales leader in both America and the world. Apart from Ford, various other automobile manufacturers were turning out vehicles in substantial numbers. Chevrolet, Buick, Oldsmobile and Oakland, all divisions of General Motors, were among the top ten in output, together with such major independent companies as Dodge, Hudson, Willys-Overland and Studebaker. A group of lesser-known motor car builders struggled along on modest annual volumes of production and sales, with many of these destined to vanish from the marketplace within a few years as post-war competition intensified. Among the automobiles carrying relatively high price tags Cadillac led in sales by a good-sized margin during the immediate post-war period, with Franklin, Cole of Indianapolis, and Packard contending for second place. Much of Packard's volume in 1919 was represented by trucks (a holdover from the days of war production), so that its pleasure car output fell below that of the Syracuse firm. A newcomer to the luxury vehicle field in 1920 was the Indianapolis-based Duesenberg, designed by and named after two brothers who had won national acclaim for developing highly-successful racing machines. This upper-level car incorporated many technical innovations, including a high-speed straight-eight cylinder engine and four-wheel hydraulic brakes, but of particular interest to Franklin engineers was the emphasis the new Duesenberg vehicle placed on lightness. The car featured extensive use of aluminum to keep overall poundage at a low level, and through adoption of a tubular front axle an effort was made to reduce unsprung weight and improve roadworthiness, all old hat to the experienced Franklin design staff!

The automobile buyer in 1920 enjoyed an extraordinarily wide range of vehicles from which to choose, with manufacturers making extensive use of magazine and newspaper advertisements to incorporate slogans that might excite public interest. In typical ads the Haynes automobile was entitled a "character car" and the Lexington vehicle "a thoroughbred," while the Paige Company cast aside all false modesty to describe its product as "the most beautiful car in America." The Detroit-built American motor car was denoted "the balanced six" which would deliver "miles of smiles," while those considering purchase of a Hupmobile would learn that it was "endowed with something very like a personality." The Apperson was offered as an "eight with eighty less parts," and prospective Willys-Knight owners might be relieved to know that as this sleeve-valved car was driven for some time the only change would be "improvement with use." A Detroit auto manufacturer introduced a touch of romance in one of its advertisements, which portrayed a stalwart young man assisting an attractive young woman down a ladder in the middle of the night, while in the background a powerful Hudson car stood waiting to speed the eloping pair on their journey. Clearly, advertising agencies across the nation burned a vast amount of midnight oil in seeking to convince the public by one means or another of the merits of the various offerings.

Late in 1919 the Franklin firm formally announced that it would soon reenter a field which it had abandoned some years earlier, that of commercial vehicles. Design and development of a new one-ton truck, to feature pneumatic tires, a four-cylinder engine (air-cooled, of course) and a laminated wood frame was to begin immediately in a nearby rented building under the direction of James Yarian, a former Auburn Motor Co. engineer who had recently joined the Franklin staff. Company spokesmen stated that when production of the new vehicle was initiated, it would be in a plant separate and distinct from the factory utilized for the manufacture of Franklin passenger cars. As development work on this commercial vehicle commenced it was also noted by observers of the Syracuse-based auto company that H.H. Franklin was driving an attractive, experimental four-cylinder enclosed vehicle. Company officials explained that work on this small car had gotten under way during the World War I period and would be continued, but hastened to add that no immediate plans existed to put the vehicle in production.

The first full post-war year, 1919, proved to be an exceptionally satisfactory one for the Franklin organization. Total automobile production for the twelve-month period reached the 9,300 mark, a new company high, placing the firm approximately eighteenth in volume among American automobile manufacturers. Even more important, by late December 1919, nearly 300 vehicles were being completed each week, clear proof that after a year of striving a substantial production rate had been achieved in the factory. A record number of

THE POSTWAR ERA

persons were employed in turning out this large volume of cars, with 4,580 names listed on the firm's payroll at the end of the year. Net company earnings for 1919 were just over $1,800,000, also a new high.

During the early months of 1920 the Franklin company sought to build on these achievements. Production of vehicles continued at a swift tempo as the firm made a vigorous effort to deal with a continuing backlog of over 3,000 unfilled orders. Plant efficiency steadily increased as the layout of various departments was improved and the number of scrap parts sharply reduced. In April the factory was turning out 55 cars per day, often utilizing two shifts in certain manufacturing operations. Additional employees were taken on, with the total work force in factory and office combined reaching the 5,000 level in the early spring of the year. The company recruited a substantial group of well-qualified persons from sources such as other auto firms, the aircraft industry, and a variety of college campuses to fill key positions which had been generated by the expansion program. Special-

*In April 1919, Franklin employees successfully reached the goal of producing 800 cars in that month. (*The Franklin News, *May 1, 1919)*

THE FRANKLIN AUTOMOBILE COMPANY

*A fleet of Franklin vehicles was purchased by the Gillette Safety Razor Company for its salesmen in April 1919. (*The Franklin News, *May 1, 1919)*

ists in plant construction, cost control, statistics, manufacturing engineering and other technical fields became part of the Franklin team. A series of wage and salary increases granted by top management during the early postwar period enabled employees to keep abreast of the continuing sharp escalation in the cost-of-living.

As 1920 progressed, however, it became clear that the organization would not find it easy to produce the sixteen thousand cars which the ever-optimistic H.H. Franklin in his March 18 annual report to stockholders established as a goal for the year. Shortages of parts and materials continued to plague the company, with bitterly cold weather accompanied by major snow falls (all-too-frequent winter problems in the Syracuse area) often making it impossible for suppliers to achieve timely delivery of essential items. On several occasions the firm's fleet of huge Packard trucks battled snow drifts throughout upstate New York to obtain items vitally necessary for final motor car assembly. Shipments of finished cars also were severely affected, with the company forced to lease facilities at the nearby New York State Fairgrounds to store several hundred vehicles which could neither be driven away or sent by rail to numerous anxious Franklin dealers.

THE POSTWAR ERA

Strikes by railway workers in the spring compounded the firm's transportation problems, and at one point plans were developed to establish a special barge service on the New York State Canal in order to make possible continued on-time shipments of bodies from a Buffalo supplier. These difficulties for the most part vanished with the coming of warm weather, however, and by late May and early June output of finished cars achieved peak levels, enabling the Franklin factory to break all former production and vehicle shipment records during the first half of 1920. The firm proudly announced that total volume of sales for the January-June period had reached $17,239,000, or a resounding ninety-two percent increase over the corresponding six months in 1919!

Despite these indications of prosperity at Franklin and numerous other auto companies, however, economic storm clouds were swiftly gathering on the horizon across the nation. The prices of motor vehicles established by the various manufacturers had continued to escalate throughout the second half of 1919 and the early months of 1920, and now had reached almost unbelievable levels. The cost of a Franklin touring car by the summer of 1920 had shot up to a very stiff $3,100, with the price tag of a sedan an astonishing $4,350! A federal excise tax of five percent, first imposed on pleasure cars during the wartime period, added to vehicle cost to the consumer.

As early as the end of May and beginning of June 1920, auto buyers were tending to rebel against such whopping prices, and demand for Franklins and other motor vehicles began to taper off. At the same time concern over raging inflation had caused the Federal Reserve Board to take steps to tighten credit, and to require its local member banks to do the same. With bank loans to finance car sales drying up, motor vehicle dealers across the nation found themselves harshly affected. What had been a seller's market changed overnight as auto purchasers suddenly became difficult to find. The sharp drop in retail sales soon impacted vehicle manufacture, with production levels trimmed heavily by all companies. Franklin by mid-summer of 1920 was turning out only 20 to 30 cars per day, often accompanied by a reduced work week, while employment at the firm was cut by a staggering 1,500 persons. At the same time the company had to deal with the problem of a huge build-up of parts and supplies on its shelves, mostly purchased at peak prices. By early September Franklin inventories had reached the unprecedented level of $11,100,000, far in excess of current needs, with sales throughout the nation falling to an almost minuscule sixteen cars per day. The firm, particularly since its building construction program also was reaching a peak, found itself compelled to borrow heavily from a number of banks and was in serious danger of becoming overextended financially.

Other automobile manufacturers, large and small, were facing problems identical to those confronting the Syracuse firm, and it had become clear that a solution must be sought promptly. The nation's major motor car producer was the first to take constructive action to deal with the crisis. On September 21, 1920, Henry Ford cut the price of all body styles, open and closed, of his famous Model T by approximately twenty per cent. H.H. Franklin was quick to emulate Ford's example. Only two days later, on September 23, he announced an equally sharp reduction in the sales price of vehicles, with the touring car slashed from $3,100 to $2,600; the two-passenger roadster from $3,050 to $2,400, and the enclosed sedan from $4,350 to $3,600. At the same time strict controls on purchases were imposed at the Franklin plant, with the goal of keeping the flow of supplies into the factory at a level well-below the amount being utilized in auto production, thus trimming inventory. Additional lay-offs of employees occurred as the tempo of vehicle manufacturing by the company was brought back in line with actual sales.

The Syracuse company displayed great courage, at a time when labor costs were at a peak and a huge inventory purchased at inflated figures had to be worked off, in initiating a price cut of the magnitude announced. Some additional automobile firms followed the Ford-Franklin lead, but a majority attempted to cling to the existing top-heavy price structure, with utterly disastrous results. It was to be a grim autumn and early winter for a large number of motor car manufacturers,

THE POSTWAR ERA

Material for wooden frames being processed at the Franklin factory.

and an even more unpleasant period for their workers. Industry-wide sales plummeted, and auto plants began operating on a two-and-three-day-a-week basis, accompanied by huge cuts in employment. Many auto companies at first maintained that reductions in personnel merely constituted a lay-off of inefficient and superfluous labor not needed under normal conditions, but as time went on this explanation developed a hollow ring. More and more plants shut down completely, and by the end of the year the industry found itself in a condition of near-collapse. The post-war depression affected Detroit's motor car industry in particularly severe fashion, with an earlier employment level of nearly two hundred thousand persons in auto and parts plants located in the great motor capital and its suburbs reduced to as few as twenty-five thousand at the beginning of January 1921.

Thanks in large part to the trail-blazing September price cut, the H.H. Franklin Company survived the depressed period of late 1920 in far better fashion than most of its competitors. Once the cost of the

THE FRANKLIN AUTOMOBILE COMPANY

vehicle to consumers was reduced Franklin dealers received a substantial number of new orders from the car-buying public, enabling the factory to accelerate its output. Early in November a production schedule of thirty cars per day was established, and this volume was sustained through the early winter. The firm, however, was compelled to take a number of steps to adjust to the more modest level of business operations it now was experiencing. Inventory liquidation continued, and contracts with suppliers of parts and materials were re-negotiated at far lower price levels. At the same time company management established a task force to analyze the cost of all outside purchases, and determine what items might be manufactured internally at a potential saving. Still further personnel cuts took place as plant executives sought to reduce operating costs. Internal management of the factory was streamlined, with positions such as division superintendent abolished and the numerous general foremen in charge of various major and minor departments required to report directly to the production manager. The large postwar construction program was halted for a time, with one new structure, Building O-R fronting on Magnolia Street, left in semi-finished condition in order to conserve funds. Body manufacturing operations carried on in leased space near the main factory were transferred to the Franklin plant or eliminated. The firm now planned to rely on outside body builders for the bulk of its requirements (Franklin at this time developed a close relationship with the Walker-Wells manufacturing company of Amesbury, Massachusetts, which soon was to become its major body supplier).[a] The policy of retrenchment also resulted in the company ending all experimental work on the proposed Franklin light truck and the four-cylinder car, with personnel from these specialized operations either absorbed into the basic factory staff or discharged.

1920 finally came to a close, with key executives of the Franklin firm undoubtedly feeling that the year, with its extraordinary ups-and-downs, had closely resembled a roller-coaster ride! The company did

---

[a] Other firms that supplied automobile bodies to the H.H. Franklin Manufacturing Company in the early 1920s included the American Body Company of Buffalo, New York; the Babcock Company of Watertown, New York; and the Baker-Raulang and Bender Body companies of Cleveland, Ohio.

well in the final months of 1920, however, with December shipments of 1,041 vehicles helping it advance in rank during the last quarter of the year to a surprising seventh place in the American automotive industry in dollar value of total sales (it held tenth place in actual number of cars shipped). At year's end the value of inventory had been slashed by three and one-half million dollars to a more moderate level of $7,615,000. This working off of excess parts and supplies purchased at high post-war prices clearly constituted an important accomplishment by Franklin management. When profit and loss for the year was calculated, it was found that despite a record sale of 10,539 cars valued at $26,403,000, the firm could claim net earnings of only $696,575. The modest nature of this 1920 profit was due largely to the necessity of re-pricing remaining inventory at market value, and writing off the cost of obsolete parts. A common stock dividend of $300,000 was paid during the year, a moderate reduction from the $388,000 of 1919.

When 1921 opened the Franklin Company sought to strengthen sales through a face-lift of its now somewhat dated Series 9 model. Case-hardening of the crankshaft had been initiated, and this plus other mechanical changes increased the durability of the vehicle. Up front the old-fashioned Renault-style "nose" was replaced by a grill in the shape of an inverted oval, which gave the vehicle a somewhat more modern, streamlined appearance. Due in part to this restyling, and also to the firm's effective promotion of its closed-body models, demand for the car stabilized at a satisfactory level, permitting a factory production rate of 40 vehicles per day through the early months of the year. The proportion of closed cars produced by Franklin steadily increased from month-to-month, with well over forty per cent of total output now consisting of enclosed models. Together with the Detroit-based Hudson Motor Company, Franklin continued to be a trailblazer in the development of the all-weather, solid-roof vehicle.

As the auto industry sought to meet the harsh challenges posed by the post-war depression of 1920-21, management and engineering personnel in practically all companies gave major attention to achieving substantial improvements in manufacturing efficiency. Franklin, with its vast new factory construction program well on the way to completion, was in an excellent position to utilize more modern techniques in the production of vehicles. Throughout 1920 company executives and engineers had visited the plants of other carmakers to examine and evaluate the most modern methods of auto-building, with the result that early in 1921 a conveyor-type moving assembly line was put in operation at the Franklin factory. The new system consisted of two sections, a chassis line on which frame and running gear were fitted together, and a 300-foot-long car-building line, where the body was dropped on the chassis and the vehicle assembled in final form. This progressive assembly system was built in duplicate, with two parallel lines giving a potential total capacity of 125 cars daily. At the present only one line was to be used, however, since this would give more than enough capacity to meet a production schedule calling for completion of approximately one vehicle every thirteen minutes (the second line would be utilized largely to transport motors).

The moving conveyor system represented a major advance in Franklin assembly technology, eliminating completely the old method of pushing a car from station to station as items of work were completed. The factory thus joined a number of other leading auto manufacturers in the utilization of modern production techniques. It should be noted, however, that the firm was compelled to adapt its new assembly line to certain rigid limitations imposed by the design of the Franklin factory. Since the buildings utilized were of relatively short length and often intersected at odd angles, the line incorporated a series of sharp ninety-degree bends, requiring the use in some instances of turntables. This consequently meant that the speed of the new line was slow, and work space a bit cramped. In short, while the new production process was a decided improvement over the old, it hardly could be considered fully competitive with the conveyor assembly systems in operation in vast, single-story structures at a number of the big-volume auto manufacturers (at this point a few of the Michigan-based auto plants had reached huge size, with Ford, Dodge, and one or two others employing as many as 10,000 to 20,000 hands under a single roof). Thanks in

THE POSTWAR ERA

part to the adoption of more modern assembly techniques, as well as to a reduced level of production, it was possible for the Syracuse firm to slash employment levels in the spring of 1921 to 3,000, a large drop from the 5,000 on the payroll a year earlier. The Franklin Company henceforth would operate with a much leaner work force.

The expansion of the Franklin Company's physical plant, and the sharp up-and-down trend of its operations during the immediate post-World War I period, resulted in top management having to pay more than normal attention to fiscal matters. While in earlier years the construction of new buildings together with purchases of innovative machine tools had been financed largely out of income, this was not the case in the 1919-1921 period. The big-scale capital expansion program of this era, together with the build-up of inventories through all of 1919 and much of 1920, made it necessary to seek other sources of financing. During 1919 a substantial amount of short-term borrowing took place, resulting in a total of $2,300,000 in outstanding notes shown on the company's books at the end of the year. Such borrowing continued through 1920, with some $4,510,000 in loans payable to banks listed on the consolidated balance sheet of the firm on December 31, 1920. This clearly was a stiff amount of short-term indebtedness for a small automobile company to be carrying, and represented a major departure from previous practices.

While borrowing from financial institutions could be utilized to meet immediate cash needs, it seemed clear early in the post-War era that a modification of the firm's overall capital structure would be necessary to provide long-term financing of the big expansion effort. In September 1919, therefore, the Franklin firm retired some $541,000 in outstanding preferred stock to make way for a larger $5,000,000 issue authorized a few weeks later. The new preferred was offered both to the general public and to company employees; by the end of the year some $2,000,000 had been subscribed and paid for. Efforts to market the preferred–sold at a par value of $100 per share and providing a 7% cumulative dividend–continued into 1920. Then, in May of that year a general recapitalization of the Franklin Company took place. Au-

THE FRANKLIN AUTOMOBILE COMPANY

thorization was given for issuance of preferred stock in the increased total amount of $15,000,000, together with a similar $15,000,000 in common, all stock to have a par value of $100 per share (the former limitation on issuance of common was a modest $2,000,000). Shortly thereafter existing common stock was converted into new no-par-value shares on a four-to-one basis, with an authorized maximum of 600,000 shares. By the end of 1920 the company balance sheet showed a total of $3,324,800 in outstanding preferred stock, together with 275,743 shares of no-par common held by stockholders.

The sale of both common and preferred stock continued throughout much of the following year, as efforts to strengthen the company's capital position continued. It was announced in mid-February of 1921 that Franklin employees to date had subscribed to more than a quarter of a million dollars' worth of the firm's stock. A few months later it was noted that 1,328 employees, or a resounding 40% of the total work force, had become shareholders. Sale of shares to the public had found an equally broad market, with Franklin outside stockholders, now 2,365 in total number, representing every state in the union plus several foreign nations.

At the end of October 1921, common stock was withdrawn from further sale, to be followed in mid-December by a similar closing of the sale of preferred shares. The company was able to announce at the end of 1921 that over the previous two and one-quarter years a total of $6,289,425 of preferred and common stock had been sold, all on a direct basis. No investment banking firm whatever had been utilized to aid in marketing the securities, since Franklin management felt that a far better net return would be obtained without use of such an agent, accompanied by the inevitable large commissions. H.H. Franklin's desire to avoid involvement with major investment banking firms closely paralleled the attitude of the head of the auto industry's largest company, Henry Ford. Of the total sold some $5,047,300 represented preferred shares, with only $1,242,125 constituting common. The four-for-one split of existing common stock, coupled with the relatively modest sale of new common shares to the general public and to employees, meant that the small top-management group of Franklin continued to be in full control of company affairs (preferred shareholders received dividends but normally had no voice in determining policies of the firm). H.H. Franklin himself retained a majority of the common shares, and thus could easily outvote anyone who might challenge his authority.

This infusion of fresh capital, together with profits earned by the firm, made it possible to retire the over-four-million-dollars in bank loans by June 30, 1921. The company thus once more found itself in the pleasant position of being debt-free. However, with the large-scale issuance of seven-per-cent preferred stock the firm henceforth would have to meet an annual dividend obligation of several hundred thousand dollars. With a nineteen per cent drop-off in sales during 1921 to 8,548 cars (even with this decline Franklin outpaced most of the remainder of the industry, which apart from Ford suffered a staggering 41% year-to-year slump), profits of the Syracuse-based enterprise dropped to an adjusted figure of $452,000 before payment of preferred dividends. Once these were included the final profit figure was a minuscule $185,000, or just over $20 per vehicle sold. Under such conditions it was clear that the generous common stock dividends of 1919 and 1920 could not be maintained. Instead the company declared a single mid-year fifty-cent dividend on the new no-par common shares, which involved a payout of some $140,000.

By the end of 1921 the Franklin firm had experienced, as had the American auto industry generally, the post-World War economic cycle of prosperity, depression and recovery. The company, while not among the top motor vehicle companies in terms of sales, nonetheless continued to be a producer of consequence. H.H. Franklin was able to announce in his Annual Report to Stockholders for 1921 that the firm during that year held 16th place in the industry in the number of cars sold, and tenth position in total value of sales. Of equal im-

THE FRANKLIN AUTOMOBILE COMPANY

For several years, the "Franklin Suggestion Contest" was a popular means of collecting employee ideas for plant and process improvements. These winners were shown in the April 1, 1924 issue of The Franklin News.

portance, during 1921 for the first time in the history of the Franklin organization sales of closed cars exceeded those of the open variety by a small margin, fifty-two to forty-eight percent. It also should be noted that in the first eight months of 1921 a full forty-three percent of company sales were to previous owners of Franklin cars, demonstrating that the firm had developed a loyal cadre of long-term supporters!. Among higher-priced cars only Cadillac surpassed Franklin in volume of sales, with Packard approximately on a par with the Syracuse firm in number of vehicles disposed of. Franklin's long-time upstate New York companion in the quality car field, Pierce-Arrow, was finding readjustment to post-war conditions anything but easy, having experienced a disastrous slump in sales of its very high-priced vehicles. Both the Pierce-Arrow and Packard firms suffered substantial operating deficits during 1921, with Packard also plagued by a lengthy strike of employees in a key department.

In Syracuse, now boasting a population of nearly 175,000, Franklin indisputably had become the city's pre-eminent manufacturing concern. Figures released by the United States Bureau of the Census for the year 1921 showed that the firm employed nearly nine per cent of the total Syracuse industrial work force. Annual compensation paid to Franklin employees, $4,809,000, represented well over eleven per cent of the total combined payroll of all industries in the community (clearly the earnings of each Franklin employee were decidedly above the average paid by manufacturing plants in Syracuse). In value of product Franklin placed even higher–its $22,543,000 in 1921 sales constituted almost exactly fifteen per cent of an overall output by Syracuse industries of $150,091,000. The air-cooled motor car firm did its share in helping fund local government, paying the very good-sized sum of $86,532 in city taxes during the year.

Several noteworthy items should be mentioned relative to company operations during the year 1921. On two occasions prices of Franklin automobiles were slashed; these cuts undoubtedly helped maintain sales at a satisfactory level throughout the year. On September 1st an across-the-board reduction in employee wages and salaries was announced by the firm. Company top management justified this step on the basis of the diminished prices being charged for Franklin cars plus a recent drop in the cost of living in the Syracuse area. Any sting from this downward revision of employee compensation was alleviated somewhat by adoption of a new retirement plan for elderly workers, plus installation of a suggestion system under which rank-and-file Franklin office and factory staff would be awarded cash prizes for recommending specific improvements in company operating methods. Seventy-seven year old Charles Mayer was the initial shop worker to lay down his tools and begin enjoying a pension (Franklin for years had retained on its payroll a group of very elderly employees, including a veteran of both the American Civil War and World War I), while a seventeen-year old machine design employee, Cornelius DeNood, found himself among the first to have suggestions for engineering improvements accepted.

With economic conditions brightening, construction work on unfinished manufacturing buildings and on the power house resumed during the spring months of 1921. These facilities were largely completed by the end of the year, giving the firm a total floor area of over 1,200,000 square feet in which to conduct office and factory operations. Due to vehicle sales remaining well below capacity of the enlarged plant, however, sections of the new manufacturing buildings remained unused for an extended period. On a personal note, executives and employees of the Franklin Company plus Syracuse community leaders joined in sponsoring an impressive ceremony on July 1, 1921, honoring John Wilkinson for his vast contributions to the firm and to the city of Syracuse.

The year 1922 opened with the exciting announcement by H.H. Franklin that experimental work on the once-shelved four-cylinder car had been reinstituted, with a number of key employees assigned to complete such development and ready the vehicle for production. Ralph Murphy, assistant to Vice-President John Wilkinson, was to take charge of the overall effort, aided by experienced engineers and manufacturing specialists drawn from throughout the Franklin organization. Company news releases indicated that initial work on the vehicle would be carried on in the small factory earlier leased for development of the abandoned Franklin truck, but that when manufacture of the four-cylinder car got under way it was expected that surplus floor area in the large new addition to the main plant would be utilized.

A week or two later further announcements on the proposed new vehicle were forthcoming. H.H. Franklin stated that the four-cylinder air-cooled machine, which he described as a "world-wide utility car," would carry a highly-competitive $1,000 price tag. Together with its low price the vehicle was to feature easy riding and handling, good roadability, and excellent gas and tire economy. Merchandising of the new automobile was to be conducted on a national and even international basis, necessitating a substantial expansion of the Franklin dealership network across America and in foreign lands. At one point company publications suggested that the total number of dealers at home and abroad might well mushroom to the 2,000 level, a fourfold increase. Initial technical specifications released for the new model disclosed that its engine, except for having two less cylinders, was to be essentially similar to the Franklin six, with many parts interchangeable. The wheelbase, however, would be an abbreviated 102 inches, and while the frame featured laminated wood construction the vehicle was to utilize lower-cost, semi-elliptic springs, overslung on the rear axle and underslung on the front. Air-cooling of the engine was to be accomplished by use of a blower fan mounted on the front end of the camshaft. The service (foot) brake was to operate on the transmission and the emergency on the rear wheels, following traditional Franklin practice.

The new model had been shown privately to Franklin dealers at a luncheon at the Commodore Hotel in New York City during the January 1922, National Auto Show, with an exceptionally enthusiastic response recorded. The impression now was given by the firm that the small car ultimately would be built in a separate plant, and that a subsidiary company might be organized to manufacture it. Volume production of the junior-sized vehicle was to be initiated in time to permit deliveries to be made at the opening of the major 1923 selling season (presumably in the early spring of that year).

Still further steps were taken late in February 1922, to implement the small car project. A financing plan adopted by the Franklin board of directors called for five million dollars to be raised in new capital, through sale of three million dollars in additional $100 par seven-percent preferred stock plus two million dollars of no-par common, the latter to be offered at $50 per share. The company would continue to seek to dispose of its stock directly to purchasers through an in-house securities department, thus once more eliminating use of a middleman. Clearly primary emphasis was to be placed on sale of both classes of stock to relatively small investors, with particularly strong efforts made to market the new securities to Franklin employees, dealers and owners. To increase feasibility of such sales prospective purchasers could take advantage of a time-payment plan, under which small sums of money might be set aside periodically with the company treasurer until enough was accumulated to pay for a share of stock. Interest would be credited to the paid-in funds prior to the actual purchase, indicating that many buyers expected to complete their acquisition of shares at a very slow pace. Of the five million dollars which would result from the stock sale, half was to be set aside for a new plant and equipment and the other half used for working capital.

Development work on the proposed new small car moved forward swiftly during the spring and early summer of 1922, with numerous technical difficulties ironed out and the staff employed to design the vehicle expanded substantially. In Syracuse and elsewhere, however, the attention of many business persons was directed primarily to the question of where a permanent plant to manufacture the automobile would be located. Industrial development committees representing various cities throughout the East, each hoping to entice the firm to place a manufacturing facility in its area, commenced besieging H.H. Franklin with offers. At one time it was reported that the company was considering the purchase of an existing plant in Elizabeth, New Jersey, erected earlier to produce another make of car. The Syracuse business community quickly became alarmed at the prospect of losing a promising new division of its largest industry, and local newspapers published editorials urging that the needs of the air-cooled auto manufacturing firm be given every possible consideration. It is doubtful, however, if H.H. Franklin ever seriously considered locating a facility outside the metropolitan Syracuse area (when the Elizabeth, New Jersey plant was auctioned in May 1922, Franklin was not among those bidding). The firm had organized a subsidiary corporation earlier, the Syracuse Land Development Company, which assembled a substantial tract of unimproved acreage located immediately northeast of the city of Syracuse, some seven or so miles distant from the South Geddes plant. The intention was to use part of the land for a modern, single-story sawtoothed-roof factory suitable for high-volume production of the four-cylinder vehicle, with other plots to be sold to supplier firms for construction of satellite plants and additional sections made available for construction of dwellings to house workers from Franklin and the parts firms.

However, neither the land development plan nor the four-cylinder vehicle would be brought to fruition. In the fall of 1922 the company abruptly ceased work on the proposed small Franklin vehicle, terminating the services of the engineer directly in charge of design activity, James Yarian, together with most of the three-hundred-person staff (a small number of employees of the unit were absorbed at the main plant). In a news release dated November 8, 1922, the company stated that plans for production of the car had been "indefinitely postponed," giving as a reason the rising cost of materials which made it impossible to build the vehicle at a targeted price of $1,000. At the same time it was announced that sale of stock to fund the new enterprise had been discontinued. The proposal for development of a planned industrial district northeast of the city of Syracuse also was suspended for the indefinite future, although the company did maintain ownership of approximately one thousand acres of land previously acquired (one supplier firm, Oberdorfer Foundry, located a plant on this site).

The determination to shelve a project announced some nine months earlier with great fanfare surprised the Syracuse business community, and undoubtedly stunned many persons in the Franklin organization. Clearly abandonment of the once-promising plan for the small vehicle was a decision of H.H. Franklin himself, who as the holder of a majority of shares of the common stock of the firm could sweep aside objections of other key executives. The reasons for closing out the four-cylinder project probably were threefold. First of all, it undoubtedly would have been difficult and perhaps impossible to utilize the existing Franklin factory, organized to produce a high-quality car in moderate volume, to build a four-cylinder vehicle in substantial quantities at relatively low cost. The profit margin on the sale of senior Franklin vehicles already was tiny; it could have been even more of a problem to achieve respectable earnings with a lower-priced car built to craft-shop standards. Secondly, to construct and equip a modern, highly-mechanized plant which might have enabled the firm to accomplish profitable large-scale production of a new small car would have cost a vast sum of money, well in excess of the five million dollars which the firm proposed to obtain from the sale of the new stock. Actually, the company had not been able, with its "direct selling" approach, to achieve anywhere near the five million dollars in sale of new shares which it had hoped for, and thus undoubtedly lacked the initial capital necessary to undertake the project. Finally, H.H. Franklin, having achieved a reasonable degree of success over a substantial period of years in the manufacture and sale of a "prestige" automobile, in all probability would have been reluctant to have his name primarily identified with a modestly-priced car. The four-cylinder model, if successful, unquestionably would have "stolen" sales from the senior series, and in a few years could have constituted the firm's only offering, a prospect certainly not alluring to H.H.[b]

The four-cylinder vehicle debacle was not the only vexing problem

---

[b] Shortly after work on the small Franklin car was terminated, the Rollin automobile was placed on the market. This high-quality, four-cylinder vehicle of modest size was designed by the noted ppioneer motor car engineer Rollin H. White of Cleveland and sold in the range of $1,000 to $1,200. Because of limited sales of the Rollin vehicle, its production ceased at the end of two years. It is possible that the Franklin "four," which also sought to compensate for modest size by featuring excellent design, might have been equally unsuccessful. American motor car buyers tended to seek the "big package" in cars they purchased, rather than superb engineering.

THE POSTWAR ERA

with which the Franklin firm was forced to contend during the year 1922. Much of the site of the big Franklin factory fronting on South Geddes Street originally was a low-lying, somewhat marshy field, bisected by a stream named Harbor Brook. As major new sections of the plant were constructed toward the rear of this land, all with foundations resting on piles driven deeply into the soft ground, Harbor Brook was enclosed in a tunnel under the buildings and yard. A series of torrential rains occurring in the late afternoon of Saturday, June 17, 1922, produced a volume of storm water far too great for the tunnel to handle, with the result that the factory yard plus the basements and first floors of nearly all the buildings were badly flooded. The new powerhouse had to be shut down; the battery of coal-burning furnaces which served the heat-treating department had their fires swiftly quenched; and the rampaging flood waters destroyed or badly damaged many thousands of dollars worth of spare parts and other stock. Only a heroic effort by a small group of supervisory personnel made it possible to save fifty-five new cars which were on the floor of the final inspection department awaiting delivery (these vehicles were hurriedly driven up a ramp to the safety of the second story as the swiftly rising water splashed against their wheels and undercarriages). The direct damage and cost of clean-up aggregated well over one hundred thousand dollars, but equally important was the loss of production caused by the effects of the sudden storm. Facilities such as heat-treating furnaces took weeks to dry out before fires could be rekindled, making it necessary to "farm out" manufacturing work to other local firms for a considerable period of time. The net result of this natural disaster, coupled with such recurring problems as lack of efficient freight service by the railroads during part of the year plus delays in the manufacture of auto bodies by such suppliers as the Walker Body Company in Amesbury, Mass., and the American Body Company of Buffalo, was that 1922 production of Franklin cars barely exceeded 8,000 units. This was a drop of 500 vehicles from the year before, and meant that Franklin failed to match the gain in production and sales achieved by the auto industry as a whole in 1922 over the depressed year 1921.

THE FRANKLIN AUTOMOBILE COMPANY

The Franklin Company, undoubtedly embarrassed by these setbacks, chose not to forward to any of the major securities rating services (Moodys, Poors, etc.) a profit and loss statement for the year. This was a most unusual omission for a public company which in August 1922, had boasted of having over 6,000 stockholders located throughout America. It seems clear, however, that the firm suffered an operating loss for 1922 in the range of $1,500,000 (a consolidated balance sheet, issued well into 1923, showed a decline in the surplus account of $1,330,000 during the year). No payment was made to holders of the company's common stock during 1922, although dividend requirements on the seven percent preferred were met on schedule (the Franklin Diecasting Corporation, a separate company since January 1, 1920, paid a dividend on its common shares). The amount of preferred stock outstanding now approached six million dollars, which meant that the firm was compelled to meet annual dividend requirements on the order of $400,000, a substantial charge for a relatively small firm. Even in profitable years the company's earnings might not be adequate to retire any large portion of the outstanding preferred shares and thus ease the payout requirement.

Despite a disastrous 1922, the Franklin Company had good reason to look forward to a potentially much improved 1923. During the summer months of 1922, while work on the soon-to-be-abandoned small car was continuing, the firm announced a new Series 10 automobile, succeeding the now obviously outdated Series 9. The overall size of the new offering was largely unchanged, with the wheelbase continued at a modest 115 inches and the weight of the touring model a very trim 2,450 pounds. Mechanically, however, the 10 bristled with innovations. The old flywheel fan, which pulled cooling air through the cylinder jackets, was replaced with a Sirocco-type blower mounted on the front end of the crankshaft. This new unit forced a far larger volume of air over the surfaces to be cooled. Despite the vastly greater capacity (a 250% increase in volume) of the new air cool-

THE POSTWAR ERA

*Franklin cars shown in 1924 at Furnace Creek Ranch in Death Valley. The company used trips through Death Valley as proof of the durability and efficiency of the air cooling system in Franklin cars.
(Courtesy of American Automobile Manufacturers Association)*

ing system, improved technical design actually resulted in a reduced power demand for fan operation. The front-mounted fan's efficiency was further increased by a carefully-designed aluminum housing, positioned above the engine, which precisely channeled the air-blast to key locations. In addition, changes in design of the fins surrounding each cylinder also helped upgrade cooling capacity. This modernized air cooling system had been thoroughly tested by trips through Death Valley in temperatures exceeding 120 degrees Fahrenheit, the company stated. With an eye to strengthening performance from an engine whose displacement had not been increased, improvements also were made to the induction system of the new power plant. The gasoline-air mixture rushing upward out of the carburetor to the intake manifold now passed through a so-called vaporizer. This device, heated by the engine exhaust fumes, insured that the incoming gases were brought to the optimum temperature for efficient engine operation. In order to reduce stresses on the case-hardened crankshaft, the connecting rods were constructed of a light aluminum alloy rather than steel. The engine, clutch and transmission were combined in a so-called unit power plant, a practice now being followed by more and more American car builders in order to achieve simplicity of construction and ease of assembly.

Certain of the technical innovations displayed by the new Franklin Series 10, particularly the forced-draft or pressurized cooling system featuring a front-mounted fan, already had been utilized by two of the company's air-cooled competitors, the previously described Holmes car plus the more recently introduced Fox. The Fox vehicle, manufactured in Philadelphia by a small company organized in the years following World War I (its chief engineer, H.O. Swanson, could claim to be yet another "alumnus" of the Franklin organization), was a luxury-class automobile with a 132 inch wheelbase and long, handsome body lines. It also featured a large displacement engine generating a power output far in excess of that achieved by the modest-sized Franklin motor. This resulted in it being able to easily out-perform products of the Syracuse firm, a fact which the Fox Company was quick to mention in its sales literature. The price tag of the Fox sedan was $4,900, however, placing it in a much higher cost range than Franklin models. Still another new air-cooled entry was announced about this time, the Detroit. This vehicle, developed in the nation's motor capital, featured a six-cylinder engine of an unusual V-configuration, with three cylinders placed on each side of the crankcase. The result was a very short, compact engine, exceptionally light in weight and incorporating a minimum of moving parts. The new Detroit air-cooled vehicle tipped the scale at only 1,700 pounds, and its designer claimed for it an ability to cover thirty miles on each gallon of gas.

While these small independent companies were developing vehicles which could be expected to offer modest competition to the new Franklin Series 10, one of the automotive giants also was preparing an assault on the air-cooled field. The distinguished chief of the General Motors Corporation research laboratories, Charles Kettering, whose reasoning on the merits of air-cooling paralleled John Wilkinson's, had initiated experimental work as early as 1918 on an engine directly cooled by the atmosphere. The new motor ultimately brought forth by "Boss Ket's" research team featured copper fins welded to the cylinders in order to aid in dissipating heat, and thus quickly gained the name "copper cooled." Kettering convinced a number of top executives of the big corporation that the new power plant, through elimination of a multitude of parts needed for cooling purposes in a water-cooled engine, would result in a lighter, lower-cost "car of the future." The heads of several operating divisions of General Motors, including Chevrolet, Oakland and Oldsmobile, were more skeptical of the merits of the air-cooled approach, however, and many months went by before approval was given for initial production of the new engine. Finally, in December 1922, the Chevrolet Division began manufacture of the copper-cooled vehicle on a limited basis. The new car was exhibited at the New York Automobile Show in January 1923, and General Motors officials expressed pleasure at the generally enthusiastic reception it received. During the early months of 1923 a number of the new air-cooled models were delivered to Chevrolet dealers, with several hundred sold at retail (the H.H. Franklin Company purchased one for purposes of comparative analysis).

Problems with the innovative vehicle quickly showed up in the manufacturing process and intensified as the car reached the highway. The Chevrolet Division, with its highly-mechanized factories geared to volume output of conventional automobiles, found it difficult to overcome initial production troubles and build the air-cooled model to exacting standards in satisfactory numbers. On the road the air-cooled motor, according to a report submitted by a hastily-mobilized committee of General Motors engineers, tended to pre-ignite, and lose compression and power when hot. This technical team felt that the car needed further development, and recommended that it be withdrawn from production. This recommendation was followed, with Chevrolet also recalling all the copper-cooled cars from the field. Strongly upset by this decision Kettering proposed building the new vehicle, after further refinement of the engine, in limited volume in a special unit attached to the corporation's research division, but nothing came of this and the air-cooled car was simply allowed to die. Nearly forty years would pass before the General Motors Corporation offered another air-cooled vehicle to the motorcar buyer. [5-1]

Franklin's other air-cooled competitors fared no better in the marketplace. The Holmes Automobile Company, after experiencing abysmally low sales of its unattractively-styled vehicle over a several-year period in the early 1920s, entered receivership and subsequently was taken over by a group of bondholders in the spring of 1923. The firm never resumed production. The Fox Motor Car Company followed Holmes into receivership a few months later, with its factory and other real estate ultimately offered for sale at public auction. Production of the Detroit air-cooled car failed to go beyond a few prototype models, and it quickly faded from memory. The Buffalo-based Parenti Company, developer of an unique air-cooled vehicle without axles and with a plywood body, gave up the ghost after selling a sprinkling of cars. In Syracuse, Julian Brown, younger son of the distinguished inventor, Alexander Brown, who had been identified with H.H. Franklin since the turn-of-the-century, designed and built a single experimental automobile featuring a rear-mounted air-cooled radial engine plus a tubular frame. Although the Julian car excited a good deal of local interest, efforts to raise capital to produce it in volume were a total failure, and it, too, vanished from sight. The project engineer of the abandoned Franklin four-cylinder car, James Yarian, also sought to interest potential Syracuse investors in the manufacture of a similar small air-cooled vehicle. While a degree of mystery surrounds the details of this venture, it appears doubtful if more than a single prototype machine ever was built before the effort was abandoned. Another interesting Syracuse-based vehicle was the Ner-a-car, assembled in a small wooden building located a block or so north of the Franklin plant. This two-wheeled unit, powered by a tiny one-cylinder, two-

THE POSTWAR ERA

An advertisement for the Series 10 Franklin Sedan. (Courtesy of the Allan Franklin Collection)

cycle air-cooled engine, was similar in many respects to a modern motor scooter. It continued in production until the late 1920s, and was exported to such foreign countries as Great Britain.

Freed from serious competition by other air-cooled vehicle manufacturers, the H.H. Franklin Company was able to take full advantage of a boom in auto demand in 1923. As it expanded production following the dismal previous year, the company was aided in marketing efforts by its industry-wide leadership in the development of enclosed models. The public now had been totally sold on the merits of the closed car, particularly in the upper-middle and high-priced fields, and several newly-styled Franklin bodies were generating substantial customer appeal. By the spring of 1923 the Franklin factory had reached the highest level of output in its history, with sixty cars per day rolling off its assembly line to meet the extraordinary buyer demand. During the first quarter of the year seventy-one percent of the vehicles shipped by the company were closed models, and in May it was announced that this percentage had jumped to over ninety. Employees laid off during the low-volume months of 1922 now found themselves recalled to help meet the needs of the busy factory. The company proudly announced that owners of the new Series 10 vehicle included Franklin P. Adams, the well-known New York City newspaper columnist, and Walter Hampden, Shakespearean actor. Perhaps a more important testimonial to the desirability of the Franklin car, however, was provided by one George Newett of Ishpeming, Michigan, whose Series 10 demi-sedan constituted his twenty-fourth purchase of a Franklin! An unique endorsement of the basic toughness of the Franklin automobile came from a far-distant country when the Norwegian state constabulary, following competitive durability tests of numerous vehicles over rugged terrain, chose a Franklin touring car for use in enforcing that nation's prohibition law!

The excellent sales of the new Franklin model did not mean, however, that the company was totally free from problems. As the Series 10 cars came off the production line a substantial number quickly developed a highly-annoying vibration period when the car was accelerated to speeds in excess of thirty miles per hour. A desperate search for both the cause of this condition and its solution was brought to a successful conclusion by the insight and mechanical skill of Franklin engineering technician John Burns. Reasoning that the roughness must be a product of the new unit-mounting of motor, clutch and transmission, Burns developed a rubber disk which, when inserted in the clutch mechanism of the car, absorbed all vibration transmitted by the engine (this invention was patented, and earned Burns a handsome income for a number of years). Other shortcomings involving weaknesses in connecting rod bearings and piston rings in the motor of the new series had to be dealt with, as did structural defects in the aluminum body panels. These problems caused the firm a considerable degree of embarrassment, particularly since certain of the defects did not come to light until numerous vehicles had reached the hands of purchasers. The Franklin Company, however, quickly dispatched members of its highly efficient service department staff into the field to correct problems encountered by customers, so that damage to the firm's reputation was held to a minimum. The testing program for new cars at the factory, always a Franklin strong point, was upgraded further, with each unit given a lengthy run over nearby highways before being approved for delivery to a buyer.

The expanded customer demand for Franklin cars in 1923 resulted in continued efforts being made by manufacturing executives to further improve the production process. Installation of additional moving conveyor lines in several areas of the multi-story factory reduced manual handling of stock and upgraded efficiency of operations. Engines, engine parts and axles now would be assembled at a stepped-up pace through use of such machinery, and a similar facility would be utilized to speed the trimming of auto bodies. The body conveyor also was operated in close proximity to the final assembly line, so that when the last item of trim was completed the body could be dropped on a chassis and the vehicle quickly given the finishing touches necessary to make it ready for the road. It was obvious that these improvements, probably considered revolutionary by old-time shop men working in the factory, were absolutely essential if the Franklin firm was to compete effectively in what was becoming an increasingly mechanized automobile industry. Careful hand-fitting of many parts still would be emphasized, and both sub-assemblies and the finished vehicle would undergo rigorous quality checks by sharp-eyed inspectors, but the Franklin car now was far more a mass-produced product than it had been a few years earlier.

Together with advances in plant technology came improvements in the overall organizational structure of the Franklin Company. On occasion new units were established to provide expertise in certain specialized fields, including a commercial research division and an industrial relations department. Named to head the industrial relations operation was H.C. Blagbrough, a former private-school teacher and son-in-law of John Wilkinson. This unit assumed charge of the company employment function plus the firm's small medical care facility, undertook classification and rating studies of various jobs, and assisted heads of departments in dealing with grievances of employees. Also under the aegis of industrial relations were what might be termed a wide range of "welfare" programs sponsored by the company. These included an almost extraordinary variety of outings, picnics, dances and parties–the Valentine Day masquerade ball held in February 1923, was attended by no less than 1,500 employees. The Franklin firm also supported numerous company athletic teams, with the track and basketball units receiving the most attention. These squads competed in the industrial league of the city, vying for honors with representatives of such other Syracuse firms as the L.C. Smith Typewriter Co. and Brown-Lipe-Chapin Gear Co. The Franklin track team, with male and female members, scored a series of spectacular victories at the annual New York State Fair, winning the industrial league title four years in succession. The 1923 meet, conducted before a crowd of 25,000 persons perched on seats in the grandstand, saw the Franklin track squad amass more points than all its seven competitors combined!

Other programs were developed by industrial relations to strengthen employee morale. At the peak of the post-war inflationary period a grocery store plus a men's clothing outlet were established at the plant, to enable employees to obtain food and wearing apparel at prices below those charged by the city's retail shops. However, merchants operating businesses in the vicinity of the factory, undoubtedly concerned about the potential loss of patronage by company employees, occasionally entered vigorous protests to plant management about the existence of these competitive facilities. Probably due more to limited use by employees than external criticism, the grocery and clothing shops were phased out after a short period of time. The firm for several years also utilized the part-time services of a home economist, who published in the company paper suggestions on how Franklin employees and their families might live economically, and even produced recipes for a variety of tasty dishes likely to appeal to readers.

At the higher echelons of company operations H.H. Franklin, beginning with the period of intense activity which accompanied World War I, found it desirable to seek assistance in performing his steadily more demanding functions as overall head of management, finance and sales. This first person added to the top executive staff was Arthur Kemp, a Chicago banking executive, who was given the title of second vice-president of the Syracuse firm. Kemp assisted H.H. in general administration and finance, helping develop methods to upgrade company operating efficiency. His tenure was relatively brief, as he left the Franklin organization not long after the end of the Great War. A.G. Maney then was hired early in the postwar period to serve as director of distribution. In this capacity he coordinated sales, advertising and various related operations, in effect serving as the operating head of the Franklin Automobile Company. Maney departed somewhat abruptly in 1922, however. Horace Benstead, an army officer assigned to perform liaison work with the Franklin firm during the period of wartime aircraft parts production, on demobilization became a special assistant to H.H. Franklin with responsibilities in the area of finance. He resigned at the end of 1922, soon after the four-cylinder automobile project was abandoned.

In the fall of 1923 the Franklin firm announced the appointment of J.W.DuB. Gould as general manager of the company. In describing the duties of this position a company news release stated that the newly-appointed executive was to relieve H.H. Franklin of a variety of management duties that had tended to mount as the firm expanded. Gould, a New York City fiscal and management consultant, for some time earlier had acted as an external advisor to the company. In the technical and manufacturing area Ralph Murphy, a quiet-spoken native of upstate New York who had served as the company's chief engineer during the war years, in May 1920, was named assistant to vice-president John Wilkinson. In this broadened role he aided Wilkinson in directing the firm's engineering and production activities. Murphy's successor as chief engineer was Louis Stellman, originally from Vermont, who earlier played a key role in the development of vehicle testing programs.

The year 1923 proved to be an outstanding one for the automotive industry generally. Output of cars and trucks exceeded four million units for the first time, and based on dollar sales motor vehicles passed steel as the nation's leading manufactured product. The H.H. Franklin Company also could regard the year as highly satisfactory. During 1923 the firm shipped some 10,100 vehicles from its factory, a total eclipsed only by the 1921 output. The Syracuse air-cooled motor car builder continued to out-pace practically the entire automotive industry in building the now-highly-desirable closed-car. A full eighty percent of Franklin's 1923 production consisted of this type of vehicle, as the open runabout and touring car were fast losing appeal among buyers. In the financial area the company could cite a total profit after depreciation of $1,175,000 for the year, enough to meet the preferred dividend requirement of $466,000 and leave a seven hundred thousand dollar surplus. In order to conserve capital, however, for a second consecutive year no dividend payments were made to holders of common stock of the firm.[5-2]

While factory output of cars appeared to have caught up with sales in the final weeks of 1923, the opening month or two of 1924 saw the H.H. Franklin Company, together with the remainder of the American automobile industry, continue to operate at a high level of production. At one point during the winter the company even forecast that its 1924 production would exceed that of 1923. As spring neared, however, it became apparent that retail auto purchases were dropping sharply below the 1923 level, and factory output was trimmed. By early April Franklin had slashed its production schedule in half, to just over thirty cars per day. Conditions quickly deteriorated further. By late spring practically all centers of automobile manufacturing across the nation were reporting large reductions in output, coupled with substantial lay-offs of workers. In Syracuse, the Franklin plant cut back to a three-day week, with output of vehicles dropping to a level just sufficient to meet the limited number of new orders coming in from dealers. At the beginning of summer assembly lines were halted entirely for several weeks to permit the taking of inventory, a highly unusual occurrence during that time of the year.

To a degree the drop in 1924 sales of the Franklin car reflected an overall trend within the automobile industry, which now was experiencing a cyclical pattern in which an outstanding sales year almost invariably was followed by one of a not so satisfactory nature. However, it also was apparent that the Franklin firm's problems in early 1924 were more severe than those of most other auto manufacturers. Large numbers of unsold Franklin cars were piling up on dealers' lots, with the company suffering an almost catastrophic drop in demand for its vehicles. Top management ultimately was compelled to face the fact that drastic steps needed to be taken to deal with this situation. The company's engineering staff sought to provide at least an interim solution to the crisis by developing a much-improved motor for the Franklin car. This upgraded unit, featuring a new carburetor and manifold plus strengthened cooling capacity, generated increased horsepower and provided the vehicle with far better acceleration and hill-climbing ability. The new power plant together with certain chassis improvements were incorporated in an updated Franklin model, named the 10C, which was placed on the market in the early summer of 1924. However, while it was an excellent automobile mechanically, overcoming almost completely the vexing defects found in the earlier Series 10 cars, it had been apparent for some time that mechanical improvements alone would not sell the Franklin product. Shortcomings in appearance were making the car less and less appealing to buyers, thus producing serious problems for the company and its dealers.

By 1924 practically all makes of American automobiles were mechanically sound and would provide their purchasers with adequate service. Consequently, in order to achieve success in the fierce sales wars now taking place, motor car designers paid increased attention to making their products things of beauty. Lower, less-boxy-looking bodies and more attractive colors were among the features emphasized as various new models were unveiled to the public. An item of particularly concern was the front of the car, with numerous manufacturers dressing up one-time ugly radiators with nickel-plated shells of handsome design, thus giving vehicles a pleasing frontal appearance. It was in the styling area above all others that the Franklin car, with its short, downward-slanted hood and unadorned, "egg-crate" grille, was having problems competing with water-cooled vehicles.

Franklin dealers for some time had been experiencing the sharp impact of consumer sales resistance, and from this group spokesmen emerged to make factory executives fully aware of their concerns. The most vocal–and most influential–of these was Ralph Hamlin, Franklin's vigorous Southern California distributor, who for years had set a blistering pace in car sales. At a private meeting with H.H. during the summer of 1923, Hamlin shocked the president of the company by threatening to transfer his allegiance to another make of vehicle if steps were not taken to update the awkward frontal design of the Franklin car. Galvanized into action, H.H. authorized Hamlin to engage the Murphy Body Company of Los Angeles to develop a new design for the Franklin along conventional lines. The vehicle now was to have a recast appearance similar to its water-cooled competitors, with special attention given to upgrading the front section. At the same time, H.H. also retained J. Frank deCausse, a well-known custom body designer, to develop an alternate version of a restyled body (deCausse had displayed Franklins with updated fronts at a custom car salon). After some months the deCausse styling option was selected by H.H. as the basis for a face-lifted Franklin automobile.

Once the decision had been made on a new design for the car it was necessary to mobilize the Franklin factory organization to produce the vehicle, and alert the company's dealers to the fact that in the not-too-distant future they would have an attractively-restyled automobile to offer the public. At first glance these steps appeared to be relatively straightforward ones. However, putting them into effect would produce the most serious problems in the area of human relations that the staid, conservative Franklin firm ever had experienced, problems that would shake the organization to its very foundation.

Continuing the almost extraordinary turnover of Franklin top executives in recent years, J.W.DuB. Gould resigned as general manager in early 1924, citing ill health as the reason. In order to obtain a strong right arm to assist him in what now loomed as a critical area of company operations, H.H. Franklin a few weeks later named a person of broad reputation in the automobile industry as the firm's new vice president of sales. This individual, Hungarian-born Frederick E. Moskovics, after obtaining engineering training in America and abroad, worked with several small motor car companies in the areas of testing, technical development and marketing throughout the early years of the twentieth century. No staid office engineer, Moskovics helped break the world's non-stop record as an auto racing driver in 1905. Ultimately he became identified with the innovative Marmon Motor Car Co. of Indianapolis, rising to a vice-presidency with that firm. Apparently seeking additional management responsibilities Moskovics left Marmon in 1923, and thus was available to meet the Franklin organization's needs. Well-known throughout the industry as a person with a hard-driving, forceful personality, impatient of obstacles (his stocky build and broad, round face contrasted sharply with the slim-appearing, bespectacled H.H. Franklin), Moskovics as a condition of joining the Franklin organization sought and obtained a five-year employment contract giving him general control of marketing. His vice-presidency would be with the Franklin Automobile Company, the sales arm of the firm. Immediately after his arrival the quarters occupied by the company's top executive staff were totally reshuffled to permit the construction of a large private office, with glass sides, for the incoming vice-president. A merchandising bureau also was established by the company to assist Moskovics with special studies and formulation of sales plans. The wide-ranging duties of the new executive reportedly included liaison activities with the Franklin engineering staff, giving Moskovics direct contact with his old friend and SAE colleague, John Wilkinson.

The initial assignment given the new sales chief following his arrival was the provision of assistance to Franklin dealers in disposing of the large stock of unsold cars (it was estimated that the inventory totaled several thousand vehicles). A number of meetings were scheduled quickly with dealers in various parts of the country, with Moskovics delivering vigorous talks at these sessions on effective sales methods. An intensified advertising campaign was initiated, and a "bonus plan" adopted to inspire dealers to make additional sales. Letters subsequently began streaming out of company offices addressed to owners of older Franklin cars, citing the advantages of purchasing a Series 10C vehicle.

It was recognized early that complicating these efforts to dispose of the surplus Series 10C models would be the plan of the company to introduce a new Franklin automobile with major restyling, to be designated the Series 11. In order to enable the dealers to get rid of a large number of the old models before word spread of the impending new car, Moskovics apparently secured from H.H. Franklin agreement that no announcement of the Series 11 was to be made until mid-September of 1924. However, H.H., obviously under pressure to demonstrate that the firm was making swift progress in the development of a more competitive vehicle, ultimately determined to change the original schedule. On the evening of June 9, 1924, night telegrams were sent to dealers throughout the country advising them of plans for introduction of the Series 11, with these wires followed by letters and advertising material describing the new model. Moskovics was totally by-passed in this action, H.H. securing the services of H.N. Ballard of Chicago to make the announcement without the knowledge of his sales vice-president.

Following what undoubtedly was a sharp confrontation between the two men, H.H. subsequently sent his vice-president for sales a memorandum informing him that henceforth Ballard would have primary responsibility for the merchandising of cars, and advising Moskovics to cooperate in this change. Still later Moskovics received a second memo from H.H., informing him that he had been superseded by Ballard. The reaction of the tough, determined Moskovics was swift and unequivocal. He refused to carry out Ballard's instructions, resigning early in August on the ground that the contract giving him responsibility for sale of the company's automobiles had been breached and bringing suit for damages against the Franklin firm and H.H. in Federal district court in nearby Utica, New York.

A bitterly-contested legal action took place during the late fall and early winter of 1924, with Moskovics the only person testifying in his behalf. Clearly he made a highly effective witness, since a jury on December 20, 1924, found that his contract had been broken by the company and awarded him $158,883 in damages, the largest verdict ever given to that date in the Federal judicial district of Central New York in a case of this nature! A few weeks afterward the award of damages was declared excessive and reduced to $130,000 by the judge who presided at the trial. Still later, following Moskovics' appointment as President of the Stutz Motor Car Co. of Indianapolis, the parties reached an out-of-court settlement of the matter.

While the rupture of relations with Frederick Moskovics was both unpleasant and costly, the company shortly was to experience a far more staggering loss. Early in the fall of 1924, as the firm's technical staff was readying plans to place the Series 11 in production, it was observed that John Wilkinson no longer was coming to his office at the

THE FRANKLIN AUTOMOBILE COMPANY

Franklin plant. At the beginning of November the announcement was made that John was severing his connection with the organization, and shortly thereafter he resigned his positions as vice-president of both the H.H. Franklin Manufacturing Co. and the Franklin Automobile Company, together with his seats on the boards of directors of both firms. Both H.H. Franklin and John Wilkinson were tight-lipped about the reason for this abrupt resignation, but it seemed certain that events of the 1922-24 period had led to the split between the two men. John, with his continuing interest in a lighter, simpler automobile, clearly had been acutely unhappy with the unilateral decision of H.H. late in 1922 to terminate permanently the small car project. In addition, the plan to develop new styling for the Series 11 vehicle apparently had been devised without much if any consultation with Wilkinson, a course of action which must have been highly displeasing to an engineer with a top-flight national reputation in the automotive industry.

As the year 1924 ended, it was apparent that it had been a far-from-successful one for the Franklin firm. Output of vehicles dropped from over 10,000 in the previous year to a bare 6,000. Heavy cuts had been made in the work force, with the employment level of over 3,000 in January 1924, dropping by many hundreds during the course of the year. As the books of the firm were closed on December 31, the results had to be recorded in red ink. The company suffered an operating loss of over $800,000, and in addition found it necessary to write off several hundred thousand dollars in deferred and other special charges. When the preferred dividend payment also was deducted (needless to say, no dividend was declared on common shares), the firm found itself on the deficit side of the ledger to the extent of over $1,700.000.[5-3]

These losses were vexing. They meant that in the three-year period 1922-24, during which most of the well-established motor car manufacturers in America had shaken off the effects of the 1920-21 post war recession and were performing well financially, the Franklin firm had lost money two-thirds of the time. With no dividend paid on the common stock for three consecutive years, this class of securities now was receiving a mediocre rating from investment analysts. The company continued to attempt to sell its preferred stock during much of this period, but since even this class of securities was trading at less than par on the stock exchanges, the market obviously was limited.

Unpleasant as it must have been facing these financial results at the end of 1924, the loss of John Wilkinson's presence in the area of engineering and design may well have dealt the company a far more severe blow in the long-term. Since the time when it began producing automobiles the organization had relied almost completely on John as its leader in the technical area. His dominance in this sector of company operations over the years was as complete as that of H.H. Franklin in management, finance and sales. Now the great partnership, which had brought the company stability, nation-wide recognition and a considerable degree of success over nearly a quarter-of-a-century, had been torn asunder. The path to be followed by the firm in future years was to be established by one man alone, without the judgment and counterbalance provided by the other. If the concern should decide to focus its efforts totally in the field of the luxury automobile, no strong voice was to be available to point out the possible dangers of such a course. Time alone would be the judge of whether this total concentration of decision-making authority in a single person was to be beneficial to the organization.

THE FRANKLIN AUTOMOBILE COMPANY

– Six –

The Tempo of the Twenties (1925-1929)

An attractive new Franklin automobile, with sleek, up-to-the minute styling, greeted prospective motor car purchasers in the early months of 1925. The odd-shaped front end, with its stubby, sloping profile and "horsecollar" grille (auto historian Menno Duerksen aptly termed it the "droop nose effect"), for years symbolic of America's best-known air-cooled car, had been abandoned. In its place the innovative vehicle displayed a wide, imposing hood which swept forward in a straight line to merge with a massive, vertical, nickel-plated false radiator shell of exceptionally pleasing appearance. The frame of the restyled product had been dropped a full three inches to enable bodies of a low, thoroughly modern design to be fitted. Two open cars, a trim sport roadster and a fleet phaeton, were featured in the company's line-up, along with five equally striking enclosed models, a sedan, sport sedan, limousine, coupe, and cabriolet. This new offering, designated the Series 11, signaled a landmark change in the Franklin car from a clearly identifiable, utilitarian-appearing machine to an automobile which, while still featuring an air-cooled engine, now was indistinguishable in external style and design from any of the better quality water-cooled cars on the American market.

Changes in the modernized vehicle encompassed more than a smart-

THE FRANKLIN AUTOMOBILE COMPANY

The trim and sporty Franklin boattail roadster, with the vehicle body by deCausse, was displayed at an automotive salon in the mid 1920's. (Courtesy of American Automobile Manufacturers Association)

ly restyled appearance. The wheelbase of the Series 11 had been stretched to 119 inches, and the weight increased by over 400 pounds in the sedan model. Full-elliptic springing and the traditional laminated wood frame were continued, but the addition of balloon tires and Watson Stabilators resulted in an even more boulevard-smooth ride than that provided by predecessor Franklin models. An increase in the steering gear ratio permitted continued easy handling despite greater vehicle weight and use of the new large, soft tires. Standard equipment now included a dashboard gauge to show the oil level of the engine, front and rear bumpers, and even a spare tire.

Under the gleaming new hood improved cooling of the motor had been achieved by substitution of copper fins for the former steel ones surrounding the cylinders. This change also made possible a higher compression ratio, resulting in a slightly more powerful engine. The stepped-up power output meant that the new vehicle, while bigger and heavier, still would provide quickened performance for its driver, obviously essential in an era where speed had become an ever-more-important factor in automotive marketing. A smooth-operating new Brown-Lipe single plate clutch had been fitted, plus a more powerful battery and a rear fuel tank of increased capacity. The transmission-mounted service brake was continued, but an increase in its diameter from 9 1/2 to 11 inches insured increased stopping capability without the need for greater pedal pressure. In summary, the Franklin firm's new offering was a nicely-equipped, luxury-class machine, with the larger package reflected in a much stiffer price tag than formerly for most body styles. Only the coupe, now $2,700, would be priced at nearly the same level, while the sedan was marked up from $2,850 to $3,200, the limousine from $2,950 to $3,500, and the touring from $1,950 to $2,650.[6-1]

These price increases resulted in the new Franklin vehicle costing the consumer somewhat more than another high-quality six-cylinder car offered by a competitor firm, the Packard Motor Car Co. Top management at Packard, in an obvious effort to strengthen the volume of sales of the firm's junior-level offering (the company's prestigious senior-series eight competed in a much-higher range), had taken the opposite tack from Franklin and recently slashed the price tag of its six-cylinder sedan from $3,375 to $2,585, with the limousine costing only two hundred dollars more. Through this reduction Packard had effectively eliminated the cost gap between its closed and open car models–the new Packard six sedan would be priced at a level identical with the phaeton. In taking such a step the Packard firm followed the lead of the Hudson Motor Car Co., which in July of 1924 had trimmed the cost of its "Super Six" coach (a 2-door closed model) to the same level as the touring car, $1,500. These pricing policies established by two important firms in the high and medium-priced automotive fields simply confirmed what many informed persons had observed in the motor car industry by the mid-1920s, the fact that the closed car was fast achieving sales leadership (in 1925, for the first time, enclosed vehicles sold in larger volume than open types), and companies soon would have to offer it at the same cost as the old-style open models if they expected to compete effectively. The Franklin firm as a trail-

THE FRANKLIN AUTOMOBILE COMPANY

Hugh Goodhart was advertising manager of the Franklin organization for many years. (Franklin Automobile Company dealer's brochure)

blazer in closed car sales very shortly might need to re-examine its approach to pricing open and enclosed models.

A somewhat revamped Franklin organization assumed responsibility for manufacturing and marketing the new Series 11 model, together with the holdover 10C Series which also was offered to customers, usually at a considerable discount, during the first half of 1925. Giles H. Stilwell, long-time legal counsel to the company, was elected vice-president of both the H.H. Franklin Manufacturing Company and its selling arm, the Franklin Automobile Company, succeeding John Wilkinson. Stilwell, it will be recalled, had functioned as a vice-president of the manufacturing unit in the early period of motor car production, and for many years held membership on the boards of directors of both firms. Ralph Murphy, who assisted Wilkinson in directing engineering and manufacturing activities for several years prior to John's resignation, also joining the board of directors of the manufacturing unit, was named overall operations manager of the organization. In this capacity he performed many of the same functions

Edward S. Marks would rise from student engineer to chief engineer in the Franklin firm. (Franklin Automobile Company dealer's brochure)

as did Wilkinson previously, and soon would be elected second vice-president of the H.H. Franklin Manufacturing Company. The new chief engineer was to be Edward S. Marks, a slim, youthful-appearing University of Michigan graduate who had joined Franklin as a student engineer in 1917 after teaching mathematics for a time at an eastern university. The Franklin firm, having enjoyed some degree of success in developing markets for its automobile in foreign nations, organized an export department; this unit was placed under the general direction of S.E. Ackerman, the company's sales manager. Frank Barton continued as secretary-treasurer of the company, with Hugh Goodhart serving as advertising manager.

Among the prominent Franklin dealers and distributors of the period were Ralph Hamlin of Los Angeles, George Ostendorf of Buffalo, Otto Lawton of Boston, O.C. Belt of Columbus, Ohio, George H. Williams and William Sanger of Milwaukee, Wisconsin, Wallace Wilcox of Providence, Rhode Island, and Cowles Tolman of New Haven, Connecticut. While the firm could claim a number of strong dealers in various cities, large and small, throughout many parts of the nation, sales of the car now were becoming more and more concentrated along the Atlantic Seaboard, in a few states in the Great Lakes area (particularly Ohio and Illinois), and on the West Coast. Market penetration of the Franklin vehicle was weak in the majority of great plains states, somewhat surprising in light of the air-cooled car's ability to overcome the rigors of severe winter weather. Undoubtedly the high price and earlier unconventional appearance of the car restricted its appeal in the rural areas and small towns of this sparsely-populated region.

Important as was the motor vehicle industry at the moment of America's entry into the First World War, its status at that time paled into insignificance when compared with the position it had achieved in the United States by the mid-1920s. The automobile now had become an overwhelming force economically, socially and recreationally in the lives of a huge group of Americans. The number of persons across the nation enjoying lower-middle and middle-range incomes had very nearly doubled in the five-year period from 1917 to 1922, thus providing vastly increased buying power for desirable consumer items. In addition, more and more families felt that ownership of a motor car was so vital to their well-being that they readily abandoned the purchase of other items once considered important in order to channel funds into acquisition of this exciting means of speedy, individualized transportation. The sharply expanded use of credit to purchase motor vehicles through installment or "time" payments spread over a period of months or years also played a vital role in making possible broad-based auto ownership. The "used" car, a vehicle traded-in by purchasers of new automobiles, usually sold at a modest price and allowed numerous families of limited means to experience the pleasure of becoming mobile (such trade-ins also caused problems for auto dealers, but that is a separate story!). In short, possession of some type of motor car no longer was a badge of the well-to-do, but was fast becoming a standard feature of the typical American family. The population of the United States in 1925 was estimated at 115,378,000, with no less than 20,050,000 motor vehicles (cars and trucks) in the hands of owners by the end of that year, or one for every five and three-quarters persons. This wide motor vehicle ownership was not duplicated anywhere else on the face of the globe. Even in such advanced European nations as France and Great Britain only one vehicle was available for each fifty to sixty persons, with the incidence of ownership much lower still in Germany, Italy and Spain. In these countries the automobile still was considered a luxury item, while in America it fast was becoming viewed as an absolute necessity. Even in neighboring Canada, a nation geographically and culturally similar to the United States, proportionately less than half as many individuals enjoyed ownership of automobiles.[6-2]

The amazing total of 425,000 wage earners now were directly employed across America in the manufacture of motor vehicles, bodies and component parts, or some three times as many as in 1914, a scant eleven years earlier. In addition, vast numbers of persons found work in furnishing essential materials, supplies and accessories to the motor car industry, in selling and servicing vehicles, and in driving trucks and taxis, so that total auto-related employment probably exceeded three million. The domination of this great industry by 1925 can be fully appreciated when it is noted that in the same year motorcycle and bicycle firms together utilized nationwide a mere 4,200 hands, while less than 5,000 persons continued on the payrolls of companies building the now totally antiquated carriages and wagons. Even production of the newest form of transportation, the airplane, involved only 2,700 workers.[6-3]

This huge army of automotive industry employees during 1925 put in a work week which in periods of full-time activity typically stretched to 50.3 hours. The average wage paid was just over 72 cents per hour, with the large group of assembly line workers and machine operators earning some three cents less than this figure and the smaller number of elite skilled tradesmen such as tool and die makers and paint stripers receiving fifteen to twenty cents more hourly. As was true with many auto manufacturers located outside the major centers of motor vehicle production, Franklin's hourly rate of pay for most types of work ran a trifle below the industry average. However, the Syracuse firm utilized a "premium" or "incentive" pay plan for positions in some departments, enabling those employees who achieved a high volume of production to earn substantial incomes. The small number of women employed in manufacturing operations at the various auto plants (usually in sewing upholstery or other light tasks) received only two-thirds the pay of men.

The unskilled or semi-skilled automobile factory hand earned a far higher hourly wage than employees in many other industries–workers performing routine tasks in the paper mills and pottery plants located in small towns near Syracuse averaged little more than fifty cents per hour–but despite this, turnover in the typical motor car manufacturing operation reached extraordinary levels. The phenomenon of "job-jumping" in the auto industry existed to a degree unknown in many other areas of manufacturing, such as shops building railroad cars and locomotives. To a substantial extent such transiency could be attributed to the "mass-production" techniques utilized in most auto manufacturing facilities, particularly the huge Midwestern assembly plants where the great majority of hands possessed no specialized talents and simply performed repetitive tasks at top speed throughout the working day. In such auto centers as Detroit this resulted in a large number of workers with limited skills frequently moving from one auto or parts plant to another, undoubtedly in search of a few cents per hour more in pay or better conditions of employment. Such lack of stability and company loyalty in many auto industry jobs was exacerbated by the numerous layoffs which took place in practically all motor car firms when popularity of a particular make of automobile declined or a slow selling season reduced demand for vehicles generally. Production workers also were furloughed when auto companies shifted from one model to another, an annual event in most firms. Since no unemployment insurance existed in this era, the laid-off worker found himself compelled either to endure unpaid idleness or seek a temporary job of some nature to support himself and his family until the hoped-for callback came. The H.H. Franklin Company normally enjoyed a lower voluntary "quit rate" (its pay traditionally was the highest among Syracuse industries) than most auto plants, but throughout even the generally prosperous 1920s it too experienced many layoffs. Its factory work force included a "permanent cadre" who typically held jobs twelve months of the year, and "seasonal hands" who were employed only during peak production months. Except for a tiny number of highly-skilled employees in an occasional auto plant who were members of craft unions, the motor car industry during this period was totally an "open-shop" operation. A few strikes on a limited scale took place from time-to-time (the Franklin firm experienced two or three work-stoppages, involving employees in the paint and metal-finishing units) but these normally were hastily-organized affairs occurring in specific departments of factories and involving local issues. The broad-scale industrial union had signally failed to gain even a toehold in auto manufacturing plants.

While passenger car production more than doubled from 1920 to 1925, to a total approaching four million units, the gains came entirely in the low (under $1,000) and medium ($1,000 to $2,000) price ranges. The number of cars produced in the upper-middle ($2,000 to $3,000) and the high priced ($3,000-up) fields actually declined a trifle, and fell precipitously (from 7.7 to 3.4 percent) in relation to total volume of vehicles turned out. This shift in public demand toward low and moderately-priced vehicles sharply affected the fortunes of companies manufacturing more expensive automobiles, each of which now competed for a share of a slowly-declining market. The mid-twenties saw a closing of the ranks in the motor vehicle industry generally. In 1924 alone mortality among auto manufacturers reached the stunning level of twenty percent, with a disproportionate effect on the small, independent firms. Such long-established, highly reputable producers of fine motor cars as Winton in Cleveland, Haynes in Kokomo, Indiana, and Cole in Indianapolis quietly closed their doors (Cole, a well-regarded builder of high-quality automobiles, had competed strongly with Franklin and other luxury vehicle makers for a share of the prestige car market as recently as 1920, but thereafter went swiftly downhill).

The Lincoln Motor Company in Detroit, headed by that white-bearded patriarch of the automobile industry, Henry M. Leland, ran into heavy weather in the early 1920s and was saved only by a last-minute rescue on the part of the world's most successful proponent of the cheap, mass-produced vehicle, Henry Ford (who, despite Leland's early and quite unhappy departure from the bought-out firm, wisely did not attempt to lower the superb quality of motor cars produced by his new acquisition). While the initial Lincoln cars undoubtedly suffered in the marketplace from totally uninspired styling, other high-priced vehicles with technically-advanced features found the going no easier. The old-line Premier Motor Corporation of Indianapolis discovered that an electric self-shifting transmission did not generate sufficient market appeal to save it from having to discontinue passenger car production, while the more-recently organized Wills-St. Claire Company of Marysville, Michigan, found itself desperately attempting to ward off receivership despite offering superbly-crafted six and eight-cylinder vehicles. With a bankruptcy rate several times that of manufacturing firms generally, minor companies in the auto industry increasingly were viewed by the public as risky locations in which to invest funds.

Since the average price paid by the American buyer for an automobile had dropped sharply between 1920 and 1925 (from $1,270 to $870), a number of luxury car manufacturers sought to broaden market appeal by offering more competitively-priced companion lines. The six-cylinder model introduced by Packard was the most successful example of this trend, but top price-range firms such as Locomobile quickly followed suit, and even the aristocratic McFarlan Motor Car Company of Connersville, Indiana, offered a new vehicle at just over $3,000–cheap indeed compared to the $7,000 to $9,000 this firm charged for its big town cars. Interestingly, one of the very few newcomers to the motor-car roster in the 1924-25 period, Chrysler, reversed this trend. After establishing itself firmly in the ranks of automobile manufacturers with the highly-successful introduction of a well-engineered medium-priced car, this company (actually a successor to the old Maxwell-Chalmers organization) added a luxury vehicle, the "Imperial 80," which competed with Packard, Cadillac and Franklin. Quite obviously the Chrysler firm reasoned that the prestige generated by a top quality offering might well rub off on its more moderately-priced companion lines.

The motor car, as its use mushroomed, during the mid-1920s, sharply impacted nearly every facet of life of the typical American family. Among the most strongly affected was the city dweller together with his near-cousin, the suburbanite. No longer was it necessary for motor car owners in urban areas to live within walking distance of a source of employment, or in close proximity to the stopping place of an electric rail line. Availability of the automobile–and its corollary, the modern improved road–now permitted the establishment of a residence almost anywhere within commuting range of a central city. The result was a striking transformation of the demographic structure of metropolitan areas, with a thinning of population in the urban core accompanied by substantial movement of people into outlying sectors. Countless subdivisions were springing up in suburban districts across the nation as hundreds of thousands of persons sought the pleasures of a more open life style. In addition, even the design of the home itself was very sharply influenced by the motor vehicle. The ability of what might be termed the "motorized family" to seek entertainment anywhere within reasonable driving distance meant that a well-to-do household no longer need invest in such special facilities as a music room, considered *de rigueur* in the stately homes of the 1890s. An almost universal addition to any newly-constructed mid-1920s residence, however, was the garage, now viewed as a necessity for storage of the one or more cars owned by the typical middle-class family.[6-4]

The yeoman efforts of the earlier "good roads" pioneers had borne fruit in a vastly improved system of highways spanning much of the

THE FRANKLIN AUTOMOBILE COMPANY

This Franklin advertisement in The Literary Digest in June 1925 displays a vehicle intended to appeal to a typical well-to-do American family.

nation. Two key innovations, the earlier-described enactment in 1916 of Federal road-aid legislation, followed by the establishment of state highway departments, had resulted by the mid-1920s in the construction of tens of thousands of miles of hard-surfaced routes across major sections of America.[a] People throughout many of the forty-eight states finally could proclaim that they had been "brought out of the mud." These new inter-city roads would hardly be considered satisfactory by the standards of half-a-century later–literally no limited access highways with travel lanes separated by a central divider were included in any program[b]–but in comparison with what the motorist had to endure a scant fifteen years earlier, they were greeted with enthusiasm. Throughout the eastern part of America it now was possible for a businessman or tourist to journey from one major city to another entirely on paved roads–although, unfortunately, this was not yet true in some of the sparsely-populated western states. Despite these improvements the majority of time-pressed business travelers, restricted to a speed of no more than thirty-five or forty miles per hour in the typical 1925 motor car driven on a two-lane highway, continued to utilize the speedy express passenger train for trips of any length. Substantial use of the even-more-swift-moving airplane for inter-city travel would be a decade or two in the future.

Availability of the motor car to a vast number of middle-class families had totally revamped all previous approaches to recreation. Business and professional men now could shed problems of the office as they sped to their local country clubs in the late afternoon for a relaxing round or two of golf. When vacation time approached, the flexibility afforded by the family-owned vehicle resulted in major changes in plans. The old "summer hotel," immensely popular in the 1890s and

---

a Another vital factor in highway development was the reaching of general agreement by various interest groups on a tax program to fund road construction and maintenance. In the typical state, two special charges now were broadly used: one based on the weight of the vehicle and assessed through an annual registration fee, and the other a penny or two addition to the price of each gallon of gasoline purchased. "Anti-diversion" amendments to state constitutions often were adopted to ensure that the proceeds of those taxes would be used only for highway purposes.

b A few scenic, semi-limited-access routes such as the Bronx River Parkway in Westchester County in New York had been developed by this time. However, such facilities were not intended for swift movement of vehicles over long distances.

the very early years of the twentieth century as a place where family members might spend a leisurely week or two, was fast losing its appeal. Ownership of an automobile coupled with the upgrading of highways had provided hundreds of thousands of vacationing American families with previously undreamed-of-mobility–they now could visit a half-dozen or more interesting sites in the course of a ten-day trip. Although many of these tourists would continue to look to the conventional inn or hotel in town or city as a place to break the drive each evening, others would seek to prolong enjoyment of the open air by pitching their tents in a forest, park, or public campground or through staying in one of the "cabins" which were springing up by the tens of thousands across the nation to offer cheap overnight accommodations. At this time in American history the motor car also made it possible for a large group of long-distance travelers to flee the harsh northern winter and journey to that land of perpetual sunshine, Florida.

While the automobile thus provided its vast army of owners with a speedy, flexible and often enjoyable means of transportation, it also brought in its wake problems of a nature and on a scale unforeseen two decades earlier. Many of these were concentrated in the large and medium-sized cities of America, where the enormous expansion of motor vehicle ownership had come to dominate urban life. The influence of automobile clubs and other civic groups over the previous two decades had resulted in the resurfacing of most of the ill-maintained city streets of the 1880s and 1890s, so that driving in a substantial degree of comfort now was possible. By the mid-1920s, however, the sheer volume of pleasure car and truck traffic threatened to totally overwhelm the street systems in many of the nation's key municipalities, and new approaches for regulating and channeling this great flow of vehicles became essential. At street intersections conflicts between two or more converging streams of vehicles along with pedestrians in crosswalks were becoming increasingly difficult to manage. The police officer, who for decades sought to exercise control through arm-and-hand movements, was being replaced by the electrically-operated traffic light incorporating easily-understood green and red

THE TEMPO OF THE TWENTIES

signals. Parking of vehicles on public streets while owners shopped or conducted business affairs also had become a major problem, with various types of regulation, none very satisfactory, being attempted in various cities. Early urban planners thus faced problems of crisis proportions in attempting to make it possible for a motorcar-burdened city to continue functioning in a satisfactory manner. The mounting death toll from auto-related accidents, now approaching 20,000 annually, also was generating concern across the nation, with numerous "safety" conferences held to explore ways of checking this alarming loss of life.

In the city of Syracuse attempts to insure a smooth flow of auto traffic were compounded by a unique problem, the wide-scale use of important streets as rights-of-way for passenger trains. From the beginning of the railroad era the various lines had been permitted to utilize such space, a practice which did not generate unusual difficulties in the horse-and-buggy period but produced irritating traffic-tie-ups plus hazards to safety when automotive use reached major proportions. Various recommendations were advanced to deal with this ever-worsening problem, with a special city commission, headed for many years by Franklin board-of-directors member Alexander T. Brown, struggling to find a solution which would be palatable to the various interests involved. Proposals for elevated structures, below-grade rights-of-way, and rerouting of rail lines outside the city each had supporters and opponents, but due to cost and other factors a remedy would not be found until the mid-1930s.

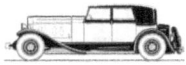

The year 1925 proved to be an excellent one for many automobile manufacturers, and particularly for the surviving independent producers. Not only were a record number of motor vehicles built and sold (total car and truck output in the United States and Canada surpassed the four-million level by several hundred thousand units, an outstanding achievement by past standards), but equally important, most firms could point to a handsome increase in profit over the previous year. The H.H. Franklin Company was no exception to the rule, with its president, in his annual report to stockholders, declaring 1925 to have been the best year in the history of the firm. H.H. related that company earnings after depreciation achieved an all-time high of $2,019,000, or well over $200 on each vehicle sold. Total number of cars produced by the Syracuse firm reached only 8,600, below the levels attained in 1919, 1920 and 1923, but an increased price per unit helped insure the company a solid profit. Franklin's output, however, was one-quarter of one percent of total industry passenger car production, in contrast to over one-half of one percent five years earlier, a mildly disquieting factor. Dividends on preferred stock in the amount of $449,000 were paid from earnings, but despite the vastly improved fiscal picture once again no distribution was made to common shareholders. This passing of any dividend on common shares, while undoubtedly disappointing to holders of such stock, did result in the company generating a very strong balance sheet at the end of 1925, with working capital reaching the level of $6,033,000. Effects of the 1924 loss had been fully overcome.[6-5]

Satisfying as was the record of the Franklin firm in 1925 to its chief executive, one of its Detroit competitors in the luxury car field fared a great deal better. The Packard Motor Car Company achieved an outstanding level of factory production of cars–24,246 units–and was able to announce a profit of $12,191,000 for the year, some five hundred dollars per vehicle.[6-6] With such a splendid earnings record this firm experienced no difficulty in retiring a multi-million dollar issue of preferred stock, and also paying a whopping $4,746,000 in dividends to its common shareholders. The title of leading independent producer of high-grade motor cars, a honor for which Franklin had mounted a serious challenge in 1920 and 1921, now clearly belonged to Packard.

The Packard success story of the 1920s makes informative reading. Under the leadership of Alvan Macauley, its stern and hard-driving chief executive, the firm began modernizing plant production facilities on a broad-scale immediately after the close of the First World War. Recovering swiftly from a disastrous 1921, when it suffered a large operating loss, Packard subsequently decided to terminate the manufacture of its truck line, choosing to concentrate entirely on what Macauley believed would offer the greatest potential for profit, the high-quality pleasure car. This decision proved to be a totally sound one. Year after year through the mid-nineteen-twenties the company could boast of handsome profits, a substantial portion of which invariably was shared with its stockholders. In order to promote its image as the builder of a leading prestige automobile the company invested heavily in crisply-written, beautifully-illustrated advertisements in America's leading weekly and monthly magazines, extolling in an understated, conservative manner the virtues of its product.

While viewed across the nation as a producer of high-grade automobiles in somewhat limited numbers, the Packard factory was organized and operated in a manner strikingly similar to plants of the big-volume Detroit auto manufacturers. Under Macauley's firm hand the company sought to achieve a steadily-increasing output of vehicles, while holding unit costs at the lowest possible level. This was accomplished in part by far greater mechanization of the production process than was the case with other independent builders of top-flight cars, such as Franklin, and also through a policy of keeping wages at modest levels for many employees, particularly those performing tasks of a routine nature (Macauley could be very tough indeed in employee relations matters).[6-7] The firm, however, wisely retained on its payroll at relatively high rates a substantial cadre of skilled craftsmen, usually with long tenure, who were responsible for putting the "finishing touches" on the luxury sedans and limousines purchased by well-to-do customers. The Packard plant also was quick to order parts from outside suppliers rather than producing them in-house if costs could be shaved a trifle through such a policy (Macauley was known as a man who would not hesitate to make a change to save a quarter of a cent per item, so long as quality was maintained).[6-8] Packard, like Franklin, invested heavily in engineering and research activities, although a substantial proportion of the Detroit-based manufacturer's technical budget was devoted to the development of aircraft engines, a potential area of diversification for the firm. The company sought to maintain buyer loyalty through a conservative styling policy, with a minimum of year-to-year design changes in the dignified, sedate vehicles it manufactured. Such an approach clearly produced success in the market place, since in city after city across America, including Syracuse, the Packard motor car had become the preferred vehicle of a large number of socially prominent families.

Franklin's fellow upstate New York luxury car maker, Pierce-Arrow, during the early and mid-1920s found itself totally unable to emulate Packard's formula for prosperity. The Pierce firm, whose products in earlier decades had stood at the very pinnacle of the American prestige car field, now was encountering hard times. A corporate reorganization during the period of the First World War burdened the Buffalo-based company with a top-heavy capital structure, and declining demand through the early 1920s for its ponderous, expensive and somewhat outdated vehicles compounded the problem. By 1925 the firm was hopelessly delinquent in dividend payments on a major issue of preferred stock, and had distributed nothing to common shareholders since 1919. Despite introduction of its more moderately-priced Series 80 line in mid-1924, sales by the company invariably trailed those of the H.H. Franklin firm on a year-to-year basis, with Pierce hard-pressed to keep its large, extensively-equipped motor car factory operating at a profitable level.

Other surviving independent manufacturers of prestige vehicles also found the going difficult as the decade of the 1920s swept along. The Cleveland-based Peerless Motor Car Company, which in an earlier period had vied with Packard and Pierce Arrow (the famous "Three P's" of American motordom) for the title of the nation's foremost luxury automobile, in recent years had encountered a rapidly shrinking market for its big eight-cylinder vehicles. Seeking to exploit a more popular price-range through the introduction of a downsized six-cylinder car, it would discover that even this venture was no guarantee of a respectable year-to-year corporate profit. The high quality—and equally high-priced—vehicles produced by the old-line Marmon Company were finding fewer and fewer purchasers by 1925; the firm shortly would begin development of a junior-sized automobile in an effort to appeal to buyers of more modest means. Other small-volume manufacturers of motor cars in the middle and upper-middle price ranges, including Jordan in Cleveland, Moon and Gardner in St. Louis and Kissel in tiny Hartford, Wisconsin, also were learning that it was not easy to develop a sound formula for annual profitability despite the widespread prosperity existing throughout the nation. An occasional manufacturer or two, such as the Indiana-based Stutz and Auburn firms, turned with moderate success to high-performance or high-style vehicles in an endeavor to carve out a special niche in the automotive marketplace. The few surviving producers of steam and electric vehicles now were approaching the end of the road, with the old-line Stanley steam car about to fade from existence, and the tiny number of firms still building units powered by electric storage batteries compelled to limit their annual output to a handful of mostly special-order machines. About this time, a Syracuse-based firm, the Stumpf Una-flow Engine Company, sought to develop and market a highly-efficient steam powered motor for automotive purposes, without appreciable success.

While numerous independent motor car builders struggled to remain competitive, the auto industry's major conglomerate in 1926-27, the huge, far-flung General Motors Corporation, now was assuming the role of a pace-setter. Under the leadership of such individuals as Alfred Sloan, Donaldson Brown and Charles Kettering, the big company had developed engineering research programs plus manufacturing management approaches which enabled it to take full advantage of its great size and multi-divisional structure. G.M.'s automotive research laboratory, serving all its operating units, now was achieving major technical breakthroughs, which before long would leave engineering staffs of many minor automotive manufacturers in the dust. The massive firm, in addition to enjoying significant economies of scale due to large vehicle production, also commenced an important program whereby its several automotive divisions would to a degree share common parts. This approach resulted in what one business historian has aptly termed economics of scope–the conglomerate could produce even greater volumes of parts more efficiently, and at the same time, achieve lower prices on its prestige vehicle lines by raiding various parts bins of its cheaper cars.[6-9] This approach was quickly put into effect when the company unveiled its new Pontiac automobile in 1926, a car which contained a considerable number of Chevrolet parts. A year later the big firm brought out the attractively-styled LaSalle vehicle, a product of its Cadillac division, at a price below that charged by the H.H. Franklin Company and similar firms for competitive models. The vast conglomerate, using its strengths, thus would have the ability to provide fearsome competition to the independent motor car builders, placing many of them in increasingly precarious positions in the years to come.

Buoyed by a successful 1925 the H.H. Franklin Company entered the following year in an overall spirit of optimism. Most segments of the motor car industry were anticipating another twelve-month period of high-level production and sales, and Franklin executives confidently looked forward to full participation in such an era of prosperity. A modest reduction in prices of most body styles had been made in September of 1925, and it was believed that this slash would keep the firm's restyled car fully competitive with its rivals.

Once again, however, events took an adverse turn for the Syracuse-based firm, as demand for Franklin cars in the early months of 1926 dropped substantially. In response to this slowdown in sales the company determined that prices for some models needed to be cut drastically to generate additional buyer interest. The revised price schedule, announced late in April 1926, saw the tag for the four-door sedan trimmed some $300, or nearly ten percent, to a new figure of $2,790. Several other closed models–the Oxford and seven-passenger sedans plus the enclosed drive limousine–also were marked down by similar amounts. The few open models remaining in the Franklin line-up either were cut only very slightly in cost or kept at previous levels. The net result was that prices of closed and open Franklin cars were closely bunched together, with a scant one hundred dollars separating the sedan and the runabout. The enclosed business coupe (lacking a rumble seat) now could be purchased at very nearly the same figure as the open touring car. Franklin thus found it advisable to follow a number of industry leaders in reducing prices of once far-more-costly closed cars to a level even with or very close to that of open models. Franklin sales responded in a gratifying manner to this price slash, spurting upward in the late spring period and continuing at a satisfactory level through most of the summer.

During early 1926 the Syracuse firm also found it essential to give strengthened support to its dealer organization through a new plan for financing inventory. This approach called for the factory to fund as much as 80 percent of the wholesale price of the car for a period of up to four months, at an interest rate of eight percent. Clearly those dealers encountering problems in obtaining financing from local lending institutions for cars held in stock pending retail sale would benefit from the new program. Soon thereafter the company took additional steps to upgrade its marketing effort. A. M. Taylor, who earlier had been an assistant in the advertising department of the Franklin firm and subsequently served as advertising manager of the small Midwest motor car company, Velie, now rejoined the Syracuse manufacturer as its advertising chief. New district managers were named for areas in which sales of the air-cooled automobile traditionally had been slow, the South and Midwest. While seeking to promote a more intensive coverage of sales territories across the nation, the Franklin company also attempted to strengthen its small-town dealer network. Some sixty distributor points were established, making it possible for minor dealers to have ready access to good-sized stocks of automobiles as a means of expediting sales (the typical low-volume dealer often did not keep showroom models on hand for immediate delivery). Trained sales personnel representing both the factory and distributors also were made available to discuss marketing and service problems with small-scale dealers, and propose solutions.

Sales and other business problems of the firm were set aside during the first week of July 1926, however, as Franklin celebrated its twenty-fifth anniversary of manufacturing air-cooled vehicles. The company proudly announced that it was the sixth oldest manufacturer of automobiles in America, and now the nation's only motor car firm utilizing an air-cooled engine. It also was noted that the Franklin company was one of a very few of the early auto manufacturers which still was headed by the executives who had organized it (one key person, John Wilkinson, was of course missing). On July 3rd all factory and office employees met in the company recreation hall to hear talks by Franklin executives and by the Chancellor of Syracuse University, Charles Flint. At this session special recognition was given a group of "old-timers," employees who had been with the air-cooled automobile builder for a period of twenty years or more. On the same day, in a project reminiscent of an earlier era, two hundred Franklin dealers across the nation got underway with a 100-mile low-gear test of the vehicle, which typically took some eight hours or more to complete.[6-10]

This period of the 1920s saw an intensification of technological progress in auto plants across the nation. Endless numbers of specialized machine tools were being developed to help increase production, with the result that by 1925 output per employee in the automotive industry was nearly triple that of 1914. Constantly increasing use was being made of the conveyor in moving materials swiftly and efficiently, with such equipment to a considerable degree also serving as a pacemaker for the worker's efforts. Vastly improved paint processes, highlighted by introduction of the new DuPont "Duco" quick-drying product, reduced the time required for painting automobile bodies from days to a few hours. Such new painting techniques thus made it possible to step-up production volume and at the same time expand the range of color choices available to customers. Upgraded manufacturing methods plus careful step-by-step scrutiny of various parts during the machining process helped reduce "scrappage" in the typical plant. In the inspection and quality control areas the Franklin organization tended to be especially strong. Throughout its history the Syracuse company consistently devoted substantial resources to the development of testing and inspection devices which insured that components of Franklin automobiles met exacting standards of quality, thus helping strengthen appeal of the vehicle to the more demanding purchaser. Special machines had been introduced to make possible the checking of both rear axles and transmissions for strength, rigidity and quietness. In order to eliminate the element of personal judgment in noise evaluations, the Franklin company instituted the use of a radio loud speaker plus an accompanying recorder, which together would amplify and record the intensity of sound coming from a rear axle undergoing tests in the "quiet room." The inspector then needed only to examine the readings to determine if the axle would meet the desired standard of noise-free operation! Clearly, this constituted an extraordinary example of high technology being used to insure quality of product in an auto plant at an early date.

The automobile industry in this era monitored its manufacturing costs with increasing care as it turned out ever-larger volumes of vehicles for sale to the public. Each firm continuously studied factory operations in an intensive effort to achieve all possible production economies. Numerous motor car companies, having invested heavily a short time earlier in physical expansion, now more and more sought to increase output through better utilization of space, more careful internal organization, and the installation of highly-efficient manufacturing equipment. Factory managers also watched closely for any excessive accumulation of inventory, making every possible effort to insure that any sudden falling-off in demand would not find them carrying large stocks of unnecessary items. Numerous firms sought to carefully schedule delivery of parts from outside suppliers so that they arrived exactly when needed and in the specific quantity required for a day's production (an early version of "just in time" planning!). Profitable manufacture of motor cars, rather than output at any cost, was being adopted as a standard.

Throughout the year 1926 and the first half of 1927 the Franklin firm,

THE FRANKLIN AUTOMOBILE COMPANY

despite its tradition of fine craftsmanship, had been compelled to recognize that efficiency of operations was a matter of major consequence. The Syracuse company was finding that overall demand for its vehicles had stabilized in the range of 8,000 units annually, far below the numbers attained by such competing makes as Packard and Cadillac-LaSalle (sales of expensive automobiles once more were increasing as the nation enjoyed unprecedented prosperity). Such a modest volume of sales made it difficult for Franklin to get its unit costs down to a satisfactory level, particularly since its bodies were produced several hundred miles away in a New England factory which continued to perform many functions by hand.[6-11] With marketing wars continuing to rage throughout the industry, however, disposing of a respectable number of cars required that Franklin sale prices be kept in line with those charged by builders of competitive products. The result was that the firm's profit at times tended to approach the vanishing point. Net operating income after depreciation of the H.H. Franklin Manufacturing Company and its subsidiaries for 1926 was just over $72,000, far from enough to meet the preferred dividend payment of $434,000. A similar situation existed during the first eight months of 1927, with the firm doing no better than barely breaking even financially. However, cautious overall fiscal management, and especially careful monitoring of inventories (they had been reduced $1,800,000 during the year 1926, and would be cut another $1,000,000 in 1927), gave the firm a very clean, sound balance sheet, with a ratio of current assets to liabilities of approximately ten-to-one, a splendid figure.[6-12]

Top-level Franklin policy-makers finally determined that a number of steps needed to be taken to strengthen the competitive position of the organization. A change in manufacturing management was made in May 1927, triggered by the resignation of the popular and personable William Dunk as production chief (he would trade automobile building for retailing, opening a new furniture store, Dunk and Bright, in downtown Syracuse). Ralph Murphy, now vice-president in charge of all Franklin engineering and manufacturing functions, brought in as Dunk's successor Lewis Purdy, formerly production manager of GM's Oakland Motor Division. The importance the company attached to the new appointment can be judged by the fact that Purdy's starting salary exceeded that of all other executives in the firm except H.H. Franklin himself! Purdy, a tall, rangy man with a somewhat caustic personality, arrived bearing the reputation of being a very tough person to work for, a title which he would quickly live up to. Longtime heads of the various production departments in the Franklin factory found their operating procedures subjected to sharp questioning by the new manufacturing chief, and in numerous instances incumbent supervisory personnel were replaced by individuals who more fully enjoyed Purdy's confidence. A number of the activities which had helped make the Franklin organization a pleasant place in which to be employed suddenly were terminated, including the company band and much of the athletic program. Plans gradually were developed for increasing the mechanization of production operations through the installation of more efficient, highly-specialized machine tools. In

Lewis J. Purdy had a reputation for being a touch and caustic production chief. (Franklin Automobile Company dealer's brochure)

THE FRANKLIN AUTOMOBILE COMPANY

addition, less emphasis now would be placed on such features of the Taylor System as use of impartial studies to determine a fair day's output for production employees, and more on pure and simple speeding up of job activity. In short, production approaches common to the giant Midwestern auto factories were introduced into the conservatively-run Franklin shops. The firm, however, continued to manufacture the majority of mechanical parts required for a Franklin car in its own plant, even though a number of items could have been purchased from outside suppliers at lower prices. This policy gave the company complete control over quality—a factor which it prized highly—but made it difficult in many instances to compete with other auto firms which placed greater emphasis on cost reduction.

Along with increased manufacturing efficiencies the company during this period also sought to strengthen substantially its methods of marketing the Franklin car. The United States Advertising Company of Toledo, Ohio, was retained as official "ad agency" for the Syracuse auto manufacturer, replacing a New York City concern used earlier. William Leininger, a vice-president of the Toledo-based agency known widely for receptivity to new ideas, now was to be the person primarily responsible for servicing the Franklin account. Leininger quickly established a close liaison with the Franklin engineering staff, reasoning that the advanced technology incorporated in the air-cooled vehicle, if presented effectively to the public, would be of decided help in selling the product. He further sought to update the heretofore somewhat bland advertising copy used by the Syracuse auto manufacturer with the goal of making it more eye-catching, especially to the 40-and-under age reader. The new advertising account executive also spent a substantial amount of time visiting Franklin dealers in the field, seeking to generate an expansion of traditionally underfunded local advertising budgets so that the marque's name might become better-known among potential fine-car-buyers.

Undoubtedly the most striking contribution made by Leininger, however, was the identification of the air-cooled Franklin vehicle with the exploits of the nation's new air hero, Charles A. Lindbergh. "Bill"

Leininger, himself a distinguished World War I combat flyer, as commanding officer in the mid-1920s of an Air National Guard squadron had befriended "Slim" Lindbergh when the financially-strapped young aviator needed assistance in rebuilding a damaged plane. Ultimately Lindbergh joined Leininger's air unit, later taking leave from it to undergo Army Air Force flight training at Brooks Field in Texas, which culminated in the airman receiving a reserve officer's commission. As a result of his fabulously successful solo trans-Atlantic flight from New York to Paris in May 1927, Lindbergh's name became known overnight throughout America. While the trail-blazing young pilot was relaxing in Paris after completing the historic journey, Leininger induced executives of the Syracuse company to offer Lindbergh

Colonel Charles Lindbergh, his pug, his Series 11 sedan with wire wheels, and the Spirit of St. Louis.
(Courtesy of The H.H. Franklin Club Library)

THE FRANKLIN AUTOMOBILE COMPANY

Lindbergh riding in a Franklin roadster during a visit to Ottawa in 1927. (Photos from the archives of the Canada Aviation and Space Museum)

the present of a Franklin car, and played a key role in convincing the youthful flyer–notably reluctant throughout his career to accept gifts of any importance for fear of being placed under obligation to the donor–to take the vehicle.[c] Lindbergh later visited Syracuse in mid-summer of 1927, and after receiving a 140-piece set of locally-manufactured chinaware as a memento of the occasion, was escorted throughout the city to a succession of functions by Franklin Company officials. On meeting H.H. Franklin, the young airman, as an acknowledgment of the gift of the car, presented the auto chief with a small piece of the outer "skin" of his famous plane, the "Spirit of St. Louis." In subsequent advertising the company pointed out in vigorous fashion that Franklin engines were cooled in a manner identical to the motor which successfully powered Lindbergh's plane in the across-the-ocean flight. Unquestionably company officials and dealers believed that this identification with aircraft technology would help make the Franklin car, as the lone air-cooled make among a host of water-cooled competitors, more acceptable in the eyes of the car-buying public.

For the H.H. Franklin Company to compete effectively with other auto manufacturers, it was compelled to bring to market at frequent intervals updated versions of its air-cooled passenger car. In January 1927, a "Twenty-Fifth Anniversary Model," incorporating a number of improvements and designated the Series 11B, was introduced at the New York Auto Show. A slightly roomier body with a wider rear seat was featured in the sedan, with narrow "clear vision" front pillars utilized in all closed-car styles. The engine, while unaltered in displacement, now incorporated a heavier crankshaft plus a redesigned intake manifold to provide a modest improvement in acceleration. Additional features included twin-beam headlights, a combination cigar lighter and inspection lamp, and counterweighted wheels with slightly larger tires.

---

c   Lindbergh used his Franklin sedan extensively during the next several years, particularly in courting his future wife, Anne Morrow.

Courtesy Allan Franklin Collection

While the new model represented a more advanced Franklin car, competing companies were by no means standing still. Progress in automotive development during the final years of the 1920s was spectacular, with each manufacturer periodically unveiling to the public vehicles with a variety of innovative features, often at prices sharply slashed from year-to-year. The Peerless firm had introduced a light six-cylinder car with an engine identical in size to that of Franklin, selling at half the cost of the air-cooled vehicle. The products of other auto manufacturers competing in the middle and upper-middle price ranges featured ever-larger engines, capable of developing substantial power and providing excellent over-the-road performance on the nation's constantly-upgraded highways. Practically all firms were emphasizing high top speeds, frequently seventy to seventy-five miles per hour, with at least one car builder claiming that its vehicles had achieved the almost unheard-of-pace of one hundred miles per hour in tests! These great increases in power and speed would be matched by improved stopping capabilities. Most manufacturers by this time had adopted four-wheel brakes, and sought to convince motorcar purchasers that their personal safety could well depend on the availability of this feature on any new vehicle.

Franklin engineers and designers thus found themselves compelled to continuously develop more advanced models which could meet the challenge of competing marques. A new 1928 line, labeled the "Airman" (a name obviously intended to exploit the similarity of the Franklin air-cooled engine to the power plant used in most planes), was introduced at the beginning of October 1927, well in advance of the forthcoming January 1928, National Auto Show. Mechanical changes in this vehicle, the Series 12, seemed almost revolutionary by previous Franklin standards. Four-wheel Lockheed internal hydraulic foot brakes replaced the transmission-based unit utilized on previous Franklins, and while the wood frame was continued on the standard 119-inch wheelbase car, a lengthened 128-inch chassis used for limousine bodies featured a steel understructure. The company was quick to note that the new steel-supported chassis incorporated only a few cross-members and thus offered substantial flexibility, but its use nonetheless represented a major shift in vehicle design.

Underneath the hood of the new model equally important advances could be observed. The displacement of the engine had been upped

THE FRANKLIN AUTOMOBILE COMPANY

The Franklin firm attempted to associate its Airman series of vehicles with Charles A. Lindbergh's trans-Atlantic flight, which also was powered by an air-cooled engine. (Courtesy National Geographic Magazine)

from the modest 199 cubic inches which had characterized Franklin power plants since 1916 to a more impressive 236. This increase had been accomplished by lengthening the stroke from four to four-and-three-quarter inches, while the bore of each cylinder continued at three-and-one-quarter-inches. Net engine output shot upward from the very modest thirty-three horsepower in the former Series 11 model to a much more robust forty-six. While weight of the vehicle increased substantially–the five-passenger sedan jumped from 3,320 to 3,600 pounds–the generous increase in engine power resulted in decidedly improved performance, both in terms of acceleration and maximum speed. Franklin cars at long last were capable of attaining speeds well in excess of sixty miles per hour! Upgrading of the cooling system by company engineers made possible the swift dispelling of extra heat generated by the more powerful engine. A host of additional power plant improvements–a fully counterbalanced crankshaft, chromium-plated piston pins, a redesigned pressure lubrication system, and a novel crankcase ventilator–insured durability and long-life for the new unit. All-in-all this innovative model, coupling increased power with the traditional Franklin qualities of precise handling and superb roadability, would be fully competitive with other makes as an efficient long-distance car. The under-powered, slow-moving Franklin of earlier years now remained only a memory!

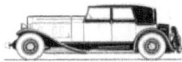

Introduction of the new Series 12 model produced a decided increase in Franklin sales during the final quarter of 1927. Fiscally this resulted in the firm achieving an operating profit during the full year of some $227,000, a modest improvement over 1926. However, the company once again had to contend with the payment of dividends of $423,000 on its outstanding preferred stock, resulting in a net charge to surplus of $196,000.[6-13] Quite obviously no payout to the holders of some 299,000 shares of common stock could be considered under these circumstances, thus this group for the sixth consecutive year saw no return on its investment. A number of other small auto manufacturers, however, fared far worse than Franklin, with the Moon Motor Company reporting a 1927 loss of $292,000, Paige Motors a deficit of $4,643,000 and Peerless a red ink figure of $726,000.[6-14]

Despite such unsatisfactory financial results on the part of certain of the lesser independent companies, plus the drop of some nine hundred thousand units in motor vehicle sales in 1927 from the preceding year (this decline largely was due to the long-lived Ford Model T reaching the end of the road, without its maker having a replacement vehicle immediately available), many motor car manufacturers confidently anticipated a major rebound in the automotive market as the year 1928 dawned. However, the group which would share in any such improved prospects was constantly shrinking–the total number of builders of passenger cars exhibiting new models at the January 1928, National Auto Show in New York City was only 43, exactly half the 86 companies which had displayed their products seven years earlier. Attrition among auto manufacturers thus continued at a frightful pace, with small independent producers almost invariably being the victims. As 1928 unfolded, however, and favorable economic conditions blossomed throughout much of the nation, many of the companies which had survived the shakeout found themselves doing very well indeed. A number of the larger independent motor vehicle producers, particularly firms in the medium-priced field such as Hupmobile, Nash and Hudson, had no problem earning highly satisfactory profits. An occasional smaller independent company which featured an attractive car line generating solid customer appeal–Auburn was an excellent example–also enjoyed prosperity. In the higher-priced ranges the Packard Motor Car Company of Detroit once again was the trailblazer. At the close of its fiscal year in August 1928, this firm reported the almost unbelievable profit of $21,855,000 on total sales of $94,677,000.[6-15] No other maker of prestige vehicles, whether independent or part of a conglomerate, found itself able to challenge Packard's continuing sales supremacy, although the Cadillac-LaSalle Division of General Motors, with two separate models to offer the public, was making a determined effort to do so. The Ford Motor Company's high-priced entry, the Lincoln, had been unable to match even the more modest sales level of Franklin.

Midway through the year the other upstate New York automobile manufacturer of consequence, the Pierce-Arrow Motor Car Company, was finally compelled to recognize that its position as a small independent builder of luxury-level motor cars had become untenable. The Pierce firm in August 1928, reached agreement with the good-sized independent motor car producer, Indiana-based Studebaker, on merger terms granting Pierce a substantial degree of continued autonomy, but enabling it to achieve manufacturing economies plus the opportunity for expanded sales through utilization of the far superior factory facilities and marketing network of the South Bend firm. Other merger developments saw the old-line Dodge Brothers Company acquired by Chrysler, thus marking the emergence of another powerful conglomerate in the automotive arena.

H.H. Franklin and his key associates determined during the early months of 1928 that the time had come for their company to make an all-out effort to improve its competitive position in the auto industry. In order to bring to the attention of the public in an aggressive manner the increased performance capabilities of the Franklin Series 12 car, the firm retained the services of the well-known over-the-road driver, Erwin "Cannon Ball" Baker. This renowned speed merchant had been utilized throughout the 1920s by a number of other motor car manufacturers to undertake performance and endurance runs with their vehicles (he even piloted the tiny, Syracuse-built motor scooter, the Neracar, from coast-to-coast!), and now was to perform a similar function for Franklin. Using carefully-tuned but otherwise stock models of the Series 12 car, Baker, a lanky, raw-boned man whose physical make-up seemingly enabled him to journey for days on end with little in the way of food or sleep ("He munched sacks of peanuts and drank endless jugs of coffee as he sped swiftly across America," later recalled a Franklin official), promptly set a transcontinental speed record for the Syracuse firm. This run was followed by numerous other record-breaking dashes from one city to another, which all-in-all should have dispelled any lingering belief on the part of the public that the Franklin was a stodgy automobile. These exploits were recounted by Baker himself–contemporary accounts describe him as a somewhat crude but effective speaker–to groups of Franklin dealers and salesmen assembled in Syracuse, with considerable enthusiasm generated as a result. Public attention was drawn to this succession of record-shattering runs through a series of advertisements prepared by "Bill" Leininger and placed by the company in a number of magazines of national circulation.

Baker's speed records coincided with the introduction of still another new Franklin model, the Series 12B Airman Limited, displayed to the public in the early summer of 1928. Power of the engine once again was upgraded modestly by an increase in the compression ratio plus refinements in the fuel feed system. Interiors of the new models were made more attractive by use of high-quality broadcloth upholstery and provision of folding center arm rests in the rear seats of all closed cars. The false radiator shell now appeared a bit more imposing thanks to an increase in the height of the vertical grille panels. While these improvements hardly could be considered of great significance, they did serve the useful purpose of keeping a freshly-styled Franklin automobile in the public eye. The advertising theme used to help market the new model, "Airman Limited–Luxurious Fast Travel," again emphasized the strengthened performance capabilities of the Franklin car.

Within the organization itself important steps were initiated to develop additional new Franklin power plants for use in future models. For some time rumors had been rippling through the auto industry that engines containing twelve cylinders arranged in a vee-shape (six on a side), popular during the First World War era but abandoned in the early 1920s by their initial developer, Packard, in favor of the more-economical-to-produce straight-eight motor, soon would be making a comeback in luxury-class vehicles. H.H. Franklin, apparently reacting to these reports and concerned that his small firm keep abreast of industry trends, directed the company engineering staff to begin the design of such a huge power plant. An aviation engine specialist, Glen Shoemaker, arrived on the scene to spearhead development work, and experimental versions of the multi-cylinder unit were produced and tested. The cost of manufacturing such a massive motor, together

John E. Williams served as vice-president in charge of sales activities for the Franklin organization. (Franklin Automobile Company dealer's brochure)

with concern about the extent of demand on the part of buyers, finally caused the company to place the entire project on the shelf for the time being. Of greater immediate importance, an effort by the Franklin engineering department to unleash the full performance potential of the tried-and-true six-cylinder engine also was initiated during this period. Franklin technical personnel led by research engineer Carl T. Doman developed an improved method of cooling, involving a blast of air being forced through the side of the engine and across the cylinders rather than from the top down. Experiments showed that this so-called side-draft system upgraded cooling capabilities sufficiently to make possible higher compression ratios and other motor refinements, resulting in vastly greater power output. Research engineers immediately subjected the new engine to a wide variety of field tests, with the intention of readying it for use in a stock vehicle at the beginning of the 1930s.

The new and more daring business approach adopted by the H.H.

THE FRANKLIN AUTOMOBILE COMPANY

Franklin Co. during 1928 went well beyond the introduction of speedier cars and development of more powerful engines. As the year neared its end additional major investments were made within the factory in improved production and assembly facilities, with the goal of enabling the firm to build, on a regular basis, some seventy or more cars per working day or nearly four hundred each week. A huge press capable of turning out fenders and similar large sheet metal parts was purchased, requiring that two floors of one of the manufacturing buildings be removed to permit its installation. Additional up-to-date machine tools also were ordered to increase the output of key engine components and other vital parts.

In another sector of company affairs it was announced early in September 1928, that John E. Williams, for the previous year-and-one-half merchandising and advertising counsel to the Franklin organization and earlier an executive of the United States Advertising Company of Toledo, the firm's ad agency, had been appointed vice-president in charge of all sales activities. This appointment promised to lend stability to a sales department which had continued to experience heavy turnover of top level staff in the years following the departure of Frederick Moskovics. A few weeks later the announcement was made that Raymond A. Dietrich, renowned as a custom body designer in both Europe and America, had become associated with the Syracuse firm as a design consultant. Clearly, attractive styling as well as brisk performance was to be given close attention in Franklin cars of the future! In addition, the company now had become interested in making its chassis available to firms producing custom bodies, with a number of such stylish vehicles appearing during 1928. On occasion such specially-fabricated units were displayed at exclusive salons across the country.

Finally, an early-summer news release by H.H. Franklin in the financial area produced major interest among the firm's shareholders and industry stock analysts. Citing the splendid cash position achieved by the company in mid-1928, thanks to what was termed "unprecedented buyer acceptance of the new Series 12 model," H.H. stated that the firm would share this prosperity with stockholders by resuming the payment of a dividend on the common stock.[d] A fifty-cent-per-share quarterly payout was made on July 20, followed by distribution of a like amount in October. H.H. Franklin thus appeared confident that his organization had turned the corner on earlier financial problems, and now could anticipate entering the ranks of those auto firms which enjoyed a continuing high level of sales and profits. [6-16]

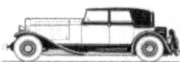

There was every indication that the great wave of automobile purchasing throughout the United States which had characterized the second half of 1928 would continue–and might well expand–as the year 1929 opened. Intense interest in new models offered by the various manufacturers was apparent, as large crowds packed auto shows held in cities stretching across the nation from Boston to Los Angeles. America appeared to be riding the crest of a totally unprecedented economic boom, accompanied by a seemingly insatiable demand for consumer goods of all types. The first few weeks of the year found automobile dealers throughout much of the country reporting increases of from six to twelve per cent in initial deliveries of new vehicles over a similar period in 1928. Motor car manufacturers quickly accelerated the pace of factory operations, with firm after firm boasting that all previous production records were being shattered. The Ford Motor Company stepped into full stride as its January output of cars and trucks reached a stunning total of 132,000, while at the other end of the price spectrum the Peerless Motor Car Company announced that a record 142 cars had left its Cleveland-based plant in a single day! Other luxury car makers claimed unprecedented levels of business, with Cadillac stating that January shipments were at an all-time high and Pierce-Arrow reporting the receipt of $3,000,000 in orders for immediate delivery. Employees shared in the boom, as numerous factory hands laid off in earlier times were rehired and substantial amounts of overtime work scheduled.

---

d The last dividend on common stock had been paid in mid-1921.

THE FRANKLIN AUTOMOBILE COMPANY

In early March Packard chief Alvan Macauley, recently elected president of the National Automobile Chamber of Commerce, announced a ten-per-cent increase in motor car business to date in 1929 compared with 1928, and predicted that this would be the best year ever in the industry. The Automobile Chamber's top executive further observed that the nation's highway improvement program now was encompassing 40,000 to 50,000 miles of new hard-surfaced road construction per year, thus helping increase demand for all types of vehicles including busses and trucks. Macauley also related that America's motor vehicle export trade, an important segment of the sales of numerous companies including Franklin, was achieving record levels.[6-17] Steel mills reported being taxed to capacity as they sought to ship sufficient full-finished sheets and other metal products to meet the voracious early 1929 demands of the automobile factories. The need for steel was intensified by the enormous increase in purchases of closed cars, with motor vehicle builders in the Franklin price class now producing over ninety-five percent enclosed models.

The H.H. Franklin Company at the very beginning of 1929 demonstrated an intent to share fully in this extraordinary wave of auto industry prosperity. On January 3 the Syracuse firm introduced a series of new models which clearly would give it the potential for far broader market penetration than ever before. Three separate lines were put on display for the car-buying public, ranging from the Model 130, with a new low price of $2,180 for a five-passenger sedan, through the medium-sized Model 135 and up to the long-wheelbase Model 137. A sedan in the Model 135 line sold for $2,485, while prices of the big Model 137 ran as high as $2,970 for a luxurious limousine. The smallest and lowest-priced car, the Model 130, utilized a six-cylinder engine identical in size to that of the 1928 Franklin, with a wheelbase extended slightly over the prior year's basic Airman Series to a full 120 inches. The two larger Models, the 135 and 137, shared a new motor (also six-cylinder) of 274-cubic-inch-displacement, some sixteen percent larger than any previous Franklin power plant. The senior-series cars featured wheelbases stretching to 125 inches in the Model 135 and 132 inches in the Model 137. In size and weight these

THE TEMPO OF THE TWENTIES

A 1929 Franklin Series 135 sports roadster (top) and a 1929 Franklin sedan (bottom). Rachael Mack, the Syracuse model shown in these photographs, was commissioned by the Franklin firm to appear in its advertisements.

two vehicles would be strikingly similar to other luxury cars of the period–and they also would have nearly as great a thirst for gasoline as their competitors! These larger models marked the end of the Franklin tradition of offering the public a light, economical, fine car. Such upsizing also meant abandoning another long-standing feature of the marque, the wood frame, as all three 1929 Franklin models shared a flexible steel foundation. A body style available later in the year was the "Speedster," an attractive model featuring a slanted windshield, racy overall appearance, and a high-speed rear axle. It was the creation of Franklin design consultant Raymond Dietrich, who produced several custom vehicle offerings for the company during 1929. Various other body builders also gave well-to-do purchasers of Franklin cars the opportunity to obtain desirable custom-styled products.

The junior Model 130, which incorporated a number of lower-cost components, undoubtedly had been designed to give Franklin dealers a series which could undercut other luxury-class automobiles in terms of price. Such a move on the part of the Syracuse firm may well have been strategically desirable in view of the steps taken by other makers of high-priced cars to seek an increased market share by offering ever-larger and more powerful vehicles to potential customers. This was typified by the action taken by the Packard Motor Car Company a few months earlier in replacing the six-cylinder engine in its junior model with a new straight-eight. Since Pierce-Arrow also had shifted to an eight-cylinder motor throughout its line, and the Cadillac, LaSalle and Lincoln automobiles utilized vee-type eighths, Franklin now would be one of the few American builders of prestige vehicles continuing to feature a lesser number of cylinders (two old-line producers of giant six-cylinder luxury machines, Locomobile and McFarlan, unable to dispose of more than a handful of cars annually, closed their doors about this time). This change by major competitors to additional cylinders might give Franklin problems in attempting to sell luxury-class cars to a public which tended to view big engines as desirable, unless some models of the air-cooled vehicle builder were offered at a cost saving. More intense competition for the Syracuse company also could be expected to come from a group of auto manu-

THE TEMPO OF THE TWENTIES

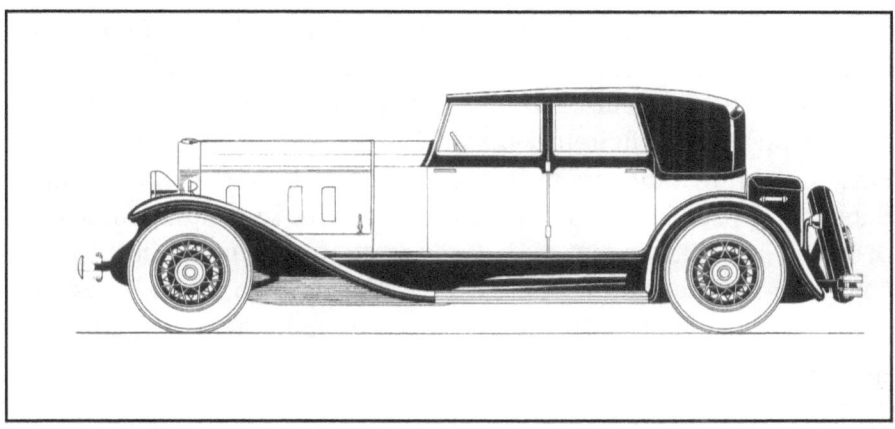

The 1929 Speedster was a custom vehicle designed by Raymond A. Dietrich, (Courtesy of American Automobile Manufacturers Association)

facturers which produced cars in a price range immediately below that of Franklin. Such well-known motor-car builders as Studebaker, Marmon, Graham-Paige and Auburn now featured recently-designed eight-cylinder models sufficiently impressive in appearance and lively in performance to cause many prospective car buyers to ask if it was necessary to consider purchase of a high-priced, luxury-class vehicle. Thus, while the 1929 auto market appeared to be virtually unlimited, it would be fought over every inch of the way by the various competing car firms. This meant that the ability of many manufacturers to achieve a decent profit on each car sold–important if firms were to maintain fiscal stability–would be tested as never before.

As the Franklin organization readied itself to do battle with its fellow auto makers for a satisfactory share of 1929 motor car sales, it first was necessary for top management to deal with the problem of funding what in 1929 was to become a substantially-expanded operation. Company production and sales in 1928, despite the proliferation of new models introduced, barely succeeded in matching levels attained by the firm in the previous two years. Profit from operations also was far from exceptional, reaching a total of only $589,000 for

THE FRANKLIN AUTOMOBILE COMPANY

the year. When preferred dividend payments of $400,000 were met, together with the reinstituted common stock payout of $299,000, the company actually incurred a "charge to surplus"–or in simple terms, a bottom-line cash deficit–in 1928 of $110,000.[6-18] This meant that the H.H. Franklin Company, during a year described by its president as outstanding, actually had been unable to achieve a significant profit on each car produced and sold. Even more important, the firm lacked any good-sized cushion of retained earnings which might be used to help fund the major costs which it faced in undertaking its ambitious new activities.

Under these circumstances the Syracuse company felt compelled to obtain outside funding to supplement its internally-generated working capital. Any one of several approaches might have been used to accomplish this, including the sale of additional common stock (it is possible that resumption of dividend payments in July 1928, was instituted in part to strengthen the standing of the company's common shares and thus improve marketability). However, while authority existed for the issuance of additional common or even preferred shares, a large amount of either would have had to be disposed of to raise the several million dollars the firm needed. Furthermore, such a sale might have taken a substantial period of time and involved large brokerage fees. In addition, issuance of new common shares could have resulted in a potential threat to H.H. Franklin's majority control of the firm. Instead, H.H. negotiated a multi-million dollar loan from a consortium of eastern and Midwestern banks (interestingly, no Syracuse lending institution was among the participants), confident that it could readily be paid back out of the firm's receipts over the next two years.

With the loan in place and essential funds now available, the company moved forward in an aggressive manner with its 1929 program. Additional factory improvements costing nearly $1,400,000 were undertaken–these basically involved upgrading of assembly facilities and installation of additional tools and machinery to bolster output rather than construction of any new buildings. Engineering research activities were expanded, looking forward to development of future

Franklin models. Equally significant, a major build-up of inventories (which had reached a low point at the end of 1928) was undertaken, in order to make possible heavy increases in production of each of the three lines of 1929 cars. In an effort to strengthen export sales H.H. Franklin and Frank Barton journeyed to Europe in February, touring Switzerland, France and England. The two men–who soon were followed across the Atlantic by engineering and manufacturing executives Ralph Murphy, Lewis Purdy and Ed Marks–sought to expand retail outlets for the Franklin car in important European auto markets.

The new models quickly began to pour off the Franklin assembly line in constantly increasing numbers. Slightly over 1,000 automobiles were shipped by the factory in January, with this figure swelling to 1,300 during the second month of the year. In early spring the company triumphantly announced that 1,566 cars had been built and sent to dealers during March, a gain of 140 per cent over the same month in 1928. Total first quarter output broke all company records, and actually was greater than the number achieved in the relatively sedate entire first half of the preceding year! This blistering pace of production and shipments by the modernized factory continued through April and May, with over 1,600 cars sent out in the former month and some 1,700 shipped in the latter. A slight tapering off was noted in June, but early in July the firm was able to proclaim that factory shipments in the range of 8,700 cars during the first half of 1929 were by far the highest in firm history. Franklin management kept assembly lines moving at a substantial pace through the summer months, traditionally a time when all auto manufacturers tended to reduce output sharply.

Up to the early summer period of 1929 the retail sales picture across the nation for the overall automobile industry was viewed by most knowledgeable persons as excellent, although a few observers, particularly Col. Leonard Ayres of the Cleveland Trust Co., expressed some degree of concern about heavy use of credit in the automotive marketplace.[6-19] While consumer purchases of cars in the early part of the year did not equal manufacturers' shipments to dealers (a not unusual condition in the winter period), overall momentum and the anticipation of large spring and early summer retail deliveries appeared to justify the enormous factory output of vehicles. By late May and early June, however, the expected swelling of consumer demand had not occurred, except in the very lowest price field. As a result, unsold cars were piling up in vast numbers on the lots of many dealers. This cooling-off in the retail market became even more apparent during the mid-summer months, with buyer resistance continuing to make itself felt, especially in the medium and upper-price ranges. Apart from the Ford Motor Company, which still was attempting to meet pent-up demand for its relatively new Model A automobile, the motor car industry by mid-August found itself compelled to slash production volume. Dealers early in that month reported the disquieting news that their stocks of unsold cars now were approximately seventy per-cent higher than in 1928, and saw no need to add to inventories.

As sales continued to weaken, further reductions in output on the part of nearly all manufacturers took place in September, with this trend continuing into early October. Certain ominous signs of a faltering economy now began to appear. Factory employment in industrial cities in states such as Ohio commenced dropping sharply, in many instances falling well below the level of a year earlier, with car sales in America's mid-western heartland also plunging downward. At this point a few of the more conservative chief executives of auto manufacturing companies began questioning current industry policies, with the president of the good-sized Willys-Overland firm in Toledo expressing a fear that production of automobiles clearly had become excessive in relation to demand and asking if this might not undermine the financial and credit structure of the country.[6-20] Then with horrifying suddenness came the stunning stock market crash of late October 1929, which shook the nation to its very foundation. Following this highly unsettling event it became clear that the vast rush to purchase automobiles was over for the present. Factory output in the entire motor car industry plummeted during the final two months of the year, with the December figure the poorest since 1921. Of particular concern to manufacturers of luxury cars was the fact that the proportion of 1929 sales in the $2,000-and-up category had fallen off from previous years.

Franklin retail sales in the year 1929 to a substantial degree followed industry trends. By mid-February they had reached a level well above that of 1928, and during the months of March, April, May, and June all previous records were broken. In July and August, however, retail deliveries tapered off, with the downward trend intensifying through the fall months and remaining weak to the end of the year.

By earlier standards the Franklin Company experienced a very good sales year during 1929–probably the best in its history. However, whereas in 1926, 1927 and 1928 output of vehicles had been tied closely to the actual volume of dealer sales, such was not the policy followed in the current year. From almost the very beginning of 1929 factory production had been accelerated to a level where it exceeded retail deliveries on the part of the Franklin dealer network by a substantial margin. H.H. Franklin, perhaps swept along by the optimism prevalent throughout much of the automobile industry during the year, decided that his company should schedule its operations to take full advantage of a seemingly unlimited boom. The excellent Franklin sales during the period from March through June in all probability reinforced H.H.'s belief in the basic strength of the market, and thus the company continued a high volume of output longer than many other manufacturers (General Motors, which more than most motor vehicle makers followed a policy of not overloading dealers with cars, apparently noted the danger signals and at a relatively early date in 1929 trimmed output to a level close to actual sales). This heavy Franklin production resulted in dealers frequently becoming substantially overstocked, with a number of the more cautious ones refusing to accept unordered trainloads of cars. Ultimately the surplus vehicles simply backed up in the distribution system, with the Franklin firm compelled to arrange for storage of many hundreds of cars either in Syracuse or elsewhere.

Total domestic sales of the Franklin car during the twelve months of 1929 were slightly under 11,000 vehicles. When an allowance of some 600 to 900 cars is made for export to Canada and other countries, dispositions reached a maximum of 11,800 vehicles. However, the factory produced over 14,400 motorcars during the year, which meant that output exceeded sales by 2,600 or more units (average annual output in the ten-year period 1919-1928 had been 8,747 vehicles). Obviously, such overbuilding could have serious consequences for the company when the end of the year arrived and a huge stock of unsold 1929 model cars had to be dealt with.

Apart from the sharp gap between production and retail sales, operations of the firm during 1929 featured a number of interesting highlights. Employment at the Franklin company, which had dropped from the lofty levels experienced earlier in the decade to the 1,900-2,000 range during the 1926-28 period (this meant that the Brown-Lipe-Chapin Corporation of Syracuse, now a division of General Motors, may well have nudged Franklin aside to become the city's largest industrial employer), rebounded to 2,600-2,800 in the year 1929, with overtime work also scheduled frequently in many production departments. This larger force of employees undoubtedly reflected the unprecedented volume of cars manufactured during much of the year. In November 1929, H.H. Franklin issued the extraordinary statement that not one of the members of that workforce need fear the uncertainties of employment in old age. Franklin pledged that in addition to the pension plan which had been in operation at his company since 1921, those workers not of pensionable age but incapable of filling more physically demanding positions in the organization would in the future be transferred to newly-created divisions where the objective would be to fashion the job to match the abilities of the man (H.H. did not specifically identify these "newly-created divisions"). Franklin further gave assurance that the wages of such persons would not necessarily decrease with the transfer, since earnings could be scaled to individual effort under the company's piece-work plan.[6-21] It is doubtful if at any time in the history of the motor car industry, a field of manufacturing well-known for both frequent general lay-offs and some degree of prejudice against the middle-aged and older employee because of a concern about his ability to meet demanding production

THE TEMPO OF THE TWENTIES

standards, such a pledge of job security for the more mature worker ever had been given.

The wise counsel obtained by the H.H. Franklin Manufacturing Company throughout most of its existence from the senior member of the firm's board of directors ended when seventy-four-year-old Alexander T. Brown died on the first day of February 1929. Noted inventor, pillar of the Syracuse industrial community for a generation or more, Brown as president of the Franklin firm during the early auto-manufacturing years had played an important role in its ultimate success, contributing both capital and a large degree of business acumen and technical know-how. His death, (fellow board member and local business leader A. E. Parsons also died a month or two earlier) left a significant gap in the policy-making structure of the company, and meant that H.H. Franklin more than ever would make key decisions. H.H. would be assisted by Ralph Murphy, now named first vice-president and general manager of the firm.

The year 1929 saw no let-up in the vigorous promotion of the Franklin car's image. The indomitable "Cannon Ball" Baker continued to "burn up" the nation's roads as he set additional transcontinental and other records in products of the Syracuse firm. In addition to demonstrating the endurance capabilities of the air-cooled Franklin in a series of runs up Pike's Peak, the lanky stock car driver succeeded in besting various crack trains–including the Twentieth Century Limited–in races from city-to-city. However, the major publicity coup' scored by the company took place off the surface of the earth! Apprised of the performance capabilities of the new side-draft engine being perfected by the organization's talented engineering staff, "Bill" Leininger proposed to Franklin top management that this potent motor be demonstrated in an unique fashion, through utilization for airborne flight! Following solution of certain vexing technical problems, on December 14 the motor displayed its prowess by successfully powering a standard Waco airplane in several flights above Dayton, Ohio. Once again Leininger and the company were able to obtain spectacular nation-wide publicity for the Franklin car through this unique demonstration of the extraordinary versatility of its well-designed motor.

The adaptability of the Franklin air-cooled engine for a variety of purposes was further demonstrated during the year by use in still another ancillary field, as a powerplant for combat tanks of the U.S. Army. It had been discovered in tests conducted during the First World War and afterward that operation of tanks as fighting vehicles placed exceptional demands on the engines powering these units. Literally every tank motor which depended on circulation of water to maintain an effective operating temperature at one time or another developed problems with its cooling system, resulting in the vehicle either breaking down in service or requiring an extraordinary amount of attention to keep it functioning. The chief testing officer for the Army Tank Corps, Captain George Rarey, consequently decided to undertake a thorough trial of an air-cooled engine in a standard light combat tank. H.H. Franklin, informed of the project, quickly offered to provide without cost to the government a Series 13 motor for a comprehensive series of tests. The air-cooled Franklin power plant, modified slightly by long-time Franklin engineers Carl Doman and John Burns to adapt it to this specialized use, was installed in the tightly-confined engine compartment of a small seven-ton army tank. It proved to be a highly-effective power source, passing all tests with ease and demonstrating its clear superiority to any water-cooled motor, particularly for hot weather operation. Impressed with the test results the U. S. War Department subsequently ordered six additional engines with the side-draft cooling system developed during 1929 by the Franklin engineering department. These new and powerful motors also easily outperformed their water-cooled competitors in an intensive battery of follow-up tests conducted during 1930.

As the year 1929 reached an end it was necessary for the firm to unveil to stockholders and the business community its fiscal status. The December 31 financial statement of the H.H. Franklin Manufacturing Company–actually issued early in 1930–contained information which appeared to be almost wildly contradictory. On the one hand H.H. Franklin could point to an operating profit after depreciation of

THE TEMPO OF THE TWENTIES

Close-up of the Franklin Series 14 engine installed in the Waco airplane in which it flew. Note the bell housing that was left on the crankcase assembly. (Courtesy of the late David T. Doman)

$1,282,000 for the year 1929 (roughly $90 per car produced), enough to meet a charge for preferred dividends of some $386,000, permit payment of the sum of $597,000 in common dividends (these were declared at the rate of fifty cents in each of the four quarters, thus reaching a total of $2.00 per share for the year), and still leave a net credit to surplus of $299,000. However, a careful examination of the firm's balance sheet disclosed a number of highly disquieting items.

Listed among the current assets was the sum of $4,622,100 for inventories, an increase from a year earlier of over $2,100,000. Even more important, some $1,685,000 of the overall inventory credit represented the value, at cost, of cars stored by warehouses or dealers on the final day of 1929. This meant that some 1,000 or more vehicles belonging to the company were in storage on the above date. In addition, the Franklin firm carried as an asset some $2,713,463 in sight drafts against bills of lading–in other words, charges to dealers for cars shipped by the H.H. Franklin Company which as yet had not been paid. It can be assumed that this large pool of vehicles for the most part were piled up on dealers' premises unsold–and that until they were disposed of the drafts would not be honored. The company balance sheet listed cash and marketable securities of just over $1,600,000, a decided drop from the December 1928, figure of close to two million dollars and an even larger decline from the 1927 level of nearly $2,300,000. The company thus was weaker in liquid assets than in immediately preceding years. On the deficit side of the ledger current liabilities included some $3,500,000 in loans payable. This represented the substantial unpaid balance of the loan made by Franklin from the consortium of banks very early in the year. Repayment of this sum could loom as a major problem for the Syracuse firm if future sales should fall and income sharply diminish. Other accounts payable had jumped from the figure of $1,240,000 a year earlier to $2,382,000, a stiff increase and undoubtedly indicative of a lessened ability of the company to deal with its bills in a prompt fashion.

The certified balance sheet of the firm contained two footnotes included by the auditors, both of which gave additional cause for concern. It was noted that the H.H. Franklin Manufacturing Company was contingently liable as endorser on certain dealers' obligations to banks in the amount of $1,428,000. This substantial contingent liability, a million dollars greater than in December 1928, again might result in trouble in any economic downturn which affected the fiscal stability of the dealer network. A second footnote stated that no provision had been made in the balance sheet for allowances that might be made to dealers after December 31, 1929 for the sale of 1929 models. This note made it all-too-clear that the big surplus of unsold 1929 model Franklins undoubtedly would have to be disposed of at a loss during 1930, with a potentially serious effect on the firm's fiscal position.

The end-of-the-year fiscal summary thus demonstrated that a record volume of business had not resulted in an improved financial position for the firm, in fact quite the reverse. The "clean" balance sheets of the previous two or three years now had been succeeded by one which, when examined closely, showed the firm substantially overextended, with a large short-term debt hanging over its head, thousands of 1929 model cars unsold, and various contingent liabilities existing. The H.H. Franklin Company would need an excellent sales year in 1930, coupled with careful attention to expenses, if it was to retrieve its former sound fiscal status. The abilities of the firm's top management staff, and especially those of its president, H.H. Franklin, soon would be tested as never before.

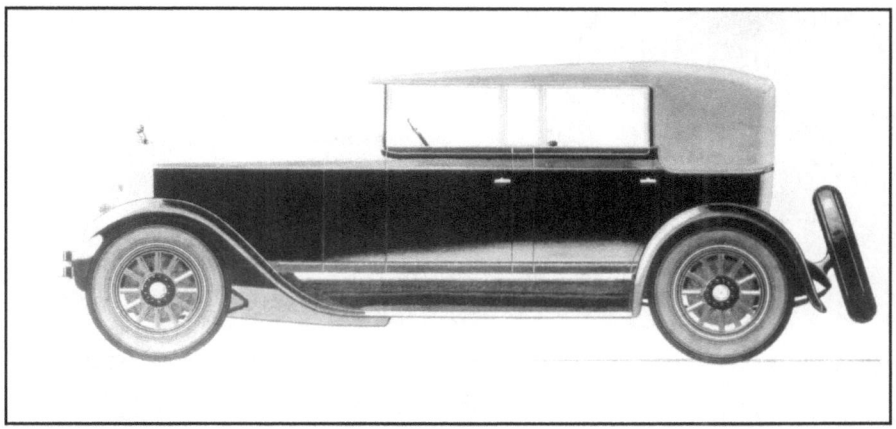

Series 12 Franklin convertible sedan with custom body, circa 1928. (Courtesy of American Automobile Manufacterers Associaiton)

THE FRANKLIN AUTOMOBILE COMPANY

– *Seven* –

The Years of Decline
(1930-1933)

The first day of January 1930, marked both the dawn of a new year and the beginning of the fourth full decade of production of the American automobile. It also saw the old-line H.H. Franklin Manufacturing Company, like other builders of motor vehicles, facing a cluster of vitally important questions affecting its future. The first and foremost of these related to the economy–would the devastating stock market collapse of the previous October trigger a general business recession of some magnitude, equal to or perhaps even worse than the sharp but blissfully short-lived set-back experienced by the nation and most auto manufacturers in 1920 and 1921? If recession or depression should come, and consumer buying shrink, what effect might this have on a massive industry which had experienced three decades of literally uninterrupted expansion and in the process revolutionized not only the transportation system of the country but most aspects of its social structure as well? Would the people of America still be able to maintain their usual travel patterns without the annual purchase of a very substantial number of new motor cars?

More specifically in terms of the Syracuse company, how might an economic slowdown affect a relatively small auto manufacturer such as Franklin, which increasingly was having to compete with three gi-

THE FRANKLIN AUTOMOBILE COMPANY

ant multi-divisional motor car companies, two (General Motors and Ford) long established, the third (Chrysler) a relative newcomer but quickly becoming a pacesetter in many areas of activity, particularly engineering? Could an independent builder of automobiles in modest numbers continue to exist alongside these huge concerns, with their vast financial resources, in a business where large-scale vehicle output and sales more and more determined the ability of a firm to earn a satisfactory profit? What effect might the relative geographic isolation of the Syracuse-based company, one of a tiny handful of motor vehicle producers still located outside the key Midwestern auto-manufacturing states of Michigan, Indiana, Ohio, and Wisconsin, have on its ability to compete with the balance of the industry? Would the total number of independent producers, already subject to heavy attrition during the decade of the 1920s, shrink even further in the years to come? Might any cut-backs in the level of consumer purchasing affect with particular severity the luxury car field, to which Franklin now almost irrevocably was committed? If Franklin's market should shrink for a time, could it ride out an economic storm in a manner which would enable it to move ahead with the next upswing in the business cycle?

The Franklin firm and its sister motor-car manufacturing companies pondered these questions with some degree of apprehension as they readied their 1930 models for unveiling at that glittering annual pageant, the New York Automobile Show. This early January event, held as usual at the Grand Central Palace in the very heart of New York City, featured displays of forty-six makes of passenger cars. This total was a trifle misleading, as a number of the marques exhibited actually were companion cars produced by well-known manufacturers–Marquette built by Buick, Blackhawk by Stutz, Erskine by Studebaker, Roosevelt by Marmon and Viking by Oldsmobile. Several of the companies participating in the show–Cunningham, Du Pont, Elcar, Gardner, Kissel, Jordan, and Moon–were producing cars in such insignificant numbers that they would be highly vulnerable to any reduction in overall demand on the part of purchasers of motor vehicles. Only two foreign builders, Voisin of France and Mercedes-Benz of

THE YEARS OF DECLINE

Germany, bothered to display vehicles at the general show, an indication of the almost total lack of interest by the typical American auto buyer in cars produced abroad. A few weeks earlier, several European luxury car manufacturers joined a number of top-drawer American makes (including Franklin) in displaying custom-bodied vehicles at a special show, the Automobile Salon. This exhibit, held annually for many years in New York and a few other cities across the country, was of interest primarily to a handful of patricians who sought only the finest in motor vehicles (attendance was by invitation only in New York City!).[7-1] In addition, the Franklin firm now displayed several highly attractive special body styles at its own "Salon" held (usually in dealers' showrooms) in a number of American cities.

Automobiles displayed at the general show featured a variety of mechanical improvements plus attractively-styled bodies which more and more incorporated the rudiments of streamlining. Unquestionably the pace-setter at the New York exhibition was the massive new sixteen-cylinder Cadillac, which would establish for upper-price-bracket vehicles a standard difficult for any competitor to equal.[a] The huge, multi-cylinder engine of this imposing motor car guaranteed extraordinarily smooth performance, with a lengthy 148-inch wheelbase insuring maximum passenger comfort and the syncro-mesh transmission plus vacuum-assisted brakes helping provide ease of handling. Other luxury motor vehicle manufacturers, while hard-pressed to match the sheer size and multiplicity of new features incorporated in this offering of the Cadillac firm, nonetheless displayed models which were intended to excite the interest of individuals willing to invest substantial sums in top-quality personalized transportation. The front-drive Cord automobile, actually introduced some months earlier, might readily appeal to those seeking the unconventional in a motor vehicle. This innovative car combined a unique method of propulsion through its front wheels with a body height reduced to an almost unbelievably-low sixty-one inches, close to a foot beneath the roofline of standard rear-drive machines. The powerful Stutz automobile of-

---

a   Somewhat ironically, Cadillac had begun automobile production almost 30 years earlier with a tiny, single-cylinder power plant, in contrast with Franklin's initial "four."

fered high-spirited, sports-car performance for the tiny minority desiring a vehicle which seemed better-fitted for the racetrack than the nation's typical narrow, winding highways. More conventional luxury cars such as Lincoln, Packard and Pierce-Arrow emphasized smooth riding qualities plus engines which, while only of an eight-cylinder variety, still could generate far more power than normally might be used in everyday driving. The long, stately bodies of these top-level marques reflected conservative good-taste, while their hand-crafted interiors featured the finest grades of upholstery set off by dashboards and window frames of highly-polished walnut or mahogany.[7-2]

The new 1930 Series 14 Franklin models, announced during the final days of 1929, incorporated a key mechanical feature which the firm's engineers had labored long and hard to perfect, the side-draft engine. This new motor, although still merely six-cylinders in size, generated 95 horsepower as compared to the 67 available in the senior-series Franklin line of the previous year, a huge increase in that era. The company boldly labeled the new unit an "airplane-type" engine, in reference to its utilization in powering the flight of the Waco aircraft late in 1929. Whatever name might be most appropriate to describe this innovative power plant, it enjoyed the unquestioned ability to propel the new Franklin over the road at the blistering speed of eighty-plus miles-per-hour. The car thus was as fast or faster than the majority of its competitors, and bore little resemblance to the sedate, low-powered vehicles built by the company a scant five or so years earlier, which struggled hard to reach even a sixty-mile-per-hour clip. With a heavy investment in this potent new engine the company found itself in no position to expend any large additional sum on chassis or body changes. An increase in rear spring length plus upgraded shock absorbers improved riding qualities, but apart from a few superficial styling changes–principally a redesigned false radiator shell incorporating glittering chrome external shutters and a slimmer profile–most bodies bore a close resemblance to those of the preceding year. One highly attractive model displayed by the company at the New York Auto Show was a convertible phaeton, named the Pirate. Designed by consultant Ray Dietrich it featured sleek streamlining and incorpo-

The sleek 1930 Pirate model Franklin, designed by consultant Raymond A. Dietrich, was displayed at the New York Auto Show. (Courtesy of American Automobile Manufacturers Association)

rated doors which extended far lower than normal, concealing the running boards. This vehicle, plus the earlier-introduced Speedster, kept Franklin very much in the forefront of advanced motor car styling.

A key difference between 1929 and 1930 Franklin models involved the abandonment by the firm in 1930 of its least-costly line of vehicles. The discontinuation of the trim, easy-to-handle Series 130, which had accounted for over fifty per cent of all company sales the preceding year, unquestionably surprised many people, particularly those in the dealer network. In all probability this decision was based on the fact that the junior-series, while priced several hundred dollars below the level of the larger Franklin models, was not appreciably less costly to produce and thus despite good sales may have contributed little to company profits. However, the elimination of this model plus a $100 per-car increase over the 1929 level in the prices of the two surviving senior-series vehicles resulted in Franklin no longer having an automobile available in or near the $2,000 range. The lowest-cost offering at the beginning of 1930, the Series 145 sedan, carried a factory tag of $2,585, placing it in the general price range of the LaSalle, the least-expensive Packard and the smallest Pierce-Arrow. Since the number of persons capable of purchasing a car dropped sharply as its price level rose, this meant that through its new policy Franklin had eliminated itself from consideration by a large number of buyers. Should the recession deepen to the point where incomes of middle and upper-middle-class business and professional persons were sharply affected, the marketing of Franklin vehicles could well become increasingly difficult.

As the new 1930 Franklin models went on display at the National Auto Show, the traditional company-sponsored annual luncheon for Franklin dealers was held at New York City's Commodore Hotel on January 6. Surprisingly, H.H. Franklin was not in attendance, but did send to the five hundred assembled sales personnel a cablegram of greeting from San Remo, Italy, where he was spending the holiday period with his sister, the recently-widowed Caroline Moser. The Franklin-powered Waco biplane which had been flown at Dayton, Ohio, was unveiled for the benefit of those present (due to adverse weather conditions, however, it had been trucked to New York). Both H.H. Franklin in his cablegram and company sales chief John Williams during a speech hailed the flights as demonstrating a significant affinity between the standard engine available in the Franklin automobile and air-cooled power plants used by the world's leading aircraft manufacturers. The well-known airplane designer, William Stout, was among the guest speakers, and after pointing out the importance of an interchange of ideas between the aircraft and automobile industries he noted that lightness in a motor vehicle was becoming recognized as important, and praised the long-standing Franklin policy of keeping bulk to a minimum. At the close of the meeting it was announced that Stout had joined the Franklin organization as a consulting engineer. Two overseas Franklin representatives attended the luncheon and the Auto Show, Frederick Blow of France and the Count of Torrubia from Spain.

The opening days of 1930 also were highlighted by an interesting article featuring a plea for better roads, written by H.H. Franklin and appearing in a newspaper of national circulation.[7-3] H.H., noting that persons in business more and more wished to use the powerful cars now produced by American automobile manufacturers for speedy, long-distance travel, observed that a genuine need existed throughout the nation for a highway system which would make such journeys possible. The air-cooled vehicle manufacturer felt that numerous business people would like to leave their offices late in the afternoon, drive swiftly on modern roads to another city some three or four hundred miles distant, and secure a restful night's sleep at a favorite hotel before arising refreshed in the morning to go about a full day's work. What would greatly facilitate such trips, Franklin maintained, would be the development of improved transcontinental express highways featuring separated, one-way traffic lanes, which would enable the motorist to speed along at sixty to eighty miles per hour with the same degree of safety as travel at thirty miles per hour could be undertaken on the narrow roads of the period. This article offered a splendid vision of a vast new national network of limited-access motorways, which ultimately would be built in America but unfortunately several decades after H.H. suggested such an approach in this pioneering article.

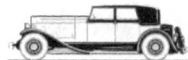

The critical problem confronting the H.H. Franklin Manufacturing Company in the early months of 1930 lay in the area of merchandising. The Syracuse firm together with its dealer network faced the formidable task of disposing of a large number of leftover 1929 vehicles, while at the same time seeking to stimulate sales of the new, high-performance 1930 Series 14 side-draft model. This dual undertaking would not be easy to carry out. The major improvements made in the 1930 Franklin power plant meant that the 1929 model now was a technologically-outdated vehicle, as well as a year-old chronologically. Very heavy price slashes might well be required to dispose of these cars, and in light of the number of vehicles involved the "clean-up" period could extend over many months.

At the beginning of 1930 a number of motor car manufacturers, including the H.H. Franklin firm, were encountering a backlash with respect to merchandising policies often imposed on their dealer organizations. The practice of "dumping" on dealers many more vehicles than could be disposed of under normal conditions, an approach used by numerous manufacturers during the second half of the 1920s and particularly 1929, while producing a short-term jump in sales also had resulted in the weakening of numerous retail outlets. Franklin, in early years quite careful to avoid overstocking, pushed excessive numbers of vehicles on many of its dealers and distributors through much of 1929, an action which produced resentment plus financial difficulties in the dealer organization. At least one important dealership closed its doors, and another switched to selling a different make of car during that year. Consequently, the Franklin firm in the opening months of 1930 was compelled to realize that it must rethink its 1929 policies. A large-volume producer of a popular motor car was in a position to drive its dealers hard, with the implied threat of replacing anyone unable to dispose of a specified number of vehicles with another who could. A small company such as Franklin, however, building an unique, high-priced car, could not gamble on having a distribution network with permanently impaired marketing capabilities. The air-cooled auto manufacturer's dealers in many instances had been with the company for a number of years, were known in their respective communities as representatives of the Syracuse firm, and could not readily be replaced, particularly in light of the traditional modest sales of the car. Furthermore, a big proportion of the Franklin dealerships were small-volume operations, with limited amounts of capital behind them. The company thus needed to work closely with its dealers in solving the overstocking problem, so that they did not collapse or turn in large numbers to selling other makes of vehicles. This was a common difficulty faced by many of the small independent auto manufacturers–the Cole Motor Company, before it went out of business a few years earlier, found itself compelled to provide direct financial support to a number of its weaker dealers.[7-4]

While the leftover stock of 1929 Franklin cars was substantially whittled down during the first six months of 1930 (a number were sold to

Franklin company employees at "fire sale" prices), the need to market so many previous-year vehicles heavily impacted sales of the new model, with the company soon required to adjust production accordingly. As a result, while retail deliveries of Franklin cars in early 1930 were strong, actually exceeding those made during the corresponding period a year earlier, factory output of the 1930 model totaled only 2,503 units from January through April, less than half the number of vehicles produced in the initial four months of 1929. The sharply-reduced sales level of the 1930 Franklin line continued through the spring months (a lower-cost "Transcontinent" sedan, introduced in May, failed to strengthen sales appreciably), resulting in the factory being placed on shortened work weeks. A substantial number of production workers found themselves furloughed throughout the first half of 1930, with few ever called back. Ultimately additional orders for cars were received (the "Speedster" model sold well during most months, with thirty delivered in May alone), and the company maintained a modest level of 1930-model production into the early fall. The experience, however, must have been a sobering one for H.H. Franklin and other key executives of the firm, who now had been forced to recognize that the company could be facing a far-from-bright future.

These marketing and production problems swiftly affected company finances, with the Franklin firm from the very beginning of the new year compelled to take steps to conserve its assets. Following a board of directors meeting held in Syracuse in January 1930, the announcement was made that the common stock dividend, paid on a quarterly basis throughout 1929, was to be suspended.[7-5] Worse was yet to come. With output of the 1930 models falling well below expectations as the year progressed and losses mounting, it also became necessary for the firm to consider eliminating payment of the dividend on its preferred stock. Despite concern as to the effect this would have on the general reputation of the company and on its standing in the financial world, such action ultimately was taken, with the final payout on preferred shares made on August 1. This was a stunning reversal of circumstances for a company which throughout 1929 had boasted of setting records in factory output and retail deliveries.

The H.H. Franklin Company was not the only automobile producer to experience difficulties in this period. As the year 1930 progressed it became clear that demand for new motor cars on the part of the public had slumped significantly from the 1929 peak. Manufacturers now were recognizing that the high-volume merchandising of 1929 models to a considerable extent had been achieved at the expense of future automobile markets. Sales of a number of firms held up well for the first few months of the year–as with Franklin, many of those retail deliveries undoubtedly involved heavily-discounted 1929 models–but by early summer a sharp downward trend became evident. At the same time general business conditions throughout the nation worsened and the stock market, which had enjoyed a moderate recovery from the late 1929 crash, once again began to fall sharply. By mid-summer many automobile firms decided to close their doors for several weeks in order to allow, in the words of some, an opportunity to take inventory and schedule employee vacations. More realistically, the shut-downs permitted the various companies to work off the excess vehicles stockpiled on their dealers' lots and start up again with a relatively clean slate. New motor car production, however, resumed at a decidedly lower level than in earlier months, and at little more than half the pace of the corresponding period of 1929.

Long before the end of 1930 certain trends were becoming evident that must have alarmed many of the small independent producers of motor vehicles. The so-called "Big Three"–General Motors, Ford and Chrysler–at this point were accounting for an ever-increasing proportion of the nation's total production of passenger cars. In 1925 some sixty-four per cent of all vehicles were built by the three conglomerates (Chrysler, of course, was a far smaller firm at that time), while during the first half of 1930 the figure had jumped twenty points to eighty-four out of each hundred. This meant that the large group of independents would battle over the modest sixteen per cent of the market remaining, hardly a pleasant prospect. This continuing fight over a declining market share already had hit the small producers hard–even the boom period of 1929 had seen their net earnings drop below the level of the previous several years.[7-6] Because of the exceptionally keen competition among the various motor car manufacturers, intensifying with the advent of "hard times" it was not possible for the small firms to raise prices to a degree sufficient to offset the drops in sales volume now being experienced. A few independent companies, particularly Packard in the high-priced field and Nash in the medium-cost range, had entered the 1930s with huge cash reserves, and thus could continue to be effective competitors for some time to come. The majority of the small auto manufacturers, however, were in far less-satisfactory financial condition, and might well find themselves pinched for operating funds if the sales decline continued. Tightened budgets also would make it more and more difficult for many independents to design and produce innovative new models which might appeal to the reduced number of persons still in the market for a new car, thus further endangering sales. Like Franklin, many firms during the euphoria of the 1928-29 boom had installed expensive new machinery or expanded their factories, and now were forced to contend with additional overhead costs.

As the second half of 1930 unfolded, a combination of adverse conditions in the United States plus problems arising internationally contributed heavily to the worsening prospects for sales of new motor vehicles. A natural rather than a man-made disaster during the period had severely injured the economy of much of the vast central heartland of the country. By the late summer of 1930 farm owners in a substantial number of states throughout the Midwest and Great Plains regions found themselves reeling from the effects of a widespread and long-continued drought. Agricultural districts in states such as Ohio, Illinois, Iowa, and Missouri reported crop losses in the hundreds of millions of dollars due to lack of rain, causing a severe plunge in purchasing power among both farm families and the many small-town business and professional persons whose well-being depended on a healthy rural economy.

Outside America one industrial nation after another, concerned about the shrinkage of jobs in domestic manufacturing industries caused by the deepening international economic slump, began to consider ways and means of limiting imports. At this point the government of the United States helped trigger such action by enactment of the ill-considered Smoot-Hawley Tariff Act of 1930. This legislation, adopted over the protests of a thousand American economists from one hundred and seventy universities who predicted that the act would produce bitterness in international relations and result in major injury to the nation's export trade, stiffened tariff barriers on goods entering America and thus invited sharp retaliatory steps by foreign nations.[7-7] Such action was not long in coming, as European countries with local auto industries to protect promptly raised tariff rates on imported motor vehicles in all price ranges, with some also imposing outright quotas. France and Italy were the initial leaders in this movement, but other nations were quick to follow. Even Canada, with an automotive industry closely related to that of the United States, ultimately joined in raising import duties so that Canadian workers hopefully might continue to be employed. The effect of these steps on American auto manufacturers, and particularly on the smaller firms which did not maintain foreign assembly plants, was severe, resulting in continuing attrition of important export markets. Franklin, which had appointed several new foreign distributors early in 1930 in the hope of expanding exports, was among those hit. The prediction of a number of industry leaders in 1929 that the market for automobile sales abroad literally was unlimited soon would have little meaning.

This swift reversal of years of extraordinary expansion by America's premier manufacturing industry affected all involved groups as 1930 wore on. Motor car firms now had to contend with ominous drops in demand, making it difficult to keep plants operating on anything like a profitable scale. The response to this problem by the typical automobile producer was to slash payrolls, particularly among the blue collar workforce, causing severe social effects. The difficulties encountered by the large number of laid-off auto workers in Detroit and other major motor car centers quickly became serious. No unemployment insurance of any type existed in the auto manufacturing field, as such

THE YEARS OF DECLINE

programs had been vigorously opposed by top executives in the motor car industry on the ground that they would impose an unfair burden on business. Thus out-of-work factory hands were forced to turn to their own usually limited personal resources to support themselves and their families. The federal government and most individual states at the time were totally unprepared to deal with the critical human problem of mass unemployment, and as a result many city governments found themselves compelled to fill the gap. In the early fall of 1930 Mayor Frank Murphy of Detroit[7-8] convened an emergency meeting of the chief executives of a number of auto and auto-related companies headquartered in that city to discuss what might be done to assist the many former auto employees now walking the streets. Direct relief to such persons appeared to be the only immediate answer, and various companies provided help with cash contributions. The retail automobile dealers, having entered the depression period in a none-too-healthy condition because of the earlier-described over-stocking of vehicles by manufacturers plus their own large investments in showrooms and other capital facilities, also were finding the going difficult. By the end of 1930 a majority were conducting business at a loss, with a considerable number simply closing their doors and ceasing operations. Such a reduction in local sales outlets resulted in further damage to the marketing capabilities of many motor car manufacturers.

Despite these critical problems besieging the motor vehicle industry and the people depending on it for their livelihood, use of the automobile, based on recorded gasoline consumption, actually increased in the initial depression year of 1930.[7-9] This meant that the desire to benefit from the convenience of the motor car continued unabated–what was lacking was the willingness, or more often the fiscal ability, to purchase many new vehicles. Automobile sales in America, which in the past had substantially outpaced increases in personal income, in this recessionary period were falling off far more swiftly than any drop in the overall income level. In short, major clusters of motor car customers were fast vanishing throughout the entire country. The nation's lower economic groups, who in the mid-to-late 1920s had begun to purchase motor vehicles in considerable numbers, now due to economic adversity no longer could continue to do so. Only a relatively lenient repossession policy on the part of lending institutions and other motor car financing agencies, which had no desire to be burdened with a glut of unsaleable vehicles, made it possible for many families who defaulted in time payments to retain the cars they had ordered in more prosperous times. The majority of individuals in the middle and upper classes had been affected less severely than those on the lower rungs of the income ladder, and thus for the time being were continuing to purchase a moderate number of new motor cars. However, should the economic recession continue to deepen, even these more advantageously-situated persons could be expected either to eliminate such purchases or reorient their buying plans toward lower-priced makes of motor vehicles. Firms in the motor car industry consequently might be required to modify earlier policies in merchandising and especially pricing of vehicles in order to survive.

As 1930 neared a close the Franklin firm found itself facing problems every bit as severe as those which confronted its major competitors. Demand for the 1930 model, despite its heavily-advertised "aircraft" engine and the wide range of body styles offered (including a variety of custom bodies), continued to be disappointing. In the early fall factory production was cut again from earlier levels, with numerous additional employees laid off. The company undoubtedly felt compelled to take these steps to prevent a repetition of its 1929 mistake of maintaining production far in excess of consumer demand, with resulting unpleasant consequences. Repayment date for outstanding bank loans was extended to mid-1931, as the firm lacked funds to meet these big obligations. A pay cut of ten percent was imposed on all salaried employees–justified, the company stated, by reductions in the current cost of living–with hourly rates of factory hands slashed proportionately (earlier in the year H.H. Franklin had denounced such wage trimming[7-10]). For the first time in years layoffs affected office employees, and even struck the engineering and technical staffs. The

THE YEARS OF DECLINE

> *Effective December 1, 1930, a 10% reduction in salary of all of the officers and salaried employes of the Franklin Automobile Company and the H. H. Franklin Manufacturing Company will be made.*
>
> *The Company regrets very much that business conditions have finally made this action necessary. Fortunately the cost of living has also been appreciably reduced this year.*
>
> *The Company is sure that the present conditions are but temporary and is confident of your continued loyal support.*
>
> Syracuse, N. Y., November 28, 1930.
>
> President.

This notice, signed by H.H. Franklin, told employees of a 10-percent salary reduction in late 1930. (Courtesy of Leo Gerst)

H.H. Franklin Company, which throughout much of the 1920s had offered employment each June to a number of new college graduates, no longer would provide such young persons with initial opportunities in the automotive field.

Of particular concern to Franklin executives was the fact that the company during 1930 had been less successful than several major competing makers of top-drawer cars in maintaining earlier levels of output. Packard and Cadillac, while experiencing a slackening of business from the boom period of 1929, still were enjoying satisfactory years, and Pierce-Arrow to a substantial degree was continuing its impressive 1929 comeback. In contrast, Franklin production had plummeted to less than half that of the previous year. The air-cooled vehicle builder was finding the new economic slowdown far more difficult to adjust to than the initial post-World-War-I slump of 1920-21. H.H. Franklin apparently did not feel his company could afford the trailblazing price cuts which it utilized so effectively to stimulate business during the earlier depression, presumably because income from auto sales during 1930 was down sharply and the firm deeply mired in debt. In addition, competition among all fine-car manufacturers in the early 1930s had become increasingly intense. Unlike 1921, when

THE FRANKLIN AUTOMOBILE COMPANY

Packard had not achieved the important status in luxury car sales that it later would enjoy, and Pierce-Arrow was offering an outdated vehicle, these two marques together with Cadillac-LaSalle and Lincoln now stood at the pinnacle of the fine car field. In several respects during the early 1930s Franklin found itself at a decided disadvantage in attempting to compete with other top-quality makes. While continuing to offer only a six-cylinder engine (by late 1930, Cadillac would provide purchasers with a choice of eight, twelve, or sixteen-cylinder models), and in the eyes of many not fully enjoying the high prestige of other luxury-class vehicles, it nonetheless charged near-top-level prices. Not too surprisingly, therefore, it was finding satisfactory sales figures increasingly difficult to achieve.

The Syracuse firm made every possible effort to fight back. Late in October it sponsored a novel show at its plant, primarily emphasizing military uses of Franklin products. Army personnel plus over two hundred company sales and distribution people attended the event. Exhibits included a seven-ton army tank, a new armored cavalry reconnaissance car capable of traveling fifty miles-per-hour, and a truck for airport emergency use, all powered by the basic Franklin air-cooled engine. One guest who attended, Captain George Rarey of the United States Army Tank School, noted that Franklin power plants had stood up well under armed services tests, and voiced a belief that their use would be extended. H.H. Franklin and other company spokespersons forecast a return to more normal levels of general business and automobile sales during the year 1931, and expressed confidence that an ever-widening acceptance of air-cooling by the public would provide excellent future prospects for the firm.[7-11]

Toward the end of November 1930, the Syracuse auto producer took an important step toward strengthening its top management structure. With considerable fanfare the company announced that Frederick J. Haynes, onetime manufacturing manager of the firm and subsequently president of both Dodge Brothers and Durant Motors, would rejoin Franklin as vice-president, general manager, and a member of the board of directors. On his arrival the big, bluff returning Syracusan expressed solid confidence in the future of the air-cooled car, and also voiced an optimistic belief that the auto industry would take the lead in overcoming the economic slump and returning the nation's business to another period of prosperity. Haynes unhesitatingly declared that a continuing increase in the number of cars in America was inevitable due to a growing population, better roads and more vehicles utilized by each family. The new Franklin vice-president looked forward to growth in the motor vehicle export business, stating that countries such as China awaited only an adequate road system to become a vast automotive market. Haynes urged dealers to continue to work hard, remarking that a selling approach incorporating confidence and courage would help dispel the existing panic and produce increased buying by the public.[7-12]

With the sharp drop in sales experienced by auto manufacturers as the second half of 1930 unfolded, several companies sought to strengthen

Frederick J. Haynes, former manufacturing manager at the Franklin firm, joined the automobile builder as a vice president, general manager, and a member of the board of directors.
(Dealer's Bulletin, *December 11, 1930)*

their competitive positions by accelerating the introduction of 1931 models. In the luxury-car field the Chrysler Corporation in mid-summer of 1930 announced its new eight-cylinder Imperial Series, replacing a previous six-cylinder version. Of striking design this vehicle incorporated a deep Vee-type radiator grille up front, while its robust 125-horsepower engine provided impressive performance. The 1931 Cadillac-LaSalle cars were introduced by this General Motors division a few weeks after the debut of Chrysler's new entry. In addition to rounding out its line with a twelve-cylinder model the Cadillac Motor Car Co. also managed to slash prices drastically, offering the LaSalle sedan at $2,295. Other fine-car builders, including Lincoln and Stutz, followed on the heels of these early leaders with their own upgraded vehicles. In almost every case the 1931 models featured engines of greater power than formerly, with prices often set at reduced levels. Another independent motor car builder, the Marmon Company, confirmed the trend toward huge multiple-cylinder offerings when it exhibited a new "sixteen" at the Chicago Automobile Salon in November. This technically-advanced vehicle, utilizing an aluminum-block motor and mounted on a 145-inch wheelbase, combined a superbly-smooth ride with a top speed of fully one hundred miles per hour. Not to be outdone, the old-line Reo Motor Co. of Lansing, Michigan, unveiled a luxury-class vehicle, the "Royale" featuring a big eight-cylinder power plant plus bodies of striking appearance. It remained to be seen, however, how such costly new entries would fare in a fast-declining fine car market.

The Franklin firm joined these competitor makes in the early introduction of next-year cars by displaying its 1931 offerings at the beginning of November 1930. The company's new vehicles, designated the Series 15, incorporated Transcontinent and DeLuxe models. The Transcontinent line, the lower of the two in price (with the sedan tagged at $2,295, it was directly competitive in cost with the LaSalle), utilized a 125-inch wheelbase chassis except for the seven-passenger, roadster and salon models. The DeLuxe and the larger Transcontinents featured an extended 132-inch wheelbase, with longer and wider bodies than those used in comparable 1930 models. Since the body also was

THE YEARS OF DECLINE

positioned a trifle lower, and a slanting windshield adopted for use in all closed types, the DeLuxe displayed an especially attractive appearance. Interiors of a more luxurious nature added a touch of sparkle to the new Franklin offerings, particularly in the DeLuxe Series. Both Transcontinent and DeLuxe shared the company's traditional six-cylinder air-cooled engine, now featuring a more efficient blower for cooling plus rubber pads inserted at the rear engine mounts to smooth out vibration. This power plant developed a full one hundred horsepower, and in the DeLuxe series was mated to a Warner four-speed transmission for greater flexibility of performance. The Franklin factory quickly swung into production of the new models, hoping that they would trigger a strong sales surge in the final weeks of 1930 and the opening days of 1931.

As the end of the first full year of the economic slump arrived H.H. Franklin submitted to stockholders his report on the operations of the company during the preceding twelve-month period, and outlined its financial status as of December 31, 1930.[7-13] This document did not make for pleasant reading. The firm's South Geddes Street factory had built a very modest 6,043 Franklin automobiles during all of 1930, a far lower number than in any year in recent company his-

The 1931 Transcontinent Pursuit model Franklin was a nicely styled vehicle that could compete with the LaSalle and other luxury cars. (Courtesy of American Automobile Manufacturers Association).

THE FRANKLIN AUTOMOBILE COMPANY

tory. While some 7,700 cars were sold at retail by the dealer network, the additional vehicles largely were 1929 models disposed of at huge discounts to bargain-hunters. A staggering operating loss of some $4,200,000 was recorded for overall 1930, a sum greater than the aggregate profit earned by the company during the previous half-dozen years. While the profit-and loss statement was discouraging, an examination of the year-end consolidated balance sheet revealed equally serious problems. Short-term loans payable to banks totalled $2,900,000, only modestly below the $3,500,00 owed at the end of 1929. This meant that during 1930 the firm had been able to pay down only a fraction of the large outstanding bank debt, which in a recessionary economy loomed more and more as an albatross around the neck of the Syracuse company. The amount due on the loans plus current accounts payable reached a total of just under $3,600,000. To offset such debts the firm was able to list only $750,000 in cash plus slightly over $950,000 in current receivables. While the H.H. Franklin Company also included among its current assets some $2,600,000 in inventories, this figure meant little unless the stock of parts and raw materials that it largely represented could be converted into passenger cars for which buyers might be found. The balance sheet also listed as a liability the sum of $454,000 placed in a reserve for contingencies, but such a step undoubtedly was essential in light of the declining value of many of the physical assets of the firm. A footnote to the balance sheet reported that the H.H. Franklin Manufacturing Company once again was contingently liable as endorser on dealers' obligations to banks in the amount of $905,000.

The December 31, 1930 fiscal report showed that the Franklin firm was facing a future which suddenly had darkened. While the company had major fixed assets in its plant and machinery–fortunately free from any mortgage–there was no way of liquidating such capital facilities to help improve its seriously weakened cash position. The firm now found itself in a dilemma which all independent auto producers dreaded–its working capital (current assets minus current liabilities) was so limited that the Syracuse auto builder's future scope of operations could well be severely restricted. Prices of common and

THE YEARS OF DECLINE

preferred stock of the H.H. Franklin Manufacturing Company at the end of 1930 reflected the firm's impaired fiscal position and dubious future earnings potential. Common shares were being traded at just over four dollars, with preferred bringing a price of some thirty-nine dollars.[7-14] These were sharp drops from levels earlier in the year, when the common sold for twenty-four dollars and preferred as high as eighty. Undoubtedly the firm's elimination of all dividends during 1930 injured Franklin stock values, as did a perception in financial circles that the Syracuse air-cooled vehicle manufacturer was "in trouble!"

Among the small-scale producers of motor vehicles Franklin found itself far from alone in experiencing a year-end financial statement containing vast quantities of red ink. Sales of pleasure cars by the independent auto manufacturing firms in the full year 1930 literally had collapsed, dropping to less than half the level achieved in 1929. For many of these companies such a plunge in volume of vehicles disposed of meant sharp operating losses, with an occasional auto builder near the point of closing its doors. A number of firms had attempted to continue the payment of dividends throughout 1930, undoubtedly hoping to keep the price of company stock from declining excessively, but in most instances such a policy simply resulted in a further weakening of the cash position of these concerns. With profits vanishing and balance sheets looking far less healthy than a year or two earlier, the survival of a number of independent auto manufacturers would be dependent on a solid improvement in car sales in the immediate future.

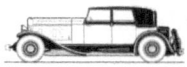

The year 1931 opened with predictions by many auto industry leaders that the discouraging year 1930 would be followed by a much-improved succeeding twelve months. Attendance at the numerous auto shows held across the nation was strong–"taking in" such events had become a tradition among many American households–and there appeared to be a fair degree of interest on the part of potential purchasers of motor vehicles in the new offerings of the various companies. A few firms slashed prices further, and nearly every motor car manufacturer could fairly claim that more value was being offered for the dollar than ever before.

However, as the second year of the economic slump unfolded it gradually became clear that the normal cycle of automobile sales experienced in the 1920s, when a down-year invariably was succeeded by one or more strong ones, was being shattered. The number of cars purchased by consumers in 1930 had dropped sharply from the peak year 1929; in 1931, after a brief upturn in the spring when the glittering new models together with pleasant weather brought a number of purchasers into automobile showrooms, the level of vehicles disposed of began falling in an even more precipitous manner. This ongoing drop in the rate of auto sales continued to exceed even the alarming slide in total income of persons employed in America. The number of unemployed, including blue-collar workers and now white-collar types as well, was mounting steadily across the nation from month to month. Persons in this unhappy position, as observed earlier, could not possibly be potential purchasers of motor vehicles, but equally important, the widespread publicity given to mushrooming unemployment figures tended to shake the confidence of many of those fortunate enough still to be working. The business and industrial sector of the nation thus continued to be sharply hit by an economic slowdown which appeared to have no bottom! Income of farm families fell further during early 1931, largely eliminating persons in this group as motor car buyers, while sales of vehicles abroad continued to decline, with only some fifteen high-priced American cars of all makes now disposed of each month in the entire nation of France.

The seemingly endless drop in total automobile sales at this point was accompanied by important changes in buying patterns of those who still were purchasing vehicles. Several manufacturers now had succeeded in developing cars which combined both attractive lines and powerful eight-cylinder motors, while carrying price tags in the one-thousand-dollar range. One of the leaders in this trend was an Indiana-based firm producing a medium-priced vehicle which in 1929 and 1930 had enjoyed a level of sales a trifle higher than those of Franklin. The Auburn Motor Car Company, a division of a small conglomerate put together by a relative newcomer to the ranks of top-level auto chiefs, brash, dynamic Errett L. Cord, introduced an automobile drastically redesigned for the 1931 model year. The new vehicle featured semi-sports car styling of a striking nature plus a high-performance motor, a combination which understandably appealed strongly to a public badly depressed in spirit by the economic slump. Equally important, the big, impressive Auburn sedan sold at the incredibly low price of $995. The Buick Division of General Motors also introduced a new series of cars incorporating straight-eight engines and attractive body lines, with the lowest priced model available at the modest figure of $1,035. Both the Auburn and Buick products sold in large numbers throughout the depression year 1931, and undoubtedly took away numerous customers from various higher-priced marques, including Franklin.

During the gloomy economic period of the early 1930s those persons still able to purchase automobiles in the middle and high-priced ranges more and more tended to choose cars capable of meeting basic transportation needs at the most reasonable possible cost. The social prestige factor, which without question played a major role throughout the 1920s in helping sell luxury-class motor products, now was shrinking sharply in importance. By 1931, a considerable number of upper-class families began to feel that in light of the nation's critical unemployment problem it might be indiscreet to appear on the streets in an ostentatiously expensive vehicle! This concern about "conspicuous consumption" would soon result in the almost total destruction of the market for custom-bodied vehicles, with the annual "salon" at which such high-priced motor cars were displayed shortly to fade out of existence (Franklin continued to promote custom body sales in 1931, with only modest results). In addition, the auto industry for several years had been encountering increased competition for the consumer dollar from a variety of products which promised to make life in the American home more enjoyable. The radio, introduced in the early-to-mid 1920s, now was selling in huge numbers as families discovered its entertainment value. The electric refrigerator had heavily invaded middle-class households, as had power-driven washing machines and portable vacuum cleaners. Undoubtedly by the 1930s a considerable amount of discretionary income which earlier might have been used for automobile purchases was being spent for these attractive new home-oriented items.

The Franklin firm continued to make every possible effort to sell its relatively high-priced products during 1931. Frederick Haynes, noted for his ability while chief executive of Dodge to work effectively with dealers, sought to shore-up the distribution network of the Syracuse company against the sharp inroads of a depression economy. Discounts to dealers were improved, thus giving them additional leeway in negotiating with prospective purchasers of Franklin cars. In the early spring Haynes took personal charge of all manufacturing operations of the company, accepting the resignation of Lewis Purdy as factory manager. Named to assist Haynes in the area of vehicle production was Frank Lederle, credited during the previous decade with having developed an outstanding service and spare parts division of the Franklin firm. Haynes and Lederle quickly developed an operating plan which would enable the company to achieve a profit on an output of only 6,000 vehicles annually. Efforts to publicize the merits of the air-cooled automobile continued, although the firm terminated the somewhat costly services of "Cannon Ball" Baker, who had gone far toward establishing performance supremacy of the Franklin car on the nation's highways. The company now utilized a well-known aviator, Captain Frank Hawks, on his numerous flights abroad to advocate the merits of the Syracuse product. Hawks, who had set a number of speed and distance records in the air, sought to convince potential luxury-class automobile purchasers in several European nations of the value of driving a motor car which incorporated a power plant similar in principle to those used in many of the world's leading aircraft. The firm also provided vehicles for Amelia Earhart, the nation's best known woman flyer, and continued to reap public relations benefits

THE YEARS OF DECLINE

*Famous aviator Captain Frank Hawks, who set many speed and distance records in the air, advocated Franklin cars because of their efficient air-cooled engines (*Dealer's Bulletin *September 11, 1930)*

The Dealers' Bulletin *of May 1931 boasted that famous flyer Amelia Earhart drove a Franklin car.*

THE FRANKLIN AUTOMOBILE COMPANY

The Franklin firm reaped public relations benefits from the use of its products by celebrities such as Charles Lindbergh. This photo of Lindbergh and his wife appeared in the Dealers' Bulletin *of May 1931.*

from the use of its air-cooled product by the person who now had become the world's most renowned aviator, Charles Lindbergh.

However, even these valiant efforts to market the Franklin motor car in this period of economic storm and stress met with only limited success. Weak retail sales figures in the opening period of 1931 were succeeded by a modest rise in customer deliveries starting in mid-February and continuing through much of April. As subsequent spring months unfolded, however, it became clear that the firm was encountering difficulties in disposing of a respectable number of cars, with new registrations dropping to less than half the level of 1930. A substantial number of these sales involved year-earlier models, adding to company problems. At the end of May automobile production at the Syracuse plant was halted completely to permit dealers to dispose of accumulated stock. This shutdown, give unexpectedly heavy publicity in auto trade journals, undoubtedly embarrassed the company, which in a hastily-issued newsletter reassured dealers that the firm was in sound condition and still shipping cars. The plant reopened some two and one half weeks later, but as sales during early summer

THE YEARS OF DECLINE

barely exceeded the three-hundred-a-month level the pace of operations was far from brisk. Franklin dealer bulletins continued to stress purchases of the car, including some custom-bodied versions bearing Dietrich, Brunn, Derham and other prestigious nameplates, by a variety of well-known persons in business, the entertainment world and the social register. However, sales of this nature were minute in volume and did not make up for heavy drop-off in demand for the product on the part of the typical upper-middle-class citizen.

In early July the firm celebrated the thirtieth anniversary of production of the Franklin car, also proudly noting that H.H. Franklin had retained his position as head of the company longer than any other chief executive in the auto industry. Unfortunately, with the weakened condition of the Syracuse motor vehicle builder at the time–its common stock now traded for a pitiful three dollars per share–the festivities were hardly as cheerful as at earlier commemorations!

By the late summer and early fall of 1931 the entire American auto industry had been compelled to realize that it was facing a crisis of major proportions. Sales of automobiles of practically all manufacturers not only were running well below the levels of 1930, which itself had been viewed as an unpleasant "off year," but now were dropping sharply from one month to the next. During this period fewer and fewer companies were operating in anything approaching a profitable manner. The independent concerns for the most part bore the major brunt of the decline in sales and earnings, with pressures mounting on those firms which continued to build vehicles solely in the luxury field. At this point even the long-prosperous Packard Motor Car Company began feeling the full effects of the decline and commenced operating at a loss, with Pierce-Arrow also sliding into the deficit column (these two concerns had managed to show respectable profits in 1930). The sales levels of such venerable independents as Peerless and Marmon were plummeting, with both companies encountering severe problems in paying current bills as the year progressed. Two old-line St. Louis-based motor car builders, Moon and Gardner, announced plans for liquidation, with a representative of the Gardner firm stating frankly that the reason for this step was the difficulty which a small independent auto builder invariably met in seeking to compete with big manufacturers. The Jordan Motor Car Company of Cleveland, whose sparkling advertisements had excited the interest of prospective automobile buyers throughout the nineteen-twenties, entered receivership, while the Kissel Company of Hartford, Wisconsin, sought to fight off petitions by creditors asking that it be adjudged bankrupt. A well-regarded Indiana-based manufacturer, Elcar, found itself compelled to close its doors before the end of the year, and the Durant Motor Company, which had sought without success to spur sales by importing a tiny French-built motor car, the Mathis, was encountering a variety of fiscal and other problems and nearing collapse.

Unemployment in the automobile industry continued to worsen as the second half of 1931 unfolded. The Michigan State Department of Labor reported that the number of workers employed in that state by auto and parts firms in mid-September had dropped from 183,000 a year earlier to 149,000. More important, the weekly wage of a factory hand now averaged only a very skimpy $20.94, a sharp cut from the $27.35 earned twelve months earlier.[7-15] While Michigan was perhaps the hardest hit, other states also reported stiff auto-related employment cutbacks. Two medium-sized Ohio cities closely identified with the motor car field, Akron and Toledo, were affected with particular severity. Akron, center of the rubber industry, was experiencing heavy lay-offs in its many plants which built automobile and truck tires, while Toledo, with several major factories involved in both motor car and parts production, now found that manufacturing employment had dropped nearly forty percent from the 1929 level.

In Syracuse, the diversified nature of the community's industrial base for a time protected the work force, but by the late summer and early fall of 1931 conditions had drastically worsened. The city's manufacturing employment index plunged from a level of 105 in mid-1929 to 66 by August 1931, with payrolls hit even more severely–here the decline in the same period was from 112 to 53.[7-16] Franklin employment, which had slumped from the 2,600 range attained in 1929 to

THE YEARS OF DECLINE

just over 1,500 at the end of December 1930, now had fallen even further and did not exceed 800 to 1,000 persons, many of whom were working only part-time. Additional slashes were made in the pay of all Franklin salaried employees at this time, with total reductions from 1929 levels now approximating thirty percent. The Syracuse firm was far from alone in taking such action–late in September 1931, the still relatively prosperous General Motors Corporation cut the pay of its salaried staff by ten to twenty percent.[7-17] The excellent level of morale which for decades had characterized the Franklin labor force now was fast declining in this period of wide-spread layoffs and stiff pay cuts.

Innovative attempts elsewhere in the industry to stimulate auto purchases met with little or no success. The American Austin, a tiny, fourteen-brake-horsepower vehicle modeled on a small British car and offered in 1930-31 at a price below that charged for a Ford or Chevrolet, sparked almost no serious interest on the part of those persons considering purchase of a motor car. Automobiles of unconventional design also were finding very weak acceptance in the marketplace. The front-wheel-drive Model L-29 Cord car was sinking into oblivion, while those few automotive firms which featured the sleeve-valve Knight engine in their vehicles either had closed their doors or, in the case of the Willys Company, soon would switch to a power plant using conventional poppet valves. The growing hesitancy on the part of the public to purchase motor cars in any way unconventional might well have given Franklin management serious concern at this point. One interesting potential solution to the auto industry crisis was offered by a MIT faculty member, E.C. Harwood, who suggested that new opportunities might be opened up through manufacture of what in effect would be a "disposable car." His plan projected the building of an extremely cheap, simple automobile, which would last perhaps 30,000 miles or two years, at which time it would be junked. Harwood felt that no effort should be expended to make the vehicle repairable, since this was "handcraft" work which was shockingly expensive and belonged back in the Dark Ages.[7-18] While this approach might well have stimulated new car sales–at the expense of thousands of repair shops–there is no record of any manufacturer ever considering the production of such a vehicle.

Other approaches to help solve the auto industry crisis were suggested by various public officials. The articulate Thomas McDonald, chief of the U. S. Bureau of Public Roads, pointed out in numerous speeches that major highway building performed the important depression-era function of alleviating unemployment as well as upgrading the nation's road system. The Federal government moved ahead aggressively in this area by appropriating an unprecedented quarter-of-a-billion dollars for use in highway work throughout America during 1931. At the state level the governor of New York, Franklin D. Roosevelt (soon to be heard from on the national scene), championed the cause of big public works projects and in particular sought to speed the construction of new motor roads throughout the Empire State. The auto industry applauded the funding of major highway improvement programs through gasoline and other auto-related taxes, but felt otherwise when such tax revenues were used for purposes unrelated to the motor car. State governments, however, desperate for sources of money to support schools, help pay for unemployment relief programs, and construct public buildings, often sought to achieve such a diversion. Equally distasteful to auto company leaders was a proposal by the Federal Department of the Treasury to reinstate some form of direct tax on the sale of new automobiles. The earlier World War I tax on pleasure cars as "luxury products" had been dropped in the late-1920s, and the industry with an almost unanimous voice objected to its return. Meanwhile, H.H. Franklin, in yet another article in a major newspaper, continued his well-worded pleas for the construction of super-highways across America, scientifically engineered and planned in a coordinated manner.[7-19]

On several occasions during 1931 the president of a major American business enterprise outside the automotive field proposed an approach under which all branches of industry would take major steps toward stabilization of employment.[7-20] Gerard Swope, who headed the General Electric Company, urged that industry organize into trade associations functioning under government supervision for the purpose of giving the best possible service to the public together with protection of workers. As a key part of this scheme Swope advocated industry-wide adoption of a program incorporating workers' compensation (for accidents), life and disability insurance, pensions, and unemployment insurance coverage for all employees. Such benefits were to be portable in nature, thus an employee might transfer from one employer to another with the benefits following along. Funding of such a program would be achieved through modest deductions from the paychecks of employees, plus matching contributions by employers. Swope astutely noted that consumption in America was by the mass of the people, not the few, and that if workers were to buy to satisfy their needs it was essential that they not only have adequate present income but in addition be given long-term security so that they might feel safe in spending their pay. Obviously Swope was seeking to deal with a psychological factor, the depression-generated fear of the future which had gripped Americans in the early 1930s and dried up purchasing of most big-ticket items. The General Electric executive concluded by expressing the opinion that stabilization of the employment relationship could be undertaken in a more uniform manner by industry-wide associations than by the various states or even the Federal government, but warned that if business failed to demonstrate forceful leadership society might well demand action by Congress and the legislatures, and once this occurred the power of taxation would have no economic restraints.[b]

Swope's proposals met with considerable skepticism, and a degree of outright opposition, on the part of auto industry leaders. Fear of any type of governmental intrusion through public-sector supervision of industry-wide trade associations raised the hackles of some, while

---

[b] Around this time, Swope joined two other titans of industry, Myron C. Taylor of the United States Steel Corporation and Walter C. Teagle of Standard Oil of New Jersey, in a series of informal meetings at which the trio sought to pinpoint the nation's major socio-economic problems and develop realistic solutions. Each was an innovative thinker and doer, as demonstrated by Taylor a few years later when he stunned the American business world and avoided a potentially bitter and even bloody strike by recognizing the CIO's (Congress of Industrial Organization) steelworkers' union as the bargaining agent for employees of the company he headed. These three forward-looking industrialists were products of elite and traditionally conservative Eastern universities–Swope was educated at the Massachusetts Institute of Technology, and Taylor and Teagle were educated at Cornell University.

others simply felt that each company had to work out its own destiny and that the very concept of all the units in an industry cooperating was impractical. While automotive executives in general believed that the best method of dealing with unemployment was through stabilization of the production curve, a number recognized, at least in theory, that they must accept some social responsibility for the well-being of their employees, and an occasional individual expressed willingness to seriously consider unemployment insurance when normal conditions returned. Certain of the more conservative auto industry chiefs, however, were of the opinion that workmen faced the same problems as companies–their wages were subject to the law of supply and demand, and if in good times they displayed thrift, lived well within their means, and planned for the inevitable bad periods they could survive until conditions improved.[c]

As a practical matter the grim times which the auto industry was encountering invariably resulted in a decided worsening of employment conditions for hands in the typical factory. Heavy slashes in volume of production made it increasingly difficult for manufacturers to operate in the black, and in an effort to control costs harsh policies often were adopted in dealing with labor. Even those fortunate enough to retain full or part-time jobs found employers now becoming increasingly demanding, with supervisors determined to wring every possible ounce of effort from workmen tending machines or assembling vehicles, and hourly pay rates cut to the minimum. The big auto plants in Detroit, Dearborn, Flint and Pontiac, Michigan, led the way in this drive for speeded-up, low-cost production, but certain of the factories operated by small independent companies joined in the trend. The highly competitive prices of the Auburn automobile clearly were achieved to a degree by a low-wage policy on the part of the company building this car. Lack of any organization through which workers could speak with a unified voice (the auto industry continued to pride itself on being almost totally an "open shop" operation) effectively kept

---

c   In fairness to automobile company management, there existed a genuine concern that the sharp peaks and valleys of motor vehicles sales–which no one in the industry felt could be readily stabilized in a highly competitive marketplace–would make it difficult for any company to fund directly a broad program of unemployment insurance and related benefits.

factory hands, however resentful, from objecting to such unpleasant conditions. However, should broad-based industrial unions ultimately develop in auto plants, it was not difficult to foresee the possibility of serious industrial strife occurring in the years ahead.

By the early fall of 1931 executives of the H.H. Franklin Company recognized that drastic action would have to be taken in an effort to stimulate the firm's pleasure car sales. Retail deliveries had continued at a slow pace, and the uninterrupted general slump in demand across America for new automobiles indicated little prospect of an industry-wide recovery. Franklin more and more was being hurt by building only a high-cost, luxury-class car in a period when demand for such products continued to dry up. The Syracuse manufacturer to date had failed to supplement its expensive basic models with a line of moderately-priced motor cars offering broadened sales appeal in a continuing weak economy. The firm also did not produce a commercial vehicle of any nature which might help its competitive position, and despite the high hopes generated by use of its air-cooled engine in army tank and armored car experiments the Franklin Company had derived insignificant benefits from military orders. Fewer than one hundred engines were delivered to the U. S. Army during the entire 1930-31 period, as budgets for all branches of the armed services were being slashed to the bone in a depression era.

Late in September 1931, the Franklin Company announced major price cuts in its twin lines of cars. The more costly of the two models, the DeLuxe, was trimmed three hundred dollars; the less expensive, the Transcontinent, a full five hundred (a special "trade allowance" had been extended to dealers a month or two earlier, forecasting the cut in prices). The lowest-priced Franklin now was available at under two thousand dollars, with the Transcontinent sedan tagged at the bargain figure of $1,795. A year or two earlier such price reductions might well have produced an immediate surge in purchases by consumers; in the very depressed automotive market of late 1931, however, the effect was far more modest. Other companies, equally desperate to shore up badly slipping sales, took similar price-cutting steps (Packard a few weeks earlier had lowered the price of its Eighth Series vehicles by several hundred dollars), thus the competitive position of Franklin was little changed. Retail deliveries of cars did improve in November to a level roughly equal to that attained during the stronger sales months earlier in the year, but while gratifying this hardly was what the Syracuse firm needed to improve its unhappy situation.

The month of November 1931, was to record incidents of vastly greater consequence to the company than a modest upturn in the sales curve. At the very beginning of the month it was announced that Frederick J. Haynes, who had joined the firm slightly less than a year earlier, now was resigning his position as vice-president and general manager together with his seat on the board of directors and returning to Detroit. No explanation was forthcoming from either Haynes or the company for this sudden departure, but it seems clear that the experienced former Dodge chief executive had reached the conclusion that salvaging the Syracuse auto builder was a nearly-impossible task. A key factor in his decision may have been an unsuccessful refinancing effort a short time earlier by former Franklin executive Horace Benstead. Benstead, now active in the investment banking field, had launched a plan calling for Franklin dealers and owners to purchase a new issue of securities in order to provide the now-financially-impaired company with fresh working capital. Benstead later related that this approach failed when the banking firms holding Franklin notes made the marketing of new securities unfeasible by declining to relinquish in any way their status as preferred creditors of the air-cooled auto manufacturer.[7-21] Failure of the Benstead plan meant that the Franklin firm no longer could hope for rescue by outside groups, and thus would be compelled to work out its destiny with whatever internal resources it could muster.

The eight lending institutions holding Franklin notes, located in cities stretching from Boston west to Chicago, in mid-1931 had joined together in a bank creditor's committee and negotiated a new agreement with the Syracuse firm. A key provision stated that in exchange for an extension of time for repayment of the notes the committee would be kept fully informed as to the status and condition of the auto company's affairs, in order that it might act in an advisory capacity in the interests of the banks. However, it was not to exercise direction or control of the management or operations of the company. Apparently taking a broad view of its authority under this agreement, the creditor committee moved swiftly to deal with the void caused by the departure of Fred Haynes. Within a very short time a person generally recognized as the committee's representative, Edwin McEwen of Cleveland, arrived on the scene at Franklin to assume the position of vice-president and general manager and serve on the company's board of directors. So much has been said through the intervening decades about McEwen and the role he played during his two-year stay at the H.H. Franklin Company that separating fact from fiction at this date is far from easy. Critics quickly charged the new vice-president with "not being an automobile man," but this allegation clearly was false. McEwen, an Ohio native sixty-three years of age when he joined the Franklin firm, originally entered the automotive field during the first decade of the twentieth century, becoming secretary and treasurer of the Cleveland-based F. B. Stearns Company, a pioneer auto manufacturer, in 1906. Shortly after affiliating with Stearns, McEwen worked with H.H. Franklin on a committee of auto industry executives charged with advance planning of motor vehicle shows sponsored by the old Association of Licensed Automobile Manufacturers; thus the two became acquainted at an early date. In the 1920s McEwen for several years served as general manager of the Velie Motor Car Company of Moline, Illinois, which manufactured a good-quality "assembled" automobile selling in the medium-price range.[7-22] Since both Velie and Stearns had gone out of business in the two or three years prior to McEwen arriving at Franklin, he quickly was dubbed "the undertaker," a man who buried sick companies. As no specific evidence exists that McEwen performed such a function at either Velie or Stearns, both low-volume auto builders unable to compete successfully in the marketplace even during the prosperous late 1920s, branding him with this title seems unfair. Undoubtedly a more serious charge which justifiably could be levied against the new vice-president was that he displayed a substantial degree of autocratic behavior, paying little attention to the views of long-time Franklin executives ("He operated by using the big stick," recalled engineering executive Ed Marks). In addition, McEwen and H.H. Franklin clearly did not work well together, with each at times seeking to countermand the other's orders. Such divided leadership obviously hurt the Franklin firm at a time when it needed the best possible cooperation on the part of its top executives if it was to have any hope of survival.

McEwen took drastic steps to slash costs immediately after his arrival. Apparently feeling that the large and highly-qualified Franklin engineering and design staff was an unnecessary luxury, he ordered the layoffs of all but a handful of technical people. The office force also found itself subjected to a similar drastic pruning. With personnel cuts accomplished the new vice-president then cast a searching glance toward the various firms which furnished the Syracuse company with key components. By far the largest supplier dollarwise was the Walker Body Company of Amesbury, Massachusetts, which for years had produced practically all auto bodies used by the H.H. Franklin Company. A close working relationship existed between the two firms, with much of the body design performed by Franklin drafters and consultants such as Raymond Dietrich, and a number of employees of the Syracuse company stationed in Amesbury to inspect finished bodies prior to shipment. McEwen at the end of 1931 negotiated a termination of the contract with Walker, which since Franklin was its only customer promptly closed its doors to avoid heavy loss. A considerable amount of machinery used in body-building then was purchased from Walker by the Franklin firm and moved to Syracuse in the early weeks of 1932. Henceforth, Franklin would manufacture its own bodies in some 52,000 square feet of largely unused space located on the top floor of the factory. A number of key craftsmen were brought to Syracuse from Amesbury and the Midwest by the air-cooled auto maker to work on the new body-building line; other essential personnel would be obtained primarily from the large pool of

The 1932 Franklin Airman continued to use the traditional six-cylinder air-cooled engine but added "supercharging." (Courtesy of Joan Doman)

unemployed people available locally. How the new approach might work in terms of quality of bodies produced was yet to be determined, but it enabled the Franklin firm to proclaim that factory employment was being increased by some 150 body-builders and thus had reached the highest level in months.

As the year 1932 began the H.H. Franklin company announced to the public a new line of automobiles, designated the Franklin Supercharged Airman. This series of vehicles continued to use the traditional six-cylinder air-cooled engine, unchanged in displacement from the previous year but now incorporating what the company described as "supercharging." The new system did not entail the addition of a fast-revolving blower to force an atomized gas-air charge into the cylinders, such as was used in the costly Duesenberg vehicle plus a few foreign cars, but instead merely involved channeling into the carburetor slightly-pressurized air from the fan-activated cooling-system.[d] It

---

[d] Franklin's claim of "supercharging" in its new model was regarded with amusement by the remain-

was claimed by the company that "supercharging" added to engine power and efficiency, resulting in improved acceleration in the slower speed range plus a greater top speed. The new Airman series also featured a three-speed transmission with synchromesh for easy shifting from second to high gear and vice-versa, plus a "free-wheeling" unit. This latter device could be employed at the driver's option in all three forward speeds, permitting the car to "coast" when desired and making possible gear-shifting without use of the clutch. The new Franklin offered its driver "ride control a unit operated from the dashboard which permitted a softening or stiffening of the spring action to obtain the type of ride desired. In addition, a Bendix "Startex" unit was incorporated in the new vehicle; this feature made possible starting of the engine by a simple turn of the ignition key and provided automatic restart in the event of a stall. Other minor technical improvements in the engine and drive line insured smoother vehicle operation, while a number of styling and related body changes increased attractiveness of the car and produced a more quiet ride. The new model incorporated the 132-inch wheelbase used on the previous year's DeLuxe model, with no counterpart of the smaller Transcontinent series offered. This meant that Franklin prices again ranged well-above the $2,000 level, with the five-passenger sedan selling at a factory price of $2,250. The new Franklin model was exhibited at the 1932 auto shows across the nation, where because of spectacular failure rates among auto manufacturers fewer firms displayed vehicles than ever before.

The various luxury-class motor car companies which competed with the Franklin firm also has taken vigorous steps toward the development of more advanced vehicles. The Packard Motor Car Company displayed at the 1932 auto shows two new cars with potential appeal to quite distinct categories of buyers. A light eight would sell at the spectacularly low price (for Packard) of $1,750, thereby sharply undercutting Franklin's cheapest offering, while a massive V-12 model– a reincarnation of Packard's famous "twin-six" of the World-War I

---

der of the industry. Edward S. Marks, chief engineer at the time, recalled that on visits to Detroit, technical personnel from other automobile firms invariably would greet him with somewhat sarcastic inquiries about the state of health of Franklin's device.

era–competed in a totally different range, with most body styles commanding near-$4,000 prices. Packard was only one of several luxury and semi-luxury-class auto manufacturers to enter the multiple-cylinder race. Lincoln, Pierce-Arrow and Auburn also brought twelve-cylinder cars to market, with Cadillac continuing to give upper-income purchasers a choice of twelve or sixteen-cylinder vehicles and Marmon again offering its massive "sixteen." Each of those firms also offered eight-cylinder models, a size of vehicle which level-headed observers of the 1932 depression scene might reasonably have felt would meet the needs of the now-pitifully-small group of luxury car buyers. Despite the chilly fine-car climate, however, only Chrysler among the more important manufacturers resisted the temptation to move into the twelve-cylinder-and-up class.

Undoubtedly feeling that its modest six-cylinder offering could not compete against these giants, the Franklin firm–which now meant its principal decision-maker, vice-president Edwin McEwen–decided to utilize the twelve-cylinder engine originally developed by the experimental engineering staff in the late 1920s. A few recently-laid off engineers and drafters were hurriedly rehired by the company for a

The massive 1932 Franklin V-12 was the company's answer to multiple cylinder vehicles introduced by other luxury car builders in early 1932. It sold for almost $4,000. (Courtesy of American Automobile Manufacturers Association)

brief period to complete design of the new vehicle. Initially the engineering department, which had continued updating the twelve-cylinder motor during the preceding three years, anticipated a mating of the big power plant with the traditional flexible Franklin chassis and body. Such an approach would have resulted in the new car incorporating both spectacular over-the-road performance and fine riding and handling qualities. However, even though several experimental vehicles of this type had been built, road-tested ("Cannon Ball" Baker had conducted tests of a "twelve" in Florida shortly before leaving the company), and even displayed to the public in New York in January 1932, the overbearing McEwen rejected the plan. Instead he directed the development of an enlarged version, mounted on a stretched-out 144-inch wheelbase and featuring a special series of bodies designed by LeBaron. Clearly he intended the new Franklin entry to be a motor car whose sheer size might overshadow the offerings of other luxury vehicle builders.

The new twelve-cylinder model, announced formally at the beginning of April 1932, contained both good and bad features. Its imposing 150-horsepower engine, with a piston displacement of a whopping 398 cubic inches, was velvet smooth in operation and offered the potential for impressive performance (such potential was increased when Franklin announced early in August that a new "Double High" rear axle would be offered as an extra-cost option to purchasers of the twelve-cylinder model). The car's LeBaron designed bodies for the most part were strikingly attractive, with the four-passenger club brougham, featuring a huge built-in trunk, clearly a style-leader. The vehicle was heavy, however, as great quantities of lead had to be used to insure proper mating of body components, and this factor combined with conventional semi-elliptic springing and ponderous axles meant that the new product to a degree lacked the smooth ride and lithe handling qualities traditional in Franklin cars. In addition, the vehicle's newly-styled bodies were constructed by the hastily-organized, in-plant Franklin body shop, often with less than happy results. Fit and finish on a number of the vehicles produced was of substandard quality, and numerous dealers and owners reacted with vociferous com-

THE YEARS OF DECLINE

plaints. The great speed with which the new Twelve had been brought to market so that Franklin might have a vehicle competitive with those produced by other top-drawer auto manufacturers also meant that little time had been available to correct the inevitable mechanical "bugs" which plague any new product. A major cross-country test drive had been taken by Franklin engineers Carl Doman and John Burns only a week or two before public introduction of the vehicle, and the peremptory fashion in which vice-president Edwin McEwen dismissed the concerns of those experienced technical persons about shortcomings in quality boded ill for the future reputation of the Syracuse firm's big machine. An equally important question facing the company was whether the new Twelve could be sold in anything like the volume necessary to amortize development costs.

The new Franklin products, along with the offerings of nearly all other surviving motor car companies, found pitifully few receptive buyers as 1932 unfolded. If 1930 had been a gloomy year for the auto industry, and 1931 even more unpleasant, the opening months of 1932 could only be described as catastrophic. Nearly every sector of the nation's economy was near-collapse, with banks failing in unprecedented numbers, basic manufacturing industries such as steel operating at the lowest levels ever seen in the modern era, and unemployment at record highs throughout America. Passenger car sales now inched along at barely one-fourth the pace of 1929, and of these an overwhelming percentage were of the three low-cost automobiles, Ford, Chevrolet and Plymouth. The factory prices of these cars ran only a trifle over five hundred dollars, giving the trio a decided advantage in the race for sales. Builders of vehicles in the medium-price class secured much of the balance of the new car market, leaving only a tiny fraction to those firms featuring upper-bracket models. Manufacturers such as Franklin and Pierce-Arrow continued to proclaim bravely from time-to-time that they were securing larger percentages of the fine-car market than ever before, but such boasts were meaningless in light of the insignificant total of luxury-class car sales.

With demand for the new Airman and twelve-cylinder models plunging to record lows by mid-1932, vice-president McEwen determined that if Franklin was to have any hope of survival the firm needed to invade the middle-price field. However, translating such a decision into reality would not be easy. The Syracuse company at the end of 1931 had closed its books on what had been another utterly demoralizing year. Output of motor cars had dropped to less than half that of 1930, with a pitiful total of 2,821 vehicles coming off the production lines. A somewhat larger number of retail sales was achieved, in the range of 3,900, but many of these involved vehicles of previous model years, sharply-discounted. Net company operating loss after depreciation was a very grim $2,424,000.[7-23]

The consolidated balance sheet offered no more cheerful news than the operating statement. While the amount of loans payable had been cut to $2,160,500, a reduction of some $740,000 from a year earlier, total current liabilities of the company were $2,387,000, in comparison to $1,569,000 in current assets. Consequently, the firm's working capital was computed at the negative figure of $818,000. At this point due to accumulated deficits the common stock of the Syracuse auto manufacturer had little or no book value. This was reflected in the price of Franklin common shares on the New York Curb Exchange, which traded at the abysmally low figure of one and one-quarter dollars at the end of the year 1931.[7-24] The company obviously was deeply concerned about the effect these disastrous fiscal statements would have on its public image; thus many months passed before they were released to the various financial reporting services.

With the company in a negative working capital position it obviously was essential that scarce current assets be conserved for basic day-to-day operations. The Syracuse firm consequently had little in the way of funds to spare for internal development of a new, smaller vehicle, and another approach would have to be taken. What was done at that point by McEwen was quite ingenious. In the summer of 1932 he entered into an agreement with the Reo Motor Car Company of Lansing, Michigan, for purchase of a number of that auto manufacturer's "Flying Cloud" automobiles, minus engine and grille. Franklin chief engineer Ed Marks plus a single aide were hastily dispatched to Lansing to design those parts required to mate the Franklin air-cooled engine to the Reo chassis, with this development work costing the cash-starved Syracuse auto firm only a few thousand dollars. The Reo cars then were shipped to the South Geddes Street factory where engines and a few other components necessary for identification of the vehicles as Franklins were added, and emerged as fresh "Olympic" models.

To a discerning eye the new medium-priced offering, introduced in October 1932, clearly failed to maintain the Franklin tradition. Smaller and lighter than any recent product of the company it did not incorporate the full-elliptic springs utilized in the six-cylinder Airman model, and its interior was decidedly more Spartan than that of the senior-series cars. However, the Olympic featured a trim, pleasing external appearance, produced outstanding performance (the 100-horsepower Franklin engine could propel the 3,500-pound vehicle at impressive speeds), and most important of all, carried a factory price tag for the lowest-cost model of only $1,385. Needless to say, the Syracuse firm made no mention of the origin of the new offering (its wheelbase was listed at 118 inches, one inch more than the 117 claimed by Reo!), stating only that the body had been built by Hayes. Initial sales of the vehicle were brisk, and while this pace did not long continue the small profit earned on each unit disposed of was highly acceptable to the company, which continued to suffer heavy losses on production of its two larger, slow-selling models.

The willingness of the Franklin firm to risk the loss of some degree of prestige in bringing out a medium-priced car of blended ancestry was typical of the approach of the American auto industry as it reached its absolute nadir during the year 1932. Only four auto manufacturing firms–two conglomerates, Chrysler and General Motors, plus a pair of independents, Auburn and Nash–declared dividends during the first half of the year, and each of these companies was compelled to dip into its reserves to make such payments. Few motor car companies wished to discuss their employment pictures, with Auburn being an exception–in mid June the Indiana-based firm announced that some 700 hands had been recalled to help produce its twelve-cylinder model (this vehicle, priced at well-under-half the cost of similar Franklin, Pierce-Arrow or Packard "twelves was enjoying a respectable level of sales). The modest degree of prosperity being experienced by the Auburn firm was almost unique among the remaining small independent producers–at this point most were in desperate trouble, constantly struggling to raise cash to pay current bills and almost uniformly lacking the funds needed to develop new models.

Total registrations of all privately-owned passenger cars in America had declined by nearly 700,000 at the end of 1931 and would fall by an additional million-and-a quarter in 1932, the first time in the history of the American automobile that such drops had occurred.[7-25] Even the big multi-divisional auto firms now were taking serious steps to consolidate operations and eliminate units which did not pull their weight. At the end of 1931 General Motors had streamlined its Oakland-Pontiac division by terminating the Oakland nameplate; only the Pontiac vehicle now would be offered. In the first half of 1932 the giant conglomerate established a Buick-Oldsmobile-Pontiac unit, thereby hoping to reduce marketing and other costs for these medium-priced vehicles. General Motor's drive to economize harshly affected the city of Syracuse and its inhabitants. In 1932, GM president Alfred P. Sloan announced plans to transfer to the company's Flint, Michigan factories all Syracuse-based operations of the corporation's Brown-Lipe-Chapin division, which for decades had been a leading producer of automotive gears. The Syracuse community could take no pleasure in the reasons bluntly cited by Sloan to justify this plant closing–first, that it was more economical to manufacture gears at a location central to the auto industry, and second, that taxes in Syracuse were substantially higher than those in the typical city in which GM operated.[7-26]

The year 1932 saw total pleasure car sales drop to an average figure of under 100,000 per month.[7-27] While the big-volume manufacturers obviously were severely impacted by this horrendous decline, unlike most independents they nonetheless could lay their hands on the funds required both to develop new models and modernize their factories. The Ford Motor Company led the way early in 1932 by introducing for the first time in the history of the auto industry a low-priced eight-cylinder car. Its arch-rival, Chevrolet, answered with an attractively-styled 1932 model, and late in the same year the Chrysler Corporation announced that its 1933 Plymouth was to be enlarged from four to six-cylinders, and that the price of the new "six" would be less than that charged for the previous "four." This type of cost reduction could be accomplished only through the many millions of dollars which the aggressive, skillfully-managed Chrysler Corporation was able to expend in efficient new plants and labor-saving machinery. Such investment was matched by General Motors as it readied its 1933 models for introduction. The GM divisions producing medium-priced cars–Pontiac at the low end, Oldsmobile in the middle and Buick at a bit higher range–offered to prospective purchasers a variety of attractive new designs coupled with generally lower prices. In an era when the buying public had become highly-conscious of dollar-value offered in an automobile–hardly surprising, since per-capita income in America by the summer of 1932 had shrunk to roughly one-half of that enjoyed in 1929–such freshly-styled, moderate-cost vehicles would offer devastating competition to other makes, particularly to the dwindling number of independent producers. With General Motor's Pontiac unit offering a new 1933-model eight-cylinder sedan at a factory price of under $700–made possible by utilization of a number of components produced in huge volume for other GM divisions and by building the car in part on several Chevrolet branch-plant assembly lines–not many families could justify the payment of perhaps twice this sum for a product of one of the independent firms.

The H.H. Franklin company struggled through the fall of 1932 and into the year 1933, continuing to make every possible effort to keep afloat. The die-casting division of the concern, H.H. Franklin's initial venture into the manufacturing field, largely had been disposed of early in 1932 to Precision Castings Corp., of Syracuse. Late in the same year, as a condition for further renewal of the air-cooled auto manufacturer's short-term notes (Franklin had totally ceased making payments on these obligations) the creditor banks obtained an assignment of the firm's interest in property owned by the subsidiary Syracuse Land Development Company. This included the good-sized tract on the northeast side of Syracuse originally acquired as a factory site for production of the ill-fated Franklin four-cylinder car. H.H. Franklin from time-to-time sought new financing sources for his company, but investors generally were in a state of shock induced by the depression, and not inclined to consider risking money in a small, off-the-beaten-track automobile builder.

Production lines of the company ran intermittently through late 1932 and early 1933 to fill the sprinkling of new orders which trickled in. Employees assembling vehicles could expect to be paid only when the line was in actual operation, but in order to preserve their jobs often were required to report on a daily basis. On a slow day workers who traveled some distance on the interurban trolley would be fortunate to recoup travel expenses. By April 1933, total company employment had dwindled to a mere 236–which meant that less than one out of every ten persons on the company payroll a few years earlier continued to have a job. The assurance given by H.H. Franklin in late 1929 that no one in the firm need fear unemployment in old age thus came back to haunt him in this bitter era. Heat and light in the Franklin plant were cut to a minimum (visitors commented on its gloomy appearance), such items as broken toilets went unrepaired, and no soap was furnished in the washrooms.

The engineering department, once the pride of the Franklin firm, had been totally dismantled. Executive engineer Robert Lay left in mid-1931 when his position was eliminated. Senior body designer Kent Haven, seeing little need for his talents in a cut-back period, joined another Syracuse firm at about the same time. Research engineer Carl Doman resigned in the very early days of 1933; his departure was followed by that of chief engineer Ed Marks a month or two later. Such outstanding technical people as John Burns, the company's key troubleshooter, and Leo Gerst, long-time head of the drafting room, found themselves dropped from the Franklin organization. The status of vice-president Ralph Murphy had been sharply downgraded to that of assistant manager during the Fred Haynes era; soon afterward he was dropped completely from the executive staff. Beginning in 1932 H.H. Franklin and other top executives served largely without pay (they may have taken promissory notes for salary due them). The firm at this point was unable to meet municipal taxes levied on its property and also fell behind on paying state taxes; these overdue charges soon would amount to a substantial sum. Membership in such a key local business organization as the Syracuse Manufacturer's Association was abruptly terminated by the company, obviously for financial reasons.

In November 1932, the citizens of America rejected the continued leadership of incumbent president Herbert Hoover and chose to place the future of the nation in the hands of Franklin D. Roosevelt, the personable and articulate governor of New York state. To a considerable degree the now unpopular Hoover undoubtedly had been made the nation's scapegoat for the depression. His views hardly were as reactionary as often has been thought–at the very beginning of the economic slump, in 1930, he pleaded with business leaders not to cut salary and wage rates, noting that this simply would destroy purchasing power and insure a business setback turning into a full-scale depression. However, with unemployment in mid-1932 reaching the horrendous level of fifteen-million persons–one out of four normally employed Americans–few were willing to give Hoover an additional opportunity to stabilize the country's economy. The interregnum between the November 1932, election and the inauguration of the new president in March 1933, saw a continuation of the depression accompanied by a collapse of many of the nation's financial institutions. The banking crisis began in Detroit, where the threatened failure of one of the city's major trust companies resulted in Governor Comstock of Michigan declaring an eight-day "bank holiday." The Detroit-based automobile companies were compelled to take the lead in reorganizing the shaky banks in the nation's auto capital in order to have local financial institutions able to process payrolls and business checks as well as to prevent the total destruction of confidence in the banking system on the part of local citizens. As the fiscal crisis spread across America a national "banking holiday" was proclaimed quickly by the new president upon his taking office. Since the nation's credit system literally ceased to function, auto manufacturing operations everywhere came to a near-standstill in early March of 1933.

The lesser automobile firms located outside Detroit at this point were in no position to provide assistance to sick banks in their own communities—most of them now found themselves involved in a day-to-day struggle to stay alive. Early in 1933 two of the leading independent motor car companies, Willys-Overland of Toledo and Studebaker of South Bend, Indiana, were compelled to go into receivership. Willys, which had encountered heavy operating deficits since 1929, saw its production rate drop over 90 per cent in three years and was deeply indebted to banks and parts suppliers. The final blow came when the firm lacked cash even to pay its workers. The Studebaker receivership, which stunned the auto industry—the firm had been viewed as a rock-solid, well-managed entity—also was triggered by heavy bank loans and large accounts payable to suppliers. Studebaker until recent years had earned excellent profits, but at this stage of the depression its inability to market successfully a low-priced car hurt it badly. Fortunately for the South Bend firm several capable receivers, including Paul Hoffman and Harold Vance, managed to continue production while the underlying financial difficulties were resolved; thus the company ultimately was able to climb back on its feet. The disaster, however, resulted in Studebaker's chief executive, the well-known Albert Erskine, taking his own life. Willys-Overland's problems would require more time for resolution, but ultimately this firm too was to succeed in staying afloat.

Such continuing attrition among the independent producers had one clear-cut effect, the even greater centralization of the automobile industry in southeast Michigan. By 1933 auto production in Cleveland, a city once second only to Detroit as a motor vehicle center, essen-

THE YEARS OF DECLINE

tially had ceased. The last of the Cleveland-based firms to close its doors, the old-line Peerless Company, was to see its plant converted to production of beer and ale when the nation voted to end prohibition.[e] Indianapolis, formerly an important automobile town, also lost its principal motor car company as Marmon ended production. Another of that city's well-known auto firms, Stutz, struggled to build an occasional car for an additional year or two, while elsewhere in Indiana the Auburn Company now was experiencing swiftly-declining sales of its once-popular semi-sports cars.

In New York State the Rochester-based Cunningham firm had terminated its tiny output of very costly pleasure cars, although continuing in the ambulance and custom body business. Famed luxury vehicle producer Pierce-Arrow of Buffalo, having taken advantage of the Studebaker debacle to regain its independence, still built annually a limited number of big sedans, town cars and limousines. Only the Wisconsin-based Nash Motor Company remained relatively healthy, displaying an extraordinary ability to earn a modest profit through much of the depression despite sharply falling sales. Even in Michigan independent auto firms, regardless of size, found it difficult to continue marketing a respectable number of pleasure cars and achieve anything resembling profitability. Sales by the Hupp, Hudson and Graham firms had dropped precipitously from earlier levels; the aristocratic Packard Motor Car Company in most years was compelled to draw on the cash surplus built up in the pre-depression era to fund its activities; and the Reo Motor Company of Lansing found its production dwindling to a paltry three or four thousand units annually. Fortunately, Reo also produced a popular line of trucks whose sales helped stabilize company finances.

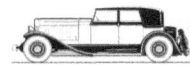

Whether sparked by a series of vigorous steps taken by the new ad-

---

[e] Peerless had built clothes-wringers and bicycles in the 1890s, prior to entering automobile manufacturing.

ministration in Washington to deal with the nation's economic crisis (even the stock market caught fire and achieved a respectable gain!), or simply due to the fact that many aging vehicles were wearing out, the late spring period of 1933 finally saw a modest turning of the tide in the American automobile industry. New car sales in May showed a measurable increase over earlier months of the year, and the upward trend continued in June. This surge in purchases of new passenger cars across the nation was confined entirely to those vehicles having factory list prices of less than $750, however. Sales of cars tagged at $750 or more actually dropped sharply during the first six months of the year, confirming the fact that the lower-cost automobile more and more was dominating the motor vehicle market.

This decisive shift in the pattern of automobile acquisitions by consumers toward vehicles with modest price tags was reflected in the continuing downward trend of Franklin sales. Retail purchases throughout America of vehicles built by the Syracuse-based auto manufacturer had dwindled to just over 1,800 units in all of 1932, less than half the 1931 number. This downturn continued as 1933 unfolded, despite the availability through the entire winter and spring of the more moderately-priced Olympic series. Budgetary constraints had precluded the Franklin firm from restyling its vehicles in January 1933 (the Series 16B Airman received one or two insignificant modifications); thus the cars offered during the previous year were continued for the present. The financially-strapped company also did not schedule its annual January Auto Show luncheon for sales personnel at New York City's Commodore Hotel, for years a traditional Franklin activity. Perhaps at this period of company history H.H. Franklin, never at ease before an audience, had little desire to attempt to strike a spark among a generally disheartened group of dealers and salespersons. Prices of senior-level cars were trimmed somewhat, however, as the 1933 selling season got under way. The Airman now carried a price tag of $1,935, a bit below the level of such competing makes as Packard, LaSalle and Pierce-Arrow (Packard somewhat surprisingly had abandoned its lowest-priced "eight"), while the big 12-cylinder Franklin was reduced a full $1,000, and now sold–in the club brougham and five-passenger sedan models—for as low as $2,885.

Financial reports for the year 1932 were not released by the Syracuse auto firm until June 1933. The reason for this tardiness became all-too-apparent when the income statement and accompanying balance sheet of the company were examined. Franklin had suffered a $1,127,000 operating loss in calendar 1932, with total cash on hand as of December 31 of that year the tiny sum of $47,000.[7-28] Company stock prices were dismal, with common shares trading at a fraction of one dollar, and preferred at just over four dollars.[7-29] The decline in number of vehicles sold thus was severely affecting the firm's financial status. Sales levels of other luxury motor car manufacturers also were dropping nearly as fast as those of Franklin, but at least two competitors, Cadillac and Lincoln, were far better positioned to ride out the financial storm. The Cadillac firm had the massive resources of General Motors behind it, while Lincoln could draw on the still substantial reserves of its sponsor, the Ford Motor Company. So long as such well-funded parent firms displayed a willingness to underwrite deficits, those two upper-bracket marques could continue production. Franklin, having no similar source of assistance, could hope only for a renewed interest on the part of the once-numerous group of quality car purchasers to aid it in returning to fiscal health.

With operating losses continuing unabated during 1933, the H.H. Franklin Manufacturing Company once again found it impossible to repay any part of the large short-term debt it owed the group of creditor banks, an obligation which now had been on the books for over four years. In early June a number of holders of good-sized blocks of preferred and common stock of the company, concerned about the dismal fiscal situation, sponsored formation of a committee to seek readjustment of the Franklin firm's financial and capital structure. The key members of the committee, Ernest B. Warriner, a New York City financier, C. Everett Bacon, partner in Spencer Trask & Company, a New York investment banking house, and B.C. Milner, Jr., chief executive of manufacturing companies located in Syracuse and Toledo, Ohio, contacted 6,000 Franklin common and preferred stockholders by mail, requesting that they deposit their stock certificates with a New York City bank under provisions of an agreement giving the committee the legal right to move forward with its work. The three-member group anticipated submitting a plan for readjustment and refinancing to the shareholders by early July 1933, or at such later date as would be agreeable to the bank creditors.

As this committee sought to deal with the H.H. Franklin Company's vexatious financial dilemma, the firm turned its attention to the development of updated models for the balance of 1933. In early July, a new Olympic series was introduced, featuring a modernized appearance through use of skirted front fenders, restyled bumpers and headlamps, and a redesigned instrument panel. These styling changes were accompanied by a variety of mechanical improvements, including a stiffened frame, rattle-free springs, and enclosure of the freewheeling unit in the transmission. The upgraded Olympic model was followed some two months later by the announcement of a new Franklin Airman line, denoted the Series 19. The key feature of this senior six-cylinder car was the adoption of bodies similar in many respects to those utilized in the twelve-cylinder model. Skirted fenders, rear-quarter and back panels incorporating broad, sweeping curves, lowered doors and a false radiator shell of deep-vee design helped modernize the car's appearance, while use of non-shatterable glass throughout enhanced the safety of the vehicle. A somewhat less pleasant feature of this new model was its price, which jumped to $2,185 in the lowest-cost sedan, an increase of some $250. Early in October the announcement was made that the Olympic series price-tag also would be nudged upward by some fifty dollars. Sales of Franklin cars, weak in the early months of the year, improved during the June-September period to a more respectable level.

While the rising cost during mid-1933 of many parts and supplies which were used in the manufacture of automobiles undoubtedly provided ample justification for these Franklin price hikes, the emergence of another factor made the timing of the increases unfortunate. One of the key features of the "New Deal"–the program President Franklin

D. Roosevelt unveiled to lead the country out of the worst economic slump in its history—was the National Industrial Recovery Act, popularly called NRA. This legislation sought to stabilize industrial production and to a degree also alleviate what understandably was felt to be the unhappy position of factory workers in the depression era (payrolls in the auto industry, despite the mid-1933 recovery, were one-third those of 1929). Together with other fields of manufacturing the automobile builders were to be required to adopt an industry-wide code governing practices in a number of areas, with substantial emphasis on hours worked by employees and wages paid them. The basic automobile code was submitted to President Franklin D. Roosevelt late in August 1933, and swiftly approved by him. In its initial form this new act did not deal with the subject of trade practices, particularly retailing of motor vehicles, but early in October 1933, a supplemental code covering this area was approved. Among its provisions was a formula for determining the allowance to be made by a dealer for the used car traded-in by the typical purchaser of a new vehicle. Such trade-in allowance hereafter was to be sharply limited—it could not exceed the average price paid by a purchaser at retail for such a used vehicle in a specified market area. Since dealers who handled expensive makes of automobiles almost invariably followed the practice of granting "long trades" on the cars turned in by customers on new vehicles, they were severely affected by the new regulation, with the purchaser of a high-cost car now compelled to pay a decidedly stiffer price than before. The net result was that many persons who in the past purchased top-drawer motor cars would have still another reason to consider vehicles in more moderate price brackets. Packard, Cadillac, and Pierce-Arrow, together with Franklin and other luxury-class vehicle builders, all found themselves adversely affected by this restrictive rule.

The year 1933 closed with the H.H. Franklin Company still fighting desperately for survival as a going concern. Total sales for the year of all three series of cars—Olympic, Airman and Twelve—in America reached some 1,330 units, with a handful of additional vehicles exported to other countries (curiously, the tiny Netherlands led all other nations on the European continent in Franklin sales). The company as a side business also provided a modest number of air-cooled power plants for customers such as the U.S. Army and the Davey Air Compressor Company of Ohio. However, despite fair success in marketing the Olympic model–disputes at times with the Reo Motor Car Co. over the number of units to be delivered to Franklin apparently limited availability of the Olympic to customers–the overall level of activity was not nearly adequate to enable the firm to break even financially. As a result, the Syracuse auto builder was compelled to announce another substantial operating loss, $819,000, for the 1933 period. Company assets listed at the end of the year, apart from land, buildings, machinery and inventory, largely consisted of some $41,000 in cash and $61,000 in accounts and notes receivable. The debit side of the balance sheet included the huge loan still owed to creditor banks, some $2,163,000, plus $400,000 in general accounts payable.[7-30] During a brief period in the summer of 1933 the firm managed to meet its bills for parts and supplies on a timely basis, but by the end of the year it again was far in arrears. Franklin stock on December 31, 1933, traded at pitiful prices–below one dollar for common and a fraction over a dollar for preferred.[7-31]

The condition of the Syracuse auto manufacturer thus was indeed grim as it prepared to enter the year 1934. A sprinkling of shop employees–mostly long-term hands who at one time held supervisory positions–continued to assemble a tiny number of cars in the largely deserted South Geddes Street plant, while a handful of clerks dealt with paperwork in the front office. H.H. Franklin and other top management personnel hung on, undoubtedly hoping that some new development would enable the firm to "turn the corner," but any such expectation had little basis to support it. With the continuing trend toward lower-priced vehicles even the Olympic series now was out of the range of the great majority of American new car buyers. Once again, failure of the company to market any type of vehicle in the $1,000-or-under price class told heavily against it. At this point there was no possibility of the firm developing a lower-cost car internally–it could muster neither the fiscal resources nor the engineering talent necessary to achieve such a goal.ᶠ In addition, with the Syracuse company lacking funds to purchase new machine tools since the inception of the depression four years earlier, its manufacturing methods now were decidedly inferior to those of its Midwestern competitors. Thus there appeared to be scant hope for improvement in the firm's status during the months ahead, even if the motor vehicle industry as a whole continued to enjoy a resurgence in sales. The nation's longtime air-cooled vehicle builder was nearing the end of the road.

---

f   The firm had made intermittent efforts during the 1931-1933 period to develop an en-bloc eight-cylinder engine, which might have lowered manufacturing costs and resulted in Franklin cars becoming more competitive in price. Such endeavors were abandoned because of limited availability of working capital.

THE FRANKLIN AUTOMOBILE COMPANY

– *Eight* –

The Demise of the Company
(1934-1940)

As the year 1934 opened the American nation eagerly sought to detect a few rays of light shining through the still gloomy economic overcast. During the preceding nine months the Roosevelt administration had launched one experimental program after another in a desperate effort to alleviate poverty and get the country back on its feet. A hastily-planned initial effort by the new President and Congress called for direct assistance to the vast number of citizens with no jobs and no resources, with over three-quarters of a billion dollars spent under the Federal Emergency Relief Administration to keep such destitute persons and their dependents from starving. Late in 1933 the Civil Works Administration was set up to pay the unemployed modest wages in exchange for labor on a variety of public projects, some useful and others admittedly of little more than a make-work nature. At the same time state and municipal governments were urged to move ahead quickly with federally-subsidized capital improvements, including highway and street upgrading, utility line extensions, park and playground development and even the building of airports. Such construction programs would put people to work and, it was hoped, also provide new facilities for community use.

In early 1934 the city of Syracuse was as badly in need of economic rejuvenation as any medium-sized municipality in America. The community's once-strong industrial base had been dealt a devastating series of blows by the great depression, with one firm after another severely affected. A few plants were totally closed, with many others operating at only a fraction of their normal pace. The area's labor force, particularly the big segment involved in manufacturing, was suffering from massive layoffs. Auto-related employment, standing at the 4,000 level early in 1930, had fallen to a pitiful 200 four years later. The depression held a viselike grip on the community, with the newly-elected mayor, Rolland B. Marvin, reporting to the board of directors of the Syracuse Manufacturers Association in the early spring of 1934 that 11,500 families or a total of approximately 50,000 persons in the municipality were receiving some form of direct relief, a huge number in a city with an estimated population of just over 200,000.[8-1] Whole sections of local newspapers were filled with notices of liens placed against both residential and business properties for non-payment of taxes. A year or two earlier the municipal government had decreed that married women on its payroll were to be dropped in favor of men, the rationale being that one paycheck per family was all that could be allowed in these grim times!

Both conventional and offbeat approaches were adopted in the Syracuse community to deal with the problem of severe unemployment. One of the most ingenious was termed the "man of the block" plan, under which persons in a local area who still held jobs each paid a small stipend per week (usually a half-dollar or dollar) to an unemployed neighbor in exchange for performance of useful services. The out-of-work individual kept the walks and driveways in the block cleared of snow, carried containers of garbage and trash from houses out to the curb, and even ran occasional errands for those families who compensated him. The large number of one-time Franklin factory workers now laid-off and unable to find employment with other companies sought to deal with adversity in many different ways. The relatively small group of individuals who had been test drivers and skilled mechanics probably fared best, with a number of them opening garages at which they serviced Franklins and other makes of cars. Persons

THE DEMISE OF THE COMPANY

living in the country who had been seasonal Franklin employees also adjusted well, the majority simply becoming full-time farmers. Urban dwellers with no special abilities other than those directly related to automobile manufacturing found the going more difficult, with many of them having to settle for a variety of part-time, "fill-in" jobs to keep their heads above water. At the bottom, numerous persons dropped by the Franklin firm simply wound up on the relief rolls.

As this upstate New York community sought to deal with the effects of the nation's greatest depression, a change in the ownership structure of Syracuse industry may well have compounded local economic problems. In the earlier years of the century practically all manufacturing plants in the city and suburban areas were owned by the local inventors and entrepreneurs who originally had established them, with control thus resting in Syracuse-based families. By the mid-1930s this pattern had changed radically. Over the years a considerable number of Syracuse companies had been bought-out by large national firms, and thus became merely local branches of big conglomerates. Decisions on volume of production and levels of employment in the city's industries increasingly were made at corporate headquarters hundreds of miles away, where little concern existed about the effects of a layoff. The residents of Syracuse thus found their economic futures more and more under outside control, a somewhat unnerving prospect.

The automobile shows held in numerous cities across America in the early months of 1934 were viewed by industry observers as highly successful. Big increases in attendance at these events over the previous year, together with a considerable amount of on-the-spot purchasing of new vehicles, indicated that consumers now were returning in increasing numbers to the automotive marketplace. This warm reception accorded the new models, following on the heels of a substantial improvement in sales of passenger cars experienced during the final months of 1933, gave motor car builders reason to believe that the corner had been turned and that 1934 would see the automobile industry once again climb firmly back on its feet and lead the nation toward a major economic recovery.[8-2]

At the very beginning of 1934 the industry had been compelled to recognize, however, that despite the new signs of strength in motor car sales the prices listed for automobiles would continue to be an all-important factor with the buying public. Depression psychology together with tight family budgets had turned most persons into bargain-hunters; thus while the attractive new styling of vehicles was welcomed many decisions to buy would be based largely on cost. Consequently, despite the previously-noted jump in raw material prices compared to depression lows of 1932 and early 1933, plus increased labor rates incurred by auto manufacturers under National Industrial Recovery Act regulations (hourly pay of factory hands had been upped modestly throughout the industry and stand-by time now was compensated), motor car companies did not dare risk placing substantially higher tags on the new models. Some price advances were noted, but even so one of the "low-priced three" (Ford, Chevrolet and Plymouth) could be purchased for well under six hundred dollars while buyers seeking a more impressive vehicle incorporating high levels of performance and riding comfort could choose from a wide array of makes at only a few hundred dollars more. In addition, the purchaser of even an economy-class car could expect a standard of mechanical reliability and overall quality undreamed of in such a vehicle a scant half-dozen years earlier. The engineers and manufacturing managers had done their work well; it now was unnecessary for motor car buyers to spend large sums of money to obtain an eminently satisfactory automobile. The modern, light, low-cost vehicle with its easy handling qualities particularly appealed to the increasing number of women taking the wheels of motor cars. The era of an uniformed chauffeur transporting members of the female sex around the city in a ponderous town car or limousine was fading into history. The end result of these changes in the market was that the big, over-$2,000 car was becoming an anachronism. Despite an improving national economy barely one per cent of auto purchasers chose such upper-bracket vehicles, and their number was dwindling month-by-month.

The H.H. Franklin Company entered the new year confronting obstacles almost identical to those which had plagued it in the recent past. Because of severe fiscal limitations the Syracuse firm was able to incorporate only minor styling and mechanical refinements in the cars displayed at the auto shows. The grille of the Olympic was given the attractive, deep-vee shape pioneered in the senior cars, and the six-cylinder engine common to Olympic and Airman models was updated a trifle with redesigned pistons and an improved pressure oiling system. With these insignificant changes the company's offerings totally lacked the sparkle of such competitor vehicles as the all-new 1934 LaSalle, with its beautifully streamlined, up-to-the-minute appearance. General Motors was able to produce this smart-looking automobile at a price closely competitive with that of the Franklin Olympic through the liberal borrowing of mechanical components from one of its less-costly offerings, the Oldsmobile. Other manufacturers displayed vehicles with revolutionary new lines, Chrysler incorporating in its cars the so-called "airflow" design and Hupmobile stepping forward with its "aero-dynamic" models. The Franklin firm, restricted to a somewhat dated car (its "boxy" bodies were little changed from the two previous years), thus would have to compete with numerous highly-innovative products from other companies as the 1934 sales race unfolded.

Merchandising the Franklin vehicle was made even more difficult by the steady attrition in the firm's dealer ranks occurring throughout the depression era. With the level of sales of the Syracuse product plummeting nearly ninety per cent during the four-year period 1929-1933, it was inevitable that many of the weaker dealers would drop by the wayside, with stronger ones often considering a shift in allegiance to a more popular make of motor car. It is impossible at this date to know the exact number of failures and desertions which took place among Franklin dealers during the grim depression years of 1931, 1932 and 1933, but it must have been substantial. Dwindling Franklin sales plus rumors of company fiscal instability also made it easy for dealers representing competing makes of automobiles to intimate that anyone purchasing a product of the Syracuse manufacturer faced the danger of becoming the owner of an "orphan" car.

As the top management group of the Franklin firm sought to meet these and related difficulties, its ranks were thinned by the death of an important, if controversial, executive. Edwin McEwen, in poor health during the closing months of 1933, succumbed at age 65 to an attack of pneumonia in January, 1934. His passing left three men in overall control of Franklin operations, each of whom was of relatively advanced age. Giles Stilwell, chairman of the board, now was in his early eighties, while H.H. Franklin was sixty-seven and Frank Barton, the secretary-treasurer, seventy-one. This trio was a far cry from the youthful and dynamic group which had guided the entry of the H.H. Franklin Manufacturing Company into the new field of motor vehicle building a third of a century earlier. At the time of McEwen's death the firm also lost the services, through resignation, of John Williams, vice president of sales; his position was filled by George Cuddy, formerly manager of dealer business administration. The firm totally lacked an engineering chief, an almost unbelievable gap in a company that for decades had been noted for technical excellence.

In February 1934, it was announced that the committee established earlier to seek readjustment of the capital structure of the H.H. Franklin Manufacturing Company was discontinuing its operations. H.H. Franklin quickly issued the reassuring statement that the termination of this committee's efforts would not affect extension of the company's large bank loans, nor the continuation of vehicle production by the firm. A second committee was then established to work toward revitalization of Franklin fiscal affairs, with the successor body consisting entirely of officers of local Syracuse banks. William H. Kelley, president, and F.H. Plumb, vice-president, of the Merchants National Bank and Trust Company of Syracuse, plus Harold Stone, president of Onondaga County Savings Bank, were members of the new group.[8-3] This committee immediately sought to explore fresh sources of funds for the hard-pressed auto company, with emphasis on efforts to obtain supplemental capital locally. In addition, contacts were initiated with persons in the Federal government to determine if the company might qualify for a Reconstruction Finance Corporation (RFC) loan. As the banker group moved forward with its work H.H. Franklin, assisted once again by Horace Benstead, undertook a parallel effort to seek some method of refinancing which would make it possible to keep the firm afloat.

However, while these efforts to devise a fiscal "rescue plan" were unfolding, a series of adverse events relentlessly threatened the continued existence of the H.H. Franklin Manufacturing Company. The creditor banks, which following the death of Edwin McEwen no longer had a trusted representative participating in company decision-making, now were becoming increasingly restive about the Syracuse auto firm's inability to make even token payments on the outstanding loan notes. Clearly, the seven out-of-town lending institutions were not prepared to hold off indefinitely from taking what steps they felt necessary to recover the borrowed funds. With its cash position having shrunk to the point where only a few thousand dollars remained in the till, the company also was hard-pressed to deal with bills submitted by numerous suppliers of parts and materials. Equally grave, the Syracuse firm had been encountering problems since the beginning of 1934 in meeting even the modest wage payments due the handful of employees who continued to build those few Franklin cars still coming off the production line. Actual sales of vehicles by the company throughout America during the first quarter of 1934 barely topped fifty per month, a number far below the levels achieved in the rock-bottom depression years of 1932 and 1933. These critical factors constituted a forewarning of approaching doom for the old-line auto builder.

The inevitable occurred during the early days of spring in 1934. On Tuesday, April 3, company treasurer Frank Barton drove from Syracuse to nearby Utica, where he submitted to the United States District Court on behalf of the Franklin firm a voluntary petition in bankruptcy. Filing of this petition, which expressed a willingness to surrender property for the benefit of creditors and sought appointment of a receiver, had been authorized by the company board of directors on the previous day. The petition, after describing Barton as a creditor to whom the bankrupt company was indebted in the sum of $3,000 and upwards, stated that the firm had been engaged in the manufacture of automobiles and auto parts for well over twenty-five years, and furnished products to eighty-one distributors plus 150 direct dealers in America, together with twenty-two foreign dealers. The petition noted that the company until recently had conducted a prosperous business, and built up much good will. It went on to state that liabilities largely consisted of notes to various banks, which the corporation had been obliged to renew from time-to-time as they came due, and which for some time it had been unable to pay. The petition related that the aggregate indebtedness to banks and trust companies totaled upwards of two million dollars, and that with the notes due and unpaid and the lenders pressing for payment the danger existed that these obligations would be sued on and execution issue against company property. It further noted that other creditors of the company were insisting on payment, and that the bankrupt corporation had no credit but still needed to purchase supplies and raw materials and hire workmen if it was to conduct day-to-day operations.

The document then expressed the petitioner's belief that a receiver should be appointed to continue company operations, since a closing would cause great harm to all concerned. It was stated that a considerable volume of business continued to come into the plant of the corporation, and that the only means to properly conduct this business would be through appointment of such a receiver. The petition then listed net fixed assets of the corporation of $3,813,520, and noted that the firm was assessed for tax purposes on the rolls of the city of Syracuse in the amount of $189,250 for land and $3,351,600 for improvements.[8-4]

Federal Judge Frederick H. Bryant adjudged the company bankrupt, appointed Giles H. Stilwell receiver, and granted the firm the usual protection against court actions by creditors. The order appointing as receiver the debonair, moustached Stilwell—who, it will be recalled, first acted as legal advisor to a youthful Herbert H. Franklin back in the mid-1890s—empowered him after the filing of an appropriate bond to continue the business of the bankrupt H.H. Franklin Manufacturing Company in so far as he might deem it just and proper, pending further direction of the court. The order went on to state, however, that nothing therein was to be construed as authorization to borrow money. In accepting the appointment Stilwell acknowledged publicly that a heavy burden of short-term debt coupled with the intensity of the depression had brought the Franklin firm to its present unhappy condition.

As the receiver commenced his duties an important initial order of business was the development of two key schedules, one listing all debts of the bankrupt corporation and the second various assets of the firm. These documents were filed with the court in mid-May of 1934. Heading the list of debts were good-sized property tax claims of Onondaga County and the city of Syracuse. County taxes were unpaid for 1932-33 and 1933-34, while city levies were due for 1932 and 1933. The total amount owing these public agencies (with an unpaid $650 water service bill thrown in for good measure) was some $204,000. These taxes were considered secured debts, since the public bodies involved enjoyed a lien on the real property of the Franklin firm for overdue amounts. In addition, the bankrupt company was obligated to the State of New York for slightly over $7,000 in unpaid corporate franchise taxes.

A relatively small but important debt owed by the bankrupt concern was pay due workers, with a total of 222 employees registering wage claims covering the last period of Franklin plant operation. The amounts due the workers ranged from pocket change in some cases to the sum of seventy-four dollars in one instance, with a total of $4,212 owed. The small size of the typical claim indicated clearly that these employees had been hired on a part-time, as-needed basis during the dismal final days of company life. Those with wage claims included persons long active in the Franklin organization—Harry Pettit, Ben-

THE FRANKLIN AUTOMOBILE COMPANY

jamin Countryman, Roland Tremain, Harold Emerick, Jefferson T. Santmeyer, DeForest Drexel, Ernest Rang, Roscoe Tenant, Louis J. Ripberger and Joseph Babcock. Frank Barton's son, Kenneth, who had served for a time as assistant secretary-treasurer of the firm, also submitted a claim for past-due compensation. By law wages due employees for pre-bankruptcy services were entitled to treatment as priority items in an insolvency proceeding.

A substantial number of unsecured creditors of the bankrupt company were listed as claimants. Chief among these were the seven lending institutions holding the overdue notes which had long haunted the Franklin firm. These banks were owed sums ranging in amount from $115,902 (Plainfield Trust Co. of New Jersey) to $387,285 (Guardian Trust Co. of Cleveland). Total amount owing the seven was the whopping sum of $2,213,918. In addition to the claims of this important group, other notes were held by H.H. Franklin ($45,272), former vice-president J. E. Williams ($10,805), secretary-treasurer Frank Barton ($3,240), board of directors member E. H. Dann ($10,805), and several additional persons identified with the firm. It was not entirely clear whether these notes represented sums advanced by company officials to help keep the firm afloat or some other type of obligation such as unpaid salaries.

A large number of suppliers of automotive parts and raw materials also were creditors, many of whom bore names known throughout American industry. Included were the A.C. Spark Plug Co., Aluminum Company of America, Armstrong Cork, Bendix, Delco Products, E.I. Du Pont DeNemours, Kelsey-Hayes Wheel, and the Firestone, Goodyear and B.F. Goodrich Tire Companies. Such local Syracuse firms as the Straight-Line Engine Co., for decades a supplier of castings to Franklin, and the Syracuse Glass Co. also were on the list. A few general creditors were located abroad, in such countries as Holland and Mexico.

Claims for pensions from the Franklin firm were submitted by long-time executives Giles Stilwell and Claude E. Hull. The Franklin pension plan was backed solely by general company assets (no pension trust fund existed); thus the bankruptcy essentially wiped out any equity built up by employees. Among those entitled to pensions only Stilwell and Hull bothered to file claims.

Several plaintiffs in lawsuits brought earlier against the Franklin firm joined the ranks of creditors. One action, a somewhat complex and extended piece of litigation, arose out of business dealings by Franklin with the R.H. Long Company. Long, a builder of motor car bodies and body parts, charged in a suit filed in Massachusetts that over a decade earlier, in 1921 and 1922, the Franklin company through certain misrepresentations had induced Long to reduce the price of body components furnished the Syracuse firm. A companion suit maintained that Franklin took discounts on bills submitted by Long to which it had no right whatever. A third item of litigation involved a type of claim better known in the present era–it charged Franklin with negligence in manufacturing and assembling one of its automobiles, with resulting personal injury to the plaintiff. This suit alleged that a defective axle on a Franklin vehicle snapped while it was being driven, causing the car to leave the highway and resulting in the death of one person and injury to another.

Offsetting these numerous liabilities were the assets of the bankrupt company, listed in a separate schedule. A principal item was real estate owned by the firm, which was listed at an appraised value of $3,144,630. A second important asset was the stock-in-trade–in effect, the inventory–used by the firm in automobile manufacturing. This included supplies, raw stores, completed or partly-completed motor cars, work in progress and separate finished parts in the overall amount of $541,320. A third key item was plant machinery and tools, with a total estimated value after depreciation of $632,254.

A variety of other assets were set forth in the schedule. The H.H. Franklin Manufacturing Company held stock in several subsidiary companies, including the Franklin Automobile Company (its selling arm), the Syracuse Land Development Company (this stock was still pledged with a trustee for the creditor banks, as partial security for bank indebtedness), the Franklin Development Company (a division set up in the 1920s to exploit inventions of Franklin employees having potential value throughout the auto industry); and the Franklin-Illinois Company (a factory retail branch). The amount of the Franklin firm's actual cash-on-hand, primarily deposits in the Merchants National Bank and Trust Company of Syracuse, was insignificant, reaching a total of only $4,738. A few minor amounts of money were due the company from various sources, and the firm had a modest equity in some nineteen unexpired insurance policies. Rounding out the assets was an income tax refund claim against the U. S. Commissioner of Internal Revenue.

The schedules showed total debts of the firm of $2,540,387, offset by estimated assets of $5,805,003. Based on these figures it could be alleged, as H.H. Franklin later did, that technically the company was not insolvent. However, such a claim must be viewed with extreme skepticism. The debts of the firm were due in cash, while its assets consisted almost entirely of real estate or personal property of one type or another of uncertain market value. The acid test would come when an effort was made to convert these items of property into dollars. With the depression literally devastating Syracuse, and American industry showing little interest in expansion, it might prove difficult to find purchasers for the firm's property at anything near the appraised prices.

The desired result of the bankruptcy proceedings would be the sale of the Franklin property as a total package to an organization capable of continuing the business of manufacturing automobiles. Consequently, early in June, 1934, Referee in Bankruptcy Ben Wiles named three trustees to take over the affairs of the H.H. Franklin Manufacturing Company and continue the business operations initiated by the receiver. Giles Stilwell was to remain active as one of the trustees; the other two were G. Norman Knaus, a Syracuse businessman, and Hugh S. Goodhart, for years the advertising manager of the Franklin firm. The appointment of these trustees terminated the earlier receivership

THE DEMISE OF THE COMPANY

in bankruptcy, and appeared to pave the way for a broad-scale effort to reorganize and rejuvenate the firm as an automobile manufacturing operation.

Numerous groups in the Syracuse community at the time of the bankruptcy filing expressed a desire to assist in developing ways and means by which the big Franklin factory might be kept in operation. The president of the Syracuse Chamber of Commerce, in appointing a special eight-member committee to work on the problem, declared:[8-5]

> This industry is vital to Syracuse. For months the Chamber of Commerce used all the means at its command to prevent the present situation (bankruptcy). Now that it has happened a committee is needed to work in devising some means by which the industry can be continued. This is a matter of gravest concern to every resident of Syracuse, and no stone will be left unturned to retain one of the city's most important manufacturing plants.

In addition to the Chamber of Commerce there was no lack of other Syracuse-based organizations seeking to join in the resuscitation effort. The three-member banker committee established early in the year to develop a fiscal reorganization plan for Franklin also indicated that it planned to continue its activities, but at the same time sounded a note of warning. In a tersely-worded statement this group observed that the bankruptcy action, which it attributed largely to the refusal of creditors of the H.H. Franklin Manufacturing Company to further renew their notes, while not necessarily putting an end to the committee's efforts, nonetheless would decidedly handicap it in its work. Undoubtedly the banker committee recognized that a company which had entered receivership was placed under a stigma which might well make a satisfactory reorganization difficult to achieve. It also without question was aware that bankruptcy status would terminate, at least for the time being, any hope of obtaining a RFC loan or similar Federal government assistance. A plan to aid the Franklin firm was also submitted to the New York State Senate in Albany, but no record exists of action having been taken by that body.[8-6]

THE FRANKLIN AUTOMOBILE COMPANY

Following their appointment on June 5, 1934, the three trustees of the bankrupt firm together with their attorneys, William Mackenzie and Lionel Grossman, quickly commenced a broad range of activities. Creditor claims against the company were scrutinized and either recommended for approval or objected to for various reasons. Under the earlier receivership of Giles Stilwell some seventy-nine Franklin automobiles had been assembled and sold, together with $37,967 worth of spare parts. The new trustees continued to dispose of other stockpiled cars and parts, receiving at various times an additional $92,600 through such sales. To carry on these business-related activities George Cuddy was hired as supervisor of factory and sales operations and a skeleton force of employees retained to handle orders, carry on the parts business and preserve the property. All former company officers and executives including H.H. Franklin had been dropped from the payroll; overall management of the bankrupt firm now was exercised by the trustees at their weekly meetings. Hugh Goodhart took personal charge of the remaining business operations on most days, although he was relieved on occasion by Stilwell or Knaus.

The several lawsuits against the bankrupt company were settled for modest sums. Claims of former Franklin employees for unpaid wages were paid in full pursuant to order of the bankruptcy court. The stock of the Syracuse Land Development Company, titleholder of the large parcel of real estate on the east side of Syracuse plus various lots in the vicinity of the Franklin plant, was released to the creditor banks in exchange for an offset of $201,625 against the total amount of indebtedness owed these lending institutions. The H.H. Franklin Company's federal tax claim, involving the years 1927, 1928 and 1929, proved difficult to resolve when the Commissioner of Internal Revenue flatly refused to enter into a stipulation to settle for an earlier agreed-upon amount. Ultimately the trustees were compelled to take the matter to the U. S. Board of Tax Appeals (the present day Tax Court) where they emerged victorious, with judgment given in the amount of $32,359 plus interest.

THE DEMISE OF THE COMPANY

Tax claims of the city of Syracuse and Onondaga County presented a problem of some complexity. The sums involved, over $350,000 when 1934 taxes came due, plus the existence of a tax lien, clearly constituted a major impediment to any ultimate sale of company assets. For several months, discussions were held regarding a possible compromise of overdue taxes at a small percentage of the amount outstanding, but without resolution of the issue. Finally, following numerous further conferences with Mayor Marvin of Syracuse and with county officials, an agreement was reached under which the two local taxing bodies waived and released any immediate right to payment of taxes from the proceeds of a sale of company property by the trustees. The two local governments, however, granted this interim waiver subject to full retention of their lien against the real estate of the bankrupt firm for the amount of the unpaid taxes.

As the trustees took these and other actions needed to put the affairs of the bankrupt company in order, concurrent efforts were made to interest potential investors in taking over the firm as a continuing operation. A total outsider, Harry A. Wahl of Newark, New Jersey, appeared on the scene in mid-April, 1934, offering at this early date an overall plan for company reorganization.[8-7] His proposal featured the development of a low-priced ($850) line of air-cooled pleasure cars, a truck, and a more-expensive twelve-cylinder vehicle, with factory operations to recommence during 1934. Wahl, who claimed to represent a group of eastern capitalists and bankers, proposed financing the program through the issuance of new stock, with interests of existing share-holders to be protected and claims of creditors either bought up or compromised. Although the plan was given substantial publicity locally and in national trade journals, there is no evidence that it was ever pursued. Late in the summer a rumor circulated that the E.L. Cord Corporation was negotiating for acquisition of the H.H. Franklin Manufacturing Company. This was denied promptly by L.B. Manning, vice-president of the Cord Corporation, who stated firmly that his company had no interest in such an acquisition.[8-8]

The special eight-member committee of the Syracuse Chamber of

Commerce held an intensive series of meetings during mid-1934, in an effort to develop a means by which Franklin automobile production could be revived. As a key part of its activities the chamber committee at one point sought to acquire rights to an innovative motor which had been developed by a partnership formed by two former Franklin engineers, Carl Doman and Ed Marks. On leaving the H.H. Franklin firm early in 1933, Doman and Marks carried on experimental work geared toward the development of a new generation of air-cooled engines suitable for use in cars or trucks. Their work was funded by a person who was no stranger to Franklin affairs, James Walker, chief executive of the Walker Body Company of Amesbury, Massachusetts, until recently a supplier of bodies to the Syracuse auto firm. The new eight-cylinder, air-cooled, Doman-Marks automotive power plant featured a modern unit-block design, enabling it to be produced at a far lower cost than previous Franklin engines. The motor thus appeared to offer the potential for use in an up-to-date automobile capable of competing in the $1,000 medium-priced motor vehicle market, a factor of great interest to the chamber committee.

As the months went by, however, no specific action was taken by the chamber group to purchase rights to the Doman-Marks motor and develop a plan for acquiring and reopening the Franklin plant. There appear to have been several reasons for this lack of achievement. First of all, James Walker, who held a controlling interest in the Doman-Marks partnership, placed a hefty price tag on the new air-cooled engine. Second, acquisition of the right to the Franklin plant and company assets meant that the interests of major creditors–primarily the multi-million-dollar claims of the lending institutions holding the outstanding notes–first had to be dealt with. Finally, fresh money undoubtedly would have been needed to rejuvenate the motor car manufacturing operation if it was to have any chance of future success. The resolution of these problems called for a substantial commitment of outside capital, which the chamber committee clearly found it impossible to secure.

While this committee carried on its efforts, the attorneys representing the trustees in bankruptcy also met from time-to-time with parties who had expressed an interest in acquiring either all the company assets or such specific items as machine tools. Finding prospective purchasers with the ability to enter a bid for the company as a whole proved to be difficult, however. Likewise, efforts to develop some type of workable plan for reorganization or recapitalization of the firm were unavailing. In the meantime the creditor banks indicated that they were considering disposing of the H.H. Franklin Manufacturing Company obligations held by them, and made clear their desire for prompt liquidation of the firm's assets if no sale could be arranged.

Finally, in October, 1934, it was announced publicly that the creditor banks had sold their claims against the Franklin Company for an undisclosed price to investors whose Syracuse representative was John Williams, former vice-president for sales of the air-cooled automobile firm. The identity of the purchasing group was not made public at the time, but press releases indicated that the new interests planned to take over the Franklin facility as a whole, initiate production of an already-designed vehicle not later than February, 1935, re-employ a substantial number of persons, and place a new medium-priced car on the market by April, 1935.[8-9]

Following this highly encouraging development Referee-in-Bankruptcy Ben Wiles late in November, 1934, entered an order directing the sale of all H.H. Franklin Company assets. On December 8, the date of the sale, only one bid was received and quickly accepted. This offer was submitted by the new firm of Franklin Motors, organized by the investment group which a short time earlier had purchased the bank claims. The sale price was $278,750 and in exchange all assets of the defunct H.H. Franklin Manufacturing Company passed to the new group, subject only to liens of the city and county governments for taxes and assessments. The sale encompassed land and buildings of the bankrupt firm, all machinery, tools and similar physical assets, any remaining inventory, and shares of stock in such subsidiaries as the Franklin Automobile Company, the Franklin Development Corporation and the Franklin-Illinois Company. Also included were all

THE FRANKLIN AUTOMOBILE COMPANY

patents and trademarks, cash on deposit held by the trustees in bankruptcy, and even claims of the bankrupt firm to tax rebates. The expressed goal of the sale was to dispose of the property of the insolvent firm as a single business entity, thus paving the way, it was hoped, for a swift return to auto manufacturing by the purchaser.

The sale agreement, in addition to calling for a relatively modest payment for assets of the bankrupt company, contained various provisions indicating clearly the desire of the trustees and the referee in bankruptcy to expedite disposition of the overall Franklin operation. Having purchased the notes held by the banks, Franklin Motors had now become by far the largest creditor of the insolvent H.H. Franklin Manufacturing Company, and thus enjoyed a major claim to the funds obtained from the sale of the bankrupt's property. As a result the sale was treated largely as a wash. The new firm, Franklin Motors, was not required to lay out any money directly for the purchase of H.H. Franklin Company assets, instead being given advance credit for the dividends which ultimately would be due it from the estate of the bankrupt firm. The trustees retained $75,000 of the cash on deposit to their credit at the Syracuse Trust Company to meet the claims of all other creditors.

The entire Franklin property having been struck down to the new firm, the trustees moved quickly to complete their work. Minor outstanding claims were paid, Federal and New York State tax obligations settled, and attorneys for the trustees compensated. Following a few additional adjustments an order of distribution was entered on April 19, 1935, calling for a dividend of 10.60046% to be paid on approved creditors' claims. Creditors of the company thus received just over 10½ cents on each dollar owing them. The holders of several hundred thousand shares of H.H. Franklin Manufacturing Company preferred and common stock, valued five-and-a-half years earlier at between fifteen and twenty million dollars, received nothing whatever. The trustees, their work completed, dropped out of the picture, with an order entered by the court on May 3, 1935, discharging them from any further responsibility. Legal proceedings move slowly, however, and

THE DEMISE OF THE COMPANY

not until November 12, 1937, did the United States District Court in Utica declare the Franklin bankruptcy case closed.

As the year 1934 came to an end and 1935 dawned, the Syracuse community entertained high hopes that the recently-organized Franklin Motors Company would speedily place the city back on the map as a builder of air-cooled automobiles. It now was learned that Midwest business interests comprised the key sources of funding for this new firm, with a substantial portion of the capital reportedly provided by Ward Canaday, wealthy Toledo businessman and president of the United States Advertising Company, which for years had performed services for the now defunct H.H. Franklin Manufacturing Company. Canaday remained largely in the background, however, with his attorney, George Ritter, also of Toledo, handling legal and fiscal matters for Franklin Motors and John Williams serving as executive head of the operation in Syracuse.

The opening period of 1935 swiftly became an era of renewed promise for the American automobile industry. The grim, low-volume depression years began to fade from memory as demand for new motor vehicles across the nation accelerated from week-to-week. At long last a substantial number of owners of tired, five-to-seven-year-old motor cars summoned the courage and secured the funds to purchase current models. The 1935 offerings featured trim new styling with emphasis on sleek, flowing lines, while the drab colors of a few years earlier were replaced by bright, attractive hues. Perhaps the most important news emanating from the ranks of independent passenger car companies was the announcement that an old-line manufacturer of luxury motor vehicles, the Detroit-based Packard firm, would offer to prospective buyers a highly-attractive eight-cylinder car selling in the $1,000 price range. A vast amount of attention was given by daily newspapers and the automotive trade press to this exciting new model, and early reports indicated that it had the potential to become a "best

THE FRANKLIN AUTOMOBILE COMPANY

seller" quickly.[8-10]

While Packard with its new offering would point the way for other builders of high-quality cars to follow, a careful examination of the genesis of the Detroit-based firm's new mid-price vehicle showed it to be the product of astute company planning and a good-sized financial investment. Despite years of depression Packard was still able to draw on a large cash reserve in its treasury to underwrite much of the cost of the new venture, and thanks to an unimpaired credit rating in banking circles it readily could borrow any additional money needed. With adequate funding available the Detroit firm found it possible to hire a talented team of engineers to design the pacesetting vehicle,[8-11] plus a cadre of equally capable production executives–several enticed from other automotive firms–to direct its manufacture. Hundreds of expensive new machine tools were installed in Packard's big East Grand Boulevard plant in Detroit to make possible the building of a high-quality automobile at a competitive price, and a strong dealer organization stood ready to market the product effectively. Perhaps most important of all, the Packard firm clearly expected to rely on its image throughout America and indeed much of the world as a builder of top-drawer vehicles to help secure broad public acceptance of this new medium-priced model. The company thus was fully prepared at this point to trade prestige for sales volume!

The successor organization now installed in the red-brick factory on South Geddes Street in Syracuse, Franklin Motors Company, needed to overcome a vastly greater number of obstacles in order to bring to market a vehicle competitive with the pacesetting Packard car. Despite optimistic earlier reports the new firm did not have an innovative air-cooled vehicle ready to move from the drawing board and test track into production–in fact, it lacked even a motor suitable for installation in such an automobile. The bodies utilized by the predecessor H.H. Franklin Manufacturing Company in its 1934 offerings, with upright lines and square appearance, would be considered hopelessly out-of-date in the 1935 automotive marketplace, and something far more stylish had to be substituted. Much of the machinery in the relatively obsolete plant required major rebuilding or total replacement if a manufacturing program of any magnitude was to recommence. The old Franklin dealer network, hard-hit by the depression and subject to further attrition during the nine months in which practically all air-cooled vehicle production had ceased, needed total rejuvenation.

Early in 1935 the successor firm opened discussions with the one source able to contribute both engineering talent and the modern power plant essential for any new air-cooled car, the Doman-Marks partnership. After some months of negotiations, agreement was reached by the several parties calling for the Doman-Marks operation to move back to Syracuse from Amesbury, Massachusetts, and in effect be absorbed by Franklin Motors. Ed Marks and Carl Doman were to be hired, under written contracts, by the new automotive concern to spearhead the effort to design a completely updated vehicle and plan for its production.[8-12] A number of other former Franklin employees now on the Doman-Marks payroll were to join in the move back to their old headquarters on South Geddes Street.

Despite the retaining of this pair of highly knowledgeable former Franklin engineers and their aides, however, questions continued to arise throughout 1935 as to the degree of commitment by Franklin Motors to the swift development of a saleable air-cooled automobile. Following transfer of the assets of the old H.H. Franklin Manufacturing Company at the bankruptcy sale, persons familiar with the situation soon became concerned as to whether the successor firm was prepared to provide the substantial amount of additional capital needed to recommence automobile production. The big South Geddes Street plant sat dark and idle month after month, and few former Franklin employees found themselves called back to work.

At one point it appeared that the new firm might be seeking to interest some other automobile company in utilizing the Doman-Marks engine in a vehicle, perhaps on a joint-venture basis. This engine, temporarily placed in the chassis of another make of car, was taken to Rochester, New York, in the summer of 1935, and demonstrated to officials of the old-line Cunningham Motor Company. Cunningham, it will be recalled, had ceased production of its own high-priced pleasure cars some two or three years earlier, but continued to build an occasional special-bodied hearse or ambulance to order. The Rochester-based firm, while small, was in respectable financial condition (a most important qualification), and earlier had expressed some degree of interest in utilizing the Doman-Marks power plant in a moderately-priced passenger car. Nothing concrete resulted from this visit, however. About the same time Franklin Motors also reportedly discussed with two independent motor car manufacturers in the Midwest possible purchase of bodies used by these companies on their current automobiles, apparently with the goal of negotiating an agreement similar to the one which resulted in the Franklin Olympic in 1932. However, no positive end product emerged from such negotiations, either.

The months passed by swiftly, with the new firm failing to place a car on the market during the 1935 model year, and making no real effort to ready one for display at the 1936 auto shows (in order to stabilize motor vehicle production and employment the date for introduction of 1936 models by all manufacturers had been advanced to mid-fall of 1935). Then an astonishing development occurred when Franklin Motors entered into a decidedly ambiguous contract with a company headed by Dallas E. Winslow, a Midwestern entrepreneur and liquidator of defunct automotive concerns. This agreement authorized the Winslow interests to operate the Franklin plant for production of motor cars, but in addition granted Winslow the right to sell substantial amounts of "surplus machinery," and even lease or sell to other parties sections of the South Geddes Street factory complex.[8-13] Before long the terms of the contract became public knowledge, and despite assurances by Franklin Motors spokespersons that machinery being sold would not be essential to the building of a modernized air-cooled vehicle, perceptive Syracusans began to express concern as to whether the true intent of the contract was simply disposition of the entire manufacturing facility. Repercussions were felt quickly. Both Doman and Marks, upset by the failure of Franklin Motors to make any serious move toward automobile production and alarmed

THE DEMISE OF THE COMPANY

by the implications of the Winslow agreement, sought to be released from their contracts. Backed by James Walker in this stand they ultimately secured their independence. John Williams also submitted his resignation as president of Franklin Motors and its subsidiaries, thus removing from the new firm's ranks an automotive sales executive of broad experience. Meanwhile, top-level officials of the city of Syracuse, by now disillusioned with the inertia of Franklin Motors, decided to take aggressive action to collect the large overdue property tax bill (earlier, city representatives had offered to scale back the tax obligation if Franklin Motors would commence building cars). In December, 1935, Mayor Marvin directed the city's corporation counsel to initiate prompt action to foreclose the tax lien.

Franklin Motors officials, clearly stung by these events, attempted to place restraints on the operations of the Dallas Winslow group. The Winslow interests quickly struck back with a lawsuit, seeking to enjoin any interference in their occupancy of Franklin plant space or with activities being carried on there. Neither party emerged the clear winner in those legal maneuvers, thus producing a state of utter confusion at the South Geddes Street complex.

At this point still another group of out-of-town investors entered the picture. Arthur J. Brandt, well-known Detroit industrial engineer with a broad background in the reorganization of run-down companies (he also had served as President of the American Austin Company for a time), secured an option from Franklin Motors early in January, 1936, to purchase the South Geddes Street factory and any machinery remaining. The city of Syracuse temporarily held up tax foreclosure proceedings on the plant to permit this latest rescue effort to move forward. Ultimately a new company, named Olympic Motors, was organized to take title to the old Franklin facility. An examination of the names of officers and directors of the Olympic organization indicates that some type of merger had taken place between the Toledo-based group which originally had purchased all Franklin assets at the bankruptcy sale and individuals identified with Arthur Brandt. In addition, the Winslow organization also was apparently involved with the new entity. Among Brandt's backers was Alfred J. Glancy, formerly a vice-president of General Motors; in conjunction with Brandt, Glancy had reorganized GM's Oakland-Pontiac Motor Division in the 1920s. Local persons who participated in the organization of the new company included Ben Wiles, Syracuse attorney and the trustee in bankruptcy who earlier had supervised disposition of property of the old H.H. Franklin Manufacturing Company. Stories in trade journals at the time of incorporation of Olympic Motors (in September, 1936) stated that the new group planned to use the Franklin plant to manufacture small cars and possibly trailers.[8-14]

The hour was late, however, for this most recent coalition to successfully resume motor car production in the Geddes Street factory. No Franklin automobiles had been offered to the public in the 1935 and 1936 model years, and it quickly became apparent that none would be ready for the 1937 selling season. At this point few Franklin dealers still existed across the country, sheer economic necessity having compelled most of them either to close their doors or seek affiliation with some active auto manufacturer. Carl Doman and Ed Marks, finally free agents, had opened their own engine manufacturing operation in a nearby community in the spring of 1936, where they were soon retained by a Colorado investor to design and build a prototype model of an innovative three-wheeled, air-cooled motor car. Much of the machinery once used to build Franklin automobiles had now been disposed of, and the neglected Geddes Street plant began to assume the appearance of a derelict, with broken windows, leaking roofs, and wooden floors heaved upward in many places due to moisture.

The Midwest investor group headed by Ward Canaday, which earlier had purchased the assets of the old H.H. Franklin Company, now was clearly devoting its major effort to rejuvenation of the Toledo-based Willys-Overland Company, which had been in receivership since 1933. Such exertions were crowned with success, with a reorganization plan for that firm approved by the federal court in August, 1936, and a nicely-styled, low-priced, four-cylinder Willys automobile placed on the market late that year. Rebirth of Willys was facilitated

THE DEMISE OF THE COMPANY

This vehicle, developed by Carl Doman and Edward Marks, is shown here on its first test run in 1937. The vehicle had a four cylinder air cooled engine and only three wheels (a single wheel in the rear). Doman and Marks produced the car for Mr. Lewis, a client, in 1936-1937. (Courtesy of Elizabeth A. Doman)

by the fact that unlike Franklin the firm never completely ceased making automobiles, permission having been obtained from the court to continue vehicle manufacture on a reduced scale throughout the several years of receivership. The city of Toledo and its residents quickly experienced visible benefits from the revitalization of the company, with some 4,000 persons finding employment in the Willys factory producing the new car.

By contrast, activities at the South Geddes Street plant in Syracuse had come to a total standstill, with only an occasional watchman now seen around the facility. Despairing of auto production ever resuming, Syracuse city officials and business leaders at this point actively sought an alternate use for the one-time bustling factory. At the beginning of the summer of 1937 an extraordinary opportunity suddenly sprang up. The New Jersey-based Carrier Corporation, producer of a high-tech product of that era, the air conditioner, about this time had begun seeking a good-sized facility in which to consolidate its far-flung manufacturing operations.[8-15] A major community effort was initiated to induce Carrier to relocate to Syracuse, with a number of the city's businesses, particularly retailing establishments, offering substantial financial contributions to help underwrite the cost of the move. The city of Syracuse, having finally foreclosed the tax lien it held on the Franklin facility, could now make it available for a new use. It therefore sold the plant to Carrier for the sum of one dollar at a public auction held in early July, 1937.

The various buildings in the aging complex were tidied-up and repaired, with machinery for manufacturing the Carrier product quickly installed. Carrier assembly-line operations for the most part required relatively short lengths of factory floor; thus the layout of the old plant, while unsuitable for modern-day high-volume motor car production, proved satisfactory for air conditioner manufacturing. The vice-president and general manager of the Carrier operation was Lemuel Boulware,[8-16] whose earlier identification with the Syracuse business community (from 1925 to 1935 he had been an executive at the Easy Washing Machine Co.) may well have been an important factor in the decision by the air-conditioner firm to move to the city. Initiation of operations by Carrier resulted in the employment of a number of out-of-work Syracusans, and aided the city in climbing out of the trough of a long-lingering depression (General Motors Corporation had reopened the Brown-Lipe-Chapin factory in 1936, also helping alleviate unemployment).

Two final items of business signaled the end of any identification of the Geddes Street plant–and even Syracuse itself–with the name "Franklin." Shortly after the sale of the factory to Carrier the Doman-Marks operation, now incorporated under the name "Air-Cooled Motors," acquired the patents, trade mark and trade name of the old H.H. Franklin Company. Hereafter this firm utilized the name "Franklin" in connection with the various types of air-cooled engines it produced at its small plant in Liverpool, New York, some five miles distant from the South Geddes facility. Air-Cooled Motors had no immediate plans for reviving an air-cooled passenger car; instead focusing its efforts on

THE DEMISE OF THE COMPANY

building replacement engines for trucks plus power plants for small package delivery vans and for industrial uses.[8-17] Early in 1938 the firm also entered a challenging new field, the manufacture of small air-cooled engines for general aviation use. The Franklin replacement parts business was disposed of to the Dallas Winslow organization and ultimately moved to Auburn, Indiana, where it would be operated as part of the Auburn-Cord-Duesenberg Company, also a Winslow acquisition.

The aging Geddes Street factory saw continued use by the Carrier Corporation for a number of years in the manufacture of air-conditioners. This was not entirely a trouble-free occupancy—on at least one occasion Carrier was compelled to drive additional piles into the

Igor Sikorsky, the aeronautical engineer given much credit for the development of the modern helicopter, worked closely with Carl Doman in the development of aircraft and helicopter engines. (Courtesy of Elizabeth A. Doman)

THE FRANKLIN AUTOMOBILE COMPANY

ground in the vicinity of the Harbor Brook drain to prevent floors from subsiding. Ultimately the prosperous Carrier firm felt the need for more up-to-date facilities, and in the late 1940s acquired a plant just east of the city of Syracuse, on a site once owned by the Syracuse Land Development Company. One-by-one the various departments of the air-conditioner firm were shifted to the east side plant. After its gradual abandonment by Carrier the one-time Franklin facility was utilized for a miscellaneous array of activities–the original building fronting on Geddes Street housed various Onondaga County offices, while the structures in the rear were rented for warehousing purposes. The various old brick factory units again were allowed to slide steadily downhill, with little attention given to maintenance or repair. It was all-too-clear to local observers that the once-proud industrial plant was nearing the end of its days.

Finally the entire tract bounded by Geddes, Marcellus, Magnolia and Gifford Streets was acquired by the local school district as a site for the new Fowler Vocational High School. Project development plans called for this educational facility to be built on the rear section of the acquired land, with a large open area stretching forward to South Geddes set aside for playground use. Demolition of the entire complex of buildings thus would be necessary, with a contractor hired to undertake this good-sized task. The old steel-reinforced brick and concrete factory proved to be a very tough nut to crack, however, stoutly resisting the massive wrecking ball wielded by the demolition crew. Ultimately heavy charges of dynamite were inserted and set off by an out-of-state blasting expert to bring down the walls and make it possible to clear the site. Today no evidence remains of the plant which once housed the city's largest industry and provided employment for two generations of Syracusans.

Even before all traces of the Franklin factory had been obliterated, the once-important automotive firm vanished from the public records of New York State. The H.H. Franklin Manufacturing Company was legally dissolved by proclamation of the New York Secretary of State on December 15, 1938, undoubtedly for long-continued non-payment of the state corporate franchise tax following bankruptcy proceedings.[8-18] Other subsidiary units, including the Syracuse Land Development Company and the Franklin Automobile Company, likewise had their corporate charters terminated. The successor firm of Franklin Motors, obviously no longer of any importance to its one-time stockholders, also was allowed to die.

The H.H. Franklin Manufacturing Company built motor vehicles for American and foreign markets over a period of nearly one-third of a century, from 1902 to 1934. This thirty-two-year span saw the American automobile develop from a tiny "horseless carriage," scarcely reliable enough for its owner to be certain of returning without mishap from a short jaunt into the countryside, into a swift, comfortable and trustworthy means of personal transportation. The period also witnessed an almost unbelievable mushrooming of the number of motor vehicles registered for use in America, from the minute figure of twenty thousand in 1902 to an astonishing 24,881,000 in 1934. Such an extraordinary increase meant that by the mid-1930s the gasoline-powered automobile was relied on overwhelmingly by the typical American family as its basic means of transportation. Despite more than four years of grim depression, Americans stubbornly refused to part with what to them had become an integral part of their lives.

As the motor car achieved this predominant status throughout the nation other once-vital modes of transportation commenced to falter badly, with some ultimately dropping by the wayside. By 1934 the interurban trolley, which for decades had transported innumerable employees from small towns and farms on the periphery of Syracuse to the Franklin plant on South Geddes Street as well as to other city-based manufacturing facilities, had all but vanished. Office and factory worker alike from outlying areas now either owned an automobile or found it possible to obtain a ride to his or her place of employment with a co-worker possessing a vehicle. The interurban tracks lay rusting and abandoned; a few years later they would be torn up to supply raw materials for war production.

Within cities the streetcar was fast being replaced by the motorbus, but even the introduction of this swifter and more flexible vehicle failed to stop numerous one-time riders from abandoning municipal public transit systems. Visits to the local grocery to purchase food, and trips to the central business district to shop at department stores, see a movie or enjoy dinner at a restaurant, more and more involved the use of the family automobile. The train, now being modernized in a few instances by the introduction of streamlined, diesel-powered units, still played a significant role in transporting people on trips of several hundred miles or more. However, it was clear that once the nation followed H.H. Franklin's earlier advice and constructed a modern interstate highway system, railroads might well follow the interurban into a state of near-oblivion so far as the passenger was concerned. Use of the airplane for transport of people, mail and small freight items was expanding steadily by the mid-1930s, but it would take the Second World War to familiarize the typical American with the advantages of flight.

The motor vehicle thus had become firmly entrenched as the nation's primary means of moving people. Sales of automobiles continued to surge in the years following the disappearance of Franklin from the scene, reaching a level in 1937 which nearly equaled the boom year of 1929. A sharp downturn was experienced during the 1938 business recession, but the industry quickly recovered and once again attained impressive heights in the period immediately preceding America's entry into the Second World War. This resurgent prosperity, however, was highly selective so far as individual automobile companies were concerned. The "Big Three," General Motors, Chrysler and Ford, now totally dominated the motor vehicle industry, accounting for approximately ninety per cent of passenger car sales. The handful of independent auto firms which managed to survive the horrors of the 1930-1934 depression era met with varying degrees of success in their efforts to regain earlier strength. The old-line Studebaker Corporation successfully emerged from receivership early in 1935, a highly significant accomplishment in that period. Like Willys-Overland–and unlike Franklin–the Studebaker firm had continued to produce a substantial number of cars while under the wing of the bankruptcy court, a factor which undoubtedly impressed the financial community and greatly aided the South Bend, Indiana, auto manufacturer in climbing back on its feet. Such an uninterrupted output also meant that the company's dealer organization, 2,000 strong, largely remained intact. Under terms of the Studebaker reorganization the large number of creditors–total obligations of the old company exceeded twenty million dollars–were given a tiny amount of cash plus a substantial block of stock in the new firm as settlement for their claims. The common shareholders of the company fared much less well, but did obtain the right to purchase on reasonable terms an interest in the reorganized enterprise. With a sound balance sheet thus achieved, the Studebaker organization was fully prepared to take advantage of the automotive sales recovery in the 1935-37 period.

Two or three additional independents achieved a moderate degree of success in the mid-to-late 1930s, while others found the going much more difficult. Buoyed by the splendid sales of its new $1,000 Series 120 model, the Packard Motor Car Company largely recovered its one-time strong position in the auto industry during 1935 and the following two years. Hudson Motors learned that a return to prosperity was not easily accomplished, but by 1935 it too was earning a small profit (the strain of putting the firm back on its feet may well have taken the life of its chief executive, the legendary Roy D. Chapin, however). Sales volume at Nash never came close to achieving pre-depression levels, and profits earned by the company may have largely reflected the surging sales volume of its Kelvinator refrigerator division.

The old-line, aristocratic Pierce-Arrow Company of Buffalo managed to survive a brief plunge into receivership in mid-1934, but its sales level in the next few years proved inadequate to insure a profit and it finally succumbed early in 1938. The once-prosperous automotive empire of E.L. Cord collapsed during the 1936-37 period, despite a last-gasp effort at revival through the production of a beautifully-designed, second-generation, front-drive Cord automobile. The Hupmobile firm of Detroit staggered on through the late 1930s, but with its plant closed much of the time and company management in a state of constant turmoil it had ceased to be a factor of any importance in the industry by the end of the decade. The Graham firm, also located in the great motor city, placed several models embodying advanced concepts of streamlining on the market in 1937 and succeeding years, only to find sales faltering and its working capital gone by the beginning of the 1940s. The Toledo-based Willys-Overland firm, as noted earlier, chose to cast its lot with a very-low-priced small car, a predecessor of today's "compact" units. Annual sales of these vehicles reached only modest levels, however, and not until the company, led by its renowned chief engineer, Delmar Roos, participated in the development and production of the U.S. Army "Jeep" did it achieve stability. An even smaller vehicle, the Crosley, made its appearance just before World War II. This tiny car revived the principle of air-cooling, utilizing a small, two-cylinder power plant originally designed for non-automotive use. Inadequate performance by American standards, plus a limited dealer organization, gave the new product slim prospects of long-term survival, however.

The mid-to-late 1930s thus saw a continuation of the consolidation of the once-broad-based American automobile industry into three giants and a few independent producers of moderate size. The prestigious small company–the builder of ten thousand or so high-quality vehicles annually, such as Franklin, Pierce-Arrow, Marmon and Peerless–had disappeared and would not be replaced. The period also marked the almost complete elimination (except for branch plants) of any important auto manufacturing operations outside the three Midwestern states of Michigan, Indiana and Wisconsin. In addition, the true luxury vehicle of earlier years had vanished from the American scene by 1940. The carefully-crafted upper-bracket car, frequently incorporating a custom body, no longer was available from any source. The Cadillacs, Packards and Lincolns now emerging from their respective factories were largely the products of the same fast-moving assembly lines which churned out big-volume, low-cost vehicles, and often shared more components with the cheaper units than their makers cared to admit.

Finally, motor car manufacturers in the late 1930s found their relationships with employees totally transformed from an earlier period. The swift rise of broad-based industrial unionism, and effective use of the sit-down strike to paralyze production, marked the end of the old, open-shop industry. Management was now compelled to bargain with its workers over wages, fringe benefits and working conditions, a far cry from previous decades when such matters were determined unilaterally by management. The day of the benevolent entrepreneur in the auto-industry, represented by H. H. Franklin and a few other heads of small companies, had come to an end.

THE FRANKLIN AUTOMOBILE COMPANY

– Nine –

The People Who Built the Cars

An attentive observer standing at the corner of Gifford and South Geddes Streets in the city of Syracuse at an early morning hour during the peak production years of the H.H. Franklin Company in the middle-to-late 1920s, would see the continuous movement of large numbers of people. Beginning well before 7:00 A.M., a stream of men garbed in work clothes crowd the sidewalks, having arrived at the Franklin plant on foot, riding bicycles, by streetcar or in automobiles. Funneling into the main Gifford Street gate they pass an elderly guard, and then fan out through the manufacturing complex to the various individual buildings in which they work.

As the 7:20 A.M. factory starting hour approaches the pace of those arriving quickens, with the guard seeking to obtain the badge numbers of workers who fail to pass through the gate by the time a piercing blast of the whistle atop the huge power plant chimney signals the start of a day of manufacturing operations. Since the company punishes even brief tardiness by docking a worker a full half-hour of his pay, some latecomers attempt to dodge by the guard, concealing the tell-tale badge numbers beneath their coats. Once they punch in at a time clock and arrive at their work stations, factory hands stow their coats but often retain their head gear (caps or hats are frequently worn

THE FRANKLIN AUTOMOBILE COMPANY

in the factory), don aprons or other protective clothing, pick up their tools, and prepare for another day of activity at machine, workbench or assembly station. The slap of belts and the hum of electric motors powering machines in the various departments now can be heard, together with the clank of the chain-driven conveyor in the final assembly area. The Franklin plant has sprung into life, and is poised to commence production of from twenty-five to seventy vehicles each working day.

Shifting his vantage point to the corner of South Geddes and Marcellus Streets shortly after 7:30, our observer sees Franklin office staff, now heavily weighted toward the female gender, appear on the scene. Here too there exists a concern about tardiness, with a number of clerical employees who live in outlying areas often boarding electric interurban cars at an unusually early hour to make certain they reach their place of employment well before the eight o'clock deadline. An occasional late-arriving office worker, upset at the prospect of a possible reprimand from a superior, might even turn and go home for the day rather than report after the starting hour. Clerical staff normally utilize the canopied Marcellus Street entrance to the big, red-brick Franklin office building, which stretches along South Geddes almost

An employee luncheon held at the office of the H. H. Franklin Manufacturing Company in November 1921. (The Franklin News, *December 1, 1921*)

to the corner of Gifford. Having climbed the few steps to the first floor level, office personnel walk through the automotive show-room located at the north end of the building, and next pass the enclosed offices of H.H. Franklin, Frank Barton, and a few other key executives (prior to his departure from the company in 1924, John Wilkinson occupied one of the largest private offices). The employees then enter a vast open room encompassing the remainder of the first floor of the building, down which can be seen long lines of desks, filing cabinets, typewriters and business machines. Clerical staff, not being required to punch a time clock, greet fellow workers and supervisors with a cheerful "Good Morning," hang outer garments on clothes trees or nearby racks, and then turn their attention to the multitude of business problems which daily pour into the office of the leading industrial firm in the city of Syracuse.

Franklin factory agents gather in front of the Franklin factory. "Brint" Baker is behind the wheel, and Frank Barton has his hand on Baker's shoulder. (Courtesy of Roland P. Kemp)

THE FRANKLIN AUTOMOBILE COMPANY

Most of the specialized personnel employed by the Franklin company arrive at office or shop as promptly as factory hands or clerical workers. Engineers, many of whom are paid on an hourly basis, normally put in early appearances to get engine tests or similar activities underway, while shop supervisors and their assistants often can be found on the plant floor well before the 7:20 starting time. Employees in the small number of departments which operate on a round-the-clock basis, such as heat-treating and the power house, occasionally find it necessary to report at odd hours in order to accommodate the needs of second- and third-shift hands. Sales and other executive-level personnel in the front office, unless attending to pressing matters away from company headquarters, almost invariably can be seen busily occupied at their desks by eight o'clock.

Finally, outside the door of a shipping and receiving area toward the rear of the Franklin plant the sharp "beep, beep" of a car horn can be heard on most mornings about 8:30. This sound announces the arrival of the firm's trim, impeccably dressed chief executive officer, H.H. Franklin. A nearby employee hastens to raise the overhead door, enabling H.H. (or on occasion his chauffeur) to drive a late-model Franklin motor car, often equipped with a body of custom design, into a reserved parking area. The company president, alighting from the vehicle, strides briskly through the aisles of the factory to the front office, stopping on occasion to question some supervisor, or less frequently a shop hand, about his activities. H.H.'s arrival means that the company's work force now is one hundred per cent involved in the job of designing, building and selling America's most popular air-cooled automobile.

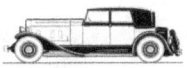

The Franklin manufacturing complex, rising as much as seven stories in the air and encompassing nearly 1,250,000 square feet of floor space (if this total area was channeled into a single-story building one hundred feet in width the structure would extend a distance of some two and one-half miles, a company spokesperson once proudly proclaimed), ranks as the largest factory in Syracuse and compares favorably in size to shops of numerous other independent companies across America producing motor vehicles during the 1920s. While smaller than the plants of the handful of large-volume producers such as Dodge, Nash, Hudson or Studebaker, the Franklin works easily surpasses in square footage the production facilities of a variety of lesser independents, including Peerless, Moon, Chandler and Jordan.[9-1]

The impressive red brick factory of the Syracuse air-cooled motor car builder does not, however, incorporate all the manufacturing facilities necessary for the production of a complete automobile. Among other things, the Franklin complex lacks a foundry in which such good-sized items as engine cylinders, crankcases and transmission housings can be cast. This deficiency, however, is largely remedied by the availability of several nearby plants which perform aluminum or iron casting operations, including the Straight-Line Engine Company located directly across Marcellus Street from Franklin, and the Oberdorfer and Cheney foundries situated a few miles distant. More striking is the absence of an internal body-building facility during this era. After terminating its short-lived venture into body-manufacturing during the immediate post-World War I period, the H.H. Franklin Company utilized for a time the products of several body-building concerns located in New York State and elsewhere. As noted previously, the firm finally has come to rely largely (except for a modest number of custom or limited-production bodies) on the Walker Body Company of Amesbury, Massachusetts, for this key item. However, Walker ships bodies to Franklin "in the white," i.e., in an unfinished condition. This meant that employees at the South Geddes plant are responsible for "trimming" the body–installing seats, upholstery, hardware, wiring and other essential items as well as painting the vehicle.

Apart from these limitations, the various departments in the Franklin factory drill, punch, cut, grind and press a vast array of key parts used in Franklin passenger cars. Gears are cut on specialized hobbers, carefully heat-treated by somewhat old-fashioned methods[9-2] to insure

THE FRANKLIN AUTOMOBILE COMPANY

durability under the strains imposed by everyday driving, and finally assembled into such major components as rear axles. Numerous small and not-so-small sheet metal parts—including by the late 1920s such items as fenders, splash aprons and even hoods—are stamped or formed on presses of varying sizes, smoothed out by finishers, painted, and made ready for installation on a vehicle. Until the introduction of steel frames in the 1928-29 period, Franklin master carpenters, after selecting top-quality cuts of timber, bond together long sections of finished wood by a heat-and-pressure process to create the famous flexible Franklin automobile frame.

A brief tour of the Franklin plant, again as seen through the eyes of our attentive observer, will be of interest at this point. Beginning in the earlier-described South Geddes Street building, the observer notes the bustle of activity in the big, open first-floor office area as the day unfolds. Sales and service personnel, seated at desks located just outside the private quarters of the top executives of the firm, are in frequent contact by telephone with distributors and dealers across the country, taking orders for new cars and seeking to adjust complaints. The telegraph is also heavily used—in a typical year some 30,000 telegrams are either sent or received by company staff.[9-3] When communication by mail is necessary, a young woman is summoned from the nearby stenographic pool to take dictation and type a letter (few executives enjoy the luxury of private secretaries). If it is essential to consult documents or retrieve correspondence from an earlier date, personnel of the filing section may be called on to locate such papers.

Something of the flavor of the Franklin office operation can be obtained from the recollections of Ralph Brown, who joined the Franklin staff in January, 1912, as a sixteen-year-old adding machine operator (at $8 per week) and ultimately rose to the responsible position of manager of accounts payable:

> Franklin office employees, both male and female, were expected to dress in conservative good taste (coats and ties were mandatory for men) and to behave on the job like ladies and gentlemen. No

one was permitted to smoke in the entire office area. Persons in the office conversed in quiet tones, and spoke on the phone in a similar manner. Most desks were equipped with two telephones, one used to contact various departments within the plant and the other to make outside calls. The only major source of noise in the vast first floor office was the comptometer operation. These business machines, used to calculate payroll and perform other bookkeeping functions for the company, were grouped in the rear of the room in order to localize the sharp clattering sound they produced.

Our observer also notes, at the extreme north end of the first floor of the South Geddes building, the showroom previously mentioned. In this area, on a nicely-carpeted floor, several striking, well-equipped examples of the current model Franklin car are displayed at all times. These sparkling vehicles, while not visible to the pedestrian on the street, nevertheless play a significant role in the Franklin sales program.

As our observer climbs the stairs to the second floor of the Geddes Street building, the scene changes quickly from a clerical atmosphere to one emphasizing technical activities. At the north end of the floor he enters a large room containing several dozen drafting tables plus an assortment of flat-topped desks, all covered with bundles of drawings and blueprints. This is the location of the mechanical design division of the Franklin engineering department, where the engine, chassis and other key components of vehicles are planned and drawn to scale. Immediately behind this room can be seen the offices of the company's chief engineer and chief metallurgist, both of which are furnished in a spartan manner. Moving further down the second floor, our observer notes the production "control boards" and then encounters the body design unit, where a small staff is intensely occupied in creating new styles for future Franklin vehicles. In this area also are located the offices of design consultants such as Ray Dietrich, plus studios where skilled stylists develop various color combinations to insure that Franklin vehicles are things of beauty.

THE FRANKLIN AUTOMOBILE COMPANY

Art and color specialist William McNabb tries new color shades on a Franklin car design.
(Courtesy of Meredith Lamson Estoff)

Ascending to the third floor of the Geddes Street building our invisible observer again finds himself in the middle of a cluster of company technical operations. At the Marcellus Street end of the building he observes more body drafters plus the tool design unit, in which machines, tools and dies essential for factory operation are laid out. Also in this area is found the purchasing department, a good-sized operation responsible for procuring annually several millions of dollars worth of parts, raw materials and other items needed to produce a finished Franklin car. Still further toward the south end of the building can be found the offices of the factory manager and plant master mechanic plus the time-study unit, while at the very rear a mailing machine room handles the many items sent out each day by the company to dealers and prospective purchasers.[a]

---

[a] Functions on the second and third floors of the South Geddes Street building occasionally were shifted. Thus, the descriptions given are correct only for one period of time.

THE PEOPLE WHO BUILT THE CARS

However, a number of extra copies of the supplement have been run off which have not been folded, and which are therefore especially well suited for framing. These unfolded copies can be obtained at the conference room on the second floor of building CM, or from Mr. Keane, office manager.

There are three hundred and nineteen faces in the group picture—count them. The flag which forms the background was loaned for the occasion through the courtesy of S. T. Betts, a well-known local real estate man. It is the largest flag in the city, and measures forty by twenty feet.

BRANCH LIBRARY IS POPULAR

That the branch of the Public Library installed in the Conference Room is well patronized is shown by the fact that from February 11 (the date when the library was installed) to April 25, one hundred and ninety-nine employes registered as borrowers, and drew out during that time nine hundred and fourteen volumes, of which seven hundred and fifty-four were books of fiction. The library at present contains between two hundred and fifty and three hundred volumes. Employes wishing any certain book not contained in the branch library may place their request through Wayne Burhans, librarian in chrage, who will ordinarily be able to secure the volume from the main public library down town. The library is open on Saturday from 12 to 12:15, and on other days from 12 to 1.

FRANKLIN LIBRARY DURING NOON HOUR. WAYNE BURHANS, WHO IS STANDING TO THE LEFT, IS KEPT BUSY HANDING OUT BOOKS

Employees making use of the employee library during lunch hour.
(The Franklin News, *May 1, 1919*)

THE FRANKLIN AUTOMOBILE COMPANY

A final climb brings our observer to the top floor of the Geddes Street structure, occupied by the company cafeteria. This facility plays a major role in allaying the pangs of hunger felt at noontime by the good-sized work force employed in the Franklin plant and office. Although many employees, particularly in the factory, eat their brown-bag lunches in the vicinity of their work places and numerous others seek a hasty meal at a nearby restaurant or even walk home for a midday bite, a large number choose to enjoy the low-cost food (typical plate lunches, such as beef stew or hot dogs and sauerkraut, are priced at a modest 25 to 35 cents) and the camaraderie found in the firm's cafeteria. This facility, in addition to serving meals, is very much a center of on-the-job social life for hundreds of workers from both office and plant. The company band often entertains listeners with a number of well-rendered tunes, with more youthful employees utilizing the music for a few minutes of dancing on the smooth hardwood floor. Many others take advantage of the tables and comfortable chairs to initiate games of cards or checkers, while more intellectually-inclined workers visit the small library located at one end of the room. One particularly appreciated feature is relaxation of the no-smoking rule enforced elsewhere in the Franklin complex, thus enabling employees to enjoy cigarette, cigar or a favorite pipe after lunch.

Our observer, however, notes the absence of a facility found in the typical large factory complex of the era, an executive dining room. While many automobile companies provide private quarters in which top-level staff can partake of a formally-served lunch, the Franklin firm, believing in equal treatment for all, eschews such an amenity. Company executives, from H.H. Franklin on down, who wish to enjoy something other than cafeteria food or who find themselves entertaining business guests from out-of-town and desire a degree of privacy, drive to downtown Syracuse to eat at a restaurant, hotel dining room or perhaps a private club.

As our observer walks across the "bridge" connecting the Geddes Street office structure with the most easterly building in the factory complex itself, he encounters a decidedly changed atmosphere. The

THE PEOPLE WHO BUILT THE CARS

An electric hoist was used to drop Franklin vehicle bodies onto the chassis.
*(*The Franklin News, *December 16, 1919).*

noise level is far higher than in the office, the air often contains the metallic and hot-oil odor common to a machine shop, and the floor is paved with small wooden blocks fitted tightly together. The various manufacturing departments now can be seen, each producing a number of parts essential to the finished motor vehicle. Lathes and drill presses emit whines and shrieks as they bite into metal, with workmen constantly kept busy feeding raw material into these ever-demanding machines and removing the finished parts. A crunching sound is produced by big milling machines as they trim the tops, bottoms and sides of such cast aluminum pieces as crankcases and transmission housings. A steady "thump, thump," can be heard from presses, some small and some towering far above the heads of the men operating them, as they punch out still other components required to build the car.

Dropping down to the ground level of the northernmost section of the factory, our observer now finds himself in the central shipping and receiving area of the Franklin complex. Adjacent to the several rail sidings which cross Marcellus Street from the north and extend deeply into the plant grounds can be observed the docks at which railroad cars–or an occasional truck or horse-drawn wagon–are unloaded. Here the big auto factory receives the vast stream of supplies needed to keep it in continuous production, ranging in size from small boxes of screws and washers to the large motor car bodies shipped to Syracuse from a distant city. This incoming torrent of essential components is balanced by an outgoing flow, as employees load completed Franklin automobiles into rail cars for shipment to distributors and dealers located across America. A smaller number of new cars, some with the steering wheels located in a unfamiliar position on the right side of the vehicle, are crated in waterproof wooden containers built by a small team of carpenters in preparation for shipment overseas.

Moving further west along Marcellus Street our observer next enters the cluster of buildings which form the core of Franklin factory operations. Denoted Buildings Y and OR, these reinforced-concrete-and-brick structures rise seven stories above ground level and extend west to Magnolia Street and south much of the way to Gifford. They contain numerous machine shops for production of parts, plus the areas where such key items as rear axles are built. Also found here is the vehicle assembly area, where the Franklin automobile takes final form.

The firm's plant operations experts have learned at an early date that in planning a multi-story factory for automobile manufacturing it is desirable to use the upper floors primarily for building the many individual components needed in a motor car, with such items then dropped down to a production line located on a lower level for final vehicle assembly. Consequently the bodies for the Franklin car, received in a unfinished state, are placed on elevators for transfer up to the fifth and sixth floors to be painted, rubbed out and polished, and then moved to the trim shop where they are upholstered and fitted with seats. Meanwhile, on the chain-driven vehicle production line on the second floor basic assembly gets underway, with the frame initially placed in an upside-down position and springs, axles and wheels securely attached. This work completed the unit then is turned over, and slowly pulled by an attached chain along the assembly line as teams of workmen install other key components of the chassis. Ultimately a motor, already run-in and thoroughly tested on a dynamometer, is placed in the chassis and the vehicle thus made capable of operation. Throughout much of the 1920s the motorized chassis without the body often is pulled from the production line for a number of miles of road testing, a process intended to insure its reliability.

With the chassis assembly complete, the vehicle moves ahead to the body drop, where a painted and trimmed automobile body is lowered from the third floor through a hole in the ceiling and attached to the chassis. Splash aprons, fenders, hood and bumpers then are attached, with headlights, taillights and similar parts also installed to produce a complete vehicle. Finally, the finished car is driven down a ramp to the ground floor of the factory and into the "glass house," a structure with windows on three sides, a wall painted white on the fourth, and strong lights overhead. Here, inspectors go over every inch of the vehicle to insure that it measures up to Franklin standards prior to being released for shipment.

Having viewed the numerous operations taking place in this major cluster of factory buildings, our observer now completes his tour by briefly visiting several auxiliary structures scattered around the overall Franklin complex. One of the most important of these is the powerhouse, a massive facility generating the bulk of the electricity and steam needed for heat, light and power throughout the entire works. Located in the center of the plant site, this large building is capped with the huge brick chimney which has become a Franklin landmark.

THE FRANKLIN AUTOMOBILE COMPANY

The powerhouse furnaces consume vast quantities of coal, brought in by railcar and deposited in a huge pile in the yard. Despite this dusty source of energy, the interior of the facility is kept spotlessly clean. Several smaller buildings can be found in the yard, including the "doghouse," a frame unit of dingy appearance and modest size in which the experimental engineering staff tests, often to the point of destruction, Franklin power plants. Another structure deserving recognition is the three-story brick building located at the northeast corner of Magnolia and Gifford Streets, housing the Franklin Die Casting Company. This operation, which also utilizes a corrugated sheet steel structure on the south side of Gifford Street to house heavy presses, was the basis for the founding of the H.H. Franklin Manufacturing Company in the 1890s. With only a hundred or so employees, it is now dwarfed by the massive automobile enterprise.

Our observer thus ends his brief tour of Syracuse's largest industry. A number of specialized functions have been by-passed on this somewhat speedy journey, but as numerous former Franklin employees recount stories of their associations with the company these missing links will shortly be filled in.

Throughout the 1920s and early 1930s, the Franklin employees in factory and office came from a wide variety of backgrounds and performed a broad range of tasks for the company. The personal descriptions by these individuals of their work and of the experiences they encountered deserve telling in their own words. The first person who will describe his recollections of work at Franklin is Leo Gerst, employed for a number of years in drafting and design activities at the South Geddes Street plant:

> I was born on the north side of Syracuse, in 1899. My father, who like my mother was a German immigrant, during my youth ran a bakery in this section of the city. Following high school I took an

ICS (International Correspondence School) course in drafting, and soon afterward obtained a position as a tracer with Continental Can Company, which had begun operations in Syracuse a few years earlier. Next I went to the New Process Gear Company, where I worked in the drafting room for two years and, incidentally, met my future wife. Then, in 1920 I began working as a draftsman in the mechanical design section at Franklin. However, my first stretch of work at the company was brief. The Franklin firm about 1921 was attempting to raise money through the sale of stock, and in an effort to improve efficiency and thus impress banks and potential buyers of stock it cut back heavily on staff, including such new employees as myself. After being laid off, I returned to work for a time at New Process Gear. In a year or so, though, I was recalled at Franklin, where I began working my way up in the drafting department. While I handled mostly minor items at first, gradually I was given more intricate assignments, culminating in the design of the front end of the Series 11 car where I repositioned the axle and moved it forward. Some time later, when Franklin dealers were beginning to feel pressure from customers for four-wheel brakes, together with another draftsman I was directed to design a new braking system for the vehicle. As this was a crash project which had to be completed in a few weeks the other man, John Rogers, handled brake design for the rear wheels while I dealt with the front. We worked day and night on this task–hours were of no consequence. After these accomplishments I was moved up to assistant head of the mechanical drafting section, and finally was appointed chief of the unit.

Somewhere around thirty men were employed in the mechanical drafting unit, with each person assigned a drawing board and usually a desk. No women were employed in any capacity in our unit. There were a lot of other activities taking place on our floor, also. The control boards were located there for a time, but finally either moved or done away with in the late 1920s. Quite a bit of space was taken up by the body design people. Bill Emonds was the chief body designer, but Ray Dietrich played a major role as a consultant. The plant cafeteria was located a couple of floors above us. I would

THE FRANKLIN AUTOMOBILE COMPANY

often eat there when the band played. Along with the food operation came a big invasion of cockroaches. We would kill them on the walls of the drafting room, and at times their dead bodies covered the place!

When the depression arrived and the company went downhill the number of draftsmen was cut back heavily. Along with this we suffered a series of stiff salary cuts. Finally, only the man who had been my boss in the drafting room earlier was kept on the job. The rest of us were let go, and just dispersed all over the place. I was called back once or twice for special projects, but that was the end of my permanent employment with Franklin.

Morale was high at the Franklin plant throughout the 1920s, since employees got the best money in town. There were layoffs at times in production departments, especially during model changeover. Other companies, though, generally would not hire laid-off Franklin people, fearing that they would leave when a call-back came.

There were lots of outside activities sponsored by the company in the 1920s. Boxing and wrestling matches were put on from time-to-time in open areas of the factory. A foreman's club held meetings in the cafeteria once a month after work. At one meeting, in order to liven things up a bit, some "hootchy-kootchy" girls were brought in to dance. H.H. Franklin got wind of this, objected strongly, and it was never done again!

When first employed at Franklin, I lived on Park Street on the Syracuse north side with my parents. I got married in 1922, and at that time rented a flat on Bellevue Avenue about a mile and a half from the plant. My pay was $37.50 a week then, and we did all right on it–in fact, we managed to save money. We did not have our own car at the time we got married. Instead, we used my father-in-law's automobile for some years before finally purchasing a Model A Ford about 1930.

THE PEOPLE WHO BUILT THE CARS

Along with Leo Gerst, a substantial number of other Franklin workers also were natives of Syracuse. Ralph Brown, the office employee introduced earlier, held several jobs as a teenager before beginning work at Franklin. He ushered in downtown theaters, delivered newspapers, and finally operated a horse-drawn delivery van for a meat market. When he entered the office at the Franklin firm Ralph lacked experience in clerical work, but soon found that this was not necessarily a disadvantage. The H.H. Franklin Company tended to bring into its office individuals who had not worked in a similar capacity elsewhere, preferring to train new people in its own system. Ralph retains many recollections of the company in its early days, prior to and during World War I.

> Very few people had motor cars when I began work at Franklin in 1912, since they could not possibly have afforded them on the wages paid at that time. In decent weather many employees rode bicycles to and from work. The company furnished several racks located just behind the main office for bike storage. No one bothered to lock his bike, as theft of a cycle from the company racks was unheard of in that era. Persons who lived within a reasonable distance of the plant often walked–people thought nothing of a mile-or-two hike to work in those days. However, a majority of Franklinites used streetcars to get to the plant or, if they lived in outlying towns as a lot did, took the interurban trolley into central Syracuse and walked the rest of the way.

> As I acquired experience and maturity I was chosen for assignments which took me out of the office. One of these tasks involved the company payroll. In this period, everyone was given his or her pay in -cash, and a large sum of money had to be drawn from a downtown bank for this purpose. When I went with the paymaster to obtain the funds, we both were armed with thirty-two caliber pistols! The payroll was made up in a tightly locked room by a small group of trusted employees, and had to balance to the penny. A second special task involved the driving of Franklin cars across upstate New York to a lake steamer anchored at Buffalo. The vehicles were

destined for the Franklin dealer in Cleveland, Clayt (C.S.) Carris. I knew very little about operating a motor car, but was able to pick up the rudiments of driving and encountered no real trouble on the trip until I pulled the Franklin onto the boat and had to maneuver it close to an already-loaded vehicle. I can still recall the deck hand yelling at me: "Move it over!" He wanted it parked within a few inches of the adjacent car, to save space.

During the period from 1912 to 1920, quite a number of restaurants, diners and saloons were located in the vicinity of the Franklin plant. These places catered to employees of Franklin, Brown-Lipe, and other nearby factories. Some served good meals, others were little more than cheap joints. In those days the saloons had their "free lunch" counters, where food was put out for the patrons to help themselves. This food almost always was salty, intended to raise a thirst for more beer!

An occasional Franklin employee came from a family with deep roots in Syracuse industry, and even in the Franklin firm itself. Frederick Kenyon's father began with the H.H. Franklin Manufacturing Company when it was still producing many key parts for its motor cars at the Lipe Machine Shop. He built early Franklin automobile engines in the Lipe facility. The father, a toolmaker who learned his trade in the 1890s, trained William Dunk and other future Franklin manufacturing executives in machine shop methods when they joined the firm during the opening days of motor car production. With a father employed at the auto firm, Fred Kenyon as a youngster lived on Marcellus Street, only a block or so from the Franklin plant. He recalls the activities in which he engaged as a youth, and his work at the Franklin factory:

> When I was a young boy I sold papers outside the Franklin factory in the early morning, before classes began at the nearby Delaware School at 9 A.M. While on the track team in grammar school I caught the eye of the coach at Syracuse Vocational High School, who convinced me to enroll there. Since I received good grades in the advanced machine shop class at Vocational High the teacher,

who worked in the Franklin plant during the summer, urged me to seek employment there as an apprentice toolmaker. I started in the tool grinding room at Franklin about 1923, where I did nothing but sharpen drills for a month straight. Finally I was moved on to more interesting assignments in the toolroom. I learned to operate lathes and milling machines, and to harden the finished tools.

The toolroom was a busy place, particularly during model change-over times. While the unneeded production workers were sent home, the toolroom went crazy with overtime work. On one special die job I pushed a 14-inch bastard file from Monday morning right through until 2 P.M. Tuesday! Another project I recall was finishing motors for display at the New York Automobile Show. Everything had to be nickel-plated, a real work of art, which often kept me going until one A.M.

I usually ate lunch in the plant cafeteria, which had good food. Often entertainment was provided, with a guitarist brought in occasionally. One noon hour I played the county checker champion, and managed to beat him–he played five persons on different checkerboards at one time.

One day I was sent downstairs to mark a table with a hammer and chisel. I accidentally hit my finger hard with the hammer, smashing it up pretty well and causing it to bleed badly. I showed it to my boss, and he fainted. They had to carry him on a stretcher to first aid, while I walked! "Doc" Lockrow, the first aid man, bandaged the finger, but it really throbbed. He dressed it every day for a week, and nature finally healed it.

Another former toolroom employee was Frank Mittins, who worked as a apprentice at the plant in the late 1920s and early 1930s. Mittins' father, also a Franklin employee, assisted him in obtaining employment. Frank has many recollections of his four years at the big South Geddes Street plant:

THE FRANKLIN AUTOMOBILE COMPANY

As toolroom apprentices we were usually moved from one machine to another every three months. However, if you developed real ability in operating a machine and your output was needed, you might be kept there a much longer time. One particular duty marked an apprentice's low status. On Saturday mornings each of us was given a bundle of waste rags and a five-gallon can of gasoline, and told to clean the various machines in the toolroom until they glistened.

Apart from this Saturday morning job, which today probably would be prohibited for health reasons, working conditions in the toolroom were good. Blowers sucked up most of the dust and fumes, so the

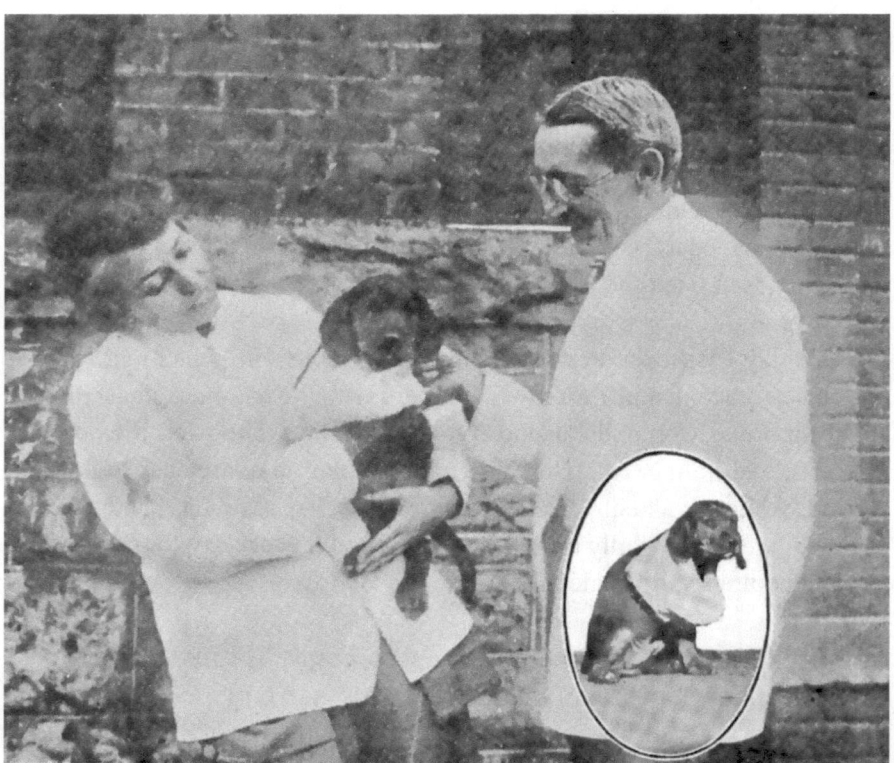

Doc Lockrow (right) handled all first-aid matters at the Franklin plant. Here, he has set the broken leg of a puppy that had been hit by a truck in front of the Franklin factory. (The Franklin News, *December 16, 1919)*

air usually was decent to breathe. No goggles or aprons were furnished–you brought your own. Every floor was equipped with a couple of rest rooms.

I began work at Franklin in 1927, after signing articles of apprenticeship. I lived at home up on Arthur Street, and usually walked the several miles to the plant every day, carrying my lunch. Once each week apprentices went down to school for classwork. My starting rate as an apprentice was thirty-three cents an hour, with increases of a few cents hourly each year. However, the work was steady, with a chance to put in a lot of overtime during model change-over periods.

The toolroom was located on the fifth floor of Y Building. About forty men worked in it, making a variety of tools and dies for departments throughout the plant and then maintaining them. There were some big machines installed in the factory in the late 1920s, including a huge press which punched out fenders and a costly crankshaft grinder. Incidentally, crankshafts during that period were stored outdoors for some months to season, and then brought in for cleanup and grinding.

A later arrival at the Franklin plant was Syracuse sheet-metal worker Armando Falso, who entered company employment in the depths of the depression. He relates his early training, and his subsequent work at Franklin:

After leaving school I worked in my father's sheet metal shop in the 1920s as an apprentice. The journeyman under whom I trained was a tough, unpleasant individual, who could be harsh with young apprentices. He often corrected mistakes with a sharp cuff on the head. With the coming of the depression and the virtual elimination of new construction in the early 1930s, my father's business dropped off to a point where he really did not need me. As I had gotten married in 1929, I had to find employment, and finally sought work at the Franklin factory in early 1932. Fortunately for me, Franklin,

THE FRANKLIN AUTOMOBILE COMPANY

after ending the purchase of car bodies from the Walker Company in Massachusetts, opened its own body shop and needed a few workers with sheet metal experience. I was one of two or three persons taken on out of a big crowd of job seekers standing at the gate of the Franklin plant.

I was sent to the sheet metal department located on a lower floor of the factory, where I began building mud aprons for the front of the car. Quite a lot of these parts were needed, both for new Franklin cars and as replacements for aprons broken in accidents involving vehicles already on the road. The superintendents and foremen during this period at Franklin were pretty hard-boiled, but since I had dealt with a domineering boss during my apprenticeship this did not bother me. Shortly after coming to Franklin I developed a new form for shaping the mud aprons, which made it possible to more than double daily production. This got a raise in pay for me but produced some animosity on the part of other workers in the small sheet metal crew, who during these hard times wanted to see the work stretched out so that it would last longer.

Working conditions in the Franklin plant were satisfactory for the time. We had adequate ventilation in our department, the lighting was good and the wood block floors were easy on everyone's feet. The company first aid station took care of even a sliver in your hand. There was some type of union in the sheet metal shop, but workers did not have to belong so I never joined. The company was very worried about theft. Each exit gate had guards assigned to it, with packages and even bulges in the pockets of employees checked as they left the plant.

I took a streetcar, and later a bus, to get to work. I did own a car, but left it at home for my wife to use. We lived in a house on Cedric Street, on the east side of Syracuse. The house had been repossessed by a bank early in the depression, and I obtained it by agreeing to pay the interest due on the mortgage. The bank was glad to get the six percent annual interest without worrying about immediate repayment of the principal. It had foreclosed on many houses throughout the city, and did not want another on its hands.

Almost every week while I was employed at Franklin the work force was cut and people laid off. Finally, after some months of employment, I came in one morning and found my operation shut down. The foreman, with tears in his eyes (he too was being laid off), handed me the final paycheck, and that was the end of my work at the Franklin plant. From that time on the company probably used up its inventory of sheet metal parts to build the small number of vehicles it turned out.

Joining the large number of Syracuse natives who were employed by the air-cooled automobile manufacturer was a substantial contingent of persons who came from outside the city. These workers lived in towns which stretched in a circular pattern around Syracuse from Elbridge, Jordan and Auburn in the west to Fulton, Baldwinsville and Liverpool in the north, Canastota and Fayetteville in the east and LaFayette and Tully to the south. Many employees lived in communities which were connected with the city of Syracuse by interurban trolley, thus easing the problem of commuting. Others sought rides to the factory with fellow-employees who owned automobiles, or lived in rooming houses near the plant during the workweek and went home only on weekends. A number of these out-of-town workers recall their experiences, among them Harold Davis, who grew up some thirty miles northwest of Syracuse. Harold describes his early life, and work at Franklin:

I was raised on a farm in the town of Hanibal, in Oswego County. I lost time at school because I helped my father work the farm, but did finish the eighth grade. About the time I reached manhood my parents moved to a much smaller farm in Martville in northern Cayuga county and no longer needed my services. I found a summer job in the public works department of the village of Hanibal, where I operated a grader and drove a truck. When fall came, a friend who worked at the H.H. Franklin Company called me and said that the

THE FRANKLIN AUTOMOBILE COMPANY

firm was hiring people. By this time I knew quite a bit about the mechanical aspects of cars through practical experience plus reading and studying auto and tractor repair manuals. I filled out an application for work at the Franklin plant, which I turned in to George Dutcher, the employment manager and was soon taken on.

I began work the first week of November, 1926, in the shipping and receiving department, where I was assigned to the raw stock section. There was no training of any kind, you simply "learned by doing." We handled Walker-built auto bodies brought in on rail cars plus all kinds of finished and unfinished parts and supplies used in the Franklin plant. Engine oil was brought in from the Quaker State Company in carload lots. After unloading these items we had to carefully count and check everything against the shipping bills and memos which were then turned in at the office. Many items received by our department were taken immediately by handcart or truck to different parts of the plant to be utilized for assembly. There was no night shift in shipping and receiving, but if finished vehicles had to be loaded on box cars late in the day, overtime was authorized. The company did not want to pay demurrage charges on rail cars sitting there overnight.

I roomed on South Geddes Street about two blocks from the plant gate during the week, going home to Martville only on weekends. The walk to work took five minutes, and snow storms presented no handicap. I ate breakfast and dinner at a nice diner, but since we were given only a half-hour break at noon I had to eat lunch at a short-order restaurant just outside the plant which gave very quick service.

Work in the raw stock section at times could be tough and dirty, so there was a large turnover of personnel. Occasionally an employee would seek to dodge a heavy unloading job by hanging around the "lunch wagon," a handcart which came through the plant twice a day where workers could purchase sandwiches, hot or cold drinks and candy. The violator usually was warned once or twice about his malingering, and if it continued he was let go.

I was only a seasonal worker at Franklin. I would be on the payroll from late fall until April or May, during the big winter and early spring car production period, and then be laid off. Some older people who had been with the company for a long time were kept on the year around. However, I was always able to obtain work with a road construction company during the outdoor months, which kept me employed until "freeze-up" time in the fall, when I would get a call-back from Franklin. I had the opportunity to work my way up in the raw stock operation, and ultimately became receiving clerk. My pay in this job was about fifty-five cents an hour. Then I was laid off in May, 1932, and never called back. By that time the company had cut down to a tiny work force, and was building only a handful of cars.

I still recall the twelve-cylinder automobile that Franklin built during the final days of my work with the company. It was a big, beautiful car, with nice lines and body shape. The motor and chassis were very good, but the body was a failure from the standpoint of quality and durability. Revamping of the plant would have been necessary to build it right, and that would have been too costly a proposition. Many of the workers in our department thought that marked the beginning of the end for the firm.

Other employees from outlying towns found that commuting to and from the plant involved a long day. Henry Burke, who lived in the village of Jordan and worked at Franklin first in 1927, and later in 1929, describes his experiences:

Our working hours at the Franklin plant were from 7:20 A.M. to 5 P.M. Monday through Friday, with an hour off for lunch. On Saturdays work ended at noon. I took the Rochester & Syracuse interurban trolley to work, which I caught in Jordan at 6:05 A.M. Even a heavy fall of snow did not stop the trolley operation, as large cars fitted with snow plows were used on the line. However, the interur-

THE FRANKLIN AUTOMOBILE COMPANY

ban dropped us off nearly a mile from the plant, which meant a long walk twice a day. It was after 6 P.M. when I got off the trolley on the evening trip back to Jordan.

Before coming to Franklin I had worked on a farm during summer months and went to school in the winter, so I had no factory experience. I was employed as a production line worker in final assembly, where I attached the rear axle to the frame. The axles were built on the third floor and lowered to the second-floor assembly line, where they were fitted to the frame when it was in an upside-down position. Two other men, William Potter and George Drake, worked with me on the axle installation team. There was no real training for assembly line work; you were put with an experienced person for about three days, by which time you got up to speed. With heavy axles being installed there was some concern about safety, but I was never really hurt on the job. I did get something in my eye once, but it was not serious.

Rate of production had increased sharply when I worked for the Franklin Company the second time. Earlier, when Bill Dunk was production manager, about 35 cars came off the assembly line each day, but in the 1929 period, under Lew Purdy, we were pushed to get the output up to 70, even if it meant working overtime. Some days when the five P.M. quitting time approached one of the straw bosses would walk up and down the assembly line shouting: "Seventy cars–stay 'til you get 'em." However, the Franklin workers were an independent bunch, and many took their coats off the hooks and left the job at five P.M. regardless of the foreman's order. On at least one occasion those leaving were threatened with punishment by Ernie Rang, head of the final assembly department, but nothing ever came of this. The job of straw boss was a pretty unpleasant one–these men had just one concern, getting production out. While I was there one of them could not take the pressure, and went back to working at the bench.

Inspections of the work you did were thorough, especially the first time I worked at the Franklin plant. The company tried to build a high-quality car, and a finished automobile would be rejected by an inspector if not up to standard. During my second period of employment there was a lot more emphasis on production–they were pushing hard for big output of cars. The motors were tested thoroughly before going in the chassis, and then the car itself was tested. In 1929, though, the testing of the car seemed to be done mostly in the plant. I noticed some cars coming through assembly with steering wheels on the right. These were for foreign shipment.

Work on the assembly line, with the constant demand for production, was tedious. Unless you could talk or joke a bit you would go crazy. One man usually acted as a lookout to see if any of the top executives of the company were approaching our area. If he shouted "number one," it meant Bill Dunk was coming into the final assembly department. No smoking was permitted anywhere in the plant. I heard that there was a brief walkout of the men in the trim shop on one occasion, involving a dispute over group bonus pay. My own pay was sixty-four and a half cents per hour at the end of my employment. A certain amount of theft of parts by employees went on while I was there. Tires allegedly were dropped through a manhole into the stream called "Harbor Brook," which ran under the plant.

On the other side of Syracuse, Harry Borszweski also journeyed to the Franklin factory each day from a small community located east of Fayetteville. He relates his work activities:

I went to work at the Franklin plant in the mid-nineteen-twenties, when I was eighteen, and was employed there about four or five years. This was my first real job. I worked in a small section with seven or eight other men, upholstering seats for the Franklin car. Our operation was located right at the top of our building, on the sixth floor.

I usually came to work by trolley car, but during winter snowstorms it wasn't always easy to get over to the car line on foot. So, my father sometimes would have to take me to the trolley stop in his horse and wagon. I took a lunch along–saw no reason to spend money on food at a restaurant or cafeteria. I remember the big whistle blowing to start the working day, and also punching in-and-out at the timeclock. One good thing about working in the upholstering department was that I could lie down on a seat cushion and take a rest at noon-time.

My job in the upholstering section involved tacking on the undercovering and felt to hold the burlap-wrapped seat springs in place. To save time, at the start of a seat job I put half a handful of tacks in my mouth, spitting one out when needed. Once I had done my part of the work the seat cushion was turned over to a skilled man who did the finishing–he put on the outside leather or cloth in a very careful manner. Working conditions in our part of the plant were pretty good, but as we were right under the roof it got very hot in the summer, and we had to keep the windows wide open for air.

The body trim line during this period was located nearby, and I was able to see the work going on. The bare body first was placed on a wooden frame with steel wheels underneath. Teams of men swarmed over it doing things inside and out–they installed wiring, tacked on interior upholstery panels, and fitted parts on the outside. The body then was pushed by hand to the next station for another work team to put on more items. Finally, the body was striped by older men sitting on stools. They did this work very neatly and carefully using tiny brushes. Franklin was a beautifully-made car.

I received fifty cents an hour when I started, but was given a raise after spending some time on the job. A lot of men, especially those doing body trim work, were paid on the group bonus plan and made good money. There were some pretty tough young fellows in the upholstery shop. I got into a tussle with one guy, a Swede, and the foreman had to separate us! You often heard threats like: "I'll be waiting for you outside after work." It was best to get out of the place darn quickly on those evenings, I can tell you!

THE PEOPLE WHO BUILT THE CARS

One Franklin employee who journeyed some distance to begin work at the company was George King, of Watertown, New York, a city located sixty miles north of Syracuse. King operated his father's farm for a time, and later worked in Watertown. Finally his father, having secured a job at the Franklin plant earlier, urged George to apply also. Taking a bus to Syracuse around the end of the summer of 1928, the young man found that the Franklin firm needed additional employees for production work, and was hired the same day. He recalls his experiences on the assembly line:

> I was part of a three-man crew working on installation of headlights and several other front-end parts. My job involved lying on a creeper underneath the car all day long, and driving bolts up through holes already drilled in the wooden frame and sheet metal to hold headlight brackets and other items in place. If the holes for the bolts did not line up, I used a heavy electric drill to run new ones through. The two men working up top then fastened the light brackets and other parts on the protruding ends of the bolts. Since the car was moving steadily along the conveyor, I put my feet up against the bottom of the chassis and it pushed the creeper ahead at the same pace. We had about fifteen minutes to do the work at our station on the line. Quite a few Franklin cars were built for export at that time, and some had right-hand steering. These were run right down the line with the others—we just had to reverse some parts of our work.
>
> The Franklin plant was kept clean, and no one pushed you too much. So long as you kept up with the line everything was fine. However, on the assembly line there were no breaks during working hours. If you took a few minutes off to go to the toilet you had to catch up with your work when you returned. Things sometimes did not get done then, and had to be taken care of later. Inspectors would check for any items overlooked. We started work early, shortly after seven A.M. I lived in a furnished room pretty close to the plant, and ate all my meals out, generally at one of about a dozen restaurants located nearby. I never ate in the company cafeteria.

Overall I would rate Franklin a pretty fair place to work at. No one tried to punish you if you missed doing something on the car, and the foremen were O.K. I got tired of production work, though, especially when it involved being on my back under the cars all day long, and quit the job around Christmas in 1928. I believe I was there altogether less than six months.

Another person with a farming background who was a member of the plant work force for several years was William James. "Bill" James was born and grew up on a farm on Onondaga Road on the west side of Syracuse, only three or so miles from the Franklin factory. He comments on his experiences at Franklin:

When I finished high school in June, 1927, I spent the summer and early fall with a maintenance crew in the state highway department. This was seasonal work, and ended on October 25. I went to Franklin about two days later, following in the footsteps of my brother Emmett who already worked there. I was not quite eighteen years old when I was hired. As I recall, a limited physical exam was given me by the plant nurse.

After being hired I reported to "Red" Countryman, head of engine assembly, who assigned me to the crankcase unit, located on the third floor of the factory building which connected to the rear of the Geddes Street office. The crankcase group included some fifteen to twenty men, who performed different tasks. Four of us worked at benches in line with each other, placing main bearings in the crankcase. These were checked for fit by inserting a crankshaft smeared with Prussian Blue compound. After the crankshaft was spun a few times the blue compound would show any high spots on the bearings, which then were hand-scraped until a proper fit was secured. When the engine was completely assembled it was moved to the adjacent test room where it was run with transmission attached. If the engine was found to be faulty it was reworked, but very few were not O.K.

While we didn't have a specific production quota to meet on the bearing job, we were expected to keep hard at work. We had little or no freedom—we could not move around, and were allowed only one three-minute break during the nearly five-hour morning work period. If an employee was late by even a couple of minutes, his name and badge number were taken by the watchman at the gate and he was docked a half-hour's pay. We had a hour off for lunch, which was nice. The food in the plant cafeteria was good, the prices were fair, and we could relax and talk at the tables as we ate. Working conditions at Franklin were satisfactory. The plant was clean, not particularly smoky or dusty, and well-lighted.

During rush periods in late 1928 and in early 1929, we often had to work seven days a week, plus some evenings. At this point it almost became a sweatshop and the men finally rebelled, leaving against orders at noon one Saturday. When we reported for work Monday morning a short but stern warning was given to everyone; "Do not come back if you do it again!" At that point morale fell pretty low. When I wanted to go hunting in the Adirondacks in the fall of 1928, in order to get a bit of time off I had to have a doctor write to the company about my health problems. He may have stretched the truth a bit when he said I needed an operation!

We had a pretty diversified bunch working in the Franklin plant, with a lot of nationalities represented. A big majority grew up in Syracuse or the surrounding area, while about ten per cent were foreign born. There were some Canadians at the factory. One person who came from Almonte, Ontario, went back there when the plant closed.

A big change in factory employment came at the end of 1929 and the early months of 1930–I would guess that as much as seventy per cent of the help was let go in a short time. By 1931 and early 1932 I found myself cut down to a day or two of work in a week, or at times even in a month. At this point I was the last one of the original four people on the bearing job still employed. Finally, later in 1932, I too

THE FRANKLIN AUTOMOBILE COMPANY

was laid off permanently. I doubt if many engines were made after that–the company mostly used up what it had on hand. I had begun going to college part-time when things slowed down, since it was obvious there was no future with the firm.

A native Canadian who spent several years working at Franklin, John Des Groseilliers, was born in 1903, in Wallaceburg, Ontario. John came to Syracuse in 1923, thinking of enlisting in the U.S. Navy. He relates what made him change his mind, and how he ultimately became associated with the automobile firm:

> I met a good-looking young redheaded woman soon after arriving in Syracuse, and abandoned any thought of leaving the city for naval service. After working for several years as a planer operator for a company which produced artificial stones, I was hired by Franklin in the mid-to-late 1920s. Edward Quirk, a service department foreman, helped me get the job. I began as a mechanic's helper in the section of final assembly where items like cowl lights were installed and the vehicle given a semi-final inspection for defects. After a year I was rated as a mechanic, and assigned some additional tasks. One time I was sent up front to the factory showroom to work on a vehicle being displayed, and while there H.H. Franklin suddenly stuck his head inside the car and asked me if I knew what I was doing! He seemed to be a nice man, with an obvious harelip.
>
> During the period I worked at Franklin final assembly was located on the second floor, with finished cars driven down a ramp into the "glass house" at ground level for a strict final check. Sometimes a smashup occurred at the end of the ramp if a car broke loose from control of the driver and hit other vehicles parked at the bottom. I knew many of the drivers who road-tested cars on Lord's Hill west of Syracuse.
>
> The Franklin automobile was a high-quality product, well put together. The conveyor in final assembly ran slowly, and people had time to do good work. There were many inspectors around con-

stantly checking on things. The company did have a bit of a problem at one time when the engines were set too tight, but this was soon corrected. All-in-all, I would describe it as a very decent outfit to work for.

When Purdy became boss of manufacturing, he bought millions of dollars worth of new machinery in an all-out effort to build up production. Many of these machines, though, were never used effectively. The Franklin plant just was not suited for turning out cars in high volume. It should have been built entirely on one floor, instead of multi-story with cars and parts always being shifted around on elevators and ramps.

After the peak year of 1929, when we often worked overtime, things really slowed down. I think the Franklin firm made a mistake in bringing out the V-12 model. It was too large a car and did not fit in with other company products. Not many were built, but I do remember one of them being sold on special order to a famous jockey, who wanted a 100-mile-per-hour car!

At the end I was the only man working as a mechanic-inspector, and often there was little to do. Finally the big boss of all car assembly operations, Harry Orchard, came in one day and said: "The vacation is over, go get your time." That was all; I found myself unemployed.

Ted Wichert was a native of Syracuse, born in 1905. After attending a technical high school he learned of a training class for young men interested in learning the painting trade. This apprentice training ultimately led to a job with the Franklin firm. He describes his experiences:

We were kept in the training school until considered good enough to go into production paint work in a factory–about one and one-half years of instruction in all. I was taught paint finishing, and also trained to do graining of interior panels. I still have my steel graining brushes from that period. When I went into the Franklin plant about 1927, the painting process involved all lacquer. The aluminum car bodies first were carefully washed with acid, and the primer sprayed on and rubbed out. Then a color coat was put on, lightly sanded down, washed and rubbed out. After this process was repeated with more color coats a mist coat of lacquer finally was applied, carefully rubbed with pumice stone and buffed. It took several hours to complete the painting work, and then the body had to pass a strict inspection. If any defect showed it went back for redoing. When steel bodies later were used the painting process was speedier. Painting was completed before the body was moved upstairs for trimming. At the time I was there, most Franklin cars were built with closed bodies. Earlier the company used color varnish in paint work, a very slow process which held down production.

Painting was done by a good-sized gang of men, probably numbering over 100. Another smaller crew striped the cars and occasionally put on the owner's initials. I enjoyed working in the paint shop at Franklin. Everybody did his job, and we helped each other. I carried my lunch, eating out in the parking lot during warm weather and at my bench if it was cold. The paint shop was a dustproof area, with a good ventilating system to remove fumes. No masks were used by the workers when I was there. Production painters were paid about ninety cents per hour, but during rush periods we worked a lot of overtime and made a great deal of money. A heavy load of overtime could become unpleasant if continued very long, and since the company switchboard shut down at 5 P.M., there was no way of calling home in the evening to let our families know how late we would be. Big overtime pay was offset by the periods when the company changed models. There was no work and no earnings whatever then!

I worked as a painter for about three years, and then went into inspection, where I spent my final two or three years with the company. Layoffs hit hard beginning in 1930, although the layoff process appeared to be fairly managed. The company continued its "perfection approach" in building cars until the end of my employment late in 1932. Once the Olympic model came in, I saw few real Franklins made afterward, and I suspect the firm mostly drew on its stock of existing parts to build these cars.

During my later years with the company I was assigned to maintain H.H. Franklin's car–it was a Pirate model. Usually Mr. Franklin drove the car to the plant himself, but if a longer trip was planned his chauffeur was at the wheel. Needless to say, I kept the car spotless! Mr. Franklin, with his harelip, tended to be a bit difficult to understand.

Jack Oswald was a youth in his mid-teens when he began his employment at the Franklin plant about 1927. He relates how he was hired and the type of work he did:

I was only sixteen when I sought employment at the Franklin plant, and had not held any real job before that. A young woman I knew who worked in the company office told the employment interviewer I was eighteen, and he took her word for it, with no further check made. I did bench work in one of the machine shops first, grinding burrs off the heads of bolts. Not much skill was needed for that kind of job; it was break-in work for a beginner. Later I was put on various production machines, Jones & Lamson, Warner & Swazey, where I turned out tie-rod ends and idler shafts. When not needed for machine-shop jobs I was given other work around the plant, including placing felt in between car bodies and fenders to prevent squeaks and rattles.

While I worked at Franklin I lived on Geddes Street about four or five blocks above the plant. I usually went home for lunch after a bad experience in the cafeteria. One noon they handed out samples of chewing tobacco, and being a foolish young guy I tried some and promptly got sick! Not too many people drove to work, as the parking lot held only about 100 to 200 cars. Quite a few workers still used bicycles. A large number, men. and women, came by streetcar. I still remember the double-headers (two streetcars attached together) waiting outside at five P.M.

I have many memories of the Franklin plant. It was nicknamed the "Daisy Farm," either because it was an easy place to work at or because so many farmers were employed there. These farm people wanted to work on the land in the summer months, and actually welcomed being laid off during that period. Often a lot of farmers would come in at the beginning of winter looking for work and willing to take a pretty low rate of pay in exchange for a job.

Cars were run up and down the hills west of Syracuse for testing purposes when I first came, but later a test track, deliberately made very bumpy, was installed inside the plant. The track was built tight up against posts and machines, so drivers had to be darn careful. When Charles Lindbergh drove over the inside test track on a visit to the plant he was supposed to have said that it was a tougher run than his flight to Paris! The Franklin was a well-built car, close to hand-made, but pretty costly to buy.

During peak work periods I made up to sixty dollars per week, which included some overtime and, later in my employment, payments under a bonus system. However, if your total earnings per hour exceeded ninety cents the company would re-time you and a new standard would be set for payment. You usually did not know that you were being retimed! There was no union I knew of in the plant except in part of the paint shop–I heard that some of the painters went out on strike at least once. I would describe working conditions at Franklin as good at all times. I continued with the company until near the end of its existence.

Management of the plant changed while I worked there. Bill Dunk was succeeded as factory boss by Lew Purdy, who I was told came from another automobile company. Purdy pushed people, seeking more efficiency, and also put in a huge press to punch out big sheet metal parts in volume. I think this was a poor decision, since the factory was laid out wrong for large production.

THE PEOPLE WHO BUILT THE CARS

Ward Sturge worked at the Franklin plant on two occasions. He also was a man with an unusual qualification–talent as a professional musician. Ward describes his activities as both a plant employee and a member of the company band.

> I had been a musician all my life, as were my father and mother. I played in an army band during World War I, and the bandmaster suggested I go to Juilliard for further training. However, when I came home from service, I went to work in a powdered milk factory. Then I heard of Franklin and applied for work there. My background as a musician was a big factor in my being hired, because the company wanted workmen who could also fill in a band members.
>
> I started with the Franklin Company in 1921, working on a gear cutter. Then I was assigned to experimental work on transmissions. During the noon hour, I played in the band in the company cafeteria. I also played bassoon in the Syracuse Symphony Orchestra, and H.H. Franklin gave me special permission to leave the plant at any time to practice with this group. I kept on with the Syracuse Symphony for 20 years, and I also played with an American Legion band and as part of a small orchestra in a Syracuse hotel. Earlier, I had played briefly on a Mississippi River steamboat, but got homesick and came back to Syracuse!
>
> The first time I was employed at Franklin I stayed only a little over a year, quitting to start a chicken farm. Then, about 1927, I went back to the Franklin plant, turning out small parts on a milling machine. I was paid on a piecework basis, and if I worked extra hours I made big money, even more than my boss. Working conditions at the plant were good but the work tended to be seasonal, with a lot of ups and downs. However, even with the layoffs people once in there did not usually want to leave. The standard pay was about sixty-five cents an hour for jobs not on piecework, but people doing special tasks often got more. There were some accidents–at one time I got steel slivers in my hand, and it became very sore. I also recall that people who worked around punch presses often lost fingers or parts

of fingers. The second time I stayed with the company until 1930, and then went back to farming.

Some three hundred or more women were employed by the H.H. Franklin Manufacturing Company throughout the years of peak automobile production. The overwhelming majority of these persons could be found in the Geddes Avenue office building. Only a tiny number were located in the manufacturing area, and all of them performed clerical duties. Top management at the Franklin firm clearly did not believe that women were suited for employment in machine shops or on assembly lines, even if the work involved required dexterity rather than physical strength. Throughout the 1920s female staff appeared to have been largely insulated from the layoffs that took place periodically among many male workers, probably because the company did not view it as wise policy to have clerical personnel come and go when they worked so closely with management.

Various women remembered their careers with the Franklin firm. One of them, Cora L. Housman, was employed by the company in a clerical capacity for a number of years. She relates her experiences:

> I started work at Franklin in 1924 as an eighteen-year-old clerk in the Geddes Street building. My father, Claude Lawton, was an assistant foreman in final assembly at the time, and my uncle, Charles Slingerland, for some years was H.H. Franklin's chauffeur. I worked in an office upstairs under Percy Hughes, where I checked the orders for new cars and parts from dealers and subdealers, working-up the discounts and stamping them on the documents.
>
> I lived in the tiny village of Warners, from which I took the interurban trolley to Syracuse, walking from the drop-off point down Geddes Street to the plant. Office hours were from 8 A.M. to 5 P.M. during the week plus a half-day on Saturday, but we had a fairly lib-

eral lunch hour–long enough for me to go downtown on the streetcar occasionally to shop at one of several department stores and even eat at a Chinese restaurant. Usually I had lunch in the company cafeteria, however, where the food was good and I quickly gained weight! I did not own a car while employed at Franklin.

After working at Franklin some time I was promoted to record clerk, where I wrote requisitions for tools, parts, oil and other items. At first records on items ordered were kept somewhat informally, but finally we used the Cardex system. I continued as a record clerk up to about the time the plant closed in the 1930s. I was among the last employees to leave the company.

Mrs. Housman was one of several women who worked in the office which handled the ordering of supplies. A second person was Marguerite "Peggy" Moore, who also describes her experiences:

I began work at the Franklin Company in the spring of 1921, starting as a typist at the rear of the main floor of the Geddes Street office building. After about a year on this job, I was moved upstairs to work in the unit which ordered supplies. I would write up orders from shop foremen for a lot of different items needed in their departments, and submit them to the assistant production manager, Bill Lane, for his signature. The orders then went to the purchasing department to be filled. Our small ordering unit was moved around quite a bit. We finally found ourselves down on the ground floor of one of the factory buildings next to the Marcellus Street shipping dock. It was an inconvenient location in one respect; as there were no women's bathrooms in the factory, we had to get permission to go through the plant up to the front office to use the restroom there!

I can still recall some of the unusual items we ordered. One was watches, both wrist and pocket types, given to top salesmen in the dealer organization as prizes. We also processed requisitions for special-order cars. Occasionally these involved installation of very luxurious cloth upholstery, plus ladies' comb and mirror sets in the rear compartments. An occasional special-order vehicle also might require leather upholstery of an unusual color throughout.

I liked my work at Franklin, since everyone there tended to be pretty nice. Executives such as Bill Dunk and Bill Lane were fine people to work for. My starting pay was fifteen dollars a week, but I finally went up to about thirty-three dollars. There were many lay-offs in the plant during slack periods, but the office force was kept on.

We had plenty of social activities. The young, unmarried women went to Tubbert's Restaurant on the north side of town for after work parties, or out to Mike Scallion's in the Split Rock area for fish dinners. A wagon came through the factory every day where we could purchase candy and soft drinks. I still remember dancing in the company cafeteria during the noon hour. I recollect H.H. Franklin paying a visit to our office one day. The city had been hit by a huge snowfall, and he came upstairs to ask Bill Lane about the storm's effect on operations in the plant. Mr. Franklin had a very hollow voice. I learned later that he had no roof in his mouth, but it was not difficult to understand him.

While our unit was still in the Geddes Avenue building I found myself close to the time study section. It was located in a special screened-in area, almost a cage. As I recall, the supervisors and men from the various factory departments usually came there to be interviewed by the time study people. I distinctly remember Stella Tague, Mr. Franklin's private secretary. She was a refined, middle-aged lady at the time I worked there, who lived on "Tipperary Hill" some distance west of the plant.

My ten years or more at Franklin ended when I was laid off in 1931. It was an enjoyable period of my life, which I still recall very well.

Yet another woman employed in the order unit was Sara Duxbury, a native of Great Britain. She recounts her experiences with the Franklin company:

I was born in Yorkshire, England, in 1907, the oldest in a family of four children. My father, a miner, decided to emigrate to America, so we moved to the Syracuse area in 1913. Dad worked at Brown-Lipe Company in Syracuse, a firm that made gears. After attending Porter Elementary School and Vocational High I worked for a time on James Street for a pill manufacturer. Then I had a chance to go to Franklin, where I was assigned to the order unit, at that time located on the ground floor of the factory building fronting on Marcellus Street.

Most of our work involved the processing of orders from factory departments for supplies and parts. If the item requested was kept in the supply room located near our office, a stock chaser would obtain it and deliver it to where it was needed. There was no real training period–you picked up the office procedure on the job. As I recall, I started at about $13.50 per week, but got increases from time to time. At first we were paid in cash, and later by check. I felt that Franklin was a good place at which to work. Morale was high in our little office.

I lived with my family on Onondaga Road, west of town. I usually rode the Auburn trolley to work. It came in from the town of Skaneatales, and took no more than twenty minutes to get to the plant. On occasion, though, I would get a ride with a Franklin test driver who had been running a car up and down the nearby hills. He would have to let me out a few blocks from the factory, however, as the testers were not supposed to have riders.

Quite often I would have the other girls who worked in the order section out to our house to sample some of my dad's "home brew." All-in-all we had a lot of fun. It came to an end, though, when the Franklin firm ran into the depression and could not sell cars. At that point everyone was laid off for good.

Another woman who worked in the Franklin office was Meredith Lamson Estoff. She describes her brief but interesting period of employment there at the end of the 1920s.

In the spring of 1929, I had pre-enrolled in Syracuse University and planned to start in the fall. However, my dad died unexpectedly around that time. Instead of heading for college, I found it necessary, due to family finances, to take a short business school course and look for a job. In the fall of 1929 I was fortunate enough to get taken on by the Franklin Company. I am sure someone spoke for me, because at that time the firm was doing a lot more laying-off than hiring.

I was assigned to a small engineering secretarial pool which was located on the second floor of the Geddes Street office building. My desk was one of several located by the window which looked out on South Geddes. The car design people were located further down in the big room, and we could see them at work. We typed letters and reports for the engineers who were located on our floor, including Ed Marks and his assistants. Since I was inexperienced I did not find it easy at first to take dictation and accurately transcribe my notes, but people were understanding and I soon improved.

With many different activities going on, the second floor certainly was an interesting place in which to work. Ray Dietrich had his big design boards nearby, and we could watch the new cars taking shape on them. Also in the area was William "Bill" McNabb, a young art and color man who came from one of the Detroit auto firms to work at Franklin. He would try a variety of different colors and shades on drawings of various Franklin car models. Still another person was a tall, good-looking young woman from a nearby office who paid us frequent visits. She would stand by the water cooler and slowly sip a glass of water while she looked over the men who worked nearby. I always thought she really had an eye for Ray Dietrich!

The Franklin firm ran into serious trouble shortly after I arrived, and cutbacks soon came. A small group of us were sent out to work for the Syracuse Franklin dealer, as I recall, sometime during the early summer of 1930. We had temporary quarters on top of the dealer's showroom in an added-on structure with a tin roof, and by the middle of summer it was so hot that it became unbearable. This job lasted only a few months, and at the end of it we were unemployed. I turned to other types of work, and had no further connection with the Franklin Company.

Numerous additional persons, some at one time employed by the H.H. Franklin Company and others related to former employees, have interesting recollections of life during the auto manufacturing era. Brothers Luke and Joe Ganley were sons of Edward J. Ganley, who about 1910 moved from Skaneatales Falls to Syracuse to work for the Franklin firm, when he ultimately became a mechanic and a test driver. In 1920, Edward left the firm and opened his own "Franklin Garage" in the southwestern section of Syracuse. The garage was constructed by Edward Ganley and a next-door neighbor in the rear of the Ganley home, and designed so that a vehicle could drive out a side door and back onto the street. Luke Ganley has interesting recollections of activities in this home-based service shop. He remembers his father using what might be termed a "mechanic's stethoscope," a device which by amplifying sounds made it possible to locate bearing knocks in engines. Luke, a mechanically-inclined youngster, also recalls being encouraged to work in the garage once he was old enough to make a definite contribution to the operation. His father, however, did not encourage Luke having his friends come in and "help out." Edward Ganley observing the horse play which often went on when two young men got together, made the significant observation: "One teenager equals half a man, but two of them together equal no man!"

The backgrounds of a number of Franklin employees were somewhat unique, but few more so than that of Henry Remmick. A nephew, Roland Janes, recalls that Remmick came from Germany, where he had been educated as an architect, in the early 1920s. He soon found that despite sound training and earlier accomplishments in architecture he could not obtain a job in his field in America; thus, swallowing his pride, he ultimately went to Franklin as a paint striper. After some time with the company he was given the title "chief of decorations," in which capacity he oversaw body striping, the placing of owner's initials on cars, and installation of special items in the interiors of vehicles. Mr. Janes roomed with the Remmick family in Syracuse during the very early 1930s, and recalls his uncle as a jolly, outgoing fellow, except when listening to music from Vienna, Austria, on his short-wave radio (often with glass of wine in hand!). On those occasions he was off by himself in another world, and did not want to be disturbed by anyone.

A few employees of the Franklin firm filled jobs not usually found in the typical automotive plant. Yet another employee, Harley Willis, now well over one hundred years of age, worked in the printing department of the Franklin firm on two separate occasions. After serving as a printing apprentice in other shops, Harley joined the Franklin organization as a printer early in 1914. He found the printing shop, which produced a variety of forms needed in the Franklin office and plant plus brochures utilized in the company's sales programs, to be a small (seven employees) but congenial place. "You were let alone and expected to provide quality work," he remembers. Harley rode a motorcycle to work, parking it on South Geddes Street in front of the Franklin office building in which the printing unit was located at that time. Harley left the firm for health reasons in 1917 ("I became a not-very-successful farmer," he recalls), but returned two years later and continued working until print shop operations were cut back sharply in 1924. Some years later he opened his own printing establishment, which has continued in successful operation in Syracuse to the present day.

Numerous other former employees of the H.H. Franklin Company carry memories of their work with the Syracuse firm. Albert Simmons over a several-year period combined duties as an assembler in the factory of the air-cooled vehicle manufacturer with farming activities.

Albert lived some miles west of Syracuse in the Elbridge area, first on the "home farm" of his parents; later on his own farm. He recalls the Franklin firm as a decent employer, where anyone willing to do a fair day's work could expect to be treated well. Working conditions in his department, he remembers, were generally good, although employees did suffer from occasional dull headaches caused by engines of fully assembled cars emitting exhaust fumes while being test-driven for short periods. After leaving Franklin as a result of its big employee cutbacks in the early 1930s, Albert owned and operated a good-sized dairy farm for 42 years.

A Franklin employee in the period before America entered World War I was Harmon Cross, the "belt man." Harmon's work with the firm involved repairing belts during the years 1915-1916, when most of the machines in the plant were powered by flat leather belts attached to a revolving overhead shaft which ran the entire length of a building. Since these belts wore out or broke frequently, Harmon's small crew of six or seven men was kept busy installing replacements and then repairing the defective ones.

In summary, the thousands of persons who were employed at the H.H. Franklin Manufacturing Company during its more-than-three-decades of automobile production can be described as an interesting and vital group. Coming from city neighborhoods, out of small towns, and off outlying farms, these individuals working together crafted one of America's quality cars. While the vast majority came from modest backgrounds, and did not enjoy the advantages of higher education, they nonetheless impress anyone meeting them as a good-quality citizens, men and women who sixty-to-seventy years ago played a vigorous role in American industry. While the passage of time tends to cause people to perhaps romanticize their earlier lives, and forget unpleasant aspects of work, it is still clear that morale must have been high and team-work very much in evidence throughout the Franklin organization in its heyday. The firm and its people formed an impressive combination by any standard of measurement.

THE FRANKLIN AUTOMOBILE COMPANY

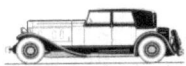

Several hundred miles east of Syracuse and some thirty miles north of Boston can be found the town of Amesbury, Massachusetts, where as noted earlier bodies for the Franklin car were produced at the Walker Company. A few other firms in the Amesbury area also built small numbers of Franklin bodies, usually on a custom basis. Amesbury could claim a long and proud history as a center of vehicle body building. For a period of several decades beginning shortly before the Civil War and continuing into the early days of the twentieth century it often was called "the carriage capital of the world." Year after year vast numbers of horse-drawn vehicles were produced and shipped throughout the nation and abroad by various local manufacturing firms.

Ultimately, as the automobile became an accepted means of transportation the focus of body building shifted steadily to it and away from wagons and carriages. As early as World War I a number of concerns of varying size produced bodies for out-of-town motor vehicle manufacturers, particularly builders of luxury cars. Several of these body shops were located in Amesbury itself, with others headquartered in the nearby community of Merrimac.

While the body-building firms in Amesbury and Merrimac had become totally motor-car oriented by the 1920s, production methods to a substantial extent mirrored those of the earlier carriage-building era. A large amount of precise hand-finishing was involved in most body-building operations, with many employees in the various firms required to possess craft-type skills not found generally among auto factory workers at the time. The fact that a big proportion of the automotive bodies manufactured by the Amesbury and Merrimac firms during much of the period incorporated easily-shaped aluminum sheets for the exterior panels made such hand craftsmanship especially feasible. Toward the end of the decade of the 1920s, however, the desire on the part of automotive companies to reduce costs and increase output cast a long shadow over such expensive and relatively slow methods of manufacture, thus signaling the beginning of the end for the New England body-building firms. As recorded previously, the decision of the H.H. Franklin Company to trim costs by establishing its own body-manufacturing department led to the swift demise of the Walker operation in the early 1930s. Adoption of a similar policy by the major purchaser of bodies from the Biddle & Smart Company of Merrimac, the Hudson Motor Car Company, caused that firm to close its doors even earlier.

The people still alive who once were employed by firms such as Walker and Biddle & Smart have stories to relate fully as interesting as those of former H.H. Franklin Company employees. One such person is Alphonse Barcelow, who describes his work building automotive bodies in the 1920s:

> I started at Walker (then called Walker-Wells) toward the end of the first World War, as a bumper's helper on the door panel job. I was about eighteen years old at the time. We had to furnish our own tools, hiring a blacksmith to make up special shears, chisels, punches and hammers needed in our work. Workers kept these items long after the plant closed, and some sets of tools are around even today;
>
> I walked from my home to work at the Walker factory, where our hours were from seven A.M. to five P.M. five days of the week. The factory also might work a half-day on Saturday depending on demand for bodies. The building I worked in at the Walker plant had four floors. Our department, or "room" as it usually was called, covered an entire floor and had about fifty workers. A superintendent and a foreman ran the department.
>
> Work on body panels was done by a skilled man called a bumper, who had two helpers to assist him. He would start with a long flat sheet of metal, which was bent to a rough shape and then bumped on a power hammer to get the proper curves and create a finished panel. The panel would be checked periodically with a wooden sweep or pattern to make sure it was being properly shaped. Somewhat later

THE FRANKLIN AUTOMOBILE COMPANY

we used forms and applications of heat to speed up the work.

The Franklin bodies turned out at Walker involved aluminum panels attached to wood framing. The woodworking room took dried lengths of lumber and sawed and shaped them, using patterns as a guide. These individual pieces then went to another room where the wood body frame was put together over a big form, with screws and glue used to hold the joints. Bodies for Franklin went out of our factory without window glass or upholstery. The bodies were shipped to Syracuse on railroad flat cars, and we covered them with canvas for protection.

After several years at Walker I moved over to Biddle & Smart, a much bigger outfit, which built a lot of bodies for Hudson. These bodies were largely of aluminum, also. At both Walker and Biddle & Smart men from the auto plants would come down and look carefully at the first job or two you did from blueprints. If these people did not like the style it would be changed until they got what they wanted.

I was paid around thirty-five dollars a week when I started at Biddle & Smart, but later went on piecework and made really good money. When models were changed in the fall most of the crews were laid off for a month or so. I usually walked home for dinner at noon, but for snacks we tossed coins out the window to young kids who would go to a nearby bakery and buy us cakes and pies. The lemon pies were really good!

I finally became boss of the experimental shop at Biddle & Smart, where we tried out new methods and worked on bodies for the future. By the end of the 1920s, though, Detroit was making dies to press out body panels cheaply and in big numbers. This meant the finish of the high-class body work here in Massachusetts.

A second person with extensive experience in automotive body-building in the Amesbury-Merrimac area was Willard Flanders. While never working directly for the Walker Company, he recalls many aspects of his work at a similar firm:

> I originally was from Boscawen, New Hampshire, about sixty miles north of the Amesbury-Merrimac area. While visiting relatives in the vicinity of Amesbury in 1915 I obtained a job at the Biddle & Smart Company. I was sixteen at the time. I started as a bench hand, learning the upholstery trimmer's trade. I needed a lot of training, so I didn't receive much in the way of pay to begin with. I upholstered the doors of touring car bodies being built for the Mercer Automobile Company. These were done entirely in Spanish leather, which involved tacking the edges all the way around. The output in the early days was about seven bodies each work-shift. From the beginning I was taught to "spit tacks" onto a magnetic hammer, and finally was able to handle two kinds of tacks in my mouth at one time. Later I was put in charge of an entire bench, and finally made an assistant foreman. In this job I managed to learn a good deal about company operations in all departments.
>
> I have heard that the shops in Amesbury received their first automobile body orders from the Stanley Steamer firm, about 1898. Currier-Cameron Company built this body, but sublet the painting and trimming to another outfit. In the early 1900s the Bailey Body Company developed an electric car with help from Edison. Much of the automotive body building in Amesbury and Merrimac was done in old abandoned woolen mills and carriage shops. Since bodies and parts often had to be moved from one building to another it was a pretty inefficient operation. About 1927 a moving conveyor system was installed at Biddle & Smart, but with five floors in the factory it did not work out well.
>
> In the early days the body panels were all aluminum, and were "hand bumped," using bumping machines made by the Pettengell Company of Amesbury. A lot of Biddle & Smart's skilled help came from European countries. I recall immigrants from Finland and Poland working there. Many of the women workers were from the

French-speaking part of Canada, and it was not easy breaking them in. Since they spoke no English we had to use sign language to communicate!

Still another person who worked in automobile body shops in the Amesbury-Merrimac area was Edward Hamel. Edward followed his father into body-building work, as he relates:

I was born in Somersworth, New Hampshire, in 1904. My father originally worked in the cotton mills in Somersworth, Exeter, and other New Hampshire towns. It was a hard way to make a living, since he was often laid off, and with four children to support he had to cut wood and sell milk to get by. He finally moved to the Amesbury area, where he held different jobs in the Biddle & Smart factory. When my older brother, Albert, and I became old enough to work my father brought us into this plant.

Biddle & Smart for years made large numbers of bodies for Hudson and Essex, and at the peak probably employed nearly five thousand persons in its plants. We were often called the "Detroit of the East." My job much of the time was "turning doors"–an aluminum sheet was put on a cast-iron form, and with a torch and hammer I shaped the door panel. However, I also worked in the experimental department under Al Barcelow. Whenever the company needed help on special jobs I would be transferred there for a time.

I lived at home until I got married, and up to the age of 21 gave my pay to my parents. We had slowdowns at Biddle & Smart, but while I was laid off at times I was never out of a job. In those slack periods I worked at other local shops building automobile bodies. One job was at the J. B. Judkins Company, where I helped build custom bodies for Duesenberg and Pierce-Arrow.

I left Biddle & Smart just before they closed, moving over to the Walker Company where we worked on Franklin bodies. However, I was not there long before they shut their doors, too. Then a friend,

Jim Arsenault, now dead, got me a job at the Franklin Company in Syracuse. When Franklin began building its own bodies it did not have people who could work with aluminum, so I was hired to do aluminum welding. I worked alongside sheet metal men from Moline, Illinois, who had been brought in to form the steel panels on Franklin cars.

I worked in Syracuse at Franklin about two or three years, finally bringing my wife and family there too. I was at Franklin when the banks closed in 1933, and we were given a kind of I.O.U. slip for pay. The body shop was located, I think, on the fifth floor of the plant, and I did not like having to go up and down all those flights of stairs on a bum leg. At the time the Franklin plant closed I had been made foreman of the body line. After the shut down I went back to Amesbury for good.

Technological change, together with the advent of the depression of the early 1930s, thus ended the once-important role played by Amesbury and the surrounding area in the American motor vehicle industry. The closing of practically all the automotive body shops in Amesbury and Merrimac, following the loss of their key customers, devastated the local economies. Willard Flanders recalls that the employment situation in the 1930s was utter disaster: "You could not buy a job in Amesbury." Some persons moved to Detroit or similar big cities in search of employment; others sought work at the few hat factories or shoe plants still operating in the area. Still others became self-employed in various tiny enterprises, with one former body-builder buying big pots of Boston baked beans and re-selling this food in small quantities to restaurants and stores. Not until the coming of World War II would economic conditions show any important improvement in the two small communities. By that time the earlier relationship of the area with automobile manufacturing was largely a memory.

THE FRANKLIN AUTOMOBILE COMPANY

– *Ten* –

The Leaders of the Organization

Men who headed American motor vehicle companies during the early decades of the twentieth century frequently shared several key characteristics. As observed previously, a substantial number of these leaders grew up under decidedly humble circumstances, often in rural or small-town environments. In relatively few instances did the educational backgrounds of pioneer automotive executives encompass college-level training, with a substantial number not even achieving high school graduation. Additionally, the rise to the top of most such motor firm presidents could be described as meteoric–frequently only a ten-to-twenty-year time period spanned the ascent of the humble mechanic, shop worker or clerk to the chief executive suite.

Herbert H. Franklin in many ways was representative of the other auto industry leaders found throughout America. However, in numerous other respects the man was completely atypical. The names of many pioneer motor car builders were on the tip of everyone's tongue, particularly in their home towns where in many instances they were their community's best-known personalities, but often across much of the nation as well. Throughout his more than 60 years of residence in Syracuse, on the other hand, Herbert H. Franklin largely remained an enigma to the people of that municipality. While holding the position of president of what, in the opinion of many, was the most important manufacturing company located in the city, no more than a handful of individuals could claim him as a personal friend or close acquaintance. H.H. was not an active member of any local church, never joined the most prestigious men's club in the community (even though it was located a mere half-dozen blocks from his home), and only infrequently participated in the activities of civic or service organizations. He was never a director of any Syracuse bank or other local business concern, letting subordinates in his firm handle such duties. By keeping bankers and other Syracuse business leaders largely at arms-length, the auto chief undoubtedly left many such persons with the impression that he wished to have little to do with them (H.H. may have paid dearly for such aloofness when his company fell into difficulties in the 1930s!) At no time did H.H. Franklin become politically active in any way, either as a candidate for public office or as a behind-the-scenes supporter of some leading elected official. While he made a handsome contribution to Syracuse University shortly after World War I to fund a faculty chair, it required some ten years of subsequent effort on the part of two chancellors of that institution to obtain the assent of the automobile company leader to serve on the school's board of trustees.[10-1.]

Outside Syracuse, H.H. tended to a greater extent to fill the role of a publicly active, high-level business executive. His service from 1903 to 1908 as an officer of the old Association of Licensed Automobile Manufacturers (ALAM) brought him into the public limelight, and on one occasion he was photographed, together with several other motor car company heads, arriving at the White House in Washington, D.C. to convey to the President an invitation to attend ALAM's forthcoming national auto show. While there is no record of H.H. holding any important office in the successor group to ALAM, the National Automobile Chamber of Commerce, he continued to be moderately involved in its affairs, participating in meetings and attending dinners both in America and abroad for chief executives of motor vehicle firms. In the mid-1920s, H.H. was awarded membership in Beta Sigma Gamma, the nation's leading business administration honor so-

THE LEADERS OF THE ORGANIZATION

ciety, undoubtedly in recognition of his activities as president of the H.H. Franklin Manufacturing Company.[10-2] At about the same time the Syracuse automotive executive received an award from a national-level advertising association, thus testifying to his accomplishments in that field. Franklin also was honored in 1925 by the National Automobile Chamber of Commerce as one of the pioneers in the automotive industry.

As described elsewhere in this book, on becoming president early in 1907 of the company bearing his name H.H. soon became widely quoted in the trade press on a variety of automotive-related subjects. After 1912, this tapered off, however, and during the period from the First World War through the early 1930s, Franklin never displayed the type of active leadership in the American automotive industry that two other heads of independent auto manufacturing companies, Roy D. Chapin of Hudson and Alvan Macauley of Packard, did. The major shift of the center of motor vehicle manufacturing to the Midwest and particularly to southeast Michigan, at a relatively early date may well have become a factor of some importance in limiting H.H's influence in this fast-developing industry. Even if he had wished to participate aggressively in industry affairs, H.H. was somewhat isolated geographically–he clearly would not have been available on brief notice for a meeting in Detroit of motor vehicle chiefs. The relatively modest growth of his company in contrast to the vast overall expansion of the auto industry in the years after 1912 also could have been an important cause of H.H.'s diminished influence during that period, as undoubtedly was the fact that his cleft palate prevented him from being an effective speaker before good-sized audiences or congressional committees. Clearly, H.H. kept in touch with Frederick Haynes during the years that Haynes headed the big Dodge Brothers organization in Detroit, but there is no indication that the Syracuse auto chief maintained frequent contact with other key auto industry leaders.

In summary, H.H., as the long-time head of the Franklin organization, might fairly be described as a minor American captain of industry. Filling the role of chief executive of a firm which during much of its

THE FRANKLIN AUTOMOBILE COMPANY

existence ranked among the 15 or 20 leading American automobile manufacturers (although usually near the bottom of such a group), he was a person of some consequence in corporate America. As noted earlier, however, during the later years of his company presidency his prestige clearly diminished, and except in one area, that of urban and regional planning and highway development–which will be discussed more fully later in this chapter–he was not a person whose opinion was regularly sought during the 1920s and 1930s on important issues by major national newspapers or magazines.[10-3] H.H., during his lifetime, was never listed in Who's Who In America, or even in similar directories containing names of New York State leaders. Once his company collapsed in 1934, the man literally dropped out of sight on the national scene, and to a major extent at the local level as well. He largely became a forgotten person, except to a small circle of relatives and friends, for the remainder of his life.

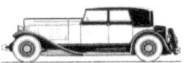

The Syracuse automotive executive, at about the time (late 1906) he became the controlling stockholder in the H.H. Franklin Manufacturing Company, acquired the commodious house at 1033 James Street which would continue to serve as his residence for the balance of his long life. This white frame two-story structure was square in shape, and while of reasonably attractive appearance lacked any particular architectural distinction. H.H. Franklin purchased this house from members of the same White family who had been plaintiffs in the sharply-contested lawsuit over John Wilkinson's services only a short time earlier! The dwelling secured by the now wealthy forty-year-old motor car manufacturer was itself far from new–while historical data is a trifle hazy, in all probability it had been built as early as the 1850s. It may well have been the first residence constructed in that section of James Street, with some early Syracusans recalling that it had been named the "hilltop house." Personal records show that H.H. immediately spent a considerable amount of money repairing and remodeling the structure to make it more suitable for luxurious living

THE LEADERS OF THE ORGANIZATION

H.H. Franklin's 1913 Model D Torpedo in front of his James Street home.

prior to moving in.

If the house purchased by the ambitious industrialist was not particularly distinctive, the same could not be said of the imposing avenue on which it fronted. James Street shortly after the beginning of the twentieth century constituted the very core of Syracuse's finest residential area. This thoroughfare, quite wide by standards of the day and surfaced with bricks, was flanked on each side by rows of magnificent elm trees whose branches, often meeting high in the air above the center of the pavement, provided a full measure of both shade and beauty. As the horse-drawn vehicle was still an important means of local travel in Syracuse in this era, the curbs were lined with stone steps on which passengers could alight from carriage or buggy, plus quaint black metal posts about three feet in height to which the horse could be hitched. "White wings"–men clothed in light-colored coveralls and wielding brooms–occasionally could be seen sweeping up horse droppings and other refuse from the surface of the street. The neighborhood clearly took great pride in its appearance.

The stately homes which bordered this pleasant avenue were owned by the business and professional elite of the city of Syracuse. Herbert H. Franklin's neighbors were listed in the Syracuse City Directory of the period as holding such positions as chief executive of a manufacturing company, president of a leading local bank, surgeon, appellate court judge and head of a prestigious law firm. One near-neighbor, Burns Lyman Smith, chose to denote his occupation simply as "capitalist." The municipal directory also occasionally listed, beneath the name of a principal male owner (except in the case of a widow, females as yet were not given recognition in this book), a second person carrying the occupational title of "coachman" or "chauffeur."

The new residence of H.H. Franklin, while not fully comparable in size to some of those owned by his neighbors, was far from small. On the first floor could be found a large, comfortable living room, a formal dining room, a music room, a library, and a solarium, the latter often used for lunches or teas to which guests were invited. In a rear extension was located a kitchen, a pantry and storage facilities, while abutting the east side of the dwelling was a *porte-cochere*, designed to give shelter from the elements to persons entering or alighting from motor vehicles. On ascending a central stairway to the second floor a guest would observe four bedrooms (each with private bath and three containing fireplaces) plus a sewing room in the main part of the house, together with living quarters for servants in the back section over the kitchen. The basement of the residence featured a produce room in which fresh vegetables were stored, together with a "putting" facility where H.H. and his guests might practice golfing techniques. At a later date, when H.H. became interested in photography, a dark room was constructed to house picture-developing activities.

The lot on which H.H.'s home stood was exceptionally deep, stretching nearly three hundred feet from front to back. Well toward the rear could be found a good-sized garage, which featured a built-in turn-

THE LEADERS OF THE ORGANIZATION

H.H. Franklin's father, Charles Risden Franklin, and his stepmother lived with Franklin in the James Street house during the final years of their lives. This photo was taken around 1910 at 1033 James Street. (Courtesy of the late J.D. Franklin)

table. This device, often utilized in the carriage era as well as in the early days of the automobile, made it possible to reverse the direction of a vehicle stored inside and thus eliminated tedious backing-out and turning. Surrounding the house almost totally, except for the crushed gravel driveway leading to the street, were gardens containing a wide variety of flowers and plants, all beautifully maintained throughout the growing season.

This substantial establishment required the services of both male and female "help" for its operation and maintenance. Inside the house could be found an upstairs maid, who dusted, made beds and kept a watchful eye on the state of H.H.'s wardrobe. Downstairs a second maid was responsible for keeping the various rooms in order and opening the door for visitors, while in the rear a cook prepared meals and cleaned up afterward. The three women who filled the above-mentioned positions on occasion acted as a team–if H.H. held a dinner party the maids would assist the cook in handling table service duties and perform related functions. While the servants put in long hours and enjoyed few holidays, H.H. clearly was regarded as a model employer, since the people holding these in-the-home positions tended to remain in his service for decades. Outside the house a groundskeeper was employed to perform gardening and general handyman tasks, while a chauffeur took charge of the Franklin automobiles and drove H.H. plus other members of the household to local or far-distant destinations.

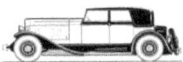

As H.H. was a lifelong bachelor, his family structure was a bit unusual by the standards of the day. During the first decade of his life at the James Street residence Herbert's unmarried sister, Charlotte, lived

H. H. Franklin's chauffeur driven 1929 Dietrich Town Car.
(Courtesy of Franklin Foundation Museum, Tucson, Arizona)

with him and took overall charge of the home. It appears that H.H.'s father and stepmother, who sold the family farm in Lisle during the early 1890s, also were part of the James Street establishment throughout most of the final years of their lives.

Both H.H.'s father and his sister Charlotte died about the time of America's entry into the first World War. Shortly thereafter the James Street household was joined by a cousin of H.H.'s, Gladys Bliss, also unmarried. Miss Bliss quickly assumed in superb fashion the position of female head of the household. Characterized by persons who knew her as a gracious, lovely lady, able to win over everyone by her intelligence and attractiveness, Gladys Bliss filled much of the vacuum created by H.H. Franklin's disinclination to participate in community activities. She served on the governing boards of local hospitals and social service agencies, was active in church work, and performed as a charming hostess at 1033 James Street.

Interesting recollections of the life of H.H. Franklin were provided by Helen Stringer, whose father, Ed Dann, was a close personal friend of the motor car manufacturer. Mrs. Stringer describes some of H.H.'s personal qualities:

> H.H. was my godfather, and thus I always called him "Uncle Herbert." He and my father became acquainted as young bachelors in the 1890s, attending together many a Syracuse social event in that now-almost-forgotten era. As my father was a part-owner of Empire Metal Company, a family firm which produced babbitt and other materials used in die-casting, a business relationship also existed between the two men.
>
> Uncle Herbert was very much a practical joker at all times, although often the person on the receiving end of the humor was not particularly appreciative of it. My father and mother were married after a long courtship, and at the beginning of their wedding trip H.H., while ostensibly helping carry their bags, contrived to partly loosen the snaps on my mother's large suitcase. As the newly married cou-

ple crossed the lobby of a New York City hotel to check in, the piece of luggage suddenly flew open, with the contents spilling out on the carpet. My mother was utterly mortified, and never completely forgave Uncle Herbert for this trick.

As a young girl I was frequently taken to the James Street home for various social activities. It was an elegant place, beautifully furnished, and due largely to the efforts of Gladys Bliss the overall atmosphere was very hospitable. Gladys was a splendid hostess– with her charm and wisdom she was a perfect foil for the reserved Herbert Franklin. I still retain some interesting memories of these visits. On one occasion I impulsively sat on Uncle Herbert's lap, something I discovered afterward he did not care for, since he was very fussy about keeping his clothes impeccably neat. As soon as I got up he carefully reset the crease in his pants! Uncle Herbert used a strong after shave lotion which frequently was mistaken for perfume by persons who did not know him.

While Herbert never married, he was very much a lady's man throughout his life. He kept in touch with a number of women living in various towns in upstate New York, visiting them at their homes from time to time. Some of these friendships apparently dated back to his days in Coxsackie. When staying at his suite in New York he frequently could be seen attending afternoon tea dances at the Plaza and other hotels. Late in his life he showed me pictures of a number of young women dressed in dancing or theatrical costumes. I very much doubt if any romantic attachment existed between a man in his eighties and these youngsters, but Herbert may well have assisted them financially in getting started with their careers. He clearly enjoyed the company of women.

H.H. Franklin should be given great credit for rising about his physical disability to become a business leader of distinction. He was a bit backward in Syracuse society but when out of town tended to assume a position of far greater importance. However, even then someone else usually did the speaking for him.

During much of his life H.H. could be described as an inveterate traveler. He was quick to board a train or enter one of the fleet of motorcars provided by the H.H. Franklin Company for a variety of destinations, journeying to New York City and Chicago to attend auto shows, to locations in the East and South to enjoy vacations, and to distant sections of the nation to survey business conditions, evaluate highways, or check on the sale of Franklin cars. In addition, the automobile company president took frequent trips abroad, in part for the purpose of spending time with his sister, Carolyn Franklin Moser, at her villa in San Remo, Italy. This was the family member at whose home H.H. lived during the entire first decade of his life in Syracuse.

Several acquaintances also recalled H.H. as a person who was accompanied by various relatives and friends–often female–when he journeyed to resort hotels for vacations. In the summer months the destination frequently was some place at or near the shore in Massachusetts, New Hampshire or New Jersey, but when biting winter weather arrived in Syracuse the almost invariable choice was Pinehurst, North Carolina. On business trips Herbert also tended to travel in the company of women who were introduced to others as his nieces. Since these persons frequently were young and attractive this practice caused a few raised eyebrows in such Midwestern industrial cities as Toledo and Detroit, where top brass at automotive companies often were viewed as a bit wild.

Other persons close to H.H. have been able to supply details of life at 1033 James Street. Florence Barton, widow of the late Kenneth Barton, was a frequent visitor at the Franklin home and recalls something of the social life there:

> When Ken and I were married, Herbert hosted a sumptuous wedding day breakfast for us. For some years afterward as a young married couple we were expected each Friday evening for a game of cards. These sessions ended quite early, however, since Herbert always wanted to reserve time to perform a series of conditioning exercises before he retired for the night!

THE FRANKLIN AUTOMOBILE COMPANY

*H. H. Franklin enjoys a golfing vacation at Pinehurst, North Carolina.
(Courtesy of Millie Franklin Moreland)*

*H. H. Franklin peruses a financial paper at the seashore.
(Courtesy of Millie Franklin Moreland)*

THE LEADERS OF THE ORGANIZATION

H.H.'s principal other source of physical activity was golf, a game which he clearly enjoyed. During his middle years he played regularly at the Onondaga Country Club, located just east of Syracuse, almost always with relatives or close friends. His trips to Pinehurst, North Carolina, also involved primarily this form of recreation, although pictures indicate that he occasionally participated in horseback riding as well. While at Pinehurst his golfing companions usually included Frank Barton and Ed Dann. Visits to Pinehurst and other resorts often extended over several-week periods, and may well have been the basis for the criticism expressed by some of the old-time employees of the company, that H.H. was an absentee company president who let others run the firm for him. Certainly when his trips abroad are also taken into account H.H. must have been absent from his office a considerable proportion of the time.

Once H.H. became wealthy he clearly displayed great generosity to a substantial number of persons. In addition to bringing his brother, Howard, and his brother-in-law, Frank Barton, into the company in high level capacities, H.H. provided direct financial assistance to various other persons related to him. One observer, distantly related to the family, recalled as a child meeting female relatives who stopped to see his father. He noted that these women wore beautiful clothes and jewelry and arrived in a new Franklin automobile, but were not employed anywhere. H.H. Franklin appeared to be their sole source of support. Together with aiding financially a number of relatives, H.H. at times was ready to assist key members of the company staff who he felt were deserving of help. Ed Marks, chief engineer of the firm, recalls that in early 1929 he was scheduled to join several other company executives on a trip to England and France to visit auto shows and meet with foreign dealers handling the Franklin car:

> Shortly before I was to leave on the overseas trip H.H. summoned me to his office and asked if my wife planned to accompany me. I told him that she would not be able to go along, as we simply could not afford the cost. "Oh, that is not fair to her," H.H. stated, "we will have to arrange things so that she can have the pleasure of taking the

trip." H.H. then adjusted the billing for a double cabin on the boat so that much of the charge was picked up by the company, and did the same for hotel rooms and various other items of expense. My wife and I were most grateful to him for this act of generosity.

H.H., who never attended college, nonetheless was strongly desirous of using a portion of his wealth to support higher education. After some discussion with key college administrators during 1919 and 1920, he established a faculty chair in transportation management at Syracuse University, making a gift of approximately $80,000 in Franklin common stock for this purpose. At a later date in the 1920s a switch in the assets of the endowment was agreed to, with H.H. taking back the stock and in its place making a gift of $80,000 in cash. In addition, H.H. established several trusts, under the terms of which female friends were granted life incomes, with Syracuse University awarded remainder interests in the assets. Practically all these trusts had to be restructured in the 1930s, however, since the value of the assets–usually real estate or stock–had shrunk to almost nothing during the great depression.

The question might be asked how H.H. could maintain such a splendid lifestyle, and financially assist so many friends and relatives, when the Franklin Manufacturing Company in many years earned only a modest profit and frequently failed to pay dividends on its common stock. It should be noted, of course, that H.H. undoubtedly was compensated handsomely for his services as the company's chief executive officer, with this salary taxed quite lightly under federal income tax laws of the 1920s (furthermore, his expense account was liberal, and fully under his control). In addition, one observer close to company affairs pointed out that the organization was structured so that the H.H. Franklin Manufacturing Company designed and built vehicles, with the Franklin Automobile Company purchasing the cars from the manufacturing unit and in turn selling them to distributors and dealers. The Automobile Company, this observer noted, would of course benefit through the mark-up on such transactions. Since the Franklin Automobile Company was controlled by H.H. Franklin and a small number of insiders, earnings would go to this group, and not be dependent on profit or loss of the manufacturing arm.

When the H.H. Franklin Manufacturing Company went through bankruptcy, as noted earlier, holders of common and preferred stock found their securities totally without value. This meant that H.H. Franklin suffered a huge personal financial loss quite late in life. However, he decidedly was not left a pauper. Life at 1033 James Street went on much as usual, with the same group of servants retained to perform household tasks and relatives and friends entertained at dinner parties. H.H. never again worked, but continued to travel to New York City frequently on what were clearly pleasure trips (he retained a hotel room on a permanent basis). However, since he could no longer requisition vehicles from a company under his control, H.H. purchased

Interior of H.H. Franklin's town car.

a Ford car for personal use. This vehicle was driven by a chauffeur, with H.H. spending his time either playing at various golf courses within driving range of Syracuse or taking pictures of scenes in the countryside (the auto executive's lengthy trips to Pinehurst for golfing vacations came to an end in the "hard times" of the 1930s).

H.H. Franklin made a final voyage to Europe in the early 1950s. Following this trip his health, which prior to that time had been excellent (he did receive unpleasant injuries to his face and jaw in an automobile accident in Ohio in May, 1930, but recovered quickly), began to go downhill. In January, 1955, he suffered a stroke, and in December of that year a second one. The second stroke left him bedridden, with nurses in attendance around the clock. H.H.'s mind began to wander during the final months of his life. On occasion he would cry out his intention to set off on a trip, and demand that his bags be packed immediately. To humor him, servants would bring a suitcase out of a closet and pretend to place his clothes in it.

H.H.'s life came to an end at his James Street home on April 16, 1956, a few months prior to what would have been his ninetieth birthday. In all probability the final years of his life were lonely ones, since his brothers and sisters plus nearly all his one-time business associates, such as Alexander T. Brown, Giles H. Stilwell and Ed Dann, had predeceased him. His funeral was sparsely attended, with the mourners consisting principally of relatives plus a sprinkling of persons once connected with the H.H. Franklin Manufacturing Company. Few representatives of the Syracuse business community were on hand for the rites, and no one from the American automobile industry put in an appearance. H.H.'s death plus his business achievements were given substantial attention by the Syracuse newspapers, but totally ignored by national level newspapers and magazines. Years later, in 1972, Herbert Franklin was given recognition for his work in the motor vehicle field by induction into the Automotive Hall of Fame.

H.H. was survived by the two most important women in his life, Gladys Bliss and his long-time confidential secretary, Stella Tague. Nei-

In October 1972, H. H. Franklin was inducted into the Automotive Hall of Fame. (Courtesy of Automotive Hall of Fame, Dearborn, Michigan)

ther ever married, and Miss Tague continued to work for H.H. after the company entered bankruptcy, coming to his James Street home each day to take dictation and type letters until nearly the very end of his life. The deceased automotive executive left an estate of over half a million dollars, a substantial sum for the mid-1950s (the James Street residence, now somewhat rundown, was part of the estate; this house soon would be demolished to permit construction of an apartment complex). A considerable part of H.H.'s assets was disposed of through trusts, with the names of the beneficiaries in many instances kept from the eyes of the curious.[10-4] In death Herbert H. Franklin continued to be every bit as secretive about personal matters as he had during most of his adult life.

John Wilkinson, the engineering leader of the H.H. Franklin Company throughout much of the period of its corporate life, shared a number of the traits of Herbert Franklin, although differing from him in many respects. John for the most part followed the lead of H.H. by displaying limited interest in the public life of Syracuse. He too never held elected office, nor did he serve on any important public board or commission in his native community. This indifference to public affairs is somewhat surprising in view of the major contributions John's grandfather made as a civic leader during the infancy of the city.

John, however, was an exceptionally active participant in community sporting events during the early years of the twentieth century. While no longer engaging in such physically demanding activities as bicycle racing, he invariably competed in municipal tennis matches and for years was ranked as the city champion in this sport. He also was a participant in Syracuse area golf tournaments, again consistently achieving a top ranking. John was an avid hunter and fisherman, often spending vacations or long weekends with fellow outdoor enthusiasts at camps located along rivers and lakes in the region around Syracuse.

Following John's earlier-mentioned marriage to fellow-Syracusan Anne Belden in 1896 (like the Wilkinson's the Belden's were an old Syracuse family), three children were born to the couple. Daughters Helen and Anne arrived in 1897 and 1900 respectively, while son John Jr. (Jack) was born some years later, in 1905. Helen married Harry Blagbrough, a Latin teacher at a private school in New England. Blagbrough subsequently joined the H.H. Franklin Company as director of employees relations. Anne married Alden Sherry, a track star at Cornell who later attended Harvard business school. Sherry, an ambulance driver and subsequently a fighter pilot in World War I,

THE LEADERS OF THE ORGANIZATION

A youthful John Wilkinson playing golf.
(Courtesy of the late Anne Wilkinson Sherry and John Sherry)

also was with the Franklin firm for a time, but ultimately went into the fields of banking and finance. Son Jack, after graduating from Cornell in 1926, and marrying Mary Van Dyne, worked for a number of firms in the Syracuse and Buffalo areas prior to his untimely death in 1945. He was never identified with the H.H. Franklin Company.

John Wilkinson constructed a beautiful residence at the corner of James and DeWitt Streets in Syracuse in 1916. A surviving daughter, Anne Sherry, recalls many details of a happy family life at this home and at a summer cottage on Skaneateles Lake:

> I was away at boarding school when our new James Street home was completed, but it immediately appealed to me when I first saw it. I can remember some of the details of life there. My mother after conferring with the cook, would order groceries from a specific

store, and they were delivered soon afterward. There was no electric refrigerator in those days; we placed a sign in the window telling the ice man how many pounds he was to deliver. A seamstress came on occasion to make children's and women's clothes for members of the household. She would take over the upstairs sewing room for several weeks at a time to complete this work.

We usually employed three servants to help mother run the house, plus a handyman who tended the furnace and did yard work. A laundress also came in two or three times a week. The family kept two cars, and later had a third one for my older sister. Father, of course, drove his own auto, but since my mother never learned to drive she had a chauffeur who came as needed, sometimes in the evening. Our family never considered itself rich, but we did live in quite a nice style.

The Wilkinson home on James Street in Syracuse, viewed from the east. (Courtesy of Hope Wilkinson Yeager)

THE LEADERS OF THE ORGANIZATION

The Wilkinson children at he family's summer home on Skaneateles Lake in 1908. (Courtesy of the late Anne Wilkinson Sherry and John Sherry)

After spending a number of summers at the seacoast in New England following their marriage, my father and mother bought land and built a summer home on the shores of Skaneateles Lake. This was largely at my father's insistence, since he did not feel he could take time away from his engineering duties at Franklin for any extended summer vacation. He drove to the Franklin plant each day throughout the summer from our lake home, usually at a very high speed. There was a story current in the early years that when women living on the Skaneateles–Syracuse road heard the roar of an approaching car and saw a vast dust cloud, they would grab their youngsters and cry: "Children look out, here comes Mr. Wilkinson!"

Life at Skaneateles Lake during the summer was very pleasant, almost like going back to an earlier era. A windmill pumped our water, and we used an icehouse to store ice cut off the lake in winter. While my dad was busy six days a week at the plant, on Sunday mornings he often would take all of us kids on a picnic. Dad built a big, fast motor boat, and we frequently went in it to the lower part of the lake for lunch or dinner at the old Glen Haven resort hotel. On one occasion our neighbor, Dr. Van Dyne, came to father and informed him that he needed to perform an urgent operation on a man living across the lake. Dad started the boat motor and drove the doctor at top speed to the sick man's home. The emergency surgery was performed and the patient recovered. We had many visitors at the lake home when I was a child. Mr. Franklin came quite often, as did Mr. Barton, Mr. Haynes, and other company officials.

On one occasion about the time of the first World War dad brought home a car with an experimental automatic transmission, and my sister and I took turns driving it. The automatic transmission did not always work, but when necessary you could screw in a lever to shift gears.

Dad had a big workshop in the basement of our James Street home, where he turned out everything from auto parts to golf clubs. He gave quite a few of these home-made golf clubs to friends. Father, despite being a very handsome man, was not too socially inclined. He tended to be a bit quiet, but did have a sense of humor. He very much enjoyed shooting partridge and pheasant, and also did a lot of fishing.

Once the H.H. Franklin Manufacturing Company began to achieve success in the production and sale of automobiles, John Wilkinson quickly attained a reputation throughout the industry as an important motor vehicle engineer. After being elected an early vice president of the Society of Automotive Engineers, John remained active in this group, delivering technical papers at the Society's annual meetings and serving on important committees. He also was a long time member of the American Society of Mechanical Engineers, participating in a prominent manner in the meetings of this organization.

Following his split with H.H. Franklin and subsequent departure from the company in late 1924, John, even though some years from normal retirement age, did not seek to become affiliated with another motor vehicle firm (reportedly he did not wish to leave Syracuse). Instead, he spent his time developing a series of experimental cars, all of which were water cooled! Probably John had no desire to become embroiled with his former employer in a tussle over rights to patents covering air-cooled vehicles. While the Wilkinson cars were given favorable publicity by Syracuse newspapers, none ever entered volume production. John also was retained in 1926 and 1927 by his old colleague, Frederick Haynes, who in those years headed the Dodge Brothers Motor Company in Detroit, to design a six-cylinder motor, also water-cooled, for the new Dodge "Victory Six." Following this effort, and the advent of the Great Depression, John appears to have gone into semi-retirement for the balance of his life. Having sold his stock in the H.H. Franklin Company not long after leaving the firm

John Wilkinson in his later years. Photo taken in Carl Doman's office at Aircooled Motors in Syracuse. (Courtesy of Elizabeth A. Doman)

THE FRANKLIN AUTOMOBILE COMPANY

An elderly John Wilkinson relaxes here with one of his prize hunting dogs. (Courtesy of Hope Wilkinson Yeager)

(when it still brought a substantial price), he was an independently wealthy man.

In an impressive ceremony held in Syracuse on November 27, 1939, John Wilkinson was awarded life membership in the Society of Automotive Engineers. The award was based on John's notable engineering achievements, with the now elderly inventor cited as a courageous pioneer who helped to establish the sound fundamentals for future growth of the automotive industries.

John Wilkinson died at his home in Syracuse on June 25, 1951. Unlike the death of H.H. Franklin, John's passing was given recognition on a national scale. In obituaries in major newspapers and news magazines he was described as an internationally-known engineer, and given credit for developing the air-cooled gasoline engine.[10-5] After years of not speaking to each other, John and H.H. Franklin resumed friendly relations shortly before John's death, reportedly at a picnic sponsored by former H.H. Franklin Company employees.

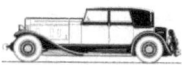

The two heads of the H.H. Franklin Company enjoyed long and productive lives during an important period of American history, one which witnessed an unprecedented revolution in the field of personal transportation. The question thus may be asked: How should each be ranked in his specialty, John Wilkinson as an automotive engineer and Herbert H. Franklin as chief executive of a motor car company of small-to-medium size?

John Wilkinson can justifiably be given high rank as a motor vehicle engineer throughout the key period of his career, the years from 1898 to 1924. He showed impressive skills during the pioneer automotive era in successfully solving problems involved in the development of a practical air-cooled gasoline motor when others were inclined to turn to the more-easily-designed water-cooled power plant. As the industry grew he also demonstrated an ability to keep the nation's only successful air-cooled car fully competitive with the water-cooled vehicles turned out in huge numbers by other companies (Franklin "firsts" in the field of automotive development are described in a subsequent chapter). Apart from his role as a technical innovator, John also merits very high rank in the automotive engineering field by his insistence on adhering to several important basic principles in motor car development. These can be summarized as: Keep the vehicle both simple and light in weight; design it carefully; build it to high standards. Few specialists in automotive engineering would question the merits of these guidelines on a long-term basis. In the over 100 years of motor vehicle production in America to date, the overall industry has perhaps fared best during those periods when the above general rules were followed.

THE FRANKLIN AUTOMOBILE COMPANY

If John had a weakness it was his tendency at times to ignore the importance of appearance in a motor vehicle. This shortcoming was most evident during his final years with the Franklin firm. As noted earlier, by 1923-24 style was playing a critical role in the popularity of a motor car, and a deficiency in this area offset, in the eyes of a significant segment of the public, technical excellence. From the end of the World War I period to the time he left the firm, John and the company both would have benefited from the services of a top-rate automotive stylist. In the period following John's departure this gap was of course filled admirably by such persons as deCausse and Dietrich.

In summary, John Wilkinson can justifiably be ranked with such important auto industry engineers of the earlier era as Howard Coffin, Jesse G. Vincent, the Lelands, Rollin H. White, Charles B. King and Howard Marmon. John, never a flamboyant individual, in the view of many observers has not been given the recognition for engineering accomplishments that he deserves. In part this may be due to the fact that he worked for a motor car company of modest size which, as noted previously, also was out of the mainstream geographically.

Assigning a rank to Herbert H. Franklin among automotive chief executives is a far more different undertaking. In any evaluation it should be noted initially that H.H. in his early days deserved to be rated as a very capable entrepreneur. When little more than a youth in his Coxsackie newspaper venture he displayed an almost uncanny ability to determine what the public wanted, and was a willing risk-taker. In addition, the man was endowed with the backbone and determination to see projects through to completion, despite initial problems and setbacks. These qualities enabled H.H. to succeed in early business ventures, and subsequently guide a pioneer auto company into a prominent place in a new industry.

It was later in the history of the motor car firm which he headed, when very different talents were needed, that H.H. Franklin encountered problems. The second major growth period of the Franklin Company began in the 1916-1918 era, followed by the large plant expansion of

THE LEADERS OF THE ORGANIZATION

1919-1921. The payroll now had become sizable, and the company structure much more complex. The need to constantly develop new products to meet the challenges of a fast-paced industry became apparent. At this point, if the firm was to retain a significant position among competing automotive concerns its chief executive would be required to display the talents of a highly competent administrator. A wide variety of activities needed to be skillfully coordinated; a sense of direction established for the firm; and capable subordinate managers recruited and utilized effectively. In attempting to fulfill these and similar responsibilities H.H. displayed marked deficiencies.

The period from 1919 through 1924 became literally a revolving door for top-level Franklin company personnel. Arthur Kemp, a well-respected business executive, was hired late in the World War I period to assist H.H. in improving efficiency in overall company operations. In less than two years he was dropped (Kemp later headed the Auburn Auto Company). A.G. Maney lasted only slightly longer as chief of merchandising activities. Various personal assistants to H.H. had very short tenures. The climax of all this came in 1924, when the Moskovics debacle occurred, followed by John Wilkinson's dramatic departure.

Quite obviously H.H. found it difficult to deal with strong subordinates. He apparently felt threatened when capable people displayed initiative in organizing and managing important segments of company operations, and chose to get rid of them. He also appeared unable to make up his mind on potential new products. The four-cylinder vehicle effort was begun, quickly shelved, re-started, and once again dropped. The truck project of the same era received similar treatment. H.H. tended to exhibit certain of the same deficiencies in the areas of high-level management and product development that another auto company head, Henry Ford, did at this time (however, in dealing with workers in his plant H.H. clearly showed far more decency than Ford).

The handling of John Wilkinson by H.H. Franklin contrasts sharply with the approach used by the capable Alfred P. Sloan in managing

THE FRANKLIN AUTOMOBILE COMPANY

a crisis involving General Motor's engineering head, Charles Kettering. Following the decision to shelve the copper-cooled Chevrolet engine project, Kettering, bitter at what he considered unfair treatment, wanted to resign. Sloan, recognizing the immense importance of Kettering's past and potential future contributions to the company, used all his talents to reassure the engineering chief that he was vital to GM, and succeeded in keeping him on board. H.H., on the other hand, either lacked the ability to make John Wilkinson feel he was essential to the future of the air-cooled vehicle firm, or simply didn't care if he left.

As observed previously, the loss of Wilkinson undoubtedly hurt the company severely in the long term. John's absence did not unduly impact the area of purely technical development, since his subordinates were able people and could continue to handle basic engineering duties with no difficulty. The real problem lay in decision-making on major company programs–whether, for example, the firm should again have considered, in the late 1920s, the development of a less-costly companion car which could have been quickly brought to market in the event of poor economic times. A second, closely-related question was whether the firm from 1929 on risked losing its basic focus as it moved toward development of ever-larger and more costly vehicles. The persons filling John's shoes, lacking important stature in the motor vehicle firm, were in no position to question H.H.'s decisions on such issues, regardless of their personal views. The company may well have paid a stiff price for this authoritarianism.

Other areas of H.H.'s executive activities justify review and comment. As the person in overall charge of company fiscal affairs (Frank Barton, while nominally the company treasurer, dealt with only minor matters), H.H. spent a substantial amount of time meeting with representatives of banking institutions, primarily in the nation's business capital, New York City, but also in such regional financial centers as Boston, Cleveland and Chicago. With the Syracuse auto manufacturing firm finding it necessary to borrow large sums of money in both the early and late 1920s to provide operating funds, H.H. on a number

THE LEADERS OF THE ORGANIZATION

of occasions was required to negotiate loans and loan extensions with a variety of lending sources. Evidence exists that he usually displayed considerable skill in carrying out this delicate task, particularly in the first half of the 1920s. Herbert Franklin has been described by his one-time aide, Horace Benstead, as a person endowed with an exceptional ability to convince hard-headed banking executives of the bright future prospects of the auto firm he headed, even when current operating results were less than satisfactory. It seems clear, however, that following the inability of Franklin to repay in timely fashion the large loan made in the boom year 1929, the banking community quickly lost confidence in H.H.'s abilities as the company chief executive. As recorded earlier, by late 1931, the creditor banks sought to keep H.H. on a very short leash, and gave him little authority over the operations of his own firm. When the company went bankrupt in 1934, and efforts were made to reorganize it and reinstitute motor car production, H.H. clearly did not play a role of any importance in such activities. At this point his reputation as an executive in all probability had dropped to a level where he no longer was consulted by either Syracuse or out-of-town business leaders.

The relationship of H.H. to the Syracuse banking community deserves notice. Whether due to the chilly feeling which existed between many Syracuse business leaders and H.H., or to the extreme conservatism of the city's financial institutions, there is little evidence that most local banks over the years were willing to assist the Franklin firm. The single exception appears to have been the Merchants National Bank and Trust Co., headed by the one Syracuse banker enjoying a close relationship with H.H. Franklin, William Kelley. Surviving correspondence indicates that when the auto firm was in desperate financial trouble in 1932, Kelley assisted H.H. in convening a meeting of the city's top bankers to discuss potential aid to the Franklin Company. No record exists as to the end result of this effort, but in all probability critically important financial assistance was refused.

H.H., particularly in the early days of the air-cooled vehicle firm, clearly showed impressive talents as the writer of the company's

THE FRANKLIN AUTOMOBILE COMPANY

advertising copy. He undoubtedly continued to either write, or at least strongly influence the composition of, company advertisements through the period of World War I and perhaps later. These interesting early advertisements, with their emphasis on practical common sense and down-to-earth reasoning, appear to be almost an extension of H.H.'s personality. In advertising and in public relations generally, Herbert Franklin displayed solid ability.

An area not directly connected to business management in which H.H. showed almost extraordinary foresight was that of urban and regional planning. In the year 1922, Franklin issued a prescient statement forecasting the development of suburban shopping centers, which he believed would be made feasible by vastly increased use of the motor car. This prediction, well in advance of its time, would take years and even decades to come about, but it demonstrated the vision of the auto executive in an important field.

Herbert H. Franklin
Courtesy of Automotive Hall of Fame

THE LEADERS OF THE ORGANIZATION

Of even greater importance than the shopping center prophecy was the series of articles written by H.H. Franklin for the *New York Times* in 1929, 1930, and 1931, urging development of a vast network of limited access, divided highways across America. As related earlier, H.H. observed that such roads would be of immense value in making it possible to fully utilize the modern automobile in speedy, safe inter-city travel. It is unfortunate that H.H.'s views on the need for a chain of superhighways throughout the nation were not listened to and acted on by top public officials in the early 1930s. This would have been a highly propitious time for the nation to commence building such a highway network, for a number of reasons. Construction costs had been pushed downward to a low level by the depression, land acquisition prices would have been minimal and a huge number of unemployed persons could have been provided with jobs. It is difficult to understand why neither President Herbert Hoover, with his background as a top-level engineer, nor his successor, Franklin D. Roosevelt, with his laudable desire to put the unemployed to work and reinvigorate the economy, considered initiating such a project during the 1931-1934 period. In addition to the physical and economic benefits which could have been gained by following H.H.'s advice, the effect of such an important program on national morale would have been incalculable. America might well have pulled itself out of a bitter, disheartening depression by its own bootstraps if the auto executive's plan of action had been followed.

H.H. Franklin thus was a decidedly complex individual. An able entrepreneur, a person with a touch of genius in producing advertising copy, he must be described as no more than an average auto company chief executive. He also has been charged by some with being a business buccaneer, an individual who used the ideas and inventions of others for his own benefit. While this charge may contain a kernel of truth, it should be noted that a large number of H.H.'s fellow industrial leaders in that era operated in a similar manner! H.H.'s surviving business and personal letters from the very early years of the twentieth century demonstrate, as noted in an earlier chapter, the outstanding ability of the man in use of the written word. A number of these epistles, however, also reflect a touch of arrogance on Herbert's part, plus a readiness to "put down" others, including persons who helped him rise in the business world. Skill in human relations was not one of H.H.'s strong points.

H.H. thus displayed a curious combination of strengths and weaknesses throughout his life. Offsetting the various shortcomings, however, was his leadership late in his career in outlining steps which should have been taken by the nation to fully exploit the potential of the motor car, and at the same time achieve a desperately-needed economic recovery. With these many contradictory personal qualities, it is perhaps best to leave any final assessment of this complex man to history.

– Eleven –

Inside the Company: Management, Marketing, and Engineering

Despite Herbert H. Franklin's problems in working with and retaining high-level executives, the H.H. Franklin Manufacturing Company itself remained an extremely stable entity during almost its entire existence. Bitter struggles for corporate control, common in both large and small auto companies through the first third of the twentieth century, seldom occurred at the Franklin firm.

There clearly were two reasons for this continued stability at the Syracuse auto manufacturing company. First, H.H. Franklin, a few years after car building commenced, achieved majority ownership of the common stock of the firm. This meant that whenever he should choose to exercise it, H.H. Franklin enjoyed full power to control decision-making at the company bearing his name. Holders of preferred stock, despite their large financial investment from 1920-on, had no voice in company affairs unless a specified number of dividends were omitted, and even when this occured as the firm took its frightful downhill plunge in the early 1930s, these shareholders took no action to challenge top management.

A second reason for the stable company environment was the makeup of the board of directors of the manufacturing firm. Membership of the board, once initially established, changed only slightly during the first twenty or more years of the auto manufacturing era. Herbert H. Franklin, Alexander T. Brown and Giles H. Stilwell were board members literally from the beginning of company operations; they were joined at an early date by John Wilkinson and Frank Barton. W.C. Lipe held a seat on the board for some years but ultimately dropped off; while Edward Dann became a board member well before 1910 and continued to serve into the 1930s. Howard L. Franklin, brother of H.H. and head of the Franklin Die Casting Corporation, came on the board in 1920 and served until his death in the mid-1920s. In addition to H.H. Franklin's large holdings, the other board members noted above also owned substantial amounts of common stock in the firm.

As the years passed two other categories of persons joined the board. One group included Syracuse business people–Herbert Hess, A.E. Parsons and, at a very late date, F.T. Delany (head of a firm which constructed most of the Franklin factory) and R.M. Tennant. A second group consisted of company executives. Arthur Holmes, chief engineer, served on the board briefly before leaving to organize the car manufacturing firm bearing his name; A P. Kemp as second vice-president held a board seat in 1917-1918; and A.G. Maney was a board member for a short period while holding the position of director of distribution. Operations executive Ralph Murphy held board membership throughout much of the 1920s, and into the 1930s, while C.E. Hull and J.E. Halligan, financial executives of the company, served briefly on the board in the late 1920s. The deaths of A.E. Parsons and Alexander T. Brown produced vacancies which were filled in mid-1929 by the heads of the sales, manufacturing and engineering divisions of the firm, John E. Williams, L.J. Purdy and Edward Marks (Purdy and Marks served only a year or so). Frederick Haynes was a key board member for a year when he rejoined the firm in 1930-31, and Syracuse attorney James Styron (a law partner of Giles Stilwell) also served in the early 1930s.[11-1]

Perhaps the most interesting feature of the board of directors of the Franklin firm was the almost total absence of out-of-town board members. The large Boston Franklin distributor, O.A. Lawton, was a board member for two years, but with this exception the membership was restricted to Syracusans until Edwin McEwen joined in late 1931. McEwen was the first individual representing out-of-town financial interests to achieve board membership (H.H. Franklin historically wanted no part of such "outside" control). As observed previously, McEwen and H.H. Franklin clashed repeatedly as executives of the automobile manufacturing company, and surviving documents indicate that they also came into sharp conflict as board of director members. McEwen, despite his powerful position, did not get his way with the board on everything. When he submitted to the directors, at the beginning of 1933, a plan calling for huge cut-backs in the company's vehicle building program, the other board members rebelled and tossed the proposal overboard.[11-2]

As noted previously, in the early days of automobile manufacturing an executive committee of board members existed, consisting of H.H. Franklin, John Wilkinson and Giles Stilwell. This small committee continued for a number of years, but ceased to exist after John Wilkinson left the firm. Thereafter H.H. during most years acted as a one-person executive body, although he was advised by various subordinate officials of the company.[11-3]

While a company of only moderate size, the H.H. Franklin firm by the mid-1920s had a decidedly complex organization structure. In addition to the manufacturing entity, the sales arm, which was the independently organized Franklin Automobile Company, also carried on an important operation. This merchandising unit was integrated with the balance of the company in many respects, but did have direct responsibility for marketing the Franklin car, and for relations with dealers. The chief operating officer of the automobile company was the vice-president of sales and marketing, although the president was H.H. Franklin. During the period that John Wilkinson was with the company the engineering and manufacturing division of the firm, while in theory reporting to H.H. Franklin as president, enjoyed a very substantial degree of autonomy. Following Wilkinson's departure the

THE FRANKLIN AUTOMOBILE COMPANY

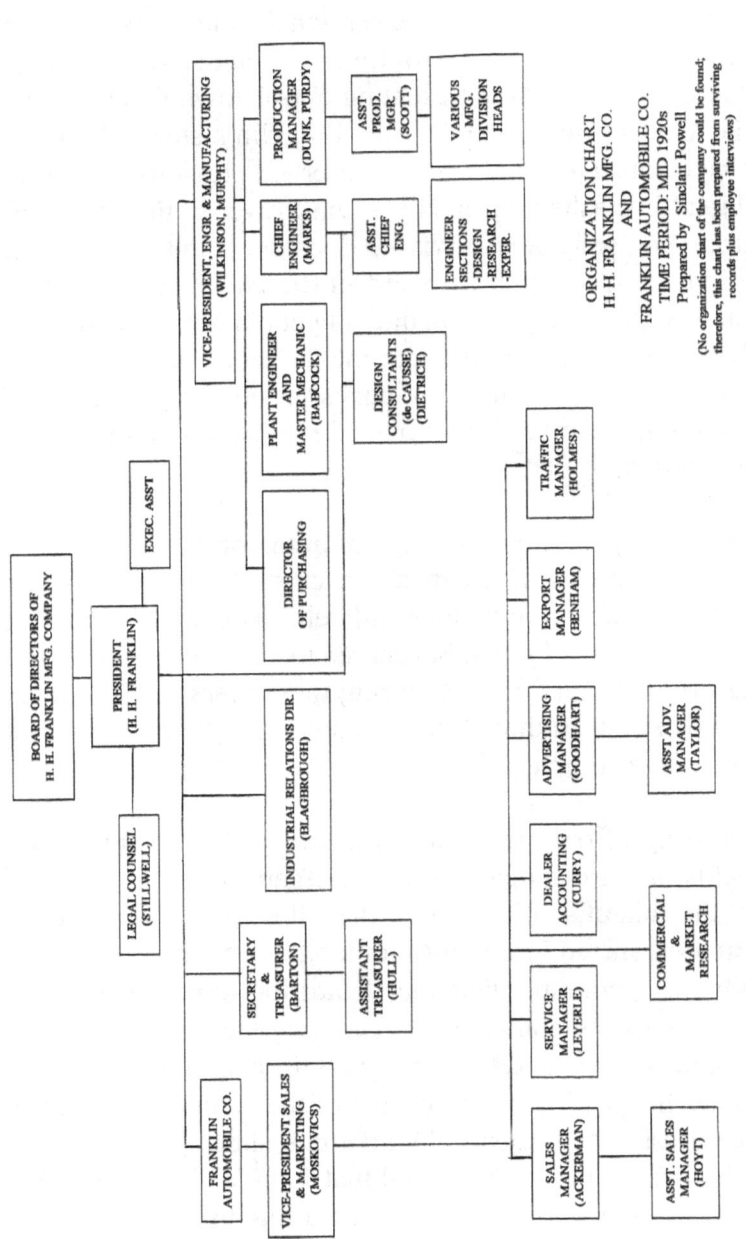

An organization chart of the H.H. Franklin Manufacturing Company and the Franklin Automobile Company, prepared by the author from surviving records and former Franklin employee interviews.

operations division became far more under the direct control of H.H.. With the very large number of persons involved in the various aspects of car manufacture, this division employed the great majority of H.H. Franklin Company personnel.

Allied with the area of sales and marketing were several units of considerable importance. These included the service department, the advertising office, the export division, and the traffic management operation. The dealer accounting office reviewed financial reports of the hundreds of Franklin dealers, and advised dealerships on effective management of business affairs.

Two divisions of the company performed what essentially were services for all other units. The treasurer's office dealt with all fiscal matters, handled accounting and payroll, and also supervised the large staff of women who were employed in the main office. Functions of the industrial relations department have been discussed in an earlier chapter, but it too was an operation which served the other divisions of the company, particularly in the areas of personnel recruitment and employment.

At least two and perhaps more divisions of the overall company were not encompassed within the basic organization. With the incorporation of the die-casting division as a separate entity a year or so after World War I, it commenced independent operations, reporting its earnings apart from the balance of the firm. The Franklin Die-Casting Corporation sold its products to numerous outside companies, and did not share its personnel with the H.H. Franklin Manufacturing Company. However, nearly all the stock of the die-casting corporation was held by the manufacturing company. Also enjoying some degree of autonomy, although less than that of the die-casting division, were the Franklin Land Development Company and the Franklin Development Company, which have been briefly mentioned earlier. Persons working with these units may have been largely on loan from the H.H. Franklin Manufacturing Company.[11-4]

THE FRANKLIN AUTOMOBILE COMPANY

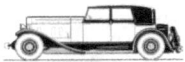

The managers of the H.H. Franklin firm, as in any moderate-sized company carrying on manufacturing operations in that era, had many concerns in dealing with rank and file employees. Productivity obviously was a vitally important factor, and by pioneering in the use of the Taylor System of scientific management the company may well have surpassed many of the other minor auto producers in both output and overall quality of workmanship. On the other side of the coin fairness in dealing with employees was important in maintaining morale among the rank-and-file. Mention has been made of both of these factors in earlier chapters, and employees of the company also commented on them at some length in their interviews. However, the one-time workers at the Franklin company made their comments some fifty-five to seventy years after being employed at the firm, when danger exists of forgetfulness or even altered perceptions.

Contemporary accounts of the automotive factory scene by discerning and unbiased observers in the early decades of the motor car industry are difficult to come by. However, this is not true with the H.H, Franklin firm. Here an astute and articulate observer, fair and balanced in his approach, worked for the firm and publicly recorded his impressions at the time. How this took place is an interesting story, unique in every way.

At the beginning of the summer of 1920, Frederick M. Davenport was a faculty member at Hamilton College, located in Clinton, New York, some thirty-five miles east of Syracuse, where he taught political science and public law. More importantly, Davenport also was a member of the New York State Senate, where he had displayed a keen interest in what were termed industrial problems. He found it difficult in his legislative work to get at the truth on key management-labor issues, since both industry and labor utilized lobbyists interested solely in presenting the point of view of their clients.

At this point Davenport unexpectedly received a letter from H.H. Franklin, who he had never met. H.H., however, had noted Davenport's interest in industrial questions in the state senate, and issued an invitation to the legislator to join the Franklin organization for the summer. In his well-phrased letter H.H. noted that be did not know what Davenport could do for the auto company, nor did he know what the firm could do for a state senator. However, H.H. expressed the feeling that the experience might be mutually beneficial.

Davenport was receptive to the idea of the Franklin firm giving a state legislator, well-meaning but with no knowledge of what went on in the auto industry, a look at things on the inside. Consequently, on July 1, 1920, the state senator reported for work at the Franklin plant, and was issued badge number 4626. He related that he was treated with courtesy, and given complete freedom in every way. He put on overalls and learned to operate a big lathe where various metals were turned down to accuracies of well under one-thousands of an inch. He rode with men testing vehicles just built, and noted their ability to detect defects so slight that they missed Davenport's ear entirely! He watched every operation being conducted in the good-sized factory, and sought to interview each leader in the Franklin organization, big or little, with preference given to persons who had come up through the ranks. The state senator looked into such areas as accounting and finance, and had an opportunity to read the confidential reports addressed to the president of the firm. He examined blue-prints with plant employees, talked with workers at their machines, and rushed to the wash-basin with them to clean up when the whistle blew at the noon-hour!

Davenport essentially was attempting to examine the human side of the auto industry. One of the key problem areas he quickly identified was the relationship between the foremen in the factory and the workers under them. He noted that some foremen, especially those who recently rose from the ranks, tended to show all the qualities of petty tyrants. He observed that in well-run industrial firms the foreman often was watched rather carefully by higher management, and soon dropped if he could not display fairness, iron out disagreements, and at the same time meet the requirements of production. He found that at a progressive plant such as Franklin a foreman did not have the final say in discharging a worker–this was done by the industrial relations office. This particular office also was available to hear the complaints of employees who felt they had received unfair treatment while on the job.

The extreme specialization of work in a modern automobile factory, with the resultant monotony, received close attention from Frederick Davenport. He soon came to realize that such monotony could ultimately be a cause of inefficient production and industrial unrest, as well as a factor in the large labor turnover experienced by many auto firms. He noted the real danger of specialization ultimately reaching the point of diminishing returns. Davenport observed that training schools (Franklin had one in its plant) could be of value in turning out persons with multiple skills, who could change from one operation to another occasionally as a relief.

At this fairly early period of auto industry development Davenport reached the conclusion that making industry more intelligent and human was what was needed. And he felt that this goal could be achieved primarily by making management more intelligent and human. He did not denigrate the genius of American industrial management, which he felt was the best in the world. However, he did feel that in many instances management took a narrow, short-term view of what its interests were, and acted accordingly. To work out effective industrial democracy, the state senator felt, would require a large degree of humaneness and vision on the part of industrial management. Lacking this, he expressed concern about militant trade unions developing and becoming engaged in deadly combat with strong employer groups, with unhappy results for all.

Davenport showed a keen awareness of the importance of what he termed "ideas from below." He noted that discoveries of ways and means to improve operations were more apt to come from individuals working on the job than from the engineering personnel at the top. He clearly looked with favor on a system within a manufacturing plant which recognized and rewarded ideas and suggestions from rank and file employees. Davenport also felt that encouraging employees to develop skills which would make them more valuable to the overall factory operation was of great importance. He cited the instance of a workman in the Franklin toolroom who on his own initiative had learned to use a highly sophisticated measuring device of that era, a sine bar. This man, with only a common-school education, nonetheless had been able to teach himself the advanced mathematical concepts required to effectively make use of this instrument. Davenport perceptively noted that it would be a loss for everyone if factory personnel displaying such initiative were not appreciated, rewarded, and given every opportunity to work up to the top.

The state senator clearly enjoyed his experiences at the Franklin plant. He noted with interest the factory hands expressing admiration for and faith in the leadership of the two men at the top in the firm (undoubtedly Franklin and Wilkinson), who they felt for years had shown the spirit of give-and-take and good will toward common workers. As he said good-by at the end of the summer Davenport described specifically such unique employees as the current chief of the Six Nations of the Iroquois, who put rear axles on the car, plus a man who was seventy-four years of age when mustered out of the British army at the end of World War I and now also was employed at the Franklin plant. He cited the "college boys" who by working at the factory were able to earn something toward their next year's cost of education, and particularly mentioned the "regulars," the Franklin employees by the thousands who would man their machines for the rest of their lives. Davenport observed, in closing his account, the comradeship and integrity he had observed in personnel at the plant.

This exceptionally interesting account of what might be termed Franklin factory life, ultimately printed in a magazine article in 1921, makes it clear that here existed an unusual auto manufacturing company, one which, while displaying various deficiencies, still was by the standards of its day a good place at which to work.[11-5] The Franklin plant may well have been relatively unique in the overall auto industry in its combination of the achievement of operating efficiency and a display of decency to the rank and file in the area of industrial and employee relations.

From the beginning of the automotive era selling the Franklin car to the American public engaged the attention of a top echelon of company officials. H.H. Franklin unquestionably spent a major portion of his time on marketing matters, particularly in the area of advertising the air-cooled vehicle. As observed previously, H.H.'s masterful talents in developing advertising copy clearly stood the company in good stead as it vigorously and successfully competed with other early automobile builders in the sale of vehicles. The Franklin firm also was fortunate in securing the services, during the first decade of automobile building, of two such vigorous sales managers as C. Arthur Benjamin and Fred R. Bump. With leadership of this caliber the firm made an impressive start in the marketing area, as demonstrated by its high rank in unit sales from 1905 to 1907 in the automobile industry.

Together with the effective use of advertising in many of the leading mass-circulation magazines of the day, the Franklin firm relied on every conceivable type of road rally and endurance contest to excite public interest in its product. The two great record-breaking cross-country trips, plus the early efforts of John Wilkinson in both racing and endurance events, have been noted in previous chapters. Even after these initial efforts the company, while it no longer sought to "show off" its products in various speed trials, continued to be strongly interested in demonstrating the capabilities of the vehicles it produced in various types of long-distance runs. One of these, made in 1910, became known to the public as the "Franklin Trek." This involved C. S. Carris, famed long-distance driver, piloting a six-cylinder Franklin car on a tour which began in Syracuse; went east to Boston; then south to New York and Washington, D. C.; west across the mountains to Ohio and Indiana; and finally on to St. Louis. The return trip involved stops at Chicago, Cleveland and Buffalo before reaching the starting point of Syracuse. The entire "Trek" involved thirteen days of travel, with some 3,500 miles covered. The purpose of this run was to demonstrate the ability of the Franklin car to furnish easy riding to its occupants on long trips made at substantial speeds, in spite of the very poor roads of the day. While the achievement of sheer speed was not a goal of the "Trek," published reports of the run did point out that on one leg of the trip the drivers of the vehicle succeeded in covering 403 miles in a single day's travel, an amazing feat in that era.

The Franklin company also benefitted from the exploits of two early women drivers of the firm's product. Mrs. Edward Prentice of Binghamton, New York, raced in "point-to-point" contests in Albany, New York, on four occasions in 1908-1909. The vehicle driven by Mrs. Prentice in this unusual activity (for a woman at this early date) was a four-cylinder 1906 Franklin. A much longer trip, across the entire country, was undertaken a few years later by another woman, Mrs. Albert W. Seaman of Brooklyn, New York. Mrs. Seaman drove a Franklin car on this extensive journey (which terminated at Ralph Hamlin's Franklin dealership in Los Angeles) covering a total of 4,150 miles. She was accompanied on the trip by her husband, but performed all the driving herself.

Franklin owners in the early days of motoring were assisted by the factory in dealing with their vehicle-related problems in a number of ways. One of these was through an *Owners' Bulletin*, published bimonthly by the Franklin Automobile Company, the selling arm of the firm, and sent to all purchasers of Franklins. This publication gave practical, down-to-earth advice to Franklin car owners. Recognizing that in this era an owner could not always return to a dealer for day-to-day service on his car, the bulletin described in detail work the owner could do to keep his vehicle in sound operating condition. Daily and weekly lubrication schedules were listed; a program whereby the owner might go over the car periodically to keep all bolts and nuts tight was outlined; and careful driving techniques were emphasized. Several issues of the bulletin described procedures which should be followed on extended trips, and advice on taking a vehicle into Canada was even included.

A second aid to owners of Franklin cars was the company service representative, a technically-trained person assigned to work in a geographic area, whose duties included inspection of every car sold after it had been in use by the owner for a specific period. This service plan obviously relieved the owner of any apprehension about things going wrong with his new vehicle. Together with this follow-up program it should be noted that the company urged owners of Franklin vehicles to let others know of their satisfaction with the car and the service rendered, thus hopefully securing for the company additional propects for purchase of the Franklin product!

By the end of World War I the merchandising and sales program of the H.H. Franklin Company had become quite sophisticated in nature. In the spring of 1919 the air-cooled vehicle builder, anxious to explore the potential overseas demand for the Franklin car, sent one of its employees, John Connolly, on an extensive tour of the Orient and South Pacific. Connolly sailed from San Francisco to Yokohama, Japan, subsequently visiting several other Japanese cities. He then went on to Seoul, Korea, and to Peking and Shanghai, China. From there he took a ship to Manila in the Philippines, where he remained an entire month. Then it was on to Melbourne and Sydney, Australia, before returning to the United States in mid-fall. Connolly expressed substantial enthusiasm on his return about the possibility of opening up the Pacific territory for sales of the Franklin car.

A second Franklin man to travel abroad in 1919 was H.D. Hekkema, originally from Holland, who returned to his native land on a combined vacation and business trip. Hekkema, aided by family contacts, was able to analyze fully the sales potential for the Franklin car in Holland, and on his return to the factory agreed to become the dealer in that country (after spending several years in Holland, Hekkema returned to North America to become the Franklin distributor in Montreal, Canada).

In the period following World War I the Franklin firm took an important step toward utilizing research techniques to aid in increasing sales of its vehicles. A commercial research office was established by the company in 1920, operating in conjunction with the sales and advertising departments and reporting to the Director of Distribution. The new office was to gather statistics on the markets in which the Franklin firm sold vehicles, and forecast economic conditions in such markets. It then was to seek to predetermine what the company sales performance should be for the total market served, and for each local district. Ultimately quotas and sales schedules would be established for the overall market and for each dealership. Records were to be kept of dealers, sub-dealers and salesmen's performance, with such sales performance to be analyzed, weaknesses pointed out, and remedies suggested. The office also was to lay out boundaries of dealers' territories along sound lines, and construct and help put into effect sales promotion plans.

The new office thus was intended to both undertake skilled market research and help develop some very practical plans to stimulate sales of the Franklin vehicle, including all-out selling drives and campaigns. An initial such selling campaign was organized and put into effect throughout the calendar year 1921. To generate competition among dealers and sales personnel, the entire dealer organization plus all its employees were mobilized into the "Franklin Army." Based on total sales achieved each salesperson might rise in rank all the way from private to general. To further stimulate competition a number of prizes, including cash bonuses plus some very fine watches were offered by the company to those achieving far more than their quota of vehicle sales. A special publication, the *Salesometer*, was put out by the company several times each month and sent to every Franklin salesperson. It contained pep talks, cartoons, listings of number of cars delivered by various dealers and salespeople, "How to do it" articles by successful salespeople (including one by a woman who worked for the

THE FRANKLIN AUTOMOBILE COMPANY

Columbia, South Carolina, Franklin dealership), and a tally of those unfortunates who found themselves mired in the "bog of no sales."

Aided by its new research office the company continued its vigorous efforts to market the Franklin car throughout the 1920s. Fortunately, two persons who worked in the sales area during that decade were able to relate their experiences. One was Robert Feeley, who spent nearly five years with the firm before and following the First World War. Bob recalls the highlights of his career at Franklin:

> I joined the Franklin firm as a finance clerk in 1917, after completing an accelerated course at Syracuse University, but left early in 1918 for Army service. On my return in 1919, I rejoined Franklin, where I was again assigned to a finance job, having responsibility for hourly worker payroll at the main factory and two small branch plants. The workers were paid in cash, and one of my functions was to distribute pay envelopes to them.
>
> After a short time I had an opportunity to aid the person who headed the new research and statisics office, by developing special reports on sales problems facing the company. My reports went to H.H. Franklin, who liked them and approved of my assignment to such work.
>
> Along with this new activity I was able to put to use a talent for drawing which I had developed as a child. At a company picnic I sketched activities involving a number of people, including Bill Dunk, the plant manager. These came to the attention of the man who ran the company newspaper, and he quickly used them. I was paid a small sum for each one that was printed. A bit later I received a more important drawing assignment. As part of the big sales promotion activity in 1921 the company put out the *Salesometer*, a little newsletter sent out to dealers and salespeople across the U. S. and Canada, and wanted cartoons and sketches for it. I supplied a number of these, and was well-paid for each. Finally, I was asked to contribute drawings to Franklin sales catalogs, for which I received

THE BIRTH OF A BOOSTER

This cartoon from the August 1921 issue of the Salesometer *boasted of the honesty and efficiency of Franklin dealers. (Courtesy of William Tuthill)*

THE FRANKLIN AUTOMOBILE COMPANY

excellent compensation. By this time I had been appointed as a staff member of the advertising department, where I worked with a Syracuse University classmate on various art items.

In general I found the Franklin organization to be a very fine one. The people who made the car were dedicated workers, and they were supervised by equally dedicated managers. The company turned out a high-quality product, as John Wilkinson would never lower his standards in any way. However, it was not difficult to see stiff competition coming in the price class in which the Franklin car sold, and obviously the company needed to prepare to meet it. Incidentally, I sold Ford cars on the side during much of the time I was with Franklin, and earned a nice extra income doing this.

H.H. Franklin was very much a "loner" at all times. He called people into his office if he wished to speak to them, and issued orders through his secretary, Stella Tague. He always ate lunch alone, at a downtown hotel.

I was promoted to an executive position in the sales department in late 1923, where I served as an assistant to S.E. Ackerman, the sales manager. However, a few weeks after receiving this appointment I received an offer to join an advertising agency as its art director, and found it too good an opportunity to pass up. At least one executive at the Franklin firm told me I had made a wise move!

Somewhat later in the history of the Franklin firm another person, Russell Smith, worked on marketing problems. Mr. Smith dealt directly with dealers and customers during several years of employment in the late 1920s and early 1930s. He describes his activities:

My specific assignment during much of the time that I worked at Franklin was that of manning the "drive away" desk, where I met and dealt with those persons who came to the factory to pick up new vehicles. Such a procedure was quite common in that period, with nearly forty per cent of the cars sold during some years driven away from the plant by either dealers or individuals who had purchased Franklins and wanted to pick them up personally in Syracuse. The dealer or individual buyer usually would arrive on the morning of the day the vehicle had been promised, and it was my duty to process the sales documents, obtain any payment due, prepare papers showing proof of ownership, and make certain that the vehicle was ready for delivery by no later than early afternoon. If the car could not be turned over to a customer on time and the person had to stay over, the company paid the hotel bill.

On occasion a customer arriving to pick up a pre-ordered Franklin literally would fall in love with one of the very attractive vehicles displayed in the company showroom, and decide to purchase it instead of the car first selected. I particularly recall a dentist from New Jersey switching his order from a rather plain-looking four-door sedan to a semi-custom model sitting in the showroom. Needless to say, the substitution was approved quickly, a check for the additional amount due obtained from the dentist by the treasurer's office, and the newly-purchased car promptly moved from the display floor to the conditioning department to be prepared for the road!

When not busy with dealers or new owners coming to pick up cars I had an opportunity occasionally to chat with "Cannon Ball" Baker, who occupied a desk next to mine in the late 1920s. Baker was a big man physically, very friendly, always ready to answer questions and well-liked and respected by the sales staff.

I recall quite well that in very early 1929 several of us in sales were astonished when we saw company schedules calling for a big increase in the number of vehicles to be produced during the year. Our initial reaction was that the firm would find it tough to ever sell that many cars, and as 1929 unfolded we discovered that these fears were justified. Later in the year a large number of new, unsold Franklins were sitting in storage in various locations, and we faced a difficult problem in disposing of them. I was responsible for suggesting that we offer some of these cars for sale to employees at big discounts, and this ultimately was done. Eventually the remaining surplus vehicles were sold through the dealers, but at greatly reduced prices. If my memory is correct it took nearly one-and-and-one-half years to dispose of the last of them.

While personnel at the home office of the H.H. Franklin Company planned sales campaigns and sought to develop overall merchandising strategies, the actual task of selling the air-cooled vehicle to the public was undertaken by the dealer network. The size of this network during the peak sales years of the Franklin car in the 1920s is not easily determined. The Syracuse firm on one occasion indicated that the total number of distributors and dealers in America and abroad exceeded 500, and a dealer directory issued about 1922 lists 486 American and 21 Canadian sales outlets. However, it is probable that a number of those listed were tiny sub-dealers, who disposed of only a handful of vehicles each year.

A small Franklin dealership in Lansing, Michigan in 1923.
(Courtesy of Lorenz Brothers)

INSIDE THE COMPANY

A substantial number of Franklin dealers did not handle this brand of vehicle exclusively–they also sold another make of car, almost always a lower-priced one. The Franklin firm did not particularly care for this practice, feeling that it tended to dilute the sales effort, but was not in a position to do a great deal about it. The companies producing popular cars which sold in large numbers often would not permit their dealers to sell a second line of vehicles built by another manufacturer.

Franklin dealers, while usually conservative in their approach to marketing the air-cooled vehicle, at times did resort to innovative methods. The Pittsburgh dealer used America's first radio station, KDKA, in 1922 to broadcast a program in which musical presentations were combined with sales messages featuring the Franklin car!

The discovery of records of early dealerships makes it possible to examine the operations of Franklin sales outlets in some depth. Two of these will now be looked at, one very large and the other relatively small.

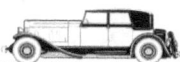

Introduced earlier as a key person in the Franklin sales network, Ralph Hamlin for nearly thirty years supplied automotive buyers in the populous Southern California region with the Syracuse-built air-cooled vehicle. Within a short time after establishing his dealership, Hamlin literally became an institution in the Los Angeles metropolitan area. The man had an astonishing ability to generate for both himself and the car he sold an extraordinary amount of desirable publicity. Use of imaginative public relations techniques, plus the exercise of considerable shrewdness as a businessperson, resulted in Hamlin during many years taking the lead in sale of cars among Franklin distributors and dealers across America.[11-6]

As noted in a previous chapter, Ralph Hamlin was at all times eager to participate in a wide range of road races and mountain climbing con-

THE FRANKLIN AUTOMOBILE COMPANY

Ralph Hamlin driving Los Angeles Mayor Alexander & U.S President William Howard Taft in a Presidential parade in 1909. Hamlin ensured Franklins were available for use of visiting dignitaries. (Courtesy of Peterson Museum)

tests, where victories resulted in newspaper headlines. He also was quick to demonstrate the advantages of air cooling through such stunts as low-gear runs across blistering-hot desert areas including Death Valley. Nor were these the only means of obtaining press coverage used by this astute merchandiser. When a new highway or bridge was to be opened for traffic in or near Los Angeles, Hamlin invariably sought the prestige of driving the first car over it. If visiting dignitaries were scheduled to participate in parades, Hamlin ensured that Franklin cars were immediately made available to transport them.

As use of the automobile expanded, Ralph sought to keep his broad circle of customers plus others in the community apprised of Franklin "happenings" through a dealer-sponsored newsletter. This publication, carrying the unique name *Franklin Camel News*, described activities of prominent persons who had purchased cars from Hamlin, and also featured interesting articles on technical aspects of the Franklin Car. Edited by a full-time public relations man who Hamlin brought on his staff it was issued once a month, with its articles frequently quoted in the local press (through friendships with reporters and editors Ralph consistently obtained prime newspaper space for Franklin-related items).

With Southern California experiencing a mushrooming of its population, Ralph Hamlin quickly realized that he needed to open branches of his Los Angeles dealership if the full market potential of the area was to be tapped. Beginning in the close-in suburbs of Los Angeles such as Hollywood and Pasadena, and later encompassing further-out communities, over a dozen satellite operating units were established at various times. These sub-dealerships often were set up as largely independent operations run by local businessmen, but if results were unsatisfactory Hamlin did not hesitate to take over a lagging facility and manage it himself. This occurred in San Diego where, when sales of Franklin cars fell off, Ralph purchased land and built an attractive showroom and service facility which he operated directly.

Hamlin recognized that rendering good service to purchasers of cars was a "secret of the business." He observed that, "you can get a customer sore awful quick" if you neglect to deal with his problems.[11-7] Ralph paid his service department personnel well, in part to keep them from showing favoritism to a few customers who were ready to hand out tips in order to get preferred treatment. He noted in interviews that while the Franklin car was highly reliable, it was not entirely trouble-free. Broken springs were a fairly common problem, particularly in the early cars which were not equipped with shock absorbers, and piston rings gave difficulties in some series of cars. Service representatives employed by the H.H. Franklin Company were of course available to Hamlin and other dealers to assist in overcoming problems which gave the local mechanics difficulty. However, Ralph did not hesitate to "go to the top" if he felt the engineering department of the Syracuse firm was slow to deal with a problem. Hamlin's leadership role in forcing changes in Franklin styling has been described previously, but on at least one other occasion his direct appeal to H.H. Franklin resulted in a reversal of an engineering department decision to continue using a vehicle part which gave trouble in the field.

As an important automotive dealer in the Southern California area Hamlin was approached at times by motor car manufacturers other than Franklin to handle their products. In the mid-teens he did take on two other franchises, Scripps-Booth and Lozier. The Scripps-Booth, a small car somewhat competitive with the Ford Model T, proved to be a reasonably saleable product (two were purchased by the Los Angeles fire department), which Hamlin continued to offer for several years. The Lozier, a large, expensive vehicle, proved difficult to sell, and Hamlin quickly gave it up. However, in connection with another major California motor vehicle dealer, Earle C. Anthony, Ralph also took on for a time the franchise for the Rauch & Lang and Baker electric vehicles. Earle Anthony, the renowned Packard dealer for all of California, was both a colleague and a vigorous business rival of Hamlin's (in addition to the electric vehicle venture the two men joined at an early date in establishing the Los Angeles Motor Car Dealers Association). In the early 1930s Hamlin for a very short period handled the Auburn car. This venture had many elements of mystery to it, never fully explained.

In his capacity as a distributor and dealer Ralph Hamlin succeeded in selling some 500 to 800 Franklin cars in a typical year during the 1920s. On one occasion he even supplied eight Franklin chassis to the J.W. Robinson Company, a Los Angeles department store. The store had special bodies built (painted an eye-catching canary yellow!) for use in deliveries. With such outstanding marketing abilities Ralph understandably was viewed by the H.H. Franklin Company as a vital link in its organization. While never offered a seat on the board of directors of the parent firm as was Earle Anthony at the Packard Motor Company, Hamlin nonetheless received respectful attention from

Syracuse-based executives. On the twenty-fifth anniversary of his becoming a Franklin dealer, March 3, 1930, the Franklin Company had a bronze plaque cast commemorating the event. The plaque, signed by H.H. Franklin, expressed appreciation for Ralph's "loyalty, enthusiasm, integrity."

Hamlin would continue as a Franklin dealer until the very end of the parent company's existence, and even in the sharply declining car market of the early 1930s succeeded in selling a respectable number of air-cooled vehicles. It must have been an unhappy experience for Ralph, however, to observe his business rival, Earle Anthony, enjoy resurgent prosperity in 1935 selling the new medium-priced Packard car, while the onetime strong Los Angeles Franklin dealership, with its parent firm bankrupt, had to content itself with a sales franchise for a minor automobile producer, Graham. There is no indication that Hamlin was at any time asked to join in the fruitless efforts during 1934-37 to revive production of the Syracuse air-cooled vehicle. Probably the vast distance separating the west coast dealer from Syracuse would have made such participation impossible under any circumstances.

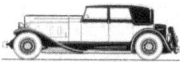

If Ralph Hamlin was representative of the major distributors of Franklin cars, a second dealership now to be examined typified the lesser sales outlets of the Syracuse auto manufacturer. Baker Brothers was a dealer of modest size, located in Glens Falls, New York, where it sold Franklin cars to customers in that municipality and the surrounding district. Glens Falls, a city with a population of just under 20,000 persons at the time, is located some fifty miles north of the state capital, Albany. The community, a small manufacturing and commercial center, has for over a century been known as the eastern "gateway" to the Adirondack resort area.

Baker Brothers operated as one of a number of Franklin dealerships

THE FRANKLIN AUTOMOBILE COMPANY

within the overall territory of the large Franklin-Klett distributorship, headquartered in Albany, New York. The Glens Falls dealership functioned with a tiny staff–the two partners, Charles H. and B. J. Baker, one or two salespeople plus a clerical in the office, and a handful of mechanics in the garage. Fortunately, surviving records and correspondence make it possible to review the operations of this small auto sales business, its relationship with the H.H. Franklin Company in Syracuse, and its dealings with customers.[11-8]

The Glens Falls' dealership began its business life by entering into a contract with the Franklin Automobile Company on December 20, 1921. This agreement, a standard one of the era, called for Baker Brothers to enjoy the exclusive right to sell new Franklin cars throughout all of Warren County, New York (in which Glens Falls is located), and in various townships of four adjacent counties. In exchange for this right to market the air-cooled vehicle in a specified area, the dealership assumed a number of responsibilities. It was required to keep on hand at all times for demonstration purposes at least one Franklin touring car or sedan, and to make all reasonable efforts to obtain the maximum amount of business from its assigned territory. Baker Brothers also was to maintain " suitable sales rooms," together with a service department adequately equipped to repair all Franklin cars in its sales district. Only repair parts purchased from the Syracuse auto manufacturer or approved by it could be used for servicing Franklin vehicles or sold over-the-counter to customers. The dealer was to report to Franklin company headquarters each week its sales of both new and used cars, and also submit twice yearly a detailed statement of its assets and liabilities.

The Glens Falls dealership would earn much of its profit from a twenty-five per cent discount from retail list price on all new Franklin cars ordered from the manufacturer (the discount jumped to thirty-three percent on most repair parts). At the same time the factory sought to bind the dealer to order a steady stream of cars. Incorporated in the contract was a schedule calling for shipment by the Franklin Company to the dealer of a specified number of vehicles for each of the ensuing nine months. Another contract clause obligated the dealer to spend a stipulated dollar amount on local advertising during the period covered by the schedule. Finally, a key provision of the agreement gave either party, manufacturer or dealer, authority to cancel the contract, with or without cause, on thirty days notice in writing. This unquestionably gave the manufacturer, as the more powerful of the two parties, the whip hand over a small dealer.[11-9]

Baker Brothers continued to operate as a Franklin dealer until the Syracuse air-cooled motor vehicle builder entered bankruptcy in 1934, and even performed a handful of dealership functions for several years after the insolvency of the parent firm. As various items of correspondence indicate, a wide range of problems were encountered by this small dealer. Since the Glens Falls firm began selling Franklin cars about the time the problem-plagued Model 10A was placed on the market, it was not long before it was required to deal with defects in customers' cars. Purchasers of the Series 10A complained about various shortcomings, including a weak clutch, defective pistons and rings, poor carburetor operation and cracks in body structure. Those faults in the various cars sold were not always easily corrected, with Baker Brothers on occasion compelled to send a vehicle back to the Franklin factory to have major repair work carried out. One customer, a prominent Glens Falls lawyer, dispatched several sharply-worded letters to both dealer and manufacturer complaining about the many defects in his wife's Franklin. Even sending a service man from the factory to literally rebuild parts of the car did not fully resolve the problem, and the vehicle's condition continued to be a touchy issue for many months. When the local attorney, in one of his letters, stated that the Franklin car was all right for his wife but that he personally preferred a "speedier, heavier and better car" for his own use, it made the relationship even more abrasive! Such sharp letters of complaint, however, were to some degree offset by an occasional word of praise. A second Glens Falls lawyer wrote to express great satisfaction with the several Franklin vehicles which he and his wife had operated through a number of seasons of "blamed blizzards" and "heaped snow-drifts" in northern New York. This letter, dated October 17, 1924, observed that the current Franklin owned by the couple (presumably a Model 10C) appeared powerful enough to "climb the side walls of the garage" should the driver choose to let it do so. Continuing in a somewhat humorous vein, the writer in closing expressed appreciation for the company's latest model, including "even the slightly inebriated lion which keeps guard over the front of the hood."

The question of the number of cars to be requisitioned by the Glens Falls dealer from the factory was a fairly constant source of friction between the two parties. Franklin sales manager S.E. Ackerman continuously urged Baker Brothers to place additional orders for vehicles so that the Glens Falls dealer would be prepared to meet "potential buyer demand." The Baker firm, as a small-scale dealer, tended to exercise caution in its orders, obviously not wanting to become overextended (at times Baker Brothers also resisted taking delivery of unpopular body styles which the factory sought to impose on it). In 1923, a good sales year for Franklin, Baker at times found itself lacking cars for delivery, and had to seek additional ones on short notice. The Glens Falls dealer did well in disposing of vehicles throughout the 1923 calendar year, winning the right to seats for the firm's two partners around a "Charmed Circle" table at H.H. Franklin's luncheon for dealers and other sales personnel held at New York City's Hotel Commodore in January 1924.

The year 1924, however, saw a swift turning of the tide in sales of the Franklin product, with the 10B series now becoming difficult to dispose of. Both the short-tenured Franklin Company vice-president, Fred Moskovics, and sales manager Ackerman constantly pressured the dealers to order more cars for sale, using both carrot-and-stick techniques. Various special bonuses were given for orders, but the threat also was made to cancel such awards if a specified quota of vehicles was not taken! This approach was continued with the 10C Franklin cars, which the Syracuse manufacturer made vigorous efforts to clear out during the second half of 1924 and the early months of 1925. By this time it was well-known throughout the company sales outlets that the drastically-restyled Series 11 would be coming out in the near future, and the factory sought to take full advantage of the dealers' interest in the new vehicle. In a letter to Baker Brothers dated January 8, 1925, sales chief Ackerman stated that for each Model 10C sold the dealer would "earn" the right to order three new Series 11 cars!

Other aspects of dealer activity in the mid-1920s are of interest. Since Baker Brothers sold cars occasionally to persons vacationing or residing for a few months of the year in the Adirondacks, the issue of a split in sales commissions with the Franklin dealer located in the hometown of the vacationing purchaser tended to arise. If the new purchaser registered the vehicle in his hometown, the local dealer was quick to claim part of the commission under a Franklin Company rule covering such transactions. The Baker Brothers firm was quite reluctant to divide its earnings, and usually had to be vigorously prodded by the manufacturer before it agreed to do so! Breakdowns suffered by vacationers driving Franklin cars at times plagued the Glens Falls dealer. In July, 1923, a Dr. Brennglass of New York City found himself stranded in the town of Lake George with an inoperative Franklin car, and demanded help. Due to a misunderstanding between factory and dealer the necessary parts were not delivered for nearly two weeks, resulting in a series of telegrams being sent to the Franklin Company by the extremely irate physician!

Sales of the Franklin car by Baker Brothers continued at a relatively steady pace throughout the 1920s (on occasion arrangements were even made to supply a custom body for a demanding purchaser). The Glens Falls dealer never was able to dispose of a large number of vehicles, with its annual sales normally running from 20 to 40 new Franklins. Its customers included various businesspersons, a local judge and several physicians. A clergyman in a nearby town also purchased a Franklin car, which was sold on an extended payment plan. Baker Brothers, holding the promissory note, occasionally had to prod the minister to catch up with an overdue installment!

During the early 1930s, the sharp drop in sales of Franklin cars quickly affected the Glens Falls dealer. A letter from the factory in early 1932 asked why Baker Brothers had not ordered at least one Series 16 Franklin car for showroom display. Despite the general atmosphere of gloom, however, a January 5, 1932, letter from the Franklin-Klett distributor in Albany to Baker Brothers urged the Glens Falls dealer to make every effort to attend the upcoming get-together of Franklin dealers and distributors at the Hotel Commodore in New York City. The letter went on to note that the 1932 Supercharged Airman and the Franklin "12" would be displayed at this function.

As the Syracuse-based Franklin motorcar builder neared the end of the road, dealers found that a number of the vehicles delivered and sold quickly developed defects in the hands of their owners. A letter of early January, 1934, enclosed a claim for refinishing of a car recently purchased by a Dr. Johnson, while another letter, dated February 13, 1934, complained of the poor mechanical quality of a 16B Franklin delivered in the fall of 1933. Later in the year 1934, still another letter referred to the fact that a pair of Wahl shock absorbers had been installed on the front of a recently-produced Franklin car, while Delco shocks were placed on the rear. Obviously, at this point the factory was using up any spare parts which could be found on its shelves to build cars! After the Franklin parent firm became insolvent Baker Brothers learned in a letter from the trustees in bankruptcy dated August 16, 1934, that no "allowances, adjustments or replacements of any kind" on cars previously sold would be made by the factory. Even earlier, on June 22, 1934, the Glens Falls dealer was informed in a communication from the Franklin-Klett distributor in Albany that a vehicle recently displayed had been sold, and that it was the last of the Franklin cars. For a few additional years Baker Brothers operated a service and repair facility for Franklin vehicles located in its geographic area. Correspondence shows, however, that the once-active Franklin dealer now had turned to selling the Hupmobile car together with the Reo truck as its principal business activity. The final curtain thus descended on this link in the once far-flung Franklin sales network.

INSIDE THE COMPANY

Even advertisements such as this one for the new Supercharged Airman which was introduced in early 1932, could not boost vehicle sales for dealers within the struggling Franklin organization.
(The Saturday Evening Post, *February 27, 1932*)

THE FRANKLIN AUTOMOBILE COMPANY

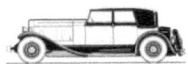

Several other Franklin dealerships, primarily located in the Midwest have been examined and in some instances their personnel interviewed. The dealer in Jackson, Michigan, Justin Fleming, for many years sold Franklin cars and served as a distributor for small sub-dealerships in the central part of that state. He found that his customers, who consisted largely of professional and business people, liked such features of the Franklin car as its comfortable ride and its ability to go through the deep snow which often accompanies a Michigan winter. Fleming also appreciated the excellent company follow-up on customer complaints. "If a purchaser felt that the paint job was not satisfactory, and the dealer agreed, the factory would quickly approve repainting," he noted. Justin Fleming recalled that he personally drove some ninety percent of the cars he sold back to Jackson from the Franklin factory in Syracuse. "This assured me the car was a completely sound runner before I turned it over to a customer," he stated. Justin was very much in favor of John Wilkinson's desire to see Franklin build a small, air-cooled car. "If this had been done Franklin might have survived the depression of the 1930s, instead of being forced out of business because of a noncompetitive price structure," he asserted.[11-10]

Donald Douglas, a classmate of Carl Doman's at the University of Michigan, spent some years in the 1920s and early 1930s in the engineering field. He was strongly interested in the Franklin car, however, and finding that there was no Franklin dealer in the good-sized city of Fort Wayne, Indiana, he left his well-paid engineering job at the beginning of 1932, went to Syracuse, met H.H. Franklin in his office, and obtained the agency. Douglas opened his doors as a dealer in the very depths of the depression, and found that the venture was a disaster from the beginning. While his relations with the factory were good, there was simply no market in Fort Wayne for a relatively high-priced car which was not well-known in the Midwest. Douglas kept his dealership alive for some time through his service business plus the occasional sale of a used car, but when the parent Franklin

INSIDE THE COMPANY

Franklin dealer Justin P. Fleming shown in 1922, above, and in 1926 below. Many of Fleming's customers were professionals. Fleming is shown below standing beside a 1926 doctor's coupe ready to be delivered. The large trunk on the rear could be used for luggage or as a rumble seat.

(Courtesy of the late Justin P. Fleming)

firm closed its doors in the spring of 1934, he decided to give up the operation.[11-11]

In the large Midwestern city of Cincinnati, Ohio, the H.H. Franklin Company began experiencing difficulty in obtaining dealer representation as early as 1930. No Franklin dealer existed in this community during the years 1930, 1931 and 1932, a serious gap in a state where sales of the Franklin car traditionally had been strong.[11-12] In 1933 this vacuum was filled when the Skulley Motor Company, handling the Franklin car, opened. This dealership quickly delivered new Franklins to the Episcopal Bishop of the Diocese of Southern Ohio, and to a prominent Cincinnati business executive and author. The Skulley firm continued Franklin operations into 1937, long after the factory closed its doors.[11-13]

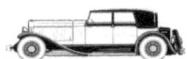

Outside the United States, a number of Franklin dealerships did business in various foreign countries. Unquestionably the leading foreign nation in terms of sales was Canada, where in a typical year during the 1920s from one hundred to two hundred Franklin cars were sold. Canadian dealerships existed in both large and small cities, from Vancouver, British Columbia, on the west coast to Halifax, Nova Scotia, on the Atlantic seaboard. Records show that several hundred Franklin vehicles were registered to owners in the Province of Quebec in the early 1930s, an indication of the success over the years of the Montreal distributorship.

The depression of 1929-on struck hard at imported American luxury cars in Canada, however, and by late 1932 the Franklin dealer network clearly had everywhere collapsed. Registration records show that in the first half of 1933 only a single new Franklin vehicle was sold at retail in the populous Canadian province of Ontario, and none at all in the Canadian maritime provinces of Nova Scotia, New Brunswick and Prince Edward Island.[11-14] In Canada, Franklin definitely had reached the end of the road even before the company entered bankruptcy.

In other parts of the world the Franklin firm appears to have met with varying degrees of success in its efforts to sell the air-cooled motor car. In Great Britain, a dealership in London sold Franklins through much of the 1920s, displaying the Syracuse product prominently at the annual British motor shows. Franklin also was represented by a dealer in Edinburgh, Scotland, which in 1929 succeeded in selling a modest number of vehicles to local physicians. It is difficult to determine the extent of market penetration of the Franklin product in Great Britain, but it probably was not large. A road test of the Franklin car conducted in the late 1920s by a British motor magazine resulted in a complimentary report, which may have helped make the vehicle better known in that nation.

On the European continent, France and Holland appeared to be the nations where the Franklin car was best known, although dealers in a number of other countries also handled the Syracuse product. In conjunction with its local dealer the Franklin firm in the very late 1920s and early 1930s sponsored an impressive display of standard and custom-bodied vehicles at the annual Paris International Auto Show. The European market dwindled in the depression years of the 1930s, however, and appeared to be largely gone by mid-1933. An active Oslo, Norway, Franklin dealer ran into financial difficulties in 1931, and the Syracuse company, which had extended credit, found itself faced with the question of whether to bring legal action to protect its interests. It finally decided that doing so would not be worthwhile.

In South America the Franklin firm made strong efforts to sell vehicles in at least two nations, Uruguay and Argentina. Year-to-year sales records in the two countries are unobtainable. In Argentina, however, registration records for all vehicles broken down by make are available for the year 1932. They show total Franklin registrations for Buenos Aires at only 51, far below the level of such competitor makes as Packard, Cadillac and Auburn.

THE FRANKLIN AUTOMOBILE COMPANY

Franklin vehicles are displayed in the showrooms of Regent Motors, Ltd., a Franklin dealer located in the West End of London, England. (Dealer's Bulletin, *September 5, 1929 (Courtesy of Gary Voxal)*

Leonard B. Clarkson, shown here with his wife, was the Franklin representative in Australia around 1930. Clarkson believed great market potential existed for air-cooled Franklins in Australia because of the scarcity of water, particularly outside the large cities.
(Dealer's Bulletin, *July 24, 1930. Courtesy of Gary Voxal)*

INSIDE THE COMPANY

Franklin vehicles were well known in France in the late 1920's and the early 1930's. This advertisement appeared in the French magazine, L'Illustration, around 1930. (Courtesy of Brooks Brierly)

THE FRANKLIN AUTOMOBILE COMPANY

In a final effort to shore-up its sagging international market in the early 1930s, Franklin officials contacted the commercial attachés at American consulates in several foreign countries, asking about sales prospects for higher-priced American cars. The responses were uniformly negative in nature. The attachés reported a collapse in sales of more costly vehicles, and saw no prospect of early improvement in light of poor economic conditions in the various nations. The foreign market thus offered no help to the beleaguered Syracuse air-cooled vehicle manufacturer as it desperately sought to avert bankruptcy in late 1933 and 1934.

The engineering department of the H.H. Franklin Manufacturing Company, as observed earlier, was from the very beginning of automobile production a vital part of the firm's overall structure Modest in size and scope initially, under the vigorous leadership of John Wilkinson it swiftly expanded to encompass a variety of activities which this able individual felt were necessary to the design and development of a sound automobile. If a special challenge was needed to bring out the best in the youth-oriented Franklin engineering staff, it was that the principle of air-cooling of an internal combustion engine demanded for its success an unusually high degree of technical effort by its designers.

The numerous advancements in the automobile pioneered or co-pioneered by H.H. Franklin Company engineering personnel indicate clearly the outstanding abilities of this group. The initial Franklin motor car, as related earlier, featured four cylinders, probably the first American production vehicle to do so (this vehicle, or the predecessor machines designed by John Wilkinson, also may have pioneered valve-in-head construction in this nation). The wooden frame, in combination with full-elliptic suspension, could well have been a Franklin "first." The float-feed carburetor together with throttle control were initiated in the 1902 vehicle, making Franklin an exceptionally smooth car to drive. Franklin co-pioneered the six-cylinder engine in 1905, and in the same year developed a straight-eight cylinder motor which may have competed briefly on the racing circuit but was never used in a production automobile. A so-called automatic lubrication system, where a pressure oil pump replaced the earlier sight-feed oiling method, was installed in Franklin vehicles at an early date, with automatic spark advance coming in 1907. Introduction of an intake yoke heater in 1913, followed by an electric carburetor primer in 1917, were innovations which aided greatly in cold weather starting and overall vehicle operation.

While several motor car companies claim to have pioneered the development of enclosed bodies, Franklin clearly was among the first American firms to produce a closed sedan on a volume basis. Availability of the V-type windshield in its vehicle bodies as early as 1916 also may well have been a Franklin innovation. The Syracuse firm either pioneered or co-pioneered the introduction of aluminum pistons about the beginning of World War I. Incidentally, the lavish use of aluminum in body and engine components probably resulted in Franklin being one of the two largest consumers of that light-weight metal in the American automobile industry (the other major user was Pierce-Arrow).

As the Franklin firm moved from pioneering days to the more sophisticated era of the 1920s, its engineering department continued to play a key role in company activities. By the 1929-1930 period some eleven sections reported to the chief engineer, with nearly 150 persons on the engineering staff–a very substantial number for a firm whose total employment during those years never exceeded 2,600, and in 1930 was far less than that figure. In 1929 the basic engineering budget was well in excess of $750,000, again an impressive figure for a small auto manufacturing firm

Various persons in the Franklin engineering department were available to describe the functions of this important unit. One was Edward Marks, who served as company chief engineer during the years 1924-

THE FRANKLIN AUTOMOBILE COMPANY

1933. Marks relates some of his experiences at the Syracuse firm:

I was a native of Auburn, New York, a small city located some twenty-five miles west of Syracuse. After earning a degree in mechanical engineering at the University of Michigan I returned to my home town to spend two years working for McIntosh and Chambers, a firm specializing in the construction of big steam and diesel engines. I then joined the Penn State faculty as a mathematics instructor, leaving academic life to come with Franklin in the early summer of 1917 as a student engineer. At that time Ralph Murphy recently had been named chief engineer of the firm, with Lou Stellman his assistant. These men reported to John Wilkinson, who headed all divisions of the company other than those concerned with administration, finance and sales.

As a student engineer I soon found I was expected to get my hands dirty, keep my eyes and ears open, and absorb all I could about company technical problems. At the end of a year of learning the ropes I was assigned to the experimental engineering section, then headed by Paul Williams, a young Cornell graduate. In this unit we tested a wide variety of engines and vehicles, and were expected to summarize our findings in concise written reports. My compensation in this period was modest–I started at a salary of $23 per week, and gradually moved up to $29. When out first baby was born I was delighted to receive a raise to $35 weekly.

After spending a few years in experimental engineering I was assigned to the service division, where engineers often were required to travel to distant cities to deal with problems in the field. The Franklin firm took pride in its vigorous follow-up of customer complaints, so I found myself in such places as Montreal, Canada and Ishpeming, Michigan, attempting to resolve cold-weather starting problems. Ultimately I returned to engineering duties at the plant, finally being named assistant chief engineer. Shortly after John Wilkinson left in the mid-1920s, and Ralph Murphy succeeded to John's position as operations head, I was named chief engineer.

This promotion did not meet with everyone's approval—Frank Barton, the company treasurer, was heard to remark that I was "far too young'" for such a position!

I had numerous responsibilities as head of engineering, but one of the most important was the advance planning of each new car the company brought out. Actually, I had help from many others in this task—we had a top-level committee made up of department heads and other key personnel which dealt with the many aspects of new vehicle development. "Looks" of the car was a major concern, with the body design people plus consultants such as Ray Dietrich usually handling this area. My key assistants and I concentrated heavily on mechanical performance of the new vehicle, while individuals in manufacturing were there to point out problems which might arise in building a car involving major changes. H.H. Franklin played an important role in new model design—he sat in on committee meetings and was quick to indicate to those persons concerned with styling, upholstery and colors what he did and did not like. On one occasion he had me completely redesign the car's front fenders just a few weeks before the New York Auto Show—he wanted a more sweeping style used. Let me tell you that implementing this last-minute change, even though it may have been desirable, took some doing, both in engineering and in manufacturing!

H.H. was very stubborn in his views on automotive design and development, and once his mind was made up no one could change it. His decision to proceed with the V-12 power plant was an example—he concluded somewhat on the spur of the moment that the firm needed a big, plush automobile to compete with Cadillac and Lincoln, and the design staff had no choice but to carry out his wishes. I served on the board of directors of the company for a short time at the end of the nineteen-twenties and the beginning of the thirties, and while there was open discussion of most issues H.H., who had stock control, made the final decisions. He also had definite ideas in areas such as employee compensation—he was totally against Christmas or year-end bonuses for staff, which he felt were nothing but a source of trouble.

In addition to an understandable concern about the design of new vehicles within his own firm, H.H. also was strongly interested at all times in what "Detroit was doing." This desire to be kept informed on the plans of competing auto companies resulted in his urging me to take fairly frequent trips to Michigan to attend technical conferences and informally visit the engineering offices of good-sized auto manufacturers located in the state. On the other hand, H.H. appeared to have no particular interest in any new ideas emerging from the Buffalo-based Pierce-Arrow Company, or for that matter from any of the small auto manufacturing firms in Midwestern states such as Ohio and Indiana, which might have been considered important Franklin competitors.

Within the engineering department I scheduled meetings of my section chiefs every Monday morning, at which we discussed the written reports submitted the Saturday before and also went over 'kicks' from the manufacturing people. There were many more complaints when Lew Purdy succeeded Bill Dunk as manufacturing chief–Purdy could be highly abrasive and difficult to get along with. In addition, he sought lower manufacturing costs even if it meant sacrificing quality, an idea which met with little favor among the engineers.

In my judgment a primary cause of the death of the company was its failure to have a low-priced car quickly available for sale when the bottom dropped out of the prestige car market after 1929-30. A company such as Cadillac was hit hard from 1931-on too, but it had a big parent organization to absorb losses. Developing the Olympic model was a late effort to stem the tide, but it was done on a shoestring–the banks were closing in on the firm by then. Incidentally, the Reo chassis and body used as the basis for the Olympic often were shipped by boat to Buffalo and trucked from there to Syracuse, probably to save the hard-up company a few dollars in transportation costs.

An engineer active in vehicle design at the Franklin firm during the 1920s was Hollis Snyder. A native of Syracuse, born in 1903, Hollis attended grade and high schools in the city and then studied engineering at Syracuse University. His association with the air-cooled automobile manufacturer began during college years:

> I started working at the Franklin plant in the summer of 1921 just after enrolling at Syracuse University, and continued during succeeding summer vacations until graduation. The jobs varied–I began as a stock clerk the initial summer, and worked on the automobile assembly line during the next vacation period. The assembly work involved hooking up the speedometer cable to a hole in the transmission, plus other routine activity. The firm was building about 20 vehicles a day on the conveyor-type assembly line, which moved quite slowly. The summer of 1923 saw me assigned to the test shed, where I wrote up the notes of test drivers after they finished their runs and changed components of engines until they ran quietly.
>
> After graduation from college I went with the Franklin Die-casting Company, where my father was the plant engineer. I spent about two years in this operation, which was independent of the car company and headed by Howard Franklin, an older brother of H.H. and a fine person to work for. My job principally involved the design of die-cast molds. The die-casting firm made many crankshaft bearings, using primarily a tin-lead alloy. These bearings were installed in all Franklin cars, of course, but die-cast products also were sold to Hudson, Packard and even divisions of General Motors.
>
> After the death of Howard Franklin in the summer of 1926, management of the die-casting company changed, and I transferred to the H.H. Franklin Manufacturing Company drafting room where I prepared wiring diagrams for the various cars produced. The mechanical drafting room was located on the second floor of the Geddes Street building, with the cafeteria two floors above. I usually ate lunch up there–while the selection was a bit limited the food was good, and the cost of a meal never exceeded fifty cents.

THE FRANKLIN AUTOMOBILE COMPANY

> My starting salary at the die-casting firm was forty dollars per week–this was after graduation from college. The best toolmakers employed by the company received one dollar per hour, although they had extra earnings through overtime. Except for the front office employees there were very few women in the workforce at Franklin. The big majority of the people working for the company were from Syracuse or the near vicinity. There was quite an ethnic mixture in the plant when I worked there, including Poles, Irish and others. Among the executives I recall Bill Dunk very well–a bit rough and ready, but a good manager. He was never a desk man, and usually could be found dealing with problems out in the plant.
>
> The Franklin firm was a very conservative organization in almost every way. It built a good-quality car, although specialized in nature. You had to want one to become an owner–and you paid for it! The sales people in the field simply were not aggressive enough in competing with dealers selling other prestige cars–in the Syracuse area particularly the customers had to come to them instead of the other way around. Major Franklin competitors in the 1920s were Packard, Pierce-Arrow, Lincoln and Peerless. The Packard small six was a nice car and gave Franklin strong competition, as did the Cadillac line. At one time I "moonlighted" as a part-time employee of the local Cadillac dealer, and we often outsold Franklin locally.
>
> I detected signs of trouble appearing in the company by the end of 1928 and beginning of 1929, and I sensed that the die-casting firm faced problems at that time also. As a result, I finally decided to leave for a position with an auto parts manufacturer in Buffalo in March of 1929.

Still another person who spent several years in the H.H. Franklin Company engineering department was W. Chapin Condit, a native of upstate New York, "Chape" describes his work:

> After graduating in engineering from Cornell, I spent a few years with a paper manufacturing company in New England. However,

INSIDE THE COMPANY

as I was strongly interested in motor cars (I owned an ancient Isotta-Frascini in college, which was used to transport numerous friends to out-of-town football games),I applied for work at the Franklin firm, and was taken on in the mid-1920s.

My duties at Franklin were primarily in the areas of experimental engineering and testing. The experimental engineering building was located on the south side of the company property, along Gifford Street. I had a desk there, where I tested and evaluated various accessories used on Franklin cars, including generators, carburetors and batteries. In the center of the factory complex was the "Dog House," a small wooden building where engines soon to go into production were tested. These motors were attached to dynamometers and run for some 100 hours, with only brief shut-downs to permit oil to be changed. I should mention that we also tested engines already in production, if some weakness developed in vehicles sold to customers. I was one of a crew of young engineers who did this work, on a day-and-night-shift basis.

I was also involved in testing of engines outside the plant. A favorite spot for road tests was Lord's Hill, where the cars had to go up an incline about two miles in length. On these runs Carl Doman and I often worked as a team. While he drove I read and recorded temperatures from sensors attached to various parts of the engine—cylinder heads, cooling fins, the cylinders themselves, and the crankcase. Along with this I road-tested prototype Franklin cars, which were run as much as 3,000 miles a week in order to spot possible defects. The route followed went from Syracuse up to Watertown, New York, and then on to the St. Lawrence River area. If we were well ahead of schedule on a road test, we might stop in Watertown to take in a short movie!

During the period I worked at Franklin (I left in early 1929 to go with an oil company), each car coming off the final assembly line was given a short test run of three or four miles. We called the principal check made of each vehicle the "mail box test!" This involved driving the Franklin up a grade, with the car cut back to ten miles per hour as it passed one mail box and then accelerated hard until it reached a second box. The vehicle had to hit twenty-five miles per hour as it reached the second box–if it did not it was sent back to the factory, usually for replacement of piston rings.

The approach in the Franklin engineering department, and indeed in the entire company, was a conservative one. Change, when it came, did so only gradually. However, the engines the firm built held up very well in service, even under hard usage. They were somewhat limited in power during much of the period I was with Franklin, but with the car's roadability it could usually hold its own against the competition.

Other persons interviewed, who worked in various sections of the engineering department including design, field service and testing, also were strongly impressed with the firm's technical operations. In summary, it can be said that during the peak years of the Franklin Company the engineering program, with its emphasis on both innovation and close attention to quality, unquestionably ranked with the very best in the motor car industry. Only when the firm commenced its downhill slide in the early 1930s did the H.H. Franklin Company lose its status as an engineering leader.

– Twelve –

Summary

The air-cooled vehicle sold by the H.H. Franklin Manufacturing Company from 1902 to 1934 could be considered first-class in nearly every respect. Built in a factory which, as observed in earlier chapters, at all times emphasized high standards of both design and workmanship, this motor car ranked among the top products of the American automobile industry. The overall merit of the car was attested to in numerous ways, among them the exceptional loyalty of Franklin owners. In some years over fifty per-cent of Franklin sales were made to previous owners of the marque.

Quality of product, however, is only one factor which makes for a successful motor car company. Other factors include the capacity to earn a satisfactory profit from year-to-year, the ability to accurately assess the motor vehicle market and achieve strong sales, and the skill to compete effectively with other firms, large and small. In these and related areas the H.H. Franklin Company encountered a variety of difficulties, a combination of which resulted in its ultimate downfall.

As with almost any firm which ultimately closes its doors, a combination of two broad elements spelled ruin for the Syracuse auto builder. One involved internal problems, the difficulties which had their origin

THE FRANKLIN AUTOMOBILE COMPANY

An early parade of members of The H.H. Franklin Club in Syracuse shows some of the various series of air-cooled vehicles produced by the Franklin company in the 1920s & 1930s. (Courtesy of Joan Doman)

within the firm itself. The other comprised external factors, ranging from major economic forces to tendencies and trends within the overall industry in which the Franklin firm competed. We will want to look at each of these causes in some detail, and in doing so also compare the H.H. Franklin Company with other firms in the automobile industry.

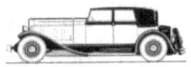

The comment often has been made of auto manufacturing companies which went to the wall that they suffered from "chronic under-capitalization." Undoubtedly many did, particularly those starting business with limited amounts of money. However, some motor car builders began with small amounts of capital and nonetheless became highly successful. In the case of the Franklin firm, it did indeed lack support from any large-scale investor when it entered automobile manufacturing. However, the Syracuse company, already well-established in another industrial field, was able to obtain funding from enough moderately well-to-do backers that it did not appear to have encountered any critical difficulty in financing its new operation. Later, in the 1919-1922 period, the firm, now with a solid reputation, was able to sell directly to investors (including its own employees) several million dollars worth of common and preferred stock. It is difficult to see where the Syracuse company from that point on could be considered to have lacked capital.

The key weakness of the Franklin firm in the financial area instead was its inability from year-to-year to achieve a sound profit margin on each car sold. With sales during the peak years from 1919 through 1929 seldom exceeding ten thousand vehicles per year, a minimum profit of $200 per car disposed of was necessary to keep the firm on a sound financial footing (this would have provided the company with funds to develop new products and carry on basic operations without the need of frequent short-term borrowing). As noted in earlier chapters, only in the year 1925, when the company unveiled a new design with obvious sales appeal, was this figure achieved. In other years the per-vehicle profit was far under $200, and in some the company suffered a deficit.

There appear to have been several reasons for this weak per-vehicle profit margin. First of all, the company may well have continued too long with its "craft-shop" approach to building vehicles. By the mid-1920s the more successful upper-bracket firms, including Packard and Cadillac, to a substantial degree had moved away from this method of operation, and did not appear to have suffered any serious loss of of quality in doing so. Second, producing many components of the vehicle in its own shops, when in at least some instances they could have been purchased elsewhere at lower cost, undoubtedly hurt the firm. Third, when Franklin in the early 1920s decided to go outside for its car bodies, it chose a relatively high-cost body builder, Walker, as its basic source of supply. While Walker gave Franklin a top-quality product, the Syracuse firm undoubtedly could have purchased fully satisfactory bodies from a major supplier such as Hayes at a decidedly

THE FRANKLIN AUTOMOBILE COMPANY

lower cost (admittedly, the Hayes bodies would have been built of steel rather than aluminum, increasing vehicle weight).

Another internal factor which caused Franklin problems was its inability in a number of cities to obtain dealers with adequate resources. When William Leininger, after taking on the Franklin advertising account in the mid-1920s, surveyed numerous Franklin dealers across the nation, he found a substantial number operating out of small, unimpressive buildings, often located some distance from their city's "automotive row." Leininger contrasted this to the imposing establishments occupied by Packard and Cadillac dealers in a large number of communities, giving them strong visibility and prestige.

H.H. Franklin's decision to throw his company heavily into debt at the beginning of 1929 in order to greatly expand output of automobiles seriously injured the firm in both the sales and fiscal areas. Whatever the basis was for his thinking, H.H. badly misjudged the 1929 market for Franklin cars priced at or near their usual levels (the 1929 Series 130 was dropped in price, but not by much). The pattern for sale of the air-cooled product in its traditional price range had been established throughout the decade of the 1920s, with sales almost invariably running from 8,000 to 10,000 units per year. It is difficult to ascertain why any reasonable person would have expected this sales pattern to change in a single year, unless a new product line was offered. If a Franklin model selling in a lower price range, from perhaps $1,200 to $1,500, had been introduced at the beginning of 1929, this undoubtedly would have created a greatly expanded demand for the vehicle and justified an expectation of heavily increased sales. However, even if its factory could have produced such a medium-priced car, this type of program was not a part of H.H. Franklin's thinking.

When the undisposed of 1929 models began backing up on the Franklin company, officials of the firm, obviously desperate to get rid of the large number of unsold cars and bring in badly needed revenue, applied what might be termed almost savage pressure on the dealer network. A recently-discovered group of letters show that company sales executives attempted to use every method possible to force substantial numbers of additional vehicles on distributors and dealers who already were awash in unsold Franklins. The company, in short, having made a bad mistake sought to push the burden on its dealers. This effort was not particularly successful. Ralph Hamlin stood firm in his refusal to accept more cars than he reasonably could expect to sell, and other dealers, perhaps encouraged by his example, usually took similar positions.[12-1] As has been related earlier, the Franklin company ultimately had to adopt a more realistic approach to the sales crisis, and grant large discounts to dealers to aid them in moving the surplus vehicles. In early 1930, advertisements by Franklin dealers openly offered reductions of up to $700 on the 1929 models (the ads, however, often did not specify the model year being discounted!). The entire affair had an adverse effect on the dealer network, since this group without question was compelled to assume a share of the discounts needed to get rid of the year-old vehicles. As a result, many Franklin dealers entered what soon was to become the depression era of the early 1930s in far from sound condition.

The parent Franklin company never recovered from the effects of overproduction of vehicles in 1929. The need to somehow dispose of the large number of carried-over 1929 cars during the year 1930 obviously must have hurt the company badly in its efforts to market its current model (in the early months of 1930 it may not have been clear to many dealers on which model, 1929 or 1930, they should expend their major effort!). With its sales effort thus partly crippled, the firm was forced to reduce production of 1930 cars to an uneconomic level. This, coupled with the whopping loss incurred in discounting the unsold 1929 models, quickly put the firm in a difficult financial bind, where it could not pay much of the indebtedness incurred in 1929. Unhappily, the process was repeated on a smaller scale in 1931, when a number of unsold 1930 models again had to be disposed of at big discounts, and production of current year vehicles trimmed. At this point, with the effects of the depression also hitting hard, the company's position became well-nigh hopeless.

THE FRANKLIN AUTOMOBILE COMPANY

Internal operating problems, coupled with a single disastrous decision at the beginning of 1929 to gamble on the company being able to sell a vastly increased number of cars that year, thus played a key role in bringing down the Franklin firm. Unquestionably there were other important factors involved. The severe economic depression from 1930 on, described in detail in Chapter Seven, will justifiably be cited by many as a key contributor to the air-cooled vehicle producer's demise. A second would be the problems which faced the smaller manufacturing firms generally as the auto industry matured and changed over the years. This area will next be examined.

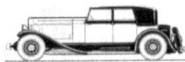

Small-scale manufacturers of motor vehicles (generally, firms which in a normal year did not produce more than 15,000 to 20,000 cars) commenced operations at the very beginning of the automotive era in America, and continued to be a factor in the auto industry until the end of the 1930s. In the pioneer years of the motor car nearly every builder of cars was relatively small, and there was little to distinguish one from the other. Rankings of companies in terms of vehicles produced and sold often changed drastically from one year to another, with the entire situation being extremely fluid.

As the second decade of motor car manufacturing neared an end, it saw the separation of motor car builders into one giant firm, a second which at the time could be described as a loosely organized conglomerate headed by an entrepreneur with few management skills, a modest number of medium-sized producers, and a large group of small companies. As observed earlier, the small independent producer in the period of the First World War was not necessarily at any great competitive disadvantage. Such builders of top-grade cars as Packard, Marmon and Pierce-Arrow prospered, as did Franklin in most years.

As the industry entered the decade of the 1920s, conditions changed to

SUMMARY

the overall detriment of the small manufacturing firm. The development of the conveyor-type assembly line often has been cited as the factor which doomed the many small producers unable to bear the cost of installing such a system, but that clearly is only part of the story. The expensive specialized machine tool which could produce tens of thousands of identical parts at low cost also gave the big volume firm which could afford such equipment a major advantage. And the conglomerate which could design parts suitable for use on several of its product lines, as noted in an earlier chapter, could reap even greater benefits from economies of scale and scope.

Were there any advantages held by small producers in the 1920s which might have helped them do battle with the giants? One or two unquestionably did exist. The minor auto manufacturers usually enjoyed greater flexibility in their operations, which enabled them to bring a new model to market more quickly than could a major company. And the small firm, not being compelled to use parts common to other models as divisions of a conglomerate might, would have had greater freedom in body design and perhaps in the field of mechanical innovation as well.

The small producer thus often was able throughout the 1920s to design and build an attractive, innovative vehicle, with considerable appeal to a fair-sized group of people having individualized tastes. However, such persons, because of the cost disadvantages of the minor company, would have had to pay somewhat more for the cars they purchased. This was not necessarily a serious burden in a period of prosperity. However, when the economic picture changed dramatically in the early 1930s, car buying habits shifted also, and the number of persons who were willing (and able) to pay for individuality dropped to the vanishing point. Vehicle builders such as Marmon, Peerless, Pierce-Arrow and Franklin felt the full effect of this shift, and the results of course were disastrous. The more standardized, big-volume car came into its own, and for decades was to totally dominate the industry.

THE FRANKLIN AUTOMOBILE COMPANY

Apart from the effects of economies of scale and related factors, the small automobile producer faced other obstacles. Many of the lesser motor car companies tended to be located in small or medium-sized communities, often a considerable distance from the center of automobile production in southeast Michigan. Such geographic isolation may have hurt these firms in terms of lack of knowledge of the latest trends in the industry. Because of this isolation small producers also without question played little or no role in the development of industry-wide policies, perhaps to their detriment.

A second major difficulty which the minor producer often had to face, especially if located in a city of modest size, was access to financing sources. Typically, banks in such communities, invariably conservative in outlook, often may have been reluctant–or because of their size, unable–to provide loans and other funding for local automotive firms. This meant that the small motor vehicle producer could have been forced to seek loans from financial institutions in major cities, where it would not be well-known and might be regarded as a poor risk. In the case of the Franklin firm, H.H. Franklin definitely felt that the major money center banks through board memberships were largely interlocked with big corporations, and thus would not deal fairly with the small auto producer standing on the outside.[12-2] Clearly, such a charge is difficult to prove or disprove.

Could the minor motor car companies have done anything to compensate for their disadvantageous position in battling the giant firms? Possible one or two approaches might have been tried. Mergers of two or more small producers were discussed on several occasions in the 1920s and early 1930s, but except for the take-over of Pierce-Arrow by the larger Studebaker firm in 1928, there was little in terms of actual achievement. Two factors made mergers among the "smalls" difficult to accomplish. First, each minor firm tended to jealously guard its independence, and was reluctant to join any combination which might cause it to lose this status. Second, all too often mergers were discussed only when the firms involved were in serious trouble. A joining of two nearly insolvent small companies obviously would

SUMMARY

not have provided a worthwhile solution to the problems of each.

Smaller firms might possibly have overcome some of their disadvantages by jointly purchasing certain essential components from parts suppliers, thus achieving to a moderate degree economies of scale. If this had been done in such areas as vehicle bodies, fairly substantial savings might well have resulted. However, each small firm usually wished to market a product identifiable solely as its own, and this would have created a barrier to any such joint effort. Use of common mechanical parts might have been more feasible (to a degree this did occur in the area of engine components, with companies such as Continental Motors supplying cylinder blocks and even entire engines to a number of independent producers). However, any extensive use of common parts probably would have involved a considerable degree of coordination among engineering and design departments of several firms, which because of distance and other factors might have been difficult to achieve.

Could small auto manufacturing companies have diversified into other fields? Franklin sought to accomplish this early-on in the area of trucks, and decades later attempted to become a significant supplier of air-cooled motors to the armed forces. Neither venture met with any particular financial success. It appears that the Franklin firm never considered production of some type of small local delivery van, such as the Stutz Pak-Age vehicle, nor a travel trailer of the variety built for a few months by Pierce-Arrow (it should be noted that these efforts failed to save the Stutz and Pierce-Arrow firms!). A merger with a household products company (washing machines, vacuum cleaners, refrigerators) also was not explored by the air-cooled auto builder. Probably from 1930-on the struggling Franklin Company had so little to offer any other firm that a consolidation offer would have been spurned.

The question was raised at the time of the Franklin Company's death struggle, and has been asked many times since: Why didn't the city of Syracuse, or some higher-level governmental body, come to the rescue of this prestigious, long-established firm which had contributed so much to the local community over the years? To answer this it must be noted initially that governmental industrial policy today differs widely from that of the 1930s era. The massive fiscal assistance granted the Chrysler firm and others by the Federal government in recent years would have been unthinkable at any governmental level in an earlier period. In addition, even if direct assistance from the municipal government to a distressed motor car builder had been legally possible in 1933-34, it would have taken a courageous group of local elected officials to move ahead with such an approach when tens of thousands of persons were on relief rolls and the city was strapped for operating funds. At the state level it also would have been politically difficult to grant aid to a single firm when dozens and perhaps hundreds of old-line companies across New York State were desperately struggling to remain alive, and equally in need of assistance.

As was observed earlier, the Federal Government through its Reconstruction Finance Corporation (RFC) appeared to offer the best source of governmental help to an ailing firm. However, the Franklin firm seemingly did not aggressively seek such aid prior to its plunge into bankruptcy. Once it was adjudged bankrupt RFC assistance, of course, was not legally possible.

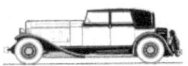

The minor producer of motor cars, after valiant efforts to survive, thus vanished from the American automotive scene. Was this loss of any real importance? The large number of persons who purchased motor vehicles quite possibly may have suffered in a variety of ways. In earlier years, when a substantial number of small companies made cars available for sale, the auto buyer could choose from among a wide variety of makes (this number reached 80 to 100 in the 1919-1920 period). The steady attrition of minor firms, however, changed this and required the motor car shopper to select a vehicle from the products of a bare handful of large companies. A number of purchasers through-

SUMMARY

out the years undoubtedly felt the lack of variety which existed earlier.

The consumer also may have been hurt by a diminished level of product quality and service following the demise of the small independent motor car builder. Evidence indicates that the small company, in producing cars, usually enforced tight standards of quality control in the manufacturing process, and often dealt with any problems that did arise when the car was in the hands of a purchaser in a quite liberal fashion. It seems clear that in the years following World War II, when a few big manufacturers dominated the motor vehicle market, such concern for the consumer largely vanished.

The disappearance of the high-quality, low-output producer from the American motor car scene thus left a gap that has not readily been filled in the years since. The minor company, typified by the fine, air-cooled vehicle builder Franklin, played a role in automotive history which was important by any standard. It fully deserves to be remembered today.

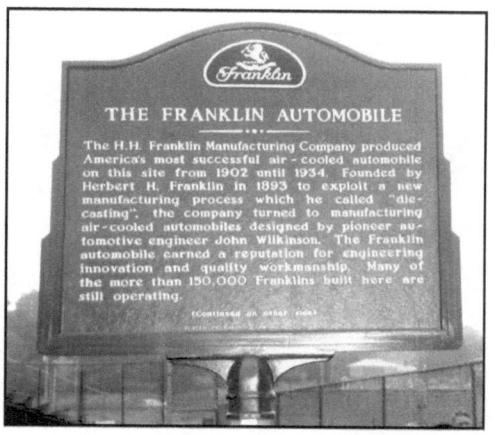

This plaque stands today at the site of the former H.H. Franklin Manufacturing Company. It reminds area visitors of the origins of the Franklin firm and the ultimate accomplishments of the company in building more than 150,000 air-cooled vehicles.

THE FRANKLIN AUTOMOBILE COMPANY

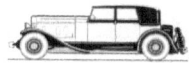

Notes

Additional detail on some of the following notes may be found in the Bibliography section of this book.

Chapter 1

1-1   Frank W. Stevens, *The Beginnings of the New York Central Railroad; A History* (New York, G.P. Putnam's Sons, 1926), pp. 147-180.

1-2   Dwight Bruce, Editor, *Memorial History of Syracuse* (Syracuse, H.P. Smith & Co., 1891), 617-681. Also, William H. Beauchamp, *Past and Present of Syracuse and Onondaga County* (Chicago, V.S.J. Clarke Pub. Co., 1908), pp. 500-516.

1-3   *The National Cyclopedia of American Biography*, Vol. 13, p. 54.

1-4   Cornell University Archives; Charles Ehle Lipe file. Also, Records of Lipe-Rollway Co., Syracuse, New York.

1-5   *The National Cyclopedia*, Vol. 35, p. 256.

THE FRANKLIN AUTOMOBILE COMPANY

1-6   Herbert H. Franklin Diary, August 18, 1883. Onondaga Historical Association Collections.

1-7   *The National Cyclopedia*, Vol. 27, p. 277

1-8   Franklin Diary, July-August, 1893. Agreement Between H.H. Franklin and H.G. Underwood, August 3,1893. Onondaga Historical Association Collections.

1-9   Shipping receipts of H.H. Franklin Mfg. Company, 1897-1899. Mildred Franklin Moreland Collections.

1-10   Cornell University Archives; John Wilkinson file.

1-11   Articles in Syracuse Newspapers from the pen of Herbert H. Franklin; Onondaga Historical Association Collections.

1-12   *Scientific American*, July 11, 1896.

1-13   Wilkinson Family Records.

1-14   It has been claimed that Syracusan F.C. Brower, a locksmith and experimenter in technical fields (he installed the first telephone in the city in the late 1870s), constructed an operable gas-powered car as early as 1890. Proof of such an achievement, however, is lacking.

1-15   *New York Automobile Co. v. H.H. Franklin, et al.*, Record of Case and Exception Taken, Supreme Court, Onondaga County; Testimony of John Wilkinson, pp. 101-164.

Chapter 2

2-1   *New York Automobile Co. v. H.H. Franklin, et al.*, Record of case & exceptions taken, Supreme Court of Onondaga County (hereafter citied as New York Automobile Co. case) Testimony of H.H. Franklin, pp. 174-183.

2-2   Revised Articles of Incorporation, H.H. Franklin Manufacturing Co., Onondaga County Corporate Records. Also see the History of the H.H. Franklin Manufacturing. Co., item 61.

2-3   U. S. Bureau of the Census, Census of Manufactures, 1905.

2-4   U.S. Census of Manufactures, 1900 (covering primarily the year 1899). Total value of motor vehicle production was $4,548,000, with some 3,700 vehicles built, the majority steam or electric-powered.

2-5   Sources include *The Automobile, Motor Age, Horseless Age*.

2-6   *The Automobile*, 1902.

2-7   The wheelbase of the initial vehicle was measured by the author and a staff member of the Smithsonian Institution at the Institution's storage facility, Silver Hill, MD, in April, 1994.

2-8   *New York Automobile Co.* case, Testimony of John Wilkinson, pp. 101-164.

2-9   The initial building leased for automobile assembly purposes was the McCarthy Shirt Factory, located at the northwest corner of Fayette and Geddes Streets. This building was largely destroyed by fire on Dec. 21, 1901. As the owners of the building decided not to rebuild, the Franklin firm then leased space in the nearby Ryan Building to store and assemble automobiles. It appears that the first Franklin production vehicle sold to S. G. Averell in June, 1902, was assembled in the Ryan facility.

2-10   Individual investors across the nation tended to be reluctant to commit funds to the pioneer auto industry, perhaps because of the all-too-frequent failure of many early motor vehicle enterprises. James Couzens, of the Ford Motor Company, related being rebuffed by one businessman after another in Detroit as he sought to raise capital for this newly-organized firm. William A. Simonds, *Henry Ford: His Life, His Work, His Genius*, (Indianapolis & New York, Bobbs-Merril, 1943), p. 79.

2-11 B.C. Forbes & O.D. Foster, *Automotive Giants of America*. (New York, B.C. Forbes Publishing Co., 1926) pp. 121-140.

2-12 Nevins and Hill, *Ford, the Times, the Man the Company*, p. 260.

2-13 Letter to editor, *Cycle and Automobile Trade Journal*, Nov. 1, 1903, p. 19.

2-14 *Scientific American*, Jan. 28, 1905.

2-15 *The American Car Since 1775*. Section on calendar year production, 1905, p. 135.

2-16 *New York Automobile Co.* Case, pp. 236 et seq.

2-17 History of the H.H. Franklin Manufacturing Company, item 195. (Hereafter cited as History)

2-18 Company brochure describing 1904 models. At an earlier date H.H. Franklin suggested that larger motors would have to be cooled by water because of the limits of air-cooling. Clearly such limitations had been overcome by the talented company engineers.

2-19 *Air-Cooled News*, Issue 24, 5; Issue 36, p. 9.

2-20 U. S. Census of Manufactures, 1905.

NOTES

2-21 *The American Car Since 1775*. section on Calendar Year Production, 1905, p. 135

2-22 Nevins & Hill, *Ford, the Times, the Man, the Company*, pp. 494-500.

2-23 History of the H.H. Franklin Manufacturing Company, item #139. Onondaga Historical Association collections, Syracuse, NY.

Chapter 3

3-1 *The Automobile*, June 21, 1906, pp. 965-967.

3-2 History of the H.H. Franklin Manufacturing Company, item 319 (hereafter cited as History).

3-3 Ibid., items 170, 229.

3-4 Kimes and Clark, *American Cars, 1805-1942*.

3-5 *The Automobile*, June 28, 1906, p. 1007.

3-6 *Motor Age*, Sept. 13, 1906, p. 7.

3-7 *Scientific American*, May 19, 1906, p. 414.

3-8 History, item 216.

3-9 Ibid., items 183, 196, 197.

3-10 Ibid., item 209

3-11 Ibid., item.160

3-12 Ibid., item 214.

3-13 Ibid., item 208.

3-14 Ibid., items 219, 220.

3-15 Ibid., item 233.

3-16 George D. Babcock and Reginold Trautschold, *The Taylor System in Franklin Management*, pp. 1-8.

3-17 *Horseless Age*, May 13, 1908, p. 583.

3-18 Ibid., August 8, 1908, p. 181.

3-19 History, item 261.

3-20 U. S. Bureau of the Census, Census of Manufactures, 1909.

3-21 *The Automobile*, June 28, 1906, p. 97.

Chapter 4

4-1 U.S. Bureau of the Census, Census of Manufactures, 1909.

4-2 Archives, Automobile Club of Syracuse: resolution adopted Sept. 24, 1909.

4-3 *Horseless Age*, Jan. 5, 1910, p. 41.

4-4 U.S. Bureau of the Census, Census of Manufactures, 1914, p. 739.

4-5 William Greenleaf, *Monopoly on Wheels*, pp. 226-231. Also see 184 *Federal Reporter*, 894, 1911.

4-6 U.S. Temporary National Economic Committee; Hearings on Investigation of Concentration of Economic Power; Part 2, Patents, 292, GPO 1939.

4-7 *Moody's Manual of Manufacturers*, 1913.

4-8 Letter of E.H. Dann to an associate, July 16, 1912.

4-9 *Moody's Manual of Manufacturers*, 1913.

4-10 Report on Factory Employment, Michigan Dept. of Labor, 1912.

4-11 Archives, U.S. Air Force Museum, Wright-Patterson Air Force Base, Dayton, Ohio; Memorandum on tests of Liberty engine, April 13, 1918. Also see *Automotive Industries*, Feb. 14, 1918, p. 386.

Chapter 5

5-1 For additional information on the "copper cooled" Chevrolet, see Stewart W. Leslie, *Boss Kettering*, (New York, Columbia Univ. Press, 1983), pp. 123-148. Through the kind assistance of H.H. Franklin Club member James Crippen, the author was also able to interview the son of the late Roland Hutchinson, a staff member at General Motors research laboratories during the period of development of this air-cooled engine.

5-2 Annual statement to stockholders, H.H. Franklin Manufacturing Company, 1923.

5-3 Ibid., 1924.

Chapter 6

6-1 *Automotive Industries*, March 5, 1925, pp. 451-454.

6-2 United States, Bureau of Labor Statistics, *Wages and Hours in the Motor Vehicle Industry*, 1925, Bulletin No. 438, Washington D. C.

6-3 Ibid.

6-4 Annals of the American Academy of Political and Social Science, 1924; *The Automobile: its Province and its Problems*. Material contained in this article has been utilized throughout section 3 of this chapter.

6-5 Annual Statement to Stockholders, H.H. Franklin Manufacturing Company, 1925.(Hereafter cited as Annual Statement)

6-6 *Moody's Manual of Manufacturers*, 1926.

6-7 John Parker, *A History of the Packard Motor Car Company from 1899 to 1929*, Wayne State University M.A. Thesis, 1949.

6-8 *Automotive Industries*, Jan. 1, 1925, pp. 38, 40.

6-9 Daniel Raff, Making Cars and Making Money in the Interwar Auto Industry, *Business History Review*, Vol. 65, Winter, 1991, pp. 721-753.

6-10 *Automotive Industries*, July 8, 1926, p. 78.

6-11 Annual Statement, 1926.

6-12 Annual Statement, 1927.

6-13 *Moody's Manual of Manufacturers*, 1928.

6-14 *New York Times*, Oct. 25, 1928, 43:1.

6-15 Ibid., June 22, 1928, 39:3.

6-16 *Automotive Industries*, March 16, 1929, 466.

6-17 Annual Statement, 1928.

6-18 *Automotive Industries*, Nov. 19, 1925, p. 885.

6-19 Ibid., Oct. 19, 1929, p. 598.

6-20 Ibid., Nov. 16, 1929, p. 742; Also see *New York Times*, Nov. 17, 1929, X, 10:7,8.

6-21 Ralph E. Jones, George H. Rarey, Robert J. Icks, *The Fighting Tanks Since 1916*, (Washington D.C., National Service Publishing Co.), 1933, pp. 157,158. The pilot model, six-Ton M 1917 A-I used the 1929 67 H.P. Franklin engine with vertical draft air cooling. The six-ton, M 1917 A-1 used the 1930-31 100 H.P. Franklin engine with side-draft air cooling.

6-22 Annual Statement to Stockholders, H.H. Franklin Manufacturing Company, 1929

Chapter 7

7-1 *Automobile Topics*, November 30, 1929.

7-2 *Automotive Industries*, Jan. 4. 1930,.pp. 1-27

7-3 *New York Times*, January 5, 1930, X 34:4. This article had been preceded by a similar one in the December 15, 1929, issue of the *New York Times*, XI, 12:2, in which H.H., citing the fact that he recently had completed a personal investigation of traffic conditions which involved 20,000 miles of travel in fourteen states, urged that roads be constructed to meet future as well as present traffic needs and that they be routed around towns rather than through them.

7-4   Howard R. Delaney, The Cole Motor Car Company, unpublished Ph.D. thesis, Indiana University, School of Business, 1954.

7-5   *New York Times*, Jan. 8, 1930, 44:6.

7-6   *Automotive Industries*, December 6, 1930, pp. 817, 818.

7-7   *New York Times*, May 5, 1930, 1:4.

7-8   A few years later as Governor Murphy he would play a key role in the handling of major auto industry sit-down strikes occurring in Flint and other Michigan cities.

7-9   *Automotive Industries*,.May 2, 1931, p. 708.

7-10 *Syracuse Herald*, July 18, 1930, p. 3.

7-11 Franklin *Dealers' Bulletin*, Franklin Automobile Company, Nov. 12, 1930.

7-12 *New York Times*, Dec. 5, 1930, 47:1. *Automotive Topics*, Dec. 6, 1930, p. 335.

7-13 Annual Report (formerly Annual Statement) of the H.H. Franklin Manufacturing Company for the year 1930

7-14 *New York Times*, Jan 1, 1931, Stock reports for year ending Dec. 31, 1930.

7-15 *Automotive Industries*, Oct. 17, 1931, p. 624.

NOTES

7-16 New York State Department of Labor, Report on Factory Employment in Selected Cities, September 1931.

7-17 *Automotive Industries*, September 26, 1931, p. 484.

7-18 Ibid., October 3, 1931, p. 495.

7-19 *New York Times*, January 4, 1931, X, 25:6.

7-20 *New York Times*, May 25, 1931, 14:2; June 12, 1931, 38;1; Oct. 18, 1931, V 9. *Automotive Industries*, Sept. 26, 1931, pp. 476 et seq.

7-21 Horace Benstead, "Franklin Automobile Company Finances," *Air Cooled News*, #50, July, 1970, pp. 3-5.

7-22 McEwen also had served on the board of directors of the Winton Motor Co. of Cleveland, another firm which went out of business!

7-23 Annual Report, 1931.

7-24 *New York Times*, Jan. 1, 1932, Stock reports for year ending Dec. 31, 1931.

7-25 *Automotive Industries*, April 23, 1932, p. 637.

7-26 Ibid., November 26, 1932, p. 687.

7-27 Police statistics for the city of Chicago showed that three times more cars were stolen in that community during November 1932, than new vehicles sold–2,738 versus 928! *Automotive Industries*, January 7, 1933.

7-28 Annual Report, 1932.

THE FRANKLIN AUTOMOBILE COMPANY

7-29 *New York Times*, Jan. 1, 1933, Stock reports for the year ending Dec. 31, 1932.

7-30 Annual Report, 1933.

7-31 *New York Times*, Jan., 1, 1934, Stock reports for the year ending Dec. 31, 1933.

Chapter 8

8-1 Minutes, Board of Directors Meeting, Syracuse Manufacturers' Association, April 25, 1934.

8-2 *New York Times*, January 7, 1934, XI, Part 1, 2-3.

8-3 Letter of H.H. Franklin to Franklin Distributors and Dealers, Jan. 30, 1934.

8-4 H.H. Franklin Manufacturing Company Bankruptcy Records, Federal Archives, Bayonne, N.J.

8-5 *Syracuse Herald*, April 4, 1934, p. 6.

8-6 Ibid., April 12, 1934, p. 4.

8-7 *Automotive Industries*, April 21, 1934.

8-8 *New York Times*, August 7, 1934, 32:3.

8-9 *Automotive Industries*, Nov. 24, 1934, p. 631.

8-10 *New York Times*, Sept. 23, 1934, IX, 8:6; Jan. 6, 1935, X, 14:3.

8-11 Ninety engineers were added to the Packard staff in the early months of 1934. *Automotive Industries*, May 26, 1934, p. 632.

8-12 Contracts, Doman & Marks with Franklin Motors. Edward Marks papers.

8-13 Contract, Franklin Motors with Dallas Winslow. Edward Marks papers.

8-14 *Automotive Industries*, Sept. 5, 1936, p. 293.

8-15 Coincidentally the brilliant Willis Carrier of the firm bearing his name, father of the modern-day air conditioner and like John Wilkinson a mechanical engineering graduate of Cornell, for many years had been a loyal owner of air-cooled Franklin cars!

8-16 Boulware later became nationally known as chief labor relations negotiator for the General Electric Company.

8-17 Air-Cooled Motors did carry on intermittent discussions up to the time of World War II with one or two small automobile manufacturers relative to the possible use of its eight-cylinder power plant in a motor car, without positive results.

8-18 Letter from N.Y. Department of State to author, May 22, 1989.

8-19 Final year for the Cadillac V-16 was 1940; for the Lincoln senior-series V-12, 1939; and for the Packard V-12, 1939. A few custom body shops did survive, one of the most notable being Derham of Philadelphia, but they had few clients.

Chapter 9

9-1 Plants somewhat similar in size to that of the Franklin firm included those of the Marmon and Auburn Motor Companies.

9-2 Coal-fired furnaces were used into the 1920s to temper steel

THE FRANKLIN AUTOMOBILE COMPANY

parts at the Franklin plant, a process viewed as outdated by most Syracuse gear manufacturers who used oil as a fuel to produce the great heat required.

9-3   *Franklin News*, Feb. 1, 1923, p. 8

Chapter 10

10-1   H.H. Franklin ultimately joined the Syracuse University Board of Trustees in mid-1929 (*New York Times*, June 8, 1929, 8:2)

10-2   Letter, James A. Viehland, Managing Director, Beta Gamma Sigma Honor Society, to the author, dated March 7, 1991.

10-3   One major newspaper occasionally sought H.H. Franklin's opinion on automotive-related matters. See *New York Times*, January 10, 1926, IX, 33:2 (Automobile Industry Outlook); January 8, 1928, X, 37:3 (Relation of Auto to Modern Life); July 22, 1933, 5:6 (H.H. Franklin Approves Recovery Agreements). Franklin's career in the motor industry was briefly covered in this newspaper in the late 1920s. *New York Times*, April 8, 1928, IX, 12:3.

10-4   Records, H.H. Franklin Estate, Surrogate's Court of Onondaga County, Syracuse, N.Y.

10-5   Wilkinson's obituary notices can be found in the *New York Times*, June 27, 1951,.29:6; in the *New York Herald-Tribune* of the same date; and in *Time*, July 9, 1951, p. 70

Chapter 11

11-1   Information on membership of the board of directors of the H.H. Franklin Mfg. Co. has been obtained from the Annual Reports of the H.H. Franklin Mfg. Co., 1913-1933.

11-2 Letter of Edward S. Marks to James Walker, Dec. 31, 1932; Edward S. Marks papers.

11-3 During the less-than-one-year period in 1930-31, when Frederick J. Haynes rejoined the H.H. Franklin Mfg. Co. as vice president and general manager, Haynes chaired the firm's executive committee.

11-4 Information on these independent .and quasi-independent units of the company has been obtained from *Moody's Manual of Manufacturers*, from Franklin bankruptcy records, and from issues of the *Franklin News*

11-5 *The Outlook*, May 4, June 22, July 27, 1921. Papers of Frederick Davenport, Division of Special Collections, Bird Library, Syracuse University.

11-6 Transcription of an interview with Ralph Hamlin (interviewer unknown) plus related written records in the Archives of the Petersen Automotive Museum, Los Angeles, CA, have been utilized for this section of Chapter XI

11-7 Ibid.

11-8 Business records of the Baker Brothers' Company, Glens Falls, NY, 1921-1937. Collection of Arnold Christiansen.

11-9 Contract between the H.H. Franklin Automobile Co., Syracuse, NY, and Baker Brothers, Glens Falls, NY, dated December 20, 1921. Collection of Arnold Christiansen.

11-10 Interview of Justin Fleming by the author, June 20, 1978.

11-11 Interview of Donald Douglas by the author, Feb. 10, 1995.

11-12 Franklin sales in Ohio collapsed in late 1930 and early 1931 (only 23 new Franklin cars were registered in the entire state in December 1930, with 26 registered in February 1931, and 11 in March of that year). *Automobile Topics*, issues of February 14, 1931, p. 122; April 11, 1931, p. 714; May 2, 1931, p. 934.

11-13 Franklin *Dealers Bulletin*, July 20, 1933 and Sept. 28, 1933; Cincinnati City Directories, 1933-34, 1934-35, 1936, 1937.

11-14 Report of American Consulate in Ottawa, Canada, 1933.

Chapter 12

12-1 File of correspondence, Ralph Hamlin with various other Franklin dealers, 1929-1932; Archives of Petersen Automotive Museum, Los Angeles, CA.

12-2 Interview with Helen Stringer, Manlius, N.Y., November 2, 1989.

12-3 A check of early RFC files by a staff member of the Federal Archives failed to disclose an application by the H.H. Franklin Manufacturing Company for assistance in 1933-1934.

Research Sources

PRIMARY SOURCES

Cornell University Olin Library, Ithaca, N.Y., Archives and Special Collections Division. Materials on Charles S. Brown,, Fred R. Bump, Frederick J. Haynes, Charles B. King, Robert E. Lay, Charles E. Lipe, John E. Sweet, Rollin H. White, John Wilkinson.

Cornell Engineering Library. Various issues of *The Crank* (student mechanical engineering journal published in 1880s and 1890s).

Detroit Public Library, National Automotive History Collection. Papers of Charles B. King and David Beecroft. Materials on H.H. Franklin Manufacturing Company.

Harvard Business School, Baker Library, Cambridge, MA. Financial reports of H.H. Franklin Manufacturing Co., 1913-1933

Michigan State University Library, Archives and Historical Collections Unit. Papers of Ransom E. Olds.

Philadelphia Free Library, Automotive Collection. Various Franklin-related materials.

THE FRANKLIN AUTOMOBILE COMPANY

Syracuse University Bird Library, Special Collections Division. Correspondence of Herbert H. Franklin with chancellors and other officials of Syracuse University, 1919-1938. Notes and related papers of Frederick Davenport dealing with his experiences at the H.H. Franklin Manufacturing Company in 1920.

Onondaga Historical Association Research Center, Syracuse, N.Y. Diary of Herbert H. Franklin; issues of *Coxsackie News* from 1886-1893; History of the H.H. Franklin Manufacturing Company 1893-1910; other papers relating to H.H. Franklin.

Franklin Foundation Museum, Tucson, Arizona. Letterbook of H.H. Franklin, 1900-1902. Miscellaneous items of H.H. Franklin Manufacturing Company.

Petersen Automotive Museum, Los Angeles, California. Transcripts of interviews with Ralph Hamlin. Correspondence of Ralph Hamlin with Franklin dealers in various American cities, 1929-1932.

National Museum of American History (Smithsonian), Washington, D.C., Transportation Division. Descriptive material on initial Franklin vehicle sold publicly (S.G. Averell car). Other material on Franklin motor cars.

The National Archives and Records Administration, United States Government, Washington, D.C. Material on H.H. Franklin Manufacturing Company and Franklin Automobile Company, particularly relating to exports.

In addition to the above, private collections of research materials were made available by the following persons: Joseph Aronson; Arnold Christianson; Mario Cuniberti; Betty Doman; J.D. Franklin; Edward Kabelac; Mildred Franklin (Mrs. John) Moreland; Marion (Mrs. Donald) Napier; Anne Wilkinson Sherry; William Tuthill.

MANUSCRIPT THESES AND RELATED PAPERS

Lay, Robert P., and Evans, L.R., "Efficiency Tests of a Franklin Air-Cooled Motor," Mechanical Engineer Thesis, Cornell University, 1907.

Parker, John, "A History of the Packard Motor Car Company from 1899 to 1929," M.A. Thesis, Wayne State University, 1949.

Smith, Howard W., "The Elasticity of Demand for the Automobile," Study undertaken for Syracuse University Graduate School, Department of Economics, 1934.

DeLancy, Howard R., "The History of the Cole Motor Car Company," DBA Thesis, School of Business, Indiana University, 1954.

PUBLIC AND OTHER DOCUMENTS

The following public documents were of value in the research study of the H.H. Franklin Manufacturing Company:

Bankruptcy records of the H.H. Franklin Manufacturing Company 1934-1937. Federal Records Center, Bayonne, New Jersey.

U.S. Census of Manufactures; various dates from 1900. See particularly report on automobiles of George E. Oller, Census of 1905.

U. S. Department of Labor, Bureau of Labor Statistics, December, 1928: Wages and Hours of Labor in the Motor Vehicle Industry: 1928.

The New York Automobile Company vs. Herbert H. Franklin, Alexander T. Brown, John Wilkinson and H.H. Franklin Manufacturing Company. Record of the case including testimony and exhibits, together with judgment and opinion of Justice W.S. Andrews, in the Supreme Court, State of New York, Onondaga County, 1906.

THE FRANKLIN AUTOMOBILE COMPANY

Raleigh Motor Car & Machine Company vs Franklin Automobile Company. In the United States District Court, Eastern District of North Carolina. Deposition of S.B. Dodge, Southern District Manager, Franklin Automobile Company, taken in Atlanta, Georgia, July 25, 1919.

New York State Department of Labor, reports of Bureau of Factory Inspection, varying dates from 1896-1914.

H. H. FRANKLIN COMPANY PUBLICATIONS

The Franklin News, 1910, 1919-1924.

Employee's Information Book; H.H. Franklin Manufacturing Company, undated, approximately 1916.

Franklin *Dealer's Bulletin*, various dates to March, 1934.

Annual reports of the H.H. Franklin Manufacturing Company, Syracuse, N.Y., various years through 1933.

Whitman, L.L., "From Coast-to-Coast in a Motor Car," 1904

Whitman, L.L., "Across America in a Franklin," 1907.

PERIODICALS, JOURNALS AND NEWSPAPERS

Very substantial use has been made of a number of trade periodicals which since the early days of the automobile in America have covered the industry. These include: *Automotive Industries* (titled *The Automobile* until 1917); *Automotive Trade Journal* (originally titled *Cycle and Automobile Trade Journal*); *Automotive Topics*; *Automotive Daily News*; *Motor*; *Horseless Age* (merged in 1918 with *Motor Age*).

RESEARCH SOURCES

Moody's Manual of Investments was examined for fiscal data on the H.H. Franklin Company and competitor firms. The *New York Times* was consulted extensively for stories on Franklin and other automotive firms, as well as for data on automotive stocks. The Syracuse newspapers were reviewed for articles on H.H. Franklin, John Wilkinson, the H.H. Franklin Manufacturing Company, and other firms producing motor vehicles in the Syracuse area.

Air Cooled News; Quarterly publication of The H.H. Franklin Club, Cazenovia N.Y., Nos. 1-131. Various articles on Franklin history found in the various issues were drawn on for this book.

Two serialized general histories of the Franklin motor car and the key persons involved with it have been produced by Menno Duerksen (in *Cars and Parts Magazine*) and by the late Thomas Hubbard (in several magazines, including *Antique Automobile* and *Air Cooled News*). Both of these serials were consulted frequently.

THE FRANKLIN AUTOMOBILE COMPANY

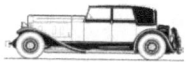

Bibliography

Anderson, Rudolph E., "The Story of the American Automobile," Public Affairs Press, Washington, D.C. 1950.

Automobile Quarterly, Kutztown, PA

- Volume 1, No. 3: "Franklin-Coast-to-Coast; Album 1904," (Courtesy of H.H. Franklin Club).

- Volume 5, No. 3; "The Case for Franklin," Hubbard, Thomas H.

- Volume 15, No. 1; "A Few Thoughts about the Franklin," Editors of Automobile Quarterly.

- Volume 17, No. 3; "The Twelve At the End of the Road," Grayson, Stan.

- Volume 19, No. 2; "J. Frank deCausse," Gosden, Walter E.

- Volume 26, No. 2: "A Matter of Principle; The Wilkinson Era at Franklin," Katz, John F.

THE FRANKLIN AUTOMOBILE COMPANY

Babcock, George D. (in collaboration with Reginald Trautschold), "The Taylor System in Franklin Management," *The Engineering Magazine*, New York, 1918.

Barber, Henry L.; *The Story of the Automobile*, A.J. Munson & Co., Chicago, 1917.

Beecroft, David; "History of the American Automobile Industry," *The Automobile*, Vols. 33-35 (Oct 1915-Aug 1916).

Bellamy, James; "Cars Made in Upstate New York," Squire Hill Publishing Company, Red Creek, NY, 1989.

Brierley, Brooks T.; *There Is No Mistaking a Pierce-Arrow*, Garret and Stringer, Inc., Coconut Grove, FL, 1986.

- *Auburn, Reo, Franklin and Pierce Arrow versus Cadillac, Chrysler, Lincoln and Packard*, Garret and Stringer, Coconut Grove, FL, 1991.

- *Magic Motors 1930*, Garret and Stringer, Coconut Grove, FL, 1996.

Chrysler, Walter P. (in collaboration with Boyden Sparks), *Life of an American Workman*, Dodd, Mead, & Company, New York, 1937.

City Directory, Syracuse, New York; R.L. Polk; 1886-1934.

Cleveland, R.M., and Williamson, S.T., *The Road Is Yours*, The Greystone Press, New York, 1951

Clymer, Floyd, *Treasury of Early American Automobiles*, Clymer Publications, New York, 1950.

Davenport, Frederick, "Out of the Toga and into Overalls," *The Outlook*, May 4, June 22, July 27, 1921.

BIBLIOGRAPHY

DeLancey, Howard R., "The Cole Motor Car Company," *Business History Review*, Vol 30 (Sept, 1956) pp. 260-273.

Denison, Merrill, "*The Power to Go*," Doubleday and Company, Garden City, NY, 1956.

Doolittle, James R.(ed), "*The Romance of the Automobile Industry*," The Klebold Press, New York, 1916.

Duerksen, Menno, "*Great American Classics*," Amos Press, Inc., Sidney, OH, 1987.

Duryea, J. Frank, "America's First Automobile," Donald F. McCauley, Springfield, MA, 1942.

Edmonds, C.C., "Tendencies in the Automobile Industry," *American Economic Review*, Vol 12 (Sept, 1923) pp 422-441.

Epstein, Ralph C., *The Automobile Industry*, A.W. Shaw Co., Chicago, 1928.

Fine, Sidney, *The Automobile Under the Blue Eagle*, The University of Michigan Press, Ann Arbor, 1962.

Flink, James J., *America Adopts the Automobile, 1895-1910*, The MIT Press, Cambridge, MA, 1970.

Georgano, G.N., Editor, *The Complete Encyclopedia of Motorcars: 1885 to the Present*, Dutton, New York 1973.

Glasscock, C.B. *The Gasoline Age*, The Bobbs-Merrill Company, Indianapolis, 1937.

Greenleaf, William, *Monopoly on Wheels; Henry Ford and the Selden Automobile Patent*, Wayne State University Press, Detroit, 1961.

THE FRANKLIN AUTOMOBILE COMPANY

Hanley, George P. and Stacey P., *The Marmon Heritage*, Doyle Hyk Publishing Company, Rochester, MI, 1985.

Hendry, Maurice D., "Franklin - The Air-Cooled Classic," *Veteran and Vintage Magazine*, July-September, 1969.

Hendry, Maurice D., *Pierce-Arrow: First Among America's Finest*, Ballentine Books, New York, 1971.

Hewitt, Edward R., *Those Were the Days*, Duell, Sloan and Pierce, New York, 1943.

Kennedy, Edward, D., *The Automobile Industry*, Reynal and Hitchcock, New York, 1941.

Kimes, Beverly Rae and Clark, Henry A., *Standard Catalog of American Cars 1805-1942*, Krause Publications, Iola, WI, 1995, 3d edition.

King, Charles B., *A Golden Anniversary, 1895-1945*, privately printed, Larchmont, NY, 1945.

Laux, James M., *The Automobile Revolution; The Impact of an Industry*, University of North Carolina Press, Chapel Hill, NC, 1982.

Lewis, Eugene W., *Motor Memories*, Alved Publishers, Detroit, 1947

Long, J.C., *Roy D. Chapin*, Privately printed, 1945.

Longstreet, Stephen, *A Century on Wheels; The Story of Studebaker*, Henry Holt & Company, New York, 1952.

MacManus, Theodore F.M. and Beasley, Norman, *Men, Money and Motors*, Harper and Brothers, New York, 1929.

Maxim, Hiram P., *Horseless Carriage Days*, Harper and Brothers, New York, 1937.

BIBLIOGRAPHY

May, George S., *R.E. Olds; Auto Industry Pioneer*, Eerdmans, Grand Rapids, MI, 1977.

Nevins, Allen, (with collaboration of Frank E. Hill), *Ford; The Times, The Man, The Company*, Charles Scribner's Sons, New York, 1954.

Pound, Arthur, *The Turning Wheel*, Doubleday, Doran and Company, Garden City, NY, 1934.

Rae, John B., *The American Automobile*, University of Chicago Press, Chicago, 1965.

American Automobile Manufacturers; The First Forty Years, Chilton Company, Philadelphia, 1959.

The Road and the Car in American Life, MIT Press, Cambridge, MA, 1970.

Ralston, Marc, *Pierce-Arrow*, A. S. Barnes, San Diego, 1980.

Scharchburg, Richard, *Carriages Without Horses*, Society of Automotive Engineers Press, Inc., Warrendale, PA, 1993.

Seltzer, Lawrence H., *A Financial History of the American Automobile Industry*, Houghton Mifflin Company, Boston, 1928.

Sinsabaugh, Christopher G., *Who, Me? Forty Years of Automobile History*, Arnold Powers, Inc., Detroit, 1940.

Sloan, Alfred P., *My Years with General Motors*, Doubleday and Co., Garden City, NY, 1964.

U.S. Federal Trade Commission, "Report on the Motor Vehicle Industry," (76th Congress, 1st Session, House Document 468) U. S. Government Printing Office, 1959.

THE FRANKLIN AUTOMOBILE COMPANY

Index

Symbols

1906 Cross Country race 88

A

Acetylene lamps 80
Ackerman, S.E.
  head of export department 205
  pressure on dealers by 454
  sales manager 155
Advertising 68
  1906 Franklin limousine 84
  1920s competition 161
  appeal to wealthy 136
  early 68
  early closed car 78
  glamour photos 241
  practical emphasis 125
  scientific light weight 132
  supercharged Airman 457
Air-Cooled Motors 336
Air-cooling 177
  advantages and competitors 86
Aircraft
  Franklin-powered Waco biplane 249, 260
  in World War I 145
  Series 14 powered Waco airplane 251
Aircraft Board Committee 145
Airman 231
  advertisement 232
  Series 12B Limited 236
  Series 19 306
  supercharged 291
Airplane
  for transport 340
Alhambra Hall
  1897 bicycle show 31
  1908 show 99
American Austin 283
American Society for Testing Materials (ASTM) 94
American Society of Automobile Engineers (SAE) 84
American Society of Mechanical Engineers (ASME) 8
Amesbury, Massachusetts
  automobiles bodies built in 390
  Depression and 395
Argentina, sales efforts 461
Armistice of November 11, 1918 147
Assembly department 370
Assembly line(s)
  300-foot long 170
  conveyor-type 128

513

Ford Motor Company 138
Franklin factory 158
post WW I 151
Assets of bankrupt Franklin company 318
Association of Licensed Automobile Manufacturers (ALAM) 66
  1911 show 113
  H.H. Franklin as officer of, 398
  John Wilkinson on technical standards committee of, 67
Auburn Motor Car Company, car sales 277
Austin vehicle 283
Australia, dealers and distributors in, 462
Auto Clubs
  Syracuse Automobile Club 110
Automobile contests 63
Automobile design 194
Automobile Salon 257
Automotive Hall of Fame 413
Automotive Industry
  by 1900 48
  by 1905 72
  by 1910 112
  cyclic nature 193
  Depression unemployment 282
  early plant organization 80
  expansion of 120
  impact on recreation 213
  mid-20s expansion 206
  mid-20s technological progress 222
  problems of small scale production 478
  retrenchment during Depression 298
  technological changes impact 395
Auto-related accidents 215
Averell, S.G.
  1913 economy run 122
  purchases first Franklin Type A 50

B

Babcock, George DeAlbert
  Frederick Haynes assistant 93
  named manufacturing chief 127
Baker, Erwin "Cannon Ball"
  1928 cross continental speed records 235
  Pike's Peak run 249
Ballard, H.N.
  appointed sales vice-president 197
Barcelow, Alphonse
  recollections from Walker-Wells 391
Barrel-hoods
  Introduction 85
Barton, Frank
  first employment with HHFMCo 59
  named Secretary 91
  with factory agents (photo) 347
Bedell, Frank
  Coxsackie realtor and HHF partner 17
Belden, Edith
  John Wilkinson's bride 33
Belt man, Harmon Cross 389
Benjamin, C. Arthur
  HHFMCo's first general sales manager 60
Benstead, Horace
  attempted restructure of finances 288
Bicycles
  early history 29
  unemployed workers move to automobile business 74
Biddle & Smart 391
Blagbrough, H.C.
  Industrial relations 190
Bliss, Gladys 405
Borszweski, Harry
  recollections 371
Brakes
  four-wheel hydraulic 231

INDEX

Brandt, Arthur J.
  Olympic Motors 333
Brayton motor 25
Brown, Alexander T. 7
  dies 249
  early life 9
Brown-Lipe Company 10
  early parts supplier 62
Brown, Ralph
  recollections 350, 361
Bump, Fred R.
  replaces Arthur Benjamin as sales manager 93
Burke, Henry
  recollections 369
Burns, John
  first work with Wilkinson 35
  photo with HHF 61

C

Cadillac
  during Depression 269
  sixteen-cylinder 257
Carris, C.S.
  1904 cross country race 64
  1906 cross country 88
  recalled by Ralph Brown 362
Changes in buying patterns 276
Chevrolet air-cooled car 185
Chrysler
  eight-cylinder 272
  introduces Imperial 210
Common School, The 17
Company Band
  Ward Sturge recollections 381
Condit, W. Chapin "Chape"
  recollections from engineering department 470
Cord
  collapse 341
  front wheel drive introduction 257
Cornell University

White, Andrew Dickson 26
Cornell University's first football team 25
Cost Control
  under George Babcock 99
Coxsackie News, The
  offices 14
  Offices (photo) 14
Cyclecars 140

D

Davenport, Frederick M., study of Frnklin factory life 434
Davis, Harold
  recollections 367
Dealer network 446
  Baker Brothers, Glens Falls, NY 451
  Justin Fleming 458
Death Valley 183
deCausse, J. Frank
  designs new look 194
  photo boattail roadster 202
DeLuxe Model introduced 272
Des Groseilliers, John
  recollections 376
Development of road system 142
Dietrich, Raymond A.
  hired as design consultant 238
Dividends
  suspended 1930 263
Doman, Carl T.
  side draft development 237
Doman-Marks
  development of new air-cooled motor 326
  three wheeled experimental vehicle 335
Duesenberg 161
Dumping practice 262
Dunk, William "Bill"
  production head 154
Duryea, J. Frank and Charles xxiii

Duxbury, Sara
  recollections 384
Dyneto
  starter generator 128

E

Earhart, Amelia
  association with advertising 278
Early automobile legislation
  Registration 111
Economy tests, 1914 123
  1919 126
Employee relations (see Chapter 9 for general description of factory life)
  employee luncheon (photo) 346
Engineering advancements by Franklin 464
Estoff, Meredith Lamson
  recollections 385

F

Falso, Armando
  recollections 365
Federal Aid Road Act in 1916 142
Federal War Industries Board 146
Feeley, Bob
  recollections in sales 442
Flanders, Willard
  recollections from Biddle & Smart 392
Ford, Henry
  quadricycle xxiii
Ford Motor Company
  Model A sales 246
  Model T impact 138
Foreign purchasers, 1919 159
Four-cylinder car
  development 176
  reasons for ending development 180

Fox Automobile 184
Fox Motor Car Company in receivership 186
Franklin Automobile Company
  commercial research office 441
  marketing arm established 92
  NYC sales branch opened 96
  overseas business 460
Franklin Automobiles
  9B update, 1917-8 154
  1910 Taxi 103
  1911 Torpedo 114
  Barrel-hoods 85
  closed car production 1923 192
  Commercial cars 116
    1912 dropped 120
  Deluxe 272
  early closed car advertisement 78
  early races 63
  early Types B & C 70
  first production Franklin 51
  light duty truck 86, 87
  Military use 1906 87
  Model M 118
  New Series
    Series 1 118
  Olympic (Series 18) 297
  One Man Top 101
  Pursuit 273
  Renault hood 118
  Series 2 & 3 121
  Series 4 121
  Series 6 128
  Series 8 129
  Series 9 133
    updating, 1921 169
  Series 10 182
  Series 10C 193
  Series 11 201
    Twenty-Fifth Anniversary Model 229
  Series 12 233

INDEX

Series 13
  Model 130 240
Series 14 258
Series 15 272
Series 19 306
Supercharged Airman (Series 16) 291
Transcontinent 263
Twelve (Series 17) 294
Type A 50
  description 51
Franklin & Bedell
  office photograph 17
Franklin, Charles Risden (photo) 403
Franklin Development Company 322, 433
Franklin Die-Casting Corporation 18, 433
  division sold 299
Franklin factory employees
  payscales, 1916 141
Franklin, Herbert H.
  1033 James Street residence 400
  as an executive 397
  as an industry leader 399
  better roads article 260
  birth and early life 11
  college endowments 410
  Coxsackie News work 13
  death 412
  die-casting business start 18
  father, Charles Risden 11
  Helen Stringer recollections 405
  industry ranking 422
  letter to Frank Bedell 56
  publisher The Common School 17
  takes controlling interest 91
Franklin-Illinois Company 322
Franklin Land Development Company 433
Franklin Motors 327, 328
Franklin, William
  Coxsackie News publisher 13
Frayer-Miller
  air-cooled competitor 86

G

Ganley, Edward J. (and sons Luke and Joe) operators of "Franklin Garage" 387
General Motors Corporation
  automotive pace-setter 219
  Buick division 277
  pay cuts 283
Gerst, Leo
  recollections 358
Goodhart, Hugh 204
Good Roads movement 211
  during Depression 284
  HHF article for NYT 260
Gould, J.W.DuB.
  as general manager 191

H

Hamel, Edward
  recollections as body worker 394
Hamlin, Ralph
  as a dealer 447
  confrontation over design 194
  leads dealer revolt 477
  Los Angeles-Phoenix race winner 124
Harris, C.B.
  cross country driver, 1906 88
Harwood, E.C.
  suggest "disposable" car 283
Hawks, Captain Frank 278
Haynes-Apperson 36
Haynes, Frank
  depression operating plan 278
  final resignation 288
  hired by HHFMCo 59
  named general manufacturing superintendent 93
  resigns to take charge of Dodge Bros. plant 127

returns to HHFMCo 270
  Wilkinson's deputy 74
Hekkema, H.D.
  Dutch dealer 440
H.H. Franklin Manufacturing Company, The
  1907-10 competition 106
  1911 business operations 120
  1913-17 financial results 135
  1916 competitors 130
  1929 factory improvements 244
  abandons "basic tansportation market" 90
  assets sold 327
  Board of Directors 430
  causes of failure 473
  competition with Big Three 264
  disposing of surplus production, 1930 261
  dividend omissions 233
  dividends resumed 239
  early finances 55, 68
  early trades employed 82
  executive churn 191
  executive revolving door 423
  files bankruptcy 317
  limps along 1932-33 300
  luxury market competition during Depression 269
  negative working captial position 296
  outside funding 244
  overproduction 248
  pay cuts, 1930 268
  plant expansion program during 1919 158
  plant tour 350
  Postwar boom 150
  production of war-related items 145
  purchases Brown-Franklin partnership 46
  stability of the company 429
  Taylor plan implemented 99
  twenty-fifth anniversary 222
  working capital limitations 274
Holmes, Arthur
  early economy test 89
  experimental engineering 93
  named chief engineer 128
  organizes Holmes Motor Car Company 160
Holmes Motor Car Company 160
  in receivership 186
Housman, Cora L.
  recollections 382
Hudson Motors
  return to prosperity 341
Hughes, Charles Evans
  NY Governor rides in 1908 Model D 100

I

in the white
  Walker bodies as shipped 349

J

James, William "Bill"
  recollections 374
Jeep
  Willys-Overland 342

K

Kallfelz Bakery 157
Kemp, Arthur 191
Kenyon, Frederick
  recollections 362
Kettering, Charles
  copper-cooled vehicle development 185
King, George
  recollections 373

INDEX

L

Labor policies 152
  post 1930s 343
  postwar pay rates 156
LeBaron
  designs 12 cylinder car 294
Lederle, Frank 278
Leininger, William
  U.S. Advertising Co. handles FAC account 226
Liberty aircraft motors 145
Lincoln Highway 142
Lincoln Motor Company
  faltering sales 234
  purchased by Ford Motor Co. 210
Lindbergh, Charles A.
  identified with Franklin 226
  photo 280
  photo, Ottawa, 1927 228
  photo with Spirit of St. Louis 227
Lipe, Charles Ehle 7
  early life 8
Lockrow, "Doc"
  handles first aid 364
Long trades
  practice prohibited 307
Los Angeles-Yosemite Economy Run 154
Lothrop, Marcus
  first metallurgist 94

M

Macauley, Alvan
  Packard leader 216
Marks, Edward S. (also see Doman-Marks)
  named chief engineer 205
  photo 205
  recalls engineering department 465
  recollection of HHF 409
Marmon Company
  Air cooled competitor 86
McEwen, Edwin
  dies 316
  named by banks to run HHFMCo 289
McNabb, William "Bill"
  color specialist (photo) 352
  recalled by Meredith Estoff 386
Military uses of Franklin product 270
Mittins, Frank
  recollections 363
Moore, Marguerite "Peggy"
  recollections 383
Moskovics, Frederick E.
  hiring fiasco 195
Moyer Wagon Works
  early Syracuse industry 6
Murphy Body Company 194
Murphy, Ralph
  John Wilkinson's assistant 192
  joins board 204

N

Nash Motor Company
  Depression era 303
National Industrial Recovery Act (NRA) 307
ndustrial relations 190
Ner-a-car 186
New York Automobile Company
  HHF asked to operate 43
  lawsuit against HHFMCo 69
  split with Wilkinson and HHF 45
  Wilkinson's first car company 39
New York Automobile Co. v. H.H. Franklin, et al. 486

O

Olympic 297
  introduced 306
Organization chart 432

Oswald, Jack
  recollections 379
Otto engine 25
Owners' Bulletin 439

P

Packard
  as competition 107
  as leading independent producer of high-grade motor cars 216
  compared to first Franklin 53
  Depression era 303
  during Depression 269
  offers $1,000 car 329
  postwar issues 175
  sales supremacy 234
  Series 120 success 341
  six-cylinder competition 203
  success of, 1912 119
Panic of 1907 96
Parenti Company 186
Physicians aware of motor car advantages 77
Pierce-Arrow 73
  during Depression 269
  failure 341
  mid-20s struggles 218
  postwar slump 175
  Studebaker merger 235
Pirate
  Dietrich design 259
Postwar boom 151
Preferred Stock Offering 171
Prentice, Mrs. Edward, winner of point to point races 1908-9 439
Production control boards 142
Production problems
  Postwar 164
Purdy, Lewis J.
  production chief 224
  recalled 380
  recalled by Henry Burke 370
  recalled by John Des Groseilliers 377
  resigns 278
Pursuit
  Transcontinent model photo 273

R

Rarey, Captain George
  U.S. Army Tank School 270
Recapitalization of the Franklin Company 171
Reconstruction Finance Corporation
  contacts for refinancing 317
Remmick, Henry
  paint striper 387
Renault-nose
  1911 introduction 119
Reo Motor Car Company
  supplier of bodies for Olympic models 296
Retirement plan 176

S

Salesometer 441
  illustration 443
Scientific light weight 131
Selden automobile patent
  Struck down 117
Selden, George
  ALAM created monopoly of patent 67
Shaw, Henry P.
  WW I employee 144
Shoemaker, Glen
  V-12 development 236
Sikorsky, Igor 337
Sloan, Alfred
  General Motors leader 219
Small car project 178
Smith, Russell
  recollections from marketing 444
Smoot-Hawley Tariff Act of 1930 266

INDEX

South Geddes Street Factory
  Carrier Corporation moves in 335
  expansion 96
  first use 53
  photo 105
  problems with 181
Speedster
  1929 Dietrich design 243
Stellman, Louis
  appointed chief engineer 192
Stilwell, Giles
  as vice-president 204
  HHF's attorney 60
  loans HHF cash for die-casting business 21
  named vice-president 91
Stout, William
  airplane designer 260
Strikes and work stoppages 209
Studebaker
  in receivership 302
Sturge, Ward
  recollections 381
Stutz 257
Sweet Artisan School
  HHFMCo helps start 94
Sweet, John Edson 7
  early life 7
Swope, Gerald
  suggests steps to stabilize employment 284
Syracuse
  Automobile Club 110
  beneficiary of nation's love for cars 140
  bicycle production 30
  Civil War expansion 5
  Depression effects 282
  early automobile business 36
  early industry 5
  Erie Canal 3
  first Franklin factory on West Onondaga Street (photo) 19
  first gasoline-powered car 36
  "Franklin Garage" 387
  impact of HHFMCo concern, 1921 175
  in late 19th Century 2
  Moyer Wagon Works 6
  post bankruptcy attempt to bring back HHFMCo 323
Syracuse Land Development Company 321

T

Tague, Stella
  continues work after bankruptcy 413
  HHF secretary hired 60
Tax claims
  city of Syracuse and county of Onondaga 325
Taylor, Frederick Winslow
  Taylor plan implemented at factory 99
Taylor Plan
  control boards 142
  implemented at plant 127
Technical innovations
  electrical laboratory established 94
  flywheel fan and vertical fins 102
  internal technical training program 128
  Low gear demonstrations 124
  Scientific light weight 131
  Series 10 182
  side draft development 237
Traffic department 93
Transcontinent 263

U

Underwood, H.G.
  hydrostatic molding 18
Union-business relations 285, 343
United States Advertising Company

retained as official ad agency 226
U.S. Army
  Franklin powered tanks 250

V

V-12 Engines
  first development 236
Vehicle registrations, 1916 137

W

Waco airplane 251
  unveiled 260
Wahl, Harry A.
  reorganization plan 325
Walker Body Company
  recollections by employees 390
  termination of contract 290
Walker, James (Walker Body Co.)
  funds Doman-Marks 326
Walker, J.E.
  named advertising manager 93
Walker-Wells Body Co 157
Webb, H.B.
  named Treasurer, HHFMCo 92
White, Andrew Dickson
  Cornell's first president 26
Whitman, L.L.
  1904 Cross country race 64
  1906 cross country 88
Wichert, Ted
  recollections 377
Wiles, Ben
  bankruptcy referee 327
Wilkinson, Forman
  Younger brother of John, executive secretary of Syracuse Automobile Club 110

Wilkinson, John
  Aircraft Board Committee 145
  bicyclist 32
  early work career 28
  Edith Belden, bride 33
  exits HHFMCo 197
  first automotive experiments 35
  first car 38
  first experimental Franklin car 45
  Franklin job 2 49
  grandfather 4
  industry ranking 422
  James Street residence 415
  life as a leader 414
  meets HHF 44
  named vice-president 128
  Ralph Murphy appointed as assistant 192
Williams, John E.
  vice-president sales activities 238
Willis, Harley
  business printer 388
Winslow, Dallas E. 332
Woman, status of in postwar years 149
Wood frame
  Franklin chassis 85
World War I
  car production had ceased 147
  effects on HHFMCo 143
  effects on the country 133

Y

Yarian, James
  development of four-cylinder $1,000 car 162
  non-Franklin car development 186

About the Author

Sinclair Powell with his Franklin 1929 Victoria Brougham.

Sinclair Powell is an automotive historian who was born in Toronto, Canada. When he was a youngster, his parents moved to Michigan, and he spent much of his childhood in Wyandotte, a suburb of Detroit. Mr. Powell graduated first from Michigan State University with

THE FRANKLIN AUTOMOBILE COMPANY

a B.A. degree in history and then from the Cornell Law School with a J.D. degree. While in the U.S. Army he also studied engineering at Lehigh University.

Mr. Powell's first exposure to the automobile industry came during his college days when he spent two summers in the machine shops of the Ford Motor Company. His work at Lincoln gave him some insight into quality vehicle construction. The older engineers at that firm could recall the cars built by Lincoln in the early and mid-1930s, and compared them with competitors such as Pierce-Arrow and the senior Packards. Mr Powell's years as a lawyer from 1950 to 1988 involved substantial work in urban and regional planning, plus activities in the area of transportation. In the 1960's and 1970s, he was retained to conduct management and legal studies of state highway departments and to evaluate methods of financing regional transportation networks.

Mr. Powell's interest in old cars began in 1966 when he joined the Pierce-Arrow Society. Membership in the H.H. Franklin Club followed a few years later. Ultimately, he realized that he was particularly interested in the history of what might be termed, "the small independent producers of quality vehicles during the first third of the twentieth century." From this came a decision to conduct in depth research into the background of the H.H. Franklin Manufacturing Company of Syracuse and ultimately develop a book on the history of the firm and the car it produced. As part of the research for this book, Mr. Powell sought to interview all persons who had worked for the Franklin firm or were related to those who once worked there. More than 125 employees and their children across America were interviewed by Mr. Powell. The interviews were accompanied by extensive research at university and other libraries, museums, historical associations, and at the federal archives and the Smithsonian Institution in Washington D.C. This book is the culmination of more than eleven years of work.

In recent years, Mr Powell also has been heavily involved in general automotive history activities. Following service on the board of direc-

ABOUT THE AUTHOR

tors of the Society of Automotive Historians, an international organization of people active in motor car history, he served in 1997-1999 as President of that group. He also is a member of the screening committee of the Automotive Hall of Fame, helping to bring the names of automotive pioneers to the attention of that organization.

www.ingramcontent.com/pod-product-compliance
Lightning Source LLC
Chambersburg PA
CBHW031842220426
43663CB00006B/472